365 Favorite Nut-Free Recipes

(365 Favorite Nut-Free Recipes - Volume 1)

Doris Naquin

Copyright: Published in the United States by Doris Naquin/ © DORIS NAQUIN

Published on December, 11 2020

All rights reserved. No part of this publication may be reproduced, stored in retrieval system, copied in any form or by any means, electronic, mechanical, photocopying, recording or otherwise transmitted without written permission from the publisher. Please do not participate in or encourage piracy of this material in any way. You must not circulate this book in any format. DORIS NAQUIN does not control or direct users' actions and is not responsible for the information or content shared, harm and/or actions of the book readers.

In accordance with the U.S. Copyright Act of 1976, the scanning, uploading and electronic sharing of any part of this book without the permission of the publisher constitute unlawful piracy and theft of the author's intellectual property. If you would like to use material from the book (other than just simply for reviewing the book), prior permission must be obtained by contacting the author at author@thymerecipes.com

Thank you for your support of the author's rights.

Content

365 AWESOME NUT-FREE RECIPES 9

1. Allergy Friendly Cookies 9
2. Alsatian Pear Kugel With Prunes 9
3. Ancho Chili Garlic Butter 10
4. Angel Hair Pasta With Vegetables And Cheese 10
5. Apricot Tarte Tatin 11
6. Arancini With Brandy Soaked Raisins 12
7. Arborio And Red Rice Risotto With Baby Broccoli And Red Peppers 13
8. Artichoke And Spinach Gratin 14
9. Arugula Piña Colada Smoothie 14
10. Asparagus Salad With Hard Boiled Eggs .. 15
11. Avocado Salad 15
12. Avocado And Tomato Salad 16
13. Baked Figs 16
14. Baked Fish En Papillotte 16
15. Baked Lobsters With A Tarragon Stuffing 17
16. Barley Risotto With Cauliflower And Red Wine 18
17. Barley, Corn And Lobster Salad 18
18. Bass Steaks With Basil Pepper Compote .. 19
19. Beef Stroganoff 20
20. Beet Green, Rice And Ricotta Blinis 20
21. Beet Greens Frittata 21
22. Beet Salad With Chèvre Frais And Caraway 22
23. Beet And Beet Green Fritters 23
24. Bibimbap With Tofu, Cucumbers, Spinach, Shiitakes And Carrots 24
25. Bing Cherry Soup 25
26. Bitter Greens With Sour Cream Dressing 25
27. Black Quinoa, Fennel And Celery Salad ... 26
28. Black And Arborio Risotto With Beets And Beet Greens 26
29. Black Eyed Pea Soup Or Stew With Pomegranate And Chard 27
30. Black Eyed Peas And Arugula Salad 28
31. Blueberry Loaf 28
32. Blueberry Pie Filling 29
33. Bozeman Flank And Beans 30
34. Braised Chard 31
35. Braised Pork Roast With Sweet Potatoes .. 31
36. Brooke's Pizza Pollo 32
37. Buckwheat Crepes With Roasted Apricots 32
38. Bulgur Pilaf With Chickpeas And Herbs .. 33
39. Bulgur Pilaf With Red Peppers And Tomatoes 34
40. Burst Vanilla Apples 35
41. Buttered Green Sugar Snap Peas 35
42. Butternut Squash Oat Muffins With Candied Ginger 36
43. Butternut Squash Puree 36
44. Butternut Squash And Sage Latkes 37
45. Cabbage, Onion And Millet Kugel 38
46. Caesar Salad 38
47. California Sandwiches 39
48. Caraway Pork Sausages With Red Wine ... 39
49. Champagne Granita With Strawberries 40
50. Chard And Sweet Corn Tacos 40
51. Chermoula 41
52. Cherry Clafouti 41
53. Chicken Breasts With Olives And Tomatoes 42
54. Chicken Breasts With Sweet Red Peppers And Snow Peas 43
55. Chicken Cacciatore 43
56. Chicken Cacciatore, New Version 44
57. Chicken Noodle Salad With Creamy Sesame Dressing 45
58. Chicken Paprikash 46
59. Chicken Soup With Lime And Avocado ... 46
60. Chicken With Apples And Ginger 47
61. Chicken With Olives, Prunes And Capers 48
62. Chicken And Sausage Jambalaya 48
63. Chili Lime Bluefish Grilled With Red Peppers And Corn 49
64. Chinese Fried Rice With Shrimp And Peas 50
65. Chunky Avocado Papaya Salsa 50
66. Cinnamon Curry Rice 51
67. Classic Irish Salad 51
68. Classic Oatmeal Raisin Cookies 52
69. Cocoa Brownies 53
70. Cod Ceviche 53
71. Cod Fillets With Cilantro Yogurt Sauce 54
72. Cold Baked Salmon With Green Mayonnaise 54

73. Cold Tomato Soup With Rosemary 55
74. Cole Slaw 56
75. Connemara Lamb Stew 56
76. Corn And Lobster Pie In A Chili Polenta Crust 57
77. Couscous Risotto 57
78. Couscous With Tomatoes, Okra And Chickpeas 58
79. Couscous With Raisins 59
80. Creamy Basil Sauce For Rigatoni 59
81. Croutons (Toasted French Bread Slices) .. 60
82. Crêpes With Grilled Peaches And Apricots 60
83. Cucumber Mint Soup 61
84. Cucumber Raita 61
85. Cucumber, Melon And Watermelon Salad 62
86. Cupid's Coupe 62
87. Curried Grilled Jumbo Shrimp 63
88. Curried Lentil And Grilled Chicken Casserole 63
89. Curry Laced Moules À La Marinière With Fresh Peas 64
90. Dandelion Greens With Crispy Onions 65
91. Dark Chocolate And Pomegranate Bark .. 65
92. Dried Fruit Compote With Fresh Apple And Pear 66
93. Duck In Red Wine Currant Sauce With Cracklings And Bacon 66
94. Duck, Wilted Spinach And White Bean Salad 67
95. Egg And Herb Salad 68
96. Enfrijoladas 68
97. Farfalle With Artichokes, Peas, Favas And Onions 69
98. Farfalle With Cabbage And Black Kale 70
99. Farofias (Poached Meringues In Lemon Custard With Cinnamon) 71
100. Farro Or Bulgur With Black Eyed Peas, Chard And Feta 72
101. Fava Bean And Asparagus Salad 72
102. Fennel And Orange Bluefish Grilled With Tomatoes, Potatoes And Fennel 73
103. Fennel And Orange Salad With Black Olives On A Bed Of Couscous 74
104. Fig Sorbet 74
105. Filet Mignon Of Beef With Roganjosh Spices 75
106. Fluke Crudo With Lime, Sea Salt And Olive Oil   76
107. Focaccia With Duck And Green Olive Ragout 76
108. French Grated Carrot Salad 77
109. Fried Green Beans, Scallions And Brussels Sprouts With Buttermilk Cornmeal Coating 77
110. Game Chips 78
111. Garden Vegetable Gratin 79
112. Garlic Spiedies 79
113. Giant Limas With Winter Squash 80
114. Ginger Vinaigrette 81
115. Gluten Free Pumpkin Muffins With Crumble Topping 81
116. Goat Cheese Salad With Pancetta, Garlic And Figs 82
117. Grated Black Radish Relish 82
118. Gratin Of Fennel And Potatoes 82
119. Greek Zucchini And Herb Pie 83
120. Green Bean Salad With Chickpeas And Mushrooms 84
121. Green Mole With Chicken 85
122. Green Pipian 86
123. Green Tomato Salsa Verde 87
124. Grilled Chicken Wings With Provençal Flavors 87
125. Grilled Fish With Tomato Cilantro Vinaigrette 88
126. Grilled Gorgonzola And Beet Green Sandwich 88
127. Grilled Leg Of Lamb With Mustard Seeds 89
128. Grilled Pizza With Grilled Fennel And Parmesan 90
129. Grilled Polenta 91
130. Grilled Porcini, Italian Style 91
131. Grilled Watermelon And Feta Salad 91
132. Grilled Or Pan Cooked Albacore With Soy/Mirin Marinade 92
133. Grits 92
134. Guacamole 93
135. Habichuelas Rojas (Red Beans, Dominican Style) 93
136. Harvest Corn Fritters 94
137. Herbed And Butterflied Leg Of Lamb 95
138. Homemade Oreos 95
139. Honey Gremolata 96

140. Honey Mustard Salad 97
141. Hot Cajun Style Crab Boil 97
142. Hot Chocolate Souffle.................................... 97
143. Hot Pepper Liquid 98
144. Indian Style Pilaf.. 98
145. Irish Whisky Pots De Creme 99
146. Jerry Anne Cardamom Cake 100
147. Jicama Relish In Chilpotle Marinade 100
148. Kale And Quinoa Salad With Plums And Herbs 101
149. King Arthur Flour's Banana Crumb Muffins 101
150. Kohlrabi Home Fries..................................... 102
151. Kohlrabi Risotto 102
152. Korean Chilled Buckwheat Noodles With Chilled Broth And Kimchi 103
153. Lamb Patties Moroccan Style With Harissa Sauce 104
154. Lasagna With Roasted Beets And Herb Béchamel... 104
155. Lasagna With Roasted Kabocha Squash And Béchamel... 105
156. Lasagna With Spicy Roasted Cauliflower 106
157. Leek Quiche 107
158. Leek And Pumpkin Soup............................. 108
159. Lemon Poundcake 108
160. Lemon And Garlic Chicken With Cherry Tomatoes 109
161. Lemon Poppy Seed Drops 110
162. Lentil Salad With Fresh Favas..................... 111
163. Lentil Soup With Cilantro (Lots Of It) ... 111
164. Lentil And Pumpkin Tagine 112
165. Lime Marinated Chicken Over 'Creamed' Corn 112
166. Linguine With Lentils And Prosciutto 113
167. Lucky's Clams Provencal 114
168. Mark Strausman's Grilled Mushrooms..... 114
169. Mashed Potatoes 115
170. Mashed Potatoes With Chives 116
171. Matchstick Potatoes...................................... 116
172. Matelote Of Monkfish (Monkfish Stew).116
173. Mediterranean Lentil Salad With Lemon Thyme Vinaigrette... 117
174. Melon Sorbet.. 118
175. Melon And Lime Parfait 118
176. Mexican Chicken Soup With Chick Peas, Avocado And Chipotles.............................. 119
177. Middle Eastern Meat Loaf 119
178. Millet And Greens Gratin 120
179. Minestrone With Giant White Beans And Winter Squash.. 121
180. Mini Bell Peppers Stuffed With Goat Cheese.. 122
181. Mini Peppers Stuffed With Tuna And Olive Rillettes 122
182. Mint Syrup 123
183. Mole Coloradito... 123
184. Momma Iquana's Fresh Vegetabel Chili. 124
185. Moroccan Cooked Carrot Salad................ 125
186. Moroccan Marinated Fish 125
187. Mousse Au Chocolat..................................... 126
188. Mushroom Stuffed Tomatoes 126
189. My Pain Catalan With Extra Tomatoes And Goat Cheese... 127
190. Noodles With Egg And Parsley Topping 127
191. Not Too Sweet Wok Popped Coconut Kettle Corn 128
192. Oats With Amaranth, Chia Seeds And Blueberries... 128
193. Octopus, Galician Style 129
194. Olive Oil Poached Bay Scallops With Chickpeas 129
195. Orange Cheese Poundcake 130
196. Orange Glaze 130
197. Orzo With Fresh Tomato 131
198. Osso Buco Alla Milanese 131
199. Oven Poached Pacific Sole With Lemon Caper Sauce.. 132
200. Oysters With Linguine................................ 133
201. Paglia E Fieno With Corn 133
202. Papaya Sorbet... 134
203. Papaya Tart... 134
204. Parsley Salad With Country Ham, Tomatoes And Asiago... 135
205. Passion Fruit Salad With White Pepper Ice Cream... 135
206. Pasta With Fresh Tomato Sauce 136
207. Pasta With Portobello Mushrooms 136
208. Pasta With Smoked Mussels And Tomatoes 137
209. Paul Buxman's Biscuits................................ 137
210. Pea Dip With Parmesan 138
211. Penne With Corn And Hot Sausage 139
212. Penne With Peas, Pea Greens And

Parmesan 139
213. Perfect White Rice, Spanish Caribbean Style 140
214. Persian Spinach, Potatoes And Peas 140
215. Pheasant With Cabernet Sauce 141
216. Pho With Carrots, Turnips, Broccoli And Tofu 142
217. Pierogi Ruskie (Potato And Cheese Pierogi) 143
218. Pimms Gelée With Raspberries And Fromage Blanc 144
219. Pissaladieres 145
220. Pizza Fantasy 145
221. Platanos Maduros (Fried Yellow Plantains) 146
222. Poached Chicken Breasts With Tomatillos And Jalapeños 146
223. Pork Burgers With Caraway 147
224. Pork Chops Baked With Apples And Onions 148
225. Pork Chops Smothered With Fennel And Garlic 148
226. Potato Gratin 149
227. Potato Lasagnas With Monkfish And Shallot Vinaigrette 150
228. Potato And Goat Cheese Pizza With Rosemary 150
229. Potato And Pea Patties With Indian Spices 151
230. Potato, Grilled Pancetta And Chive Salad 152
231. Provençal Artichoke Ragout 152
232. Prune Plum And Peach Compote 153
233. Pumpkin Ginger Pie 154
234. Pumpkin Seed Battered 'Chicken' With Cranberry Cabernet Sauce 154
235. Pumpkin Soup 155
236. Pureed Potatoes With Carrots And Onions 155
237. Puréed Beets With Yogurt And Caraway 156
238. Puréed Broccoli And Celery Soup 156
239. Puréed Trahana And Vegetable Soup 157
240. Puréed Winter Squash Soup With Ginger 158
241. Quick Chile Sauce 159
242. Quick Quesadilla With Dukkah 159
243. Quinoa And Carrot Kugel 159

244. Rabbit Fricassee With Tomatoes And White Wine 160
245. Radicchio Or Red Endive Risotto 161
246. Ramps Braised In Olive Oil 161
247. Raspberry Mousse 162
248. Ratatouille 163
249. Red Cabbage Glazed With Maple Syrup 163
250. Rhubarb Ice Cream With A Caramel Swirl 164
251. Risotto With Asparagus And Morels 164
252. Risotto With Broccoli 165
253. Risotto With Pumpkin 166
254. Risotto With Tomato Consomme And Fresh Cheese 166
255. Roast Chicken With Tarragon 167
256. Roast Cornish Hens With Herbs And Pancetta 168
257. Roasted Apple And Pear Compote With Candied Ginger 168
258. Roasted Brussels Sprouts With A Pomegranate Reduction 169
259. Roasted Carrot, Parsnip And Potato Soup 169
260. Roasted Cauliflower With Tahini Parsley Sauce 170
261. Roasted Garlic And Shallot Soup 171
262. Roasted Root Vegetables With Polenta .. 172
263. Roasted Sweet Potatoes And Fresh Figs 172
264. Roasted Vegetable Galette With Olives . 173
265. Roasted Winter Vegetable Medley 174
266. Saag Tofu (Tofu With Spinach, Ginger, Coriander And Turmeric) 175
267. Salade Niçoise With Yogurt Vinaigrette . 176
268. Salmon Fillet With Ginger And Capers .. 177
269. Salmon Tacos With Greens And Tomatillo Salsa 177
270. Sauce 178
271. Sausage Stuffing 179
272. Sauteed Wild Mushrooms With Shallots And Garlic 179
273. Sautéed Chanterelles 180
274. Sautéed Shredded Cabbage And Squash 180
275. Sautéed Spinach 181
276. Savory Bread Pudding With Kale And Mushrooms 181
277. Savory Oatmeal Pan Bread 182
278. Scallop Cakes With Artichoke Hearts 183

279. Scallop Napoleon With Crisp Potatoes ... 183
280. Scallops And Nectarines 184
281. Seared Red Rice With Spinach, Mushrooms, Carrot And Egg 184
282. Seared Sea Scallops With Lime Ginger Sauce And Caramelized Endive 185
283. Seitan Roulade With Oyster Mushroom Stuffing 186
284. Shell Bean Succotash 187
285. Show Me Bar B Q Meat Loaf 187
286. Shrimp Broth 188
287. Shrimp Stuffed With Spicy Dal 188
288. Sicilian Cauliflower And Black Olive Gratin 189
289. Skillet Collards And Winter Squash 189
290. Skillet Soba, Baked Tofu And Green Bean Salad With Spicy Dressing 190
291. Sloppy Joes 191
292. Smashed Turnips With Fresh Horseradish 192
293. Smoked Lobster Chowder 192
294. Soba And Herb Salad With Roasted Eggplant And Pluots 193
295. Soft Shell Crabs With Tomato Buttermilk Sauce 193
296. Sole With Julienne Of Pumpkin 194
297. Sour Orange Mignonette 195
298. Southeast Asian Shrimp And Grapefruit Salad 195
299. Spaghetti With Tomatoes And Garlic 196
300. Sparkling Pineapple Soup 196
301. Spartina's Roasted Cod With Nicoise Vinaigrette 196
302. Spiced Lamb Loaf 197
303. Spiced Manhattan Clam Chowder 197
304. Spicy Carrot And Spinach Latkes 198
305. Spicy Celery With Garlic 199
306. Spicy Coleslaw 199
307. Spicy Pork 200
308. Spicy Rum Punch 200
309. Spinach Bites 201
310. Spinach And Onion Tart 201
311. Spinach And Yogurt Dip 202
312. Spring Rolls With Beets, Brown Rice, Eggs And Herbs 203
313. Spring Rolls With Shredded Broccoli Stems, Vermicelli And Red Pepper 204

314. Spring Rolls With Spinach, Mushrooms, Sesame, Rice And Herbs 204
315. Steamed Fava Beans With Thyme 205
316. Stir Fried Sesame Shrimp And Spinach .. 206
317. Strata With Mushrooms And Chard 207
318. Strawberry Orange Soup 208
319. Stuffed Squid, Lisbon Style 208
320. Summer Aioli Feast 209
321. Summer Tomato Gratin 210
322. Sunchoke And Apple Salad 210
323. Suvir Saran's Guacamole With Toasted Cumin 211
324. Sweet Potato And Apple Latkes With Ginger And Sweet Spices 211
325. Sweet Potatoes Anna With Prunes 212
326. Sweet And Sour Butternut Squash Or Pumpkin 213
327. Swiss Chard Souffle With Fresh Tomato Sauce 213
328. Swordfish Hash 214
329. Taking Stock After Thanksgiving 215
330. Tangerine Sorbet 215
331. Teff And Oatmeal Pancakes 216
332. Three Greens Gratin 217
333. Tomato Bluefish Pasta 218
334. Tournedos De La Foret (Filet Mignons With Morels) 218
335. Tuna Mushroom Burgers 219
336. Turkey Normande 220
337. Turkish Pumpkin Soup 220
338. Turmeric Raisin Rice 221
339. Turmeric Rice 221
340. Two Bean And Tuna Salad 222
341. Veal In Red Wine Sauce (Meurettes De Veau) 222
342. Veal Shanks With Oriental Vegetables ... 223
343. Vegan Chocolate Chip Banana Cake 224
344. Vegan Pumpkin Tiramisu 224
345. Venison And Trotter Pie 225
346. Veracruzana Vinegar Bathed Shrimp 227
347. Warm Millet, Carrot And Kale Salad With Curry Scented Dressing 227
348. Warm Potato Salad 228
349. Warm Shrimp And Beans 229
350. Watermelon Or Cantaloupe Agua Fresca 230
351. White Bean And Shrimp Salad 230

352. White Bean Burgers 231
353. White Bean And Yogurt Green Goddess 231
354. White Beans With Clams 232
355. White Spice Poundcake 232
356. White Or Pink Beans With Beet Greens And Parmesan 233
357. Whole Grain Blueberry Buckle 234
358. Whole Wheat Focaccia 235
359. Whole Wheat Seeded Loaves 235
360. Whoopie Pies 236
361. Yogurt Or Buttermilk Soup With Spinach And Grains 237
362. Zarela Martinez's Ropa Vieja 238
363. Zrazy Zawijane (Stuffed Rolls Of Beef) .. 239
364. Zucchini Panzanella With Sun Dried Tomatoes 240
365. Zucchini Phyllo Pizza 240

INDEX 242

CONCLUSION 247

365 Awesome Nut-Free Recipes

***

1. Allergy Friendly Cookies

Serving: 2 Dozen Cookies | Prep: | Cook: | Ready in: 45mins

Ingredients

- 1 teaspoon baking powder
- ½ teaspoon baking soda
- ¾ teaspoon salt
- 1 cup whole wheat pastry flour
- ½ cup all-purpose flour
- ½ cup Earth Balance brand organic whipped buttery spread
- ¾ cup sun butter
- ½ cup brown sugar
- ¾ cup powdered sugar
- ½ teaspoon vanilla extract
- ½ cup Enjoy Life brand semi-sweet chocolate mini-chips

Direction

- Preheat oven to 350 degrees. Blend baking powder, baking soda, salt and both flours. Set aside.
- With a stand mixer, blend buttery spread, sun butter, sugars and vanilla. Gradually pour the dry mixture into the wet mixture and combine.
- Add chocolate chips.
- Refrigerate dough for 30 minutes. Remove, and use a tablespoon or a small scoop to create two dozen dough balls. With the palms of your hands, flatten balls into disks. Place on parchment-lined cookie sheet.
- Bake for 10-12 minutes. Remove from oven and place cookies on a wire rack to cool.

Nutrition Information

- 154: calories;
- 79 milligrams: sodium;
- 11 grams: fat;
- 5 grams: saturated fat;
- 4 grams: monounsaturated fat;
- 15 grams: carbohydrates;
- 9 grams: sugars;
- 0 grams: trans fat;
- 1 gram: protein;

2. Alsatian Pear Kugel With Prunes

Serving: 6 to 8 servings | Prep: | Cook: | Ready in: 3hours15mins

Ingredients

- 5 tablespoons vegetable oil
- 2 pounds ripe Bosc pears
- 2 small onions (about 1/2 pound), peeled and cut into 1-inch dice
- Salt to taste
- ½ loaf bread (about 7 ounces), cubed
- ¾ cup sugar
- 8 tablespoons butter or pareve margarine, melted
- 2 large eggs
- 2 cups pitted prunes
- 1 teaspoon cinnamon
- Juice of 1 lemon

Direction

- Preheat the oven to 350 degrees. Grease a 9-inch springform pan with 2 tablespoons of the oil.
- Peel the pears and cut all but one of them into 1-inch cubes.

- Heat the remaining 3 tablespoons of the oil over a medium-high heat in a skillet. Lightly sauté the onions until they are translucent. Remove from the heat and salt lightly, allowing them to cool slightly.
- Soak the bread for a few seconds in lukewarm water and squeeze dry. Put in a large bowl, and, using a wooden spoon or spatula, mix with 1/4 cup of the sugar and the butter or pareve margarine. Stir in the eggs, onions and half of the diced pears, setting aside the remaining pears for the sauce.
- Pour the batter into the spring form pan and bake for 2 hours.
- While the kugel is cooking, make the sauce. In a heavy saucepan set over medium-high heat, put 1 cup of water, the remaining 1/2 cup of sugar, the prunes, cinnamon, lemon juice and the remaining diced pears. Cook this compote mixture uncovered for 30 minutes.
- Finely grate the remaining pear and stir it into the cooked compote.
- When the kugel is done, remove from the oven and set on a rack to cool for about 20 minutes. Unmold from the pan onto a serving platter, and spoon half of the compote over it. Serve the remaining compote on the side.

Nutrition Information

- 529: calories;
- 23 grams: fat;
- 9 grams: saturated fat;
- 1 gram: trans fat;
- 3 grams: polyunsaturated fat;
- 80 grams: carbohydrates;
- 6 grams: protein;
- 10 grams: monounsaturated fat;
- 8 grams: dietary fiber;
- 50 grams: sugars;
- 632 milligrams: sodium;

3. Ancho Chili Garlic Butter

Serving: One-quarter cup | Prep: | Cook: |Ready in: 15mins

Ingredients

- 1 small ancho chili
- 4 tablespoons unsalted butter, softened
- 1 small clove garlic, peeled and minced
- ¼ teaspoon salt, plus more to taste

Direction

- Stem the chili, break it open and shake out all of the seeds. Bring a small saucepan of water to the boil. Lower the heat, add the chili and simmer until softened, about 5 minutes. Drain and let cool. Use a small knife to scrape the flesh of the chili from the skin. Chop the chili until it forms a paste. You should have about 1 1/2 teaspoons.
- In a small bowl, cream together the chili and the butter. Stir in the garlic and salt. Use immediately or store in the refrigerator.

Nutrition Information

- 112: calories;
- 2 grams: carbohydrates;
- 42 milligrams: sodium;
- 12 grams: fat;
- 7 grams: saturated fat;
- 0 grams: sugars;
- 3 grams: monounsaturated fat;
- 1 gram: protein;

4. Angel Hair Pasta With Vegetables And Cheese

Serving: 2 servings | Prep: | Cook: |Ready in: 35mins

Ingredients

- ¼ pound mushrooms

- 1 pound broccoli
- 2 tablespoons olive oil
- ¾ cup low-fat cottage cheese
- ¾ cup nonfat yogurt
- 1 ½ cups canned Italian plum tomatoes
- ½ teaspoon dried oregano
- ½ teaspoon dried basil
- 8 ounces fresh angel-hair pasta
- Freshly ground black pepper to taste
- ¼ cup freshly grated Parmigiano Reggiano

Direction

- Bring 3 quarts of water to boil in a covered pot.
- Wash, trim and slice mushrooms.
- Wash broccoli and remove tough stems. Cut remaining stems into thin slices and break up the florets.
- Heat the oil in a skillet and cook mushrooms and broccoli, covered, over medium-high heat for 5 minutes.
- Proces cottage cheese and yogurt in food processor until smooth.
- Break up tomatoes with your fingers and add to the vegetables with the oregano and basil. Cover and continue cooking over medium heat until broccoli is softened but still crisp.
- Cook pasta in boiling water for about 30 seconds; drain.
- Remove sauce from heat; stir in cottage-cheese mixture and pour over pasta. Season with black pepper. Serve with grated cheese.

Nutrition Information

- 738: calories;
- 3 grams: polyunsaturated fat;
- 9 grams: dietary fiber;
- 19 grams: sugars;
- 0 grams: trans fat;
- 12 grams: monounsaturated fat;
- 96 grams: carbohydrates;
- 41 grams: protein;
- 640 milligrams: sodium;
- 23 grams: fat;
- 6 grams: saturated fat;

5. Apricot Tarte Tatin

Serving: 6 to 8 servings | Prep: | Cook: | Ready in: 45mins

Ingredients

- For the pastry:
- 1 cup unbleached all-purpose flour
- 6 tablespoons cold unsalted butter cut into small pieces
- 1 teaspoon sugar
- A pinch of salt
- About 2 tablespoons ice water
- For the apricots:
- 2 pounds apricots
- 2 tablespoons unsalted butter
- ½ cup sugar

Direction

- Make the pastry. In a food processor, combine the flour, butter, sugar and salt. Process until the mixture looks like coarse bread crumbs (about five seconds). Add the cold water and process briefly, turning the machine on and off, until the mixture looks like small peas. Do not allow to become a ball in the machine.
- Turn mixture out onto lightly floured board and knead lightly until it holds together. With heel of palm of your hand, flatten it into a thick pancake about six inches across. Wrap it in plastic and refrigerate for at least 20 minutes. It will keep unfrozen up to three days before being used.
- Cut apricots in half and remove pits. Melt butter and sugar in nine-inch cast-iron skillet. Arrange apricot halves in circles on top and cook over moderate heat, without burning, until sugar begins to caramelize. Be careful not to burn. Cool completely.
- Roll out pastry into 10-inch circle. Place it on top of apricots, cutting off excess dough. Put

- edges down over fruit. Refrigerate for 30 minutes.
- Preheat oven to 425 degrees.
- Prick the pastry all over with the point of a knife. Bake for 20 to 25 minutes until the pastry is cooked.
- Cool and turn out onto a plate. Do not be dismayed if some of the apricots stick to pan; simply scrape them off and put them on top of pastry.

Nutrition Information

- 264: calories;
- 38 grams: carbohydrates;
- 24 grams: sugars;
- 40 milligrams: sodium;
- 7 grams: saturated fat;
- 0 grams: trans fat;
- 3 grams: protein;
- 1 gram: polyunsaturated fat;
- 12 grams: fat;

6. Arancini With Brandy Soaked Raisins

Serving: About 22 rice balls | Prep: | Cook: |Ready in: 1hours30mins

Ingredients

- 2 tablespoons extra-virgin olive oil
- 2 shallots, coarsely chopped
- 1 teaspoon kosher salt, more as needed
- 2 cups vegetable or chicken broth
- 2 cups arborio rice
- 2 tablespoons unsalted butter
- 6 tablespoons all-purpose flour
- ½ cup whole milk
- 5 ounces Parmesan, grated (1 1/4 cups)
- 2 teaspoons fresh thyme leaves
- 1 teaspoon finely grated lemon zest
- ¼ teaspoon black pepper, more as needed
- 2 large eggs
- ⅓ cup brandy
- ⅓ cup golden raisins
- 1 ½ cups plain dried bread crumbs or panko
- 3 ounces fontina cheese, coarsely grated
- 3 ounces fresh mozzarella, coarsely grated
- Grapeseed or safflower oil, for frying

Direction

- Heat olive oil in a medium pot over medium heat. Add shallots and cook with a pinch of salt until softened, 7 to 10 minutes.
- Stir in broth and 2 cups water and bring to a boil. Add rice and reduce heat to medium; simmer rice until it is al dente, 12 to 15 minutes. Drain, reserving 1/2 cup of the cooking liquid (there won't be much liquid left). Transfer rice to a bowl.
- Rinse out the pot and return it to medium heat. Stir in the butter and cook until foaming; whisk in 2 tablespoons flour. Cook, whisking frequently, until mixture is golden brown, 2 to 3 minutes.
- Whisk in the reserved rice cooking liquid and the milk, a little at a time, until fully incorporated, then whisk in Parmesan. Season with thyme, lemon zest, 1 teaspoon salt and 1/4 teaspoon black pepper.
- Fold the milk mixture in with the rice; taste and add more salt if needed. Let cool completely, then mix in the eggs. If you're not frying the rice immediately, cover the pan and refrigerate until needed, up to 24 hours.
- Warm the brandy in a small pot or microwave; stir in the raisins and soak 20 minutes. Drain.
- Place remaining 4 tablespoons flour (1/4 cup) in a small bowl; slowly whisk in 1/2 cup water until a smooth slurry forms. Place bread crumbs in a separate bowl. In another bowl, mix together the fontina and mozzarella.
- Scoop 1/4 cup of the rice mixture into your hands and form into a flat disk. Place several raisins and heaping teaspoon of cheese into the center of each patty. Mold the rice around the filling to fully enclose it and roll between your palms to form a ball (try not to get any cheese on the exterior of the ball). Dip the ball

in the slurry, then into the panko mixture, rolling it around to make sure it is well coated. Transfer to a baking sheet. Repeat with the remaining ingredients. (You can refrigerate the balls for up to 4 hours if you don't want to cook them immediately.)
- When ready to fry, fill a pot with several inches of grapeseed oil and heat until a drop of water added to the pan sizzles (about 375 degrees on a thermometer). Working in batches, lower a few rice balls into the oil at a time and fry, turning occasionally, until uniformly golden, about 5 minutes. Using a slotted spoon, transfer to a paper-towel-lined plate and immediately season with salt. Serve immediately.

Nutrition Information

- 294: calories;
- 8 grams: protein;
- 25 grams: carbohydrates;
- 3 grams: sugars;
- 239 milligrams: sodium;
- 17 grams: fat;
- 1 gram: dietary fiber;
- 4 grams: monounsaturated fat;
- 0 grams: trans fat;

7. Arborio And Red Rice Risotto With Baby Broccoli And Red Peppers

Serving: 6 generous servings | Prep: | Cook: | Ready in: 1hours45mins

Ingredients

- 1 cup short or medium-grain non-sticky red rice, like Bhutanese rice (3 cups cooked)
- 6 cups well-seasoned chicken or vegetable stock, as needed
- 2 tablespoons extra virgin olive oil
- ½ cup minced onion
- ¼ to ½ teaspoon red pepper flakes, to taste
- 1 red pepper, cut in small dice
- ⅔ cup arborio rice
- 1 to 2 garlic cloves (to taste), minced
- ½ cup dry white wine, like pinot grigio or sauvignon blanc
- ¾ pound baby broccoli, stems peeled and sliced, flowers torn apart into smaller pieces by hand
- Freshly ground pepper to taste
- ¼ to ½ cup freshly grated Parmesan cheese (1 to 2 ounces, optional)
- 2 tablespoons minced flat-leaf parsley

Direction

- To cook the red rice, combine with 2 cups water in a saucepan, add salt to taste and bring to a boil. Reduce the heat, cover and simmer 30 to 40 minutes, until all of the liquid has been absorbed by the rice. Remove from the heat, remove the lid from the pan and place a dish towel over the pan, then return the lid. Let sit for 10 to 15 minutes.
- Put the stock or broth into a saucepan and bring it to a simmer over low heat, with a ladle nearby or in the pot. Make sure that it is well seasoned.
- Heat the olive oil over medium heat in a wide, heavy nonstick skillet or saucepan. Add the onion and a generous pinch of salt, and cook gently until it is just tender, about 3 minutes. Add the red pepper flakes and the red bell pepper and continue to cook, stirring often, for another 5 minutes, until tender.
- Stir in the arborio rice and the garlic and stir until the grains separate and begin to crackle. Add the wine and stir until it has been absorbed. Begin adding the simmering stock, a couple of ladlefuls (about 1/2 cup) at a time. The stock should just cover the rice, and should be bubbling, not too slowly but not too quickly. Cook, stirring often, until it is just about absorbed. Add another ladleful or two of the stock and continue to cook in this fashion, stirring in more stock when the rice is almost dry. You do not have to stir constantly,

but stir often. After 10 minutes, stir in the broccoli stems and flowers and continue to add broth and stir the rice for another 10 minutes or so, until the broccoli is crisp-tender. When the rice is just about tender all the way through but still chewy, add another ladleful of stock and the red rice. Season to taste with salt and pepper. Stir together for a couple of minutes, until the stock is just about absorbed, and add another ladleful of stock, the Parmesan and the parsley, and remove from the heat. The mixture should be creamy (add more stock if it isn't). Stir for about half a minute, then serve in wide soup bowls or on plates.

Nutrition Information

- 372: calories;
- 6 grams: sugars;
- 12 grams: protein;
- 366 milligrams: sodium;
- 4 grams: dietary fiber;
- 9 grams: fat;
- 2 grams: saturated fat;
- 5 grams: monounsaturated fat;
- 1 gram: polyunsaturated fat;
- 58 grams: carbohydrates;

8. Artichoke And Spinach Gratin

Serving: 6 servings | Prep: | Cook: |Ready in: 1hours15mins

Ingredients

- For the gratin
- 3 tablespoons plus 1 teaspoon unsalted butter
- 1 medium yellow onion, peeled and minced
- 1 ½ quarts cleaned fresh spinach
- 3 large, fresh globe artichokes, trimmed and cooked, then quartered lengthwise
- 3 soft-boiled eggs, peeled and cubed
- ½ teaspoon chopped fresh thyme
- 1 tablespoon chopped fresh flat-parsley
- 1 cup Leek Crema
- ¼ teaspoon grated nutmeg
- Pinch of kosher salt
- Freshly ground pepper
- ¼ cup grated vegetarian Parmesan
- ¼ cup freshly toasted breadcrumbs
- For the Leek Crema
- 1 teaspoon unsalted butter
- 1 leek, white only, cleaned and minced
- Pinch of kosher salt
- 1 cup heavy cream

Direction

-
-

Nutrition Information

- 405: calories;
- 20 grams: carbohydrates;
- 6 grams: dietary fiber;
- 5 grams: sugars;
- 33 grams: fat;
- 0 grams: trans fat;
- 9 grams: monounsaturated fat;
- 2 grams: polyunsaturated fat;
- 11 grams: protein;
- 307 milligrams: sodium;

9. Arugula Piña Colada Smoothie

Serving: 1 generous serving | Prep: | Cook: |Ready in:

Ingredients

- ¼ cup freshly squeezed orange juice
- ½ cup light coconut milk
- 1 ¼ cups chopped pineapple (about 180 grams)
- 1 cup arugula (30 grams), rinsed
- 1 quarter-size piece of ginger, peeled
- 2 or 3 ice cubes

Direction

- Place all of the ingredients in a blender and blend for 1 full minute. Pour into a glass, garnish with an orange slice and enjoy.

10. Asparagus Salad With Hard Boiled Eggs

Serving: Serves four | Prep: | Cook: | Ready in: 15mins

Ingredients

- 1 pound asparagus
- 2 hard-boiled eggs
- 2 tablespoons champagne vinegar or sherry vinegar, or 1 tablespoon each fresh lemon juice and vinegar
- ¼ cup extra virgin olive oil
- 2 teaspoons capers, rinsed and chopped
- 2 tablespoons chopped fresh parsley or a mixture of parsley, chives and tarragon
- Salt
- freshly ground pepper to taste

Direction

- Snap the woody ends off the asparagus. Steam for five minutes. Refresh with ice-cold water, then drain and dry on paper towels. Cut into 1/2-inch pieces.
- Cut the boiled eggs in half, mince the yolks and whites separately, and season with salt and pepper
- In a salad bowl, whisk together the vinegar (or lemon juice and vinegar) and olive oil. Season with salt and pepper to taste. Add the asparagus, capers and herbs, and toss together. Add the chopped egg yolks and whites, then toss together again and serve.

Nutrition Information

- 177: calories;
- 5 grams: protein;
- 367 milligrams: sodium;
- 16 grams: fat;
- 3 grams: dietary fiber;
- 11 grams: monounsaturated fat;
- 2 grams: sugars;

11. Avocado Salad

Serving: Four to six servings | Prep: | Cook: | Ready in: 10mins

Ingredients

- 3 Haas avocados, ripe but not too soft, peeled and diced
- ¼ cup diced scallions
- 1 large red bell pepper, diced
- 1 medium red onion, peeled and diced
- 1 medium cucumber, peeled, seeded and cut into 1/8-inch slices
- 2 small tomatoes, seeded and diced
- ¼ cup fresh lime juice
- 2 tablespoons extra-virgin olive oil
- Salt and freshly ground pepper to taste

Direction

- Toss together the avocado, scallions, red pepper and onion. Add the cucumber and tomatoes. Add the lime juice and then the olive oil. Season with salt and pepper.

Nutrition Information

- 234: calories;
- 3 grams: protein;
- 13 grams: monounsaturated fat;
- 550 milligrams: sodium;
- 19 grams: fat;
- 2 grams: polyunsaturated fat;
- 16 grams: carbohydrates;
- 9 grams: dietary fiber;
- 4 grams: sugars;

12. Avocado And Tomato Salad

Serving: 4 servings | Prep: | Cook: | Ready in: 10mins

Ingredients

- 2 ripe avocados
- 4 ripe plum tomatoes
- 1 medium-size red onion, cut into thin slices
- 2 hard-boiled eggs, peeled and quartered
- 2 teaspoons finely chopped garlic
- 2 tablespoons red-wine vinegar
- 6 tablespoons olive oil
- 4 tablespoons coarsely chopped fresh coriander
- ½ teaspoon ground cumin
- Salt and freshly ground pepper to taste

Direction

- Peel the avocados and cut them in half. Discard the pit and cut each half into 4 lengthwise slices. Cut the slices into large cubes.
- Cut the tomatoes into 1-inch cubes.
- Add all the ingredients in a salad bowl. Toss well and serve.

Nutrition Information

- 400: calories;
- 8 grams: dietary fiber;
- 565 milligrams: sodium;
- 37 grams: fat;
- 6 grams: protein;
- 26 grams: monounsaturated fat;
- 4 grams: sugars;
- 15 grams: carbohydrates;

13. Baked Figs

Serving: 2 servings | Prep: | Cook: | Ready in: 25mins

Ingredients

- 6 firm ripe fresh figs
- 1 ½ tablespoons butter, melted
- 1 ½ tablespoons sugar
- Vanilla ice cream or 1 cup raspberries, 1/2 cup heavy cream and 1/4 cup confectioners' sugar

Direction

- Preheat oven to 375 degrees.
- Cut the stems off figs and place figs in a buttered baking dish. Brush with butter and sprinkle with sugar. Bake 15 minutes, until bubbly and lightly caramelized.
- With scissors or a knife, make an X in the top so that each fig opens like a flower.
- Serve figs hot with ice cream or raspberries folded into heavy cream whipped with confectioners' sugar.

Nutrition Information

- 261: calories;
- 16 milligrams: sodium;
- 7 grams: saturated fat;
- 1 gram: polyunsaturated fat;
- 43 grams: carbohydrates;
- 5 grams: dietary fiber;
- 11 grams: fat;
- 0 grams: trans fat;
- 3 grams: monounsaturated fat;
- 38 grams: sugars;
- 2 grams: protein;

14. Baked Fish En Papillotte

Serving: 1 serving | Prep: | Cook: | Ready in: 15mins

Ingredients

- For each serving:
- 1 tablespoon extra-virgin olive oil

- 1 square of kitchen parchment or aluminum foil, large enough to make a loose packet around the fish fillet
- 1 bluefish fillet
- 1 teaspoon grated lemon rind
- 1 teaspoon roughly chopped capers
- Freshly ground black pepper
- Watercress for garnish

Direction

- Preheat oven to 450 degrees.
- Use about a third of the olive oil to smear on the parchment or foil. Place the fillet on the oiled surface, and sprinkle the rest of the oil on top. Strew the lemon rind and capers over the top, and sprinkle with freshly ground pepper to taste.
- Draw the sides and ends of the paper or foil up over the fish to form a loose packet. Crimp the edges together to make a tight seal.
- Place the fish on a tray or cookie sheet. Place in the oven, and bake for 10 minutes. Serve the whole packet on a dinner plate; diners open their packets at table. Garnish with watercress.

Nutrition Information

- 462: calories;
- 23 grams: fat;
- 4 grams: polyunsaturated fat;
- 13 grams: monounsaturated fat;
- 1 gram: dietary fiber;
- 0 grams: sugars;
- 62 grams: protein;
- 229 milligrams: sodium;

15. Baked Lobsters With A Tarragon Stuffing

Serving: 4 servings | Prep: | Cook: | Ready in: 40mins

Ingredients

- 2 1 1/2-pound live lobsters
- 3 tablespoons butter at room temperature
- ½ cup finely chopped celery
- ½ cup finely chopped green onions or scallions
- ½ teaspoon finely minced garlic
- ½ teaspoon dried thyme
- Salt to taste if desired
- Freshly ground pepper to taste
- 6 tablespoons fine, fresh bread crumbs
- 1 tablespoon finely chopped fresh tarragon
- 2 tablespoons finely chopped parsley
- 1 tablespoon corn, peanut or vegetable oil
- Basil-butter sauce (see recipe)

Direction

- Preheat oven to 425 degrees.
- Place lobsters, shell side up, on a flat surface and plunge a knife quickly into the midsection where the tail joins the body. Hack away the claws and reserve them. Cut the lobsters in half lengthwise, head to tail. Remove and discard the tough sac inside the body near the eyes. Remove and discard the dark vein (the intestinal tract) from the tail section. Remove and reserve the soft coral and tomalley from each lobster. Place these in a bowl.
- Heat 1 tablespoon of the butter in a saucepan, and add the celery, green onions or scallions and garlic. Sprinkle with thyme, salt and pepper. Cook, stirring, about 1 minute. Let cool.
- To the bowl with the coral and tomalley add bread crumbs, the remaining butter, tarragon, parsley, salt and pepper. Beat well to blend. Add the celery and green-onion mixture and blend.
- Arrange lobster halves, shell side down, on a baking sheet. Scatter the claws around the halves.
- Spoon equal portions of the bread-crumb mixture into the body cavities of each lobster half. Do not cover the tail meat with the mixture. Sprinkle the tail meat with salt and pepper. Brush the tail meat with oil.
- Place in the oven, and bake 20 minutes. Serve with basil-butter sauce on the side.

Nutrition Information

- 421: calories;
- 0 grams: trans fat;
- 2 grams: polyunsaturated fat;
- 1 gram: sugars;
- 58 grams: protein;
- 1528 milligrams: sodium;
- 6 grams: monounsaturated fat;
- 15 grams: fat;
- 10 grams: carbohydrates;

16. Barley Risotto With Cauliflower And Red Wine

Serving: Serves 6 | Prep: | Cook: | Ready in: 30mins

Ingredients

- 7 to 8 cups vegetable or chicken stock, as needed
- Salt
- 2 tablespoons extra virgin olive oil
- 1 small or 1/2 medium onion, minced
- 2 large garlic cloves, minced or pressed
- 1 ½ cups barley
- 1 medium cauliflower, separated into small florets or sliced 1/2 inch thick
- 1 cup robust red wine, such as a Côtes du Rhône
- 3 tablespoons chopped flat-leaf parsley
- 2 ounces Parmesan cheese, grated (1/2 cup)
- Freshly ground pepper

Direction

- Season the stock well with salt and bring to a simmer in a medium saucepan.
- Heat the oil over medium heat in a large, heavy nonstick frying pan or a wide, heavy saucepan. Add the onion. Cook, stirring, until the onion begins to soften, about three minutes. Add the garlic, cauliflower and barley. Cook, stirring, for a couple of minutes, until the grains of barley are separate and beginning to crackle.
- Add the red wine and cook, stirring, until there is no more wine visible in the pan. Stir in enough of the simmering stock to just cover the barley. The stock should bubble slowly. Cook, stirring often, until it is just about absorbed. Add more stock and continue to cook in this fashion, not too fast and not too slowly, adding more stock when the barley is almost dry, until the barley is tender but still chewy. Taste and add salt if necessary.
- Add another ladleful of stock to the barley. Stir in the parsley and Parmesan, and immediately remove from the heat. Add freshly ground pepper, taste one last time and adjust salt. Serve at once.

Nutrition Information

- 418: calories;
- 54 grams: carbohydrates;
- 11 grams: dietary fiber;
- 19 grams: protein;
- 12 grams: fat;
- 4 grams: saturated fat;
- 1207 milligrams: sodium;
- 6 grams: monounsaturated fat;
- 2 grams: polyunsaturated fat;
- 8 grams: sugars;

17. Barley, Corn And Lobster Salad

Serving: Four servings | Prep: | Cook: | Ready in: 15mins

Ingredients

- 2 1 1/2-pound lobsters
- 2 cups cooked barley, cooled
- 2 ears corn, cooked and kernels cut off cob
- 1 tablespoon fresh lemon juice
- 2 teaspoons olive oil
- 3 tablespoons chopped fresh basil

- 1 teaspoon salt, plus more to taste
- Freshly ground pepper to taste

Direction

- Steam the lobsters until they turn bright red, about 10 minutes. Set aside until cool enough to handle. Remove the meat and cut into large chunks.
- Toss the lobster, barley and corn together. Add the lemon juice, olive oil, basil, salt and pepper. Toss until well combined. Divide among 4 plates and serve.

Nutrition Information

- 427: calories;
- 1449 milligrams: sodium;
- 0 grams: trans fat;
- 33 grams: carbohydrates;
- 4 grams: sugars;
- 60 grams: protein;
- 6 grams: fat;
- 1 gram: saturated fat;
- 3 grams: monounsaturated fat;
- 2 grams: polyunsaturated fat;

18. Bass Steaks With Basil Pepper Compote

Serving: Four servings | Prep: | Cook: | Ready in: 1hours15mins

Ingredients

- 2 cloves garlic, peeled and crushed
- ¼ cup olive oil
- 2 tablespoons fresh lemon juice
- 2 teaspoons salt
- 1 teaspoon coarse ground black pepper
- ½ cup white wine
- 1 white onion, minced
- 2 red peppers, minced
- 2 yellow peppers, minced
- 2 tomatoes, coarsely chopped
- 1 cup fresh basil leaves, coarsely torn
- 4 bass steaks (about 6 to 8 ounces each)

Direction

- In a large bowl combine the garlic, olive oil and lemon juice. Add the salt and black pepper and whisk well to combine. Slowly drizzle in the white wine. Add the onions and peppers, stir well to combine and set aside for 1 hour. Add the tomatoes and basil, stir and adjust seasoning with more salt and pepper to taste. Place the bass in this mixture and marinate for 1 to 4 hours.
- If using a charcoal grill, prepare the coals. When they are hot, remove the bass from the marinade and grill on each side for 5 to 8 minutes, depending on the thickness of the bass. After turning the fish, spoon the marinade over the bass and partially cover the grill so that the fish is allowed to smoke. Use a spatula to place each steak and its topping on plates and serve immediately. (If using a broiler, follow the same instructions, broiling the bass on one side, turning it, spooning on the marinade and broiling until done. Allow at least 4 inches between the fish and the flame to avoid burning.)

Nutrition Information

- 556: calories;
- 1164 milligrams: sodium;
- 21 grams: monounsaturated fat;
- 6 grams: sugars;
- 33 grams: protein;
- 1 gram: trans fat;
- 3 grams: polyunsaturated fat;
- 17 grams: carbohydrates;
- 4 grams: dietary fiber;
- 38 grams: fat;
- 12 grams: saturated fat;

19. Beef Stroganoff

Serving: 4 servings | Prep: | Cook: | Ready in: 1hours

Ingredients

- Kosher salt and freshly ground black pepper
- 1 ½ pounds sirloin roast, or beef tenderloin, if you're feeling fancy
- 2 tablespoons all-purpose flour
- 1 ½ teaspoons hot paprika
- 1 tablespoon neutral oil, such as canola or grapeseed
- 4 tablespoons unsalted butter
- ½ pound button mushrooms, cleaned and cut into quarters
- 2 small shallots, thinly sliced
- 12 ounces wide egg noodles
- ¼ cup dry white wine
- 1 cup heavy cream or crème fraîche
- 1 ½ teaspoons Worcestershire sauce
- 1 ½ teaspoons Dijon mustard
- Chopped fresh parsley, for garnish

Direction

- Bring a large pot of salted water to a boil.
- Cut the beef against the grain into 1/2-inch slices, pound lightly, then cut those slices into 1-inch-wide strips.
- Add the flour, paprika, 1 1/2 teaspoons salt and 1 1/2 teaspoons pepper to a large shallow bowl and toss to combine. Dredge the strips of meat in the flour mixture, shake them to remove excess flour, then transfer them to a rimmed baking sheet.
- Place a large skillet over high heat and swirl in the oil. When the oil begins to shimmer, sauté the beef slices, in two batches, until they are well browned on both sides but rare inside, 3 to 4 minutes per batch. Transfer the seared meat to the baking sheet. Turn the heat down slightly.
- Add 1 tablespoon of the butter to the pan. When it has melted and started to foam, add the mushrooms, toss to coat them with the fat, and season with salt and pepper. Cook, stirring frequently, until the mushrooms have released their moisture and are a deep, dark brown, 12 to 15 minutes. About halfway into the process, add the sliced shallots and 1 tablespoon butter and stir to combine.
- While the mushrooms cook, add the noodles to the boiling water, and cook until just done, about 10 minutes. Drain the noodles, and toss with the remaining 2 tablespoons butter. Set aside.
- When the mushrooms and shallots are soft and caramelized, deglaze the pan with the wine, scraping at all the stuck-on bits on the pan's surface. When the wine has reduced by about half, slowly stir in the cream, followed by the Worcestershire and mustard. Add the meat, along with any accumulated juices, and stir to combine. Cook, stirring occasionally, until the dish is hot and the beef is medium-rare, 2 to 3 minutes. Taste, and adjust the seasonings.
- Serve the noodles under or alongside the stroganoff; sprinkle stroganoff with parsley.

20. Beet Green, Rice And Ricotta Blinis

Serving: 24 about 2 1/2-inch cakes, serving 6 to 8 | Prep: | Cook: | Ready in: 20mins

Ingredients

- ¾ pound beet greens, or a mix of beet greens and other greens, such as chard or mustard greens, washed, stemmed and coarsely chopped (6 cups tightly packed)
- 1 cup (8 ounces) ricotta cheese
- 2 eggs, beaten
- ½ cup low-fat milk (2 percent)
- 5 tablespoons grated Parmesan
- ½ cup whole-wheat pastry flour or white whole-wheat pastry flour
- 1 teaspoon baking powder
- ½ teaspoon salt

- 1 cup cooked brown or white rice, preferably medium- or short-grain
- 2 tablespoons finely chopped chives
- 2 teaspoons finely chopped marjoram
- Freshly ground pepper
- Olive oil for the pan or griddle
- Marinara sauce for serving (optional)

Direction

- Steam the greens above an inch of boiling water for 1 to 2 minutes, just until wilted. Remove from the heat, allow to cool and squeeze out excess water. Chop fine.
- In a large bowl, beat together the ricotta, eggs, milk and Parmesan. Sift together the flour, baking powder and salt and whisk into the ricotta mixture. Stir in the greens, rice, herbs and pepper. The mixture will be thick.
- Heat a griddle or a heavy nonstick skillet over medium-high heat. Brush with olive oil, enough to coat the bottom, and drop the batter in by the heaped tablespoon. Cook for about 3 minutes, until dark brown and nicely risen, and turn over. Cook for another 2 to 3 minutes, until brown on the other side. The pancakes will be moist in the middle, but there should not be a raw flour taste. Remove from the heat and serve, or cool on a rack and heat later in a medium-low oven. Serve with a dollop of tomato sauce.

Nutrition Information

- 249: calories;
- 1 gram: polyunsaturated fat;
- 29 grams: carbohydrates;
- 329 milligrams: sodium;
- 2 grams: sugars;
- 12 grams: protein;
- 10 grams: fat;
- 5 grams: saturated fat;
- 0 grams: trans fat;
- 4 grams: monounsaturated fat;
- 3 grams: dietary fiber;

21. Beet Greens Frittata

Serving: 6 servings | Prep: | Cook: | Ready in: 50mins

Ingredients

- 2 tablespoons extra virgin olive oil
- 1 pound beet greens, stemmed and washed thoroughly
- 2 garlic cloves, minced
- 8 eggs
- Salt and freshly ground pepper to taste
- 2 tablespoons milk

Direction

- Heat a large pot of water over high heat while you stem and wash the beet greens in 2 changes of water. When the water comes to a boil, salt generously and add the beet greens. Cook for about 1 minute, until tender, and transfer to a bowl of ice water. Let sit for a few minutes, then drain, squeeze dry and chop. Alternatively, steam the greens for 2 minutes over 1 inch of boiling water. Refresh with cold water, squeeze out excess water and chop.
- Heat 1 tablespoon of the oil in a 10-inch nonstick skillet over medium heat and add the garlic. Cook, stirring, until it is fragrant, 30 seconds to a minute, and stir in the beet greens. Cook, stirring, for about 1 minute, until greens are coated with oil and fragrant. Season to taste with salt and pepper and remove from the heat.
- Using a whisk, beat the eggs in a bowl and whisk in salt to taste (about 1/2 teaspoon), freshly ground pepper and the milk. Stir in the cooked beet greens.
- Clean and dry your pan and return to the stove. Heat over medium-high heat and add the remaining tablespoon of olive oil. Hold your hand over the pan, and when you can feel the heat of the olive oil, test the heat by dropping a bit of egg into the pan. If it sizzles and cooks at once, the pan is ready. Pour in the egg mixture. Swirl the pan to distribute the

eggs and filling evenly over the surface. Shake the pan gently, tilting it slightly with one hand while lifting up the edges of the omelet with a spatula to let the eggs run underneath during the first few minutes of cooking. Turn the heat down to low, cover (use a pizza pan if you don't have a lid that will fit your skillet), and cook 10 minutes, shaking the pan gently every once in a while. From time to time, remove the lid and loosen the bottom of the omelet with a spatula, tilting the pan so that the bottom doesn't burn. It will, however, turn a deep golden brown. This is fine. The eggs should be just about set; cook a few minutes longer if they're not. Meanwhile, heat the broiler. Finish the omelet under the broiler for 1 to 2 minutes, watching very carefully to make sure the top doesn't burn (it should brown slightly, and it will puff under the broiler). Remove from the heat, shake the pan to make sure the omelet isn't sticking (it will slide around a bit in the nonstick pan) and allow to cool for at least 5 minutes and up to 15. Loosen the edges with a wooden or plastic spatula. Carefully slide from the pan onto a large round platter. Serve hot or at room temperature.

Nutrition Information

- 144: calories;
- 9 grams: protein;
- 10 grams: fat;
- 3 grams: dietary fiber;
- 0 grams: trans fat;
- 5 grams: carbohydrates;
- 2 grams: polyunsaturated fat;
- 1 gram: sugars;
- 335 milligrams: sodium;

22. Beet Salad With Chèvre Frais And Caraway

Serving: 8 servings. | Prep: | Cook: | Ready in: 4hours

Ingredients

- Roasted Beets
- 1 ½ to 2 pounds large red beets
- 1 ½ to 2 pounds large Chioggia beets
- 1 ½ to 2 pounds large golden beets
- ½ cup olive oil
- ½ cup salt
- 4 tablespoons sugar
- 3 cups red wine vinegar
- Goat Cheese Mousse
- 1 ½ cups skim milk
- 1 cup chèvre
- ¾ cup cream
- ⅔ cup sheep's milk yogurt
- 2 tablespoons lime juice
- 2 tablespoons salt
- 1 N2O charger
- Caraway Tuiles
- 2 tablespoons caraway seeds
- ⅔ cup rye flour
- ½ cup flour
- 1 teaspoon baking soda
- ½ cup butter, melted
- ¾ cup glucose syrup
- 4 egg whites
- Rye Crumble
- ½ cup butter, room temperature
- ¼ cup sugar
- 1 cup rye flour
- 1 cup bread flour
- 2 tablespoons caraway seeds
- 1 tablespoon plus 1 teaspoon salt
- 1 tablespoon milk
- Beet Vinaigrette
- 2 cups red beet juice
- ½ cup white balsamic vinegar
- 1 tablespoon caraway seeds
- 1 teaspoon black peppercorns
- 1 cup raspberries
- 1 teaspoon salt
- ¼ teaspoon xanthan gum (6/10 grams)
- 2 tablespoons olive oil
- To finish the salad
- Roasted Beets
- 2 tablespoons olive oil

- Fleur de sel
- Caraway Tuiles
- Goat Cheese Mousse
- 3 tablespoons Beet Vinaigrette
- 3 teaspoons Rye Crumble
- 32 dill blossoms

Direction

-
-
-
-
-

23. Beet And Beet Green Fritters

Serving: 16 to 18 fritters, serving 5 to 6 | Prep: | Cook: | Ready in: 2hours30mins

Ingredients

- 1 bunch beets, with greens, peeled and grated on the wide holes of a grater or food processor (about 1 to 1 1/4 pounds beets)
- Salt
- Greens from 1 bunch beets, stemmed and washed in 2 changes of water
- 2 eggs
- ½ cup chopped mixed fresh herbs, like as fennel, dill, mint, parsley
- 2 teaspoons ground cumin
- 1 teaspoon ground caraway
- 1 cup fresh or dry bread crumbs (more as necessary)
- Freshly ground pepper
- 2 ounces feta, crumbled (1/2 cup)
- All-purpose flour as needed and for dredging
- ¼ cup canola oil
- ¼ cup extra virgin olive oil
- Plain Greek-style yogurt or aioli for serving

Direction

- Salt the beets generously and leave them to drain in a colander placed in the sink or in a bowl for 1 hour, tossing and squeezing the beets from time to time (wear rubber gloves to protect your hands from the color). After an hour, take up the grated beets by the handful, squeeze out as much liquid as you can and transfer to a bowl.
- While the beets are draining, heat a large pot of water over high heat and stem and wash the beet greens in 2 changes of water. When the water comes to a boil, salt generously and add the beet greens. Cook for about 1 minute, until tender, and transfer to a bowl of ice water. Let sit for a few minutes, then drain, squeeze dry and chop fine. Alternatively, steam the greens for 2 minutes above 1 inch of boiling water.
- In a large bowl, beat the eggs and add the grated beets, herbs, cumin, caraway, beet greens, bread crumbs, salt and pepper to taste, and feta. Mix together well. Take up a small handful (one to 2 tablespoons) of the mixture, and if it presses neatly into a patty, it is the right consistency. If it seems wet, add more bread crumbs or a few tablespoons of all-purpose flour. When the mixture has the right consistency, cover the bowl with plastic wrap and refrigerate for one hour or longer.
- Combine the oils in a large frying pan and heat until rippling, about 275 degrees. Meanwhile, take up heaped tablespoons of the beet mixture and form patties. Lightly dredge in flour. Carefully transfer to the pan, taking care to fry them in batches so you don't crowd the pan, and fry until patties are golden brown on both sides. Use tongs, a slotted spatula or a spider to turn the fritters over. Remove from the oil and drain briefly on a rack, then serve, with yogurt or aioli if desired.

Nutrition Information

- 364: calories;
- 518 milligrams: sodium;
- 24 grams: fat;
- 5 grams: saturated fat;

- 6 grams: dietary fiber;
- 12 grams: sugars;
- 9 grams: protein;
- 0 grams: trans fat;
- 14 grams: monounsaturated fat;
- 4 grams: polyunsaturated fat;
- 31 grams: carbohydrates;

24. Bibimbap With Tofu, Cucumbers, Spinach, Shiitakes And Carrots

Serving: 4 servings. | Prep: | Cook: | Ready in: 1hours15mins

Ingredients

- For the tofu:
- 1 tablespoon Asian sesame oil
- ¼ cup soy sauce
- 2 tablespoons mirin (sweet Japanese rice wine)
- 1 tablespoon rice wine vinegar
- 1 tablespoon minced or grated fresh ginger
- 1 teaspoon sugar
- ¾ pound tofu (to taste)
- For the vegetables:
- 2 tablespoons rice vinegar
- 1 tablespoon sesame oil
- 2 large garlic cloves, minced or puréed
- 2 to 3 scallions, minced
- 1 tablespoon toasted sesame seeds
- Salt to taste
- Korean red pepper paste (kochujang) to taste (available at Korean markets) (optional)
- 2 Persian cucumbers or 1/2 long European cucumber, thinly sliced
- 6 ounces carrots (1 large), peeled and cut in matchsticks or grated
- 1 large bunch spinach, stemmed, or 1 6-ounce bag baby spinach
- 6 fresh shiitake mushrooms, stemmed and sliced
- Soy sauce to taste
- 1 tablespoon canola oil
- For the rice and garnishes:
- 1 ½ to 2 cups brown rice, barley, quinoa or another grain of your choice, cooked (keep hot)
- 4 eggs (optional)
- Korean red pepper paste (kochujang) to taste (available at Korean markets)
- 2 sheets nori seaweed (kimgui), lightly toasted* and cut into thin strips (optional)
- 1 tablespoon toasted sesame seeds or black sesame seeds
- Toast nori sheets (if not toasted already) by quickly passing them over a gas flame (hold with tongs) until crisp.

Direction

- Combine all of the tofu marinade ingredients in a 2-quart bowl. Whisk together well.
- Drain the tofu and pat dry with paper towels. Cut into 1/2-inch-thick dominoes, blot again with paper towels and add to the bowl with the marinade. Gently toss to coat. Cover and refrigerate for 15 minutes to an hour, or for up to a day.
- Mix together the rice vinegar, sesame oil, garlic, scallions, sesame seeds and salt to taste in a small bowl or measuring cup. Add red pepper paste if desired. Set aside.
- While the tofu is marinating, toss the cucumber with salt to taste and place in a colander in the sink for 15 to 30 minutes. Rinse and squeeze dry. Place in a bowl and toss with 2 teaspoons of the vinegar and sesame oil mixture. In a separate bowl, toss the carrots with 1 tablespoon of the vinegar and sesame oil mixture. Refrigerate both the cucumbers and carrots while you cook the tofu, spinach and mushrooms.
- Wash the spinach and wilt in a large frying pan over high heat. Remove from the heat, press out excess water and toss in a bowl with 1 tablespoon of the vinegar and sesame oil mixture.
- Heat a wok or large, heavy skillet over medium-high heat until a drop of water evaporates immediately on contact and add

the canola oil. Stir-fry the tofu for 3 to 5 minutes, until lightly browned, and remove to a plate. Add the shiitakes to the pan, let sit without stirring for 1 minute, then stir-fry for another minute or two, until tender. Remove to a plate.
- Fry the eggs in the hot pan or in a separate nonstick skillet until the whites are set and the yolks are still runny. Season with salt and pepper.
- Heat 4 wide soup bowls. Place a mound of hot grains in the middle of each one and surround with the tofu and vegetables, as well as kimchi if desired, each ingredient in its own little pile. Place a fried egg and a small spoonful of chili paste on top of the rice and garnish with the toasted nori and sesame seeds. Serve at once. Diners should break the egg into the rice. Pass the chili paste and add more as desired.

25. Bing Cherry Soup

Serving: 6 servings | Prep: | Cook: | Ready in: 1hours

Ingredients

- 4 pounds Bing cherries, washed
- ½ vanilla bean
- 6 ounces candied orange peel or slices
- 8 cups white zinfandel, or 6 cups zinfandel and 2 cups water
- Sorbet (lemon or raspberry) or vanilla ice cream or sliced fresh fruit (peaches, plums or nectarines), for serving
- Candied orange peel or biscotti, for optional garnish

Direction

- Put whole, unpitted cherries into a deep, wide, heavy pan. (No need to remove stems.) Add vanilla bean, candied orange, and wine or wine and water. Bring to a boil, lower heat and simmer 30 to 40 minutes, until thickened and reduced by half.
- Let cool for a few minutes, then transfer to a food processor in batches and pulse briefly, just until fruit is in very small pieces. Transfer fruit, pits, stems and liquid to a fine-meshed sieve placed over a large bowl. Press hard with a wooden spoon to extract all the liquid. Cover, and chill 4 hours or overnight.
- To serve, ladle into shallow bowls. Put a scoop of sorbet or ice cream or a spoonful of sliced fruit in the center. Garnish with candied orange peel or a biscotti, if desired.

Nutrition Information

- 537: calories;
- 1 gram: fat;
- 0 grams: polyunsaturated fat;
- 76 grams: carbohydrates;
- 7 grams: dietary fiber;
- 56 grams: sugars;
- 4 grams: protein;
- 19 milligrams: sodium;

26. Bitter Greens With Sour Cream Dressing

Serving: 4 servings | Prep: | Cook: | Ready in: 15mins

Ingredients

- 3 hard-cooked eggs
- 1 teaspoon sugar
- Juice of 1 lemon, or to taste
- 1 cup sour cream
- 1 tablespoon milk
- Salt and pepper to taste
- 6 cups greens, preferably romaine, endive, escarole, radicchio or chicory, roughly chopped

Direction

- Cut eggs in two and put yolks in a bowl. Mash yolks with sugar and lemon juice, and beat in the sour cream with a wooden spoon, until smooth. Thin with milk if necessary. Season with salt and pepper. (This can all be done in a food processor or a mixer, but it is easy enough by hand.)

- Slice egg whites into thin strips, and toss with greens and dressing. Serve.

Nutrition Information

- 181: calories;
- 414 milligrams: sodium;
- 2 grams: dietary fiber;
- 6 grams: protein;
- 1 gram: polyunsaturated fat;
- 7 grams: carbohydrates;
- 15 grams: fat;
- 8 grams: saturated fat;
- 4 grams: sugars;

27. Black Quinoa, Fennel And Celery Salad

Serving: Serves 4 | Prep: | Cook: | Ready in: 5mins

Ingredients

- 1 medium-size fennel bulb (about 10 ounces), quartered, cored and very thinly sliced
- 1 long or 2 shorter celery sticks, very thinly sliced
- 2 cups cooked black quinoa (about 3/4 cup uncooked)
- ¼ cup chopped flat-leaf parsley
- 2 tablespoons chopped chives
- 2 tablespoons freshly squeezed lemon juice
- 1 small garlic clove, puréed
- Salt and freshly ground pepper to taste
- 5 tablespoons extra virgin olive oil

Direction

- In a salad bowl, combine the sliced fennel and celery, the quinoa, parsley and chives.

- In a small bowl or measuring cup, whisk together the lemon juice, garlic, salt, pepper and olive oil. Toss with the salad and serve.

Nutrition Information

- 289: calories;
- 19 grams: fat;
- 3 grams: polyunsaturated fat;
- 13 grams: monounsaturated fat;
- 27 grams: carbohydrates;
- 5 grams: protein;
- 4 grams: sugars;
- 474 milligrams: sodium;

28. Black And Arborio Risotto With Beets And Beet Greens

Serving: 6 servings | Prep: | Cook: | Ready in: 2hours

Ingredients

- 1 cup black rice, like Lundberg Black Japonica or Forbidden Rice, cooked (3 cups cooked black rice)
- 1 quart chicken or vegetable stock, as needed
- 1 bunch beet greens, stemmed and washed
- 2 tablespoons extra virgin olive oil
- ½ cup finely chopped onion
- ⅔ cup arborio rice
- 2 garlic cloves, minced
- ½ cup dry white wine
- ¾ pound beets (1 bunch small), roasted, skinned and diced
- Salt
- Freshly ground pepper
- 1 to 2 ounces Parmesan cheese, grated (1/4 to 1/2 cup, to taste, optional)
- 2 tablespoons finely chopped flat-leaf parsley

Direction

- To cook the black rice, combine with 2 cups water in a saucepan, add salt to taste and

bring to a boil. Reduce the heat, cover and simmer 30 to 40 minutes, until all of the liquid has been absorbed by the rice. Remove from the heat, remove the lid from the pan and place a dish towel over the pan, then return the lid. Let sit for 10 to 15 minutes.
- Bring the stock to a simmer in a saucepan. Season well and turn the heat to low. Stack the stemmed, washed greens and cut crosswise into 1-inch-wide strips.
- Heat the oil over medium heat in a large nonstick frying pan or wide, heavy saucepan and add the onion. Cook, stirring, until the onion begins to soften, about 3 minutes, and add the rice and garlic. Cook, stirring, until the grains of rice are separate and beginning to crackle, about 3 minutes.
- Stir in the wine and cook over medium heat, stirring constantly. The wine should bubble, but not too quickly. You want some of the flavor to cook into the rice before it evaporates. When the wine has just about evaporated, stir in a ladleful or two of the simmering stock (about 1/2 cup), enough to just cover the rice. The stock should bubble slowly (adjust heat accordingly). Cook, stirring often, until it is just about absorbed. Add another ladleful or two of the stock and continue to cook in this fashion, not too fast and not too slowly, stirring often and adding more stock when the rice is almost dry, for 10 minutes.
- Stir in the greens, the diced beets and black rice and continue adding more stock, enough to barely cover the rice, and stirring often, for another 10 to 15 minutes. The arborio rice should be chewy but not hard in the middle – and definitely not soft like steamed rice. If it is still hard in the middle, you need to continue adding stock and stirring for another 5 minutes or so. Now is the time to ascertain if there is enough salt. Add if necessary.
- When the rice is cooked through, add a generous amount of freshly ground pepper, and stir in another ladleful of stock, the Parmesan and the parsley. Remove from the heat. The risotto should be creamy; if it isn't,

add a little more stock. Stir once, taste and adjust seasonings, and serve.

Nutrition Information

- 267: calories;
- 1 gram: polyunsaturated fat;
- 4 grams: dietary fiber;
- 40 grams: carbohydrates;
- 8 grams: protein;
- 768 milligrams: sodium;
- 7 grams: sugars;

29. Black Eyed Pea Soup Or Stew With Pomegranate And Chard

Serving: 4 to 6 servings | Prep: | Cook: |Ready in: 1hours15mins

Ingredients

- 1 bunch rainbow chard
- 2 tablespoons extra virgin olive oil
- ½ yellow onion, finely chopped
- 2 garlic cloves, minced
- 1 teaspoon ground turmeric
- 2 teaspoons ground cumin seeds
- ½ pound (1 1/8 cups) black-eyed peas, rinsed
- ½ cup barley
- 1 medium beet, peeled and cut in small dice
- 1 ½ to 2 quarts water (to taste)
- Salt to taste
- ¼ cup pomegranate molasses (more to taste)
- Freshly ground pepper to taste
- 1 generous bunch cilantro, chopped
- 1 cup thick yogurt
- Seeds of 1 ripe medium-size pomegranate

Direction

- Wash and stem the chard, and if the stems are wide and thick, cut the thickest parts of them into small dice (discard the thin parts). Heat the oil over medium heat in a large, heavy soup pot and add the onion and chard stems. Cook, stirring often, until the onion is very tender and lightly colored, about 10 minutes. Stir in the garlic, turmeric and cumin and cook, stirring, until fragrant, 30 seconds to a minute. Add the black-eyed peas, barley, beet and water and bring to a gentle boil. Add salt to taste and the molasses. Reduce the heat, cover and simmer 45 minutes to an hour, until the beans and barley are tender. Add freshly ground pepper, taste and adjust salt.

- Stir in the chard and the cilantro. Simmer for another 5 to 10 minutes, or until the chard is tender but still bright. Taste, adjust seasoning, and serve, garnishing each bowl with a spoonful of yogurt and pomegranate seeds.

Nutrition Information

- 229: calories;
- 7 grams: protein;
- 16 grams: sugars;
- 1159 milligrams: sodium;
- 2 grams: saturated fat;
- 0 grams: trans fat;
- 4 grams: monounsaturated fat;
- 1 gram: polyunsaturated fat;
- 38 grams: carbohydrates;

30. Black Eyed Peas And Arugula Salad

Serving: Twenty servings | Prep: | Cook: | Ready in: 40mins

Ingredients

- 1 ½ pounds black-eyed peas
- 6 cups chicken stock, approximately
- ½ cup olive oil
- ¼ cup vegetable oil
- ¼ cup raspberry vinegar
- 2 cloves garlic, minced
- 1 ½ tablespoons Dijon mustard
- 1 tablespoon honey
- ¼ teaspoon nutmeg
- Cayenne pepper to taste
- Salt and freshly ground pepper to taste
- 1 medium red onion, minced
- 3 bunches arugula, washed and dried
- 1 ¼ pounds red cabbage, finely sliced

Direction

- Pick over the peas to remove any stones or dirt. Wash thoroughly and drain. Soak overnight. Drain again.
- Place the peas in a large pot and add the chicken stock to cover them. Bring to a boil, lower the heat and simmer, covered, for 30 minutes or until done. Drain. Set aside to cool.
- In a small bowl, combine the remaining ingredients, except the red onion, arugula and cabbage. Whisk to blend.
- Place the peas, onion, arugula and cabbage in a large serving bowl. Pour the dressing over them and toss well.

Nutrition Information

- 155: calories;
- 14 grams: carbohydrates;
- 4 grams: protein;
- 437 milligrams: sodium;
- 1 gram: polyunsaturated fat;
- 0 grams: trans fat;
- 6 grams: monounsaturated fat;
- 3 grams: dietary fiber;
- 5 grams: sugars;
- 10 grams: fat;

31. Blueberry Loaf

Serving: 1 loaf | Prep: | Cook: | Ready in: 1hours30mins

Ingredients

- 1 ⅓ cups blueberries

- 1 cup plus 1 tablespoon all-purpose flour
- 8 tablespoons soft unsalted butter, plus butter for greasing pan
- 1 cup whole wheat flour
- 2 teaspoons baking powder
- ½ teaspoon baking soda
- ½ teaspoon cinnamon
- ½ teaspoon ground cardamom
- 1 cup light brown sugar
- 2 eggs
- 1 cup milk
- 1 teaspoon vanilla extract

Direction

- Preheat oven to 350 degrees. Toss one cup of the blueberries in a bowl with one-half tablespoon flour and set aside. Butter a 9-by5-by-3-inch baking pan and dust with one-half tablespoon flour.
- Sift the remaining all-purpose flour with the whole wheat flour, baking powder, baking soda, cinnamon and cardamom and set aside.
- Cream the butter and sugar together until smooth. Beat in the eggs one at a time. Stir in the flour mixture alternately with the milk. Stir in the vanilla. Fold in the cup of blueberries and spoon the batter into the prepared pan. Scatter the remaining blueberries on top.
- Place in the oven and bake about an hour and 10 minutes, until browned and a cake tester inserted in the center comes out clean. Allow to cool 10 minutes, then remove cake from the pan to continue cooling on a rack.

Nutrition Information

- 277: calories;
- 12 grams: fat;
- 0 grams: trans fat;
- 2 grams: dietary fiber;
- 5 grams: protein;
- 3 grams: monounsaturated fat;
- 1 gram: polyunsaturated fat;
- 38 grams: carbohydrates;
- 17 grams: sugars;
- 164 milligrams: sodium;
- 7 grams: saturated fat;

32. Blueberry Pie Filling

Serving: 2 quarts | Prep: | Cook: |Ready in: 1hours

Ingredients

- 1 cup sugar
- ½ cup cornstarch
- Juice of two lemons
- 4 pints blueberries
- 1 teaspoon almond extract, optional
- 4 tablespoons Grand Marnier or other orange liqueur, optional

Direction

- Fit a large pot with a rack, or line with a folded kitchen towel. Fill 2/3 with water and bring to a boil. Add 2 one-quart canning jars and boil for 10 minutes. Jars may be left in the warm water in the pot until ready to be filled. (Alternatively, you can sterilize jars by running them through a dishwasher cycle, leaving them there until ready to fill.)
- Place canning rings in a small saucepan, cover with water and bring to a boil. Turn off heat and add lids to soften their rubber gaskets. Rings and lids may be left in the water until jars are filled.
- In a large heavy pot, combine 1 cup water with sugar, cornstarch and lemon juice, and whisk until smooth. Bring to a boil and add berries; the mixture will look gloppy. Smash some of the berries with a potato masher or the back of a spoon. Return mixture to a boil for 1 minute. Add extract and liqueur, if using, and stir well.
- Remove warm jars from pot and bring water back to a boil. Ladle hot filling into jars just up to the base of the neck, leaving 1 inch at the top. Wipe jar rims clean with a damp towel. Place lids on jars, screw on rings and lower jars back into the pot of boiling water. The

water should cover the jars; if not, add more. Boil jars for 30 minutes. Transfer jars to a folded towel and allow to cool for 12 hours; you should hear them making a pinging sound as they seal.
- Test the seals by removing rings and lifting jars by the flat lid. If the lid releases, the seal has not formed. Unsealed jars should be refrigerated and used within a month, or reprocessed. (Rings and jars may be reused, but a new flat lid must be used each time jars are processed.) To reprocess, reheat filling to boiling point (as in Step 3), then continue as before.

Nutrition Information

- 108: calories;
- 0 grams: polyunsaturated fat;
- 28 grams: carbohydrates;
- 2 grams: dietary fiber;
- 20 grams: sugars;
- 1 gram: protein;
- 1 milligram: sodium;

33. Bozeman Flank And Beans

Serving: Six servings | Prep: | Cook: | Ready in: 4hours

Ingredients

- 1 pound dry pinto beans, rinsed
- 6 plum tomatoes, cut in half lengthwise
- 4 frying peppers, cut in half lengthwise, cored, deribbed and seeded
- 1 hot red pepper, seeded and cut across in 1/4-inch slices
- 1 teaspoon dry mustard
- 3 tablespoons molasses
- 4 teaspoons salt, plus more to taste
- 1 teaspoon freshly ground black pepper
- 1 teaspoon olive oil or bacon fat
- 1 medium onion, minced
- The steak:
- 1 1-pound flank steak
- 2 teaspoons kosher salt
- 1 teaspoon coarsely ground black pepper

Direction

- Place the beans in a large, heavy-bottom pot. Cover with 2 inches of water. Bring to a boil for 3 minutes. Remove from heat. Cover and let stand for 2 hours.
- Preheat the oven to 400 degrees. Place the tomatoes and frying peppers, skin side up, on a baking sheet. Roast for 25 minutes. Carefully transfer the vegetables with their juices to a food processor or blender. Add the hot red pepper. Puree until smooth. Set aside. In a small bowl, stir together the mustard, molasses, salt and pepper. Set aside.
- Drain beans, discard liquid and dry the pot. Set beans aside. Place the olive oil or bacon fat in the pot and warm over medium heat. Add the onion and cook until soft, about 5 minutes. Add the beans to the onion. Pour in enough water to barely cover the beans. Stir in the tomato-pepper puree and the molasses mixture. Cover. Bake until tender, about 1 3/4 hours, adding water as needed to keep beans very moist but not soupy. Add salt to taste.
- Fifteen minutes before serving, season the steak with 1 teaspoon salt and pepper. Set aside. 10 minutes before serving, place a cast-iron skillet over high heat. Add the remaining salt to the skillet. Heat until hot. Quickly sear the steak, allowing it to cook 2 to 3 minutes on each side, depending on its thickness and how you like your steak cooked. Remove from pan. Let stand for 5 minutes. Slice and serve around beans.

Nutrition Information

- 466: calories;
- 8 grams: fat;
- 3 grams: monounsaturated fat;
- 15 grams: dietary fiber;
- 792 milligrams: sodium;
- 1 gram: polyunsaturated fat;

- 64 grams: carbohydrates;
- 14 grams: sugars;
- 34 grams: protein;

34. Braised Chard

Serving: 4 to 6 servings | Prep: | Cook: | Ready in: 30mins

Ingredients

- 1 pound Swiss chard
- 3 tablespoons extra-virgin olive oil
- 3 cloves garlic, sliced
- ¼ cup chopped scallions
- Salt and freshly ground black pepper
- ¼ cup freshly grated Parmesan cheese

Direction

- Rinse the Swiss chard. Leave any water clinging to it. Chop it fine.
- Heat the oil in a large skillet. Add the garlic, saute for a minute or so, then add the Swiss chard. Cook, stirring, until the Swiss chard begins to wilt. Cover the pan and cook over low heat for about 15 minutes.
- Uncover and cook, stirring, a few minutes longer. Stir in the scallions, season to taste with salt and pepper. Sprinkle with cheese and serve.

Nutrition Information

- 97: calories;
- 8 grams: fat;
- 2 grams: saturated fat;
- 5 grams: monounsaturated fat;
- 1 gram: sugars;
- 4 grams: carbohydrates;
- 3 grams: protein;
- 227 milligrams: sodium;

35. Braised Pork Roast With Sweet Potatoes

Serving: 6 servings | Prep: | Cook: | Ready in: 2hours10mins

Ingredients

- 1 shoulder butt pork roast (boneless), about 3 pounds
- 2 cups water
- 2 tablespoons dark soy sauce
- ½ teaspoon Tabasco sauce
- 2 tablespoons red-wine or cider vinegar
- 2 tablespoons honey
- 1 teaspoon cumin
- 2 pounds yams (about 4)
- 1 pound onions (about 2 large)
- 6 large cloves garlic, peeled

Direction

- Place the pork roast in a cast-iron or enamel casserole with a lid. Add the water, soy sauce, Tabasco, vinegar, honey and cumin. Bring to a boil, reduce the heat to very low and boil gently, covered, for 1 hour.
- Meanwhile, peel the yams and cut into 1 1/2-inch slices. Peel the onions and cut each into 4 to 6 pieces, depending on size. Preheat the oven to 375 degrees.
- After the pork has cooked for 1 hour, add the yams, onions and garlic. Bring back to the boil and continue boiling, covered, on top of the stove for about 15 minutes. Uncover and place the casserole in the center of the oven. Cook for 45 minutes, turning the meat in the juices every 15 minutes. At the end of the cooking period, the juices should be dark and concentrated, the meat tender when pierced with a fork and the vegetables very soft.
- Serve directly from the casserole, cutting the meat at the table.

Nutrition Information

- 284: calories;
- 57 grams: carbohydrates;
- 8 grams: protein;
- 10 grams: sugars;
- 327 milligrams: sodium;
- 3 grams: fat;
- 1 gram: monounsaturated fat;
- 0 grams: polyunsaturated fat;

36. Brooke's Pizza Pollo

Serving: 4 to 6 servings | Prep: | Cook: | Ready in: 1hours15mins

Ingredients

- 3 or 4 medium zucchini, about 2 pounds
- 3 eggs, lightly beaten
- 1 cup finely chopped onion
- Salt to taste if desired
- ⅓ cup whole-wheat flour
- ½ cup finely grated mozzarella cheese
- ½ cup freshly grated Parmesan cheese
- 1 tablespoon chopped fresh basil or 1/2 that dried
- Freshly ground pepper to taste
- 1 cup red or green sweet pepper, seeded, deveined and cut into 1/4-inch cubes
- ½ cup chopped pitted black olives, preferably imported Greek or Italian
- ½ cup skinned, boneless cooked chicken breast cut into shreds, about 1/4 pound
- 2 cups fresh or canned tomato sauce
- ¼ pound cheese such as Gruyere, Fontina or cheddar, grated, about 1 cup loosely packed
- ½ teaspoon dried crumbled oregano

Direction

- Preheat oven to 350 degrees.
- Trim off ends of zucchini. Grate using food processor or hand grater. There should about 6 cups.
- Empty zucchini into clean cloth and squeeze to extract as much liquid as possible. Drained zucchini should yield 3 1/2 cups fairly firmly packed.
- Put zucchini in mixing bowl and add eggs, onions, salt, flour, mozzarella, Parmesan, basil and pepper. Blend well.
- Pour mixture into center of pizza pan 13 inches in diameter. Smooth neatly to edges. Bake 25 minutes.
- Remove pizza base from the oven and scatter cubed pepper, olives and chicken over top evenly. Spoon on tomato sauce. Sprinkle evenly with grated Grey ere and oregano.
- Return pan to oven and continue baking 25 to 30 minutes.

Nutrition Information

- 291: calories;
- 1163 milligrams: sodium;
- 8 grams: sugars;
- 0 grams: trans fat;
- 19 grams: carbohydrates;
- 1 gram: polyunsaturated fat;
- 22 grams: protein;
- 15 grams: fat;
- 5 grams: dietary fiber;

37. Buckwheat Crepes With Roasted Apricots

Serving: Yield: About 12 8-inch crepes, 15 7-inch crepes | Prep: | Cook: | Ready in: 1hours10mins

Ingredients

- For the Buckwheat Crepes:
- 3 large eggs
- 240 grams (1 cup) low-fat milk (2 percent)
- 80 grams (1/3 cup) water
- 1 tablespoon sugar (optional)
- 80 grams (2/3 cup) buckwheat flour
- 40 grams (1/2 cup) unbleached all-purpose flour
- ½ teaspoon salt

- 3 tablespoons melted butter, canola oil or grapeseed oil
- For the Roasted Apricots:
- 6 to 8 apricots, cut in half, pits removed (1 1/2 to 2 apricots per person, depending on the size)
- 1 tablespoon butter
- 1 tablespoon honey
- 1 drop almond extract
- 2 tablespoons chopped lightly toasted pistachios, plus additional for garnish
- 4 buckwheat crepes (above)
- Honey-sweetened plain yogurt or vanilla ice cream for serving (optional)

Direction

- In a medium bowl, whisk together the eggs, milk, water and sugar. Sift together the buckwheat and all-purpose flour and the salt and whisk into the liquid mixture. Add the melted butter or oil and whisk together. Insert a hand blender and blend for 1 minute. If you don't have a hand blender, blend the mixture in a regular blender for 1 minute and pour back into the bowl. Cover and let sit for 1 hour.
- Place a seasoned or nonstick 7- or 8-inch crepe pan over medium heat. Brush with butter or oil and when the pan is hot, remove from the heat and ladle in about 1/4 cup batter if using an 8-inch pan, 3 tablespoons for a 7-inch pan. Tilt or swirl the pan to distribute the batter evenly and return to the heat. Cook for about 1 minute, until you can easily loosen the edges with a spatula and the crepe is nicely browned. Turn and cook on the other side for 30 seconds. Turn onto a plate. Continue until all of the batter is used up.
- Preheat the oven to 400 degrees. Place the apricots in a baking dish large enough to accommodate them in a single layer, but not too large. Place the butter, honey and almond extract in a small saucepan or in a ramekin and heat until the butter melts, either on the stove or at 50 percent power for 25 seconds in the microwave. Pour over the apricots and toss together. Turn the apricots cut side down. Place in the oven and roast for 10 to 15 minutes, until the apricots are soft. Remove from the oven.
- Heat the crepes. Place 3 large or 4 small apricot halves on each crepe. Spoon a little of the juice in the pan over the apricots, but leave enough to spoon over the crepes. Sprinkle on some pistachios. Either roll up the crepe or simply fold over the apricots. Spoon juice from the pan over the crepe, garnish with more pistachios and serve. If you wish, serve these with a little honey-sweetened yogurt or vanilla ice cream.

Nutrition Information

- 155: calories;
- 6 grams: sugars;
- 3 grams: saturated fat;
- 22 grams: carbohydrates;
- 5 grams: protein;
- 208 milligrams: sodium;
- 0 grams: trans fat;
- 2 grams: dietary fiber;
- 1 gram: polyunsaturated fat;

38. Bulgur Pilaf With Chickpeas And Herbs

Serving: Serves four to six | Prep: | Cook: | Ready in: 1hours35mins

Ingredients

- For the bulgur pilaf with chickpeas and herbs
- 1 cup dried chickpeas, soaked in 1 quart water for six hours or overnight and drained
- Salt to taste
- 1 cup coarse bulgur wheat
- 2 tablespoons extra virgin olive oil
- 1 bunch scallions, finely chopped
- 2 large garlic cloves, minced

- ¼ cup finely chopped flat-leaf parsley, or a mixture of parsley and dill
- 2 tablespoons finely chopped fresh mint
- Juice of 1 lemon

Direction

- Drain the soaked chickpeas, and place in a pot with 1 quart water. Bring to a boil, reduce the heat and simmer one hour. Add salt to taste and continue to simmer for 30 minutes to an hour, until the chickpeas are tender.
- Place the bulgur in a 2-quart bowl. Place a strainer over the bowl, and drain the chickpeas so that the hot broth covers the bulgur. Set the chickpeas aside. Cover the bowl, and allow the bulgur to sit until fluffy, about 20 to 30 minutes. Strain and press out excess liquid.
- Heat 1 tablespoon of the oil over medium heat in a large, heavy skillet, and add the scallions. Cook, stirring, until tender, two or three minutes. Stir in the garlic, and continue to cook until fragrant, 30 seconds to a minute. Stir in the bulgur and chickpeas. Add the herbs and the remaining tablespoon of olive oil, and toss together. Remove from the heat, add lemon juice and pepper, taste and adjust salt. Add more lemon juice if desired. Serve hot or room temperature.

Nutrition Information

- 259: calories;
- 10 grams: protein;
- 223 milligrams: sodium;
- 7 grams: fat;
- 4 grams: sugars;
- 2 grams: polyunsaturated fat;
- 8 grams: dietary fiber;
- 1 gram: saturated fat;
- 42 grams: carbohydrates;

39. Bulgur Pilaf With Red Peppers And Tomatoes

Serving: Four servings | Prep: | Cook: |Ready in: 1hours15mins

Ingredients

- 1 ½ cups fine-grain bulgur
- 3 medium red bell peppers, stemmed, cored and cut into large pieces
- 1 red or green chili pepper, cored, stemmed and seeded
- 2 tablespoons water
- 1 ¼ teaspoons salt, plus more to taste
- ⅛ teaspoon sugar
- 2 medium-size ripe tomatoes
- 8 scallions, trimmed and thinly sliced
- ½ cucumber, peeled, seeded and chopped
- ¾ cup chopped Italian parsley
- 6 tablespoons fresh lemon juice
- 1 tablespoon pomegranate molasses, preferably Cortas brand (see note)
- ⅓ cup olive oil
- 1 teaspoon hot Hungarian paprika, or to taste
- Tender romaine lettuce leaves or boiled vine leaves, for garnish

Direction

- Place the bulgur in a fine sieve and shake to remove any dust. Place in a large bowl and cover with cold water. Let stand 30 minutes.
- Meanwhile, place the bell and chili peppers in a food processor with the water, 1/4 teaspoon of the salt and the sugar. Process until pureed. Transfer to a saucepan and cook over medium heat, stirring often, until reduced to a jam-like consistency, about 20 minutes. Set aside.
- Cut the tomatoes in half and squeeze gently to remove the seeds. Using the large holes of a hand grater, grate the tomato halves with the cut side facing the grater. (You should be left with just the tomato skin in your hand; discard.)
- Drain the bulgur and return it to the bowl. Add the red-pepper paste, the tomato pulp,

the remaining teaspoon salt, the scallions, cucumber, parsley, lemon juice, pomegranate molasses, olive oil and paprika. Stir to mix well.
- Cover tightly with plastic wrap and refrigerate for a few hours. Taste and season with more salt if needed. Spoon onto a platter, surround with the lettuce or vine leaves and serve.

Nutrition Information

- 422: calories;
- 12 grams: sugars;
- 9 grams: protein;
- 3 grams: saturated fat;
- 13 grams: monounsaturated fat;
- 2 grams: polyunsaturated fat;
- 59 grams: carbohydrates;
- 11 grams: dietary fiber;
- 19 grams: fat;
- 758 milligrams: sodium;

40. Burst Vanilla Apples

Serving: 6 servings | Prep: | Cook: | Ready in: 30mins

Ingredients

- 4 apples, quartered, cored and peeled (preferably Jonathans, pippins or Granny Smiths)
- 1 2-inch-long vanilla pod, split in two
- ¼ cup sugar
- 2 tablespoons water
- 3 tablespoons dark rum

Direction

- Put the apple quarters in a saucepan or saute pan just big enough to hold them in a single layer. Tuck in the vanilla sections, sprinkle the sugar over the apples and pour the water and the rum over them also.
- Cook, covered, over low heat, shaking the pan from time to time, for about 20 minutes, or until the quarters are soft and on the verge of collapse.
- Transfer the quarters to a glass serving dish, pour over their juices (the vanilla pod can be dried and reused) and serve tepid.

Nutrition Information

- 114: calories;
- 0 grams: protein;
- 25 grams: carbohydrates;
- 3 grams: dietary fiber;
- 21 grams: sugars;
- 2 milligrams: sodium;

41. Buttered Green Sugar Snap Peas

Serving: 4 servings | Prep: | Cook: | Ready in: 15mins

Ingredients

- 1 pound sugar snap peas
- Salt and freshly ground pepper to taste
- 2 tablespoons butter
- 1 tablespoon shredded fresh mint

Direction

- Pluck off and discard the string from each pea pod.
- Bring salted water to boil; there should be enough to cover peas when added. Add peas. When water returns to a boil, cook about 3 minutes. Do not overcook. Drain.
- Return peas to saucepan. Add pepper, salt, butter and mint. Stir to blend until the pieces are well coated and hot. Serve immediately.

Nutrition Information

- 100: calories;
- 9 grams: carbohydrates;

- 0 grams: polyunsaturated fat;
- 2 grams: monounsaturated fat;
- 3 grams: protein;
- 5 grams: sugars;
- 284 milligrams: sodium;
- 6 grams: fat;
- 4 grams: saturated fat;

42. Butternut Squash Oat Muffins With Candied Ginger

Serving: About 1 dozen muffins | Prep: | Cook: | Ready in: 40mins

Ingredients

- 130 grams all-purpose flour (about 1 cup)
- 100 grams whole-wheat flour (about 2/3 cup)
- 50 grams oats (about 1/2 cup)
- 55 grams light brown sugar (about 1/3 cup)
- 13 grams baking powder (about 1 tablespoon)
- 3 grams fine sea salt (about 1 teaspoon)
- 3 grams ground cinnamon (about 1 teaspoon)
- ¼ teaspoon nutmeg
- Zest of 1 lemon, finely grated
- 2 large eggs, room temperature
- ½ cup Greek yogurt, room temperature
- 10 tablespoons unsalted butter, melted and cooled
- ¼ cup maple syrup
- 130 grams finely shredded butternut squash (about 1 1/2 cups)
- 35 grams finely chopped candied ginger (about 1/4 cup)

Direction

- Heat the oven to 375 degrees and grease a muffin tin.
- In a large bowl, whisk together the flours, oats, sugar, baking powder, salt, spices and lemon zest. In a small bowl or glass measuring cup, whisk together the eggs, Greek yogurt, melted butter and maple syrup. Add the wet ingredients to the dry ingredients and gently stir with a rubber spatula until almost combined — the batter will be very thick. Then fold in the shredded squash and candied ginger.
- Spoon the batter into the muffin tin. Bake for 20 minutes or so, or until the muffins are lightly golden and spring back when touched. Cool for 5 minutes in the pan before turning them out on a wire rack.

Nutrition Information

- 251: calories;
- 5 grams: protein;
- 220 milligrams: sodium;
- 0 grams: trans fat;
- 33 grams: carbohydrates;
- 13 grams: sugars;
- 3 grams: monounsaturated fat;
- 1 gram: polyunsaturated fat;
- 2 grams: dietary fiber;
- 12 grams: fat;
- 7 grams: saturated fat;

43. Butternut Squash Puree

Serving: 4 servings | Prep: | Cook: | Ready in: 15mins

Ingredients

- 1 butternut squash, about 2 pounds
- Salt to taste
- 2 tablespoons butter
- 1 tablespoon honey
- ⅛ teaspoon freshly grated nutmeg
- ⅛ teaspoon ground allspice
- Pinch cinnamon
- Freshly ground pepper to taste

Direction

- Pare the squash, remove the seeds and cut into 1 1/2-inch cubes. Place the cubes in a saucepan, cover with water and add salt. Bring

to a boil, cover and simmer 5 minutes or until tender.
- Drain and put through a food mill or food processor. Return the puree to the saucepan and add the butter, honey, nutmeg, allspice, cinnamon, salt and pepper. Blend well until smooth. Serve hot with the ham loaf.

Nutrition Information

- 155: calories;
- 558 milligrams: sodium;
- 6 grams: fat;
- 4 grams: dietary fiber;
- 0 grams: polyunsaturated fat;
- 2 grams: protein;
- 27 grams: carbohydrates;
- 9 grams: sugars;

44. Butternut Squash And Sage Latkes

Serving: About 25 latkes, serving 6 | Prep: | Cook: | Ready in: 45mins

Ingredients

- ½ medium onion, grated
- 6 cups grated butternut squash (1 3-pound squash)
- ¼ cup chopped or slivered fresh sage (more to taste)
- 1 teaspoon baking powder
- Salt and freshly ground pepper
- 3 tablespoons oat bran
- ¼ cup all-purpose flour
- 2 eggs, beaten
- About 1/4 cup canola, grape seed or rice bran oil

Direction

- Place the grated onion in a strainer set over a bowl while you prepare the other ingredients. Then wrap in a dishtowel and squeeze out excess water, or just take up by the handful to squeeze out excess water. Place in a large bowl and add the squash, sage, baking powder, salt and pepper, oat bran, and flour. Taste and adjust salt. Add the eggs and stir together.
- Begin heating a large heavy skillet over medium heat. Heat the oven to 300 degrees. Line a sheet pan with parchment. Place a rack over another sheet pan. Take a 1/4 cup measuring cup and fill with 3 tablespoons of the mixture. Reverse onto the parchment-lined baking sheet. Repeat with the remaining latke mix. You should have enough to make about 30 latkes.
- Add the oil to the pan and when it is hot (hold your hand a few inches above – you should feel the heat), use a spatula to transfer a ball of latke mixture to the pan. Press down with the spatula to flatten. Repeat with more mounds. In my 10-inch pan I can cook 3 or 4 at a time without crowding; my 12-inch pan will accommodate 4 or 5. Cook on one side until golden brown, 4 to 5 minutes. Slide the spatula underneath and flip the latkes over. Cook on the other side until golden brown, another 3 to 4 minutes. Transfer to the rack set over a baking sheet and place in the oven to keep warm.
- Serve hot topped with low-fat sour cream, Greek style yogurt or crème fraîche.

Nutrition Information

- 252: calories;
- 12 grams: fat;
- 0 grams: trans fat;
- 4 grams: polyunsaturated fat;
- 37 grams: carbohydrates;
- 638 milligrams: sodium;
- 3 grams: saturated fat;
- 8 grams: dietary fiber;
- 6 grams: protein;

45. Cabbage, Onion And Millet Kugel

Serving: 6 servings | Prep: | Cook: |Ready in: 2hours

Ingredients

- ½ medium head cabbage (1 1/2 pounds), cored and cut in thin strips
- Salt to taste
- 2 tablespoons extra virgin olive oil
- 1 medium onion, finely chopped
- ¼ cup chopped fresh dill
- Freshly ground pepper
- 1 cup low-fat cottage cheese
- 2 eggs
- 2 cups cooked millet

Direction

- Preheat the oven to 375 degrees. Oil a 2-quart baking dish. Toss the cabbage with salt to taste and let it sit for 10 minutes
- Meanwhile, heat 1 tablespoon of the oil over medium heat in a large, heavy skillet and add the onion. Cook, stirring, until it begins to soften, about 3 minutes, then add a generous pinch of salt and turn the heat to medium-low. Cook, stirring often, until the onion is soft and beginning to color, about 10 minutes. Add the cabbage, turn the heat to medium, and cook, stirring often, until the cabbage is quite tender and fragrant, 10 to 15 minutes. Stir in the dill, taste and adjust salt, and add pepper to taste. Transfer to a large bowl
- In a food processor fitted with the steel blade, purée the cottage cheese until smooth. Add the eggs and process until the mixture is smooth. Add salt (I suggest about 1/2 teaspoon) and pepper and mix together. Scrape into the bowl with the cabbage. Add the millet and stir everything together. Scrape into the oiled baking dish. Drizzle the remaining oil over the top and place in the oven
- Bake for about 40 minutes, until the sides are nicely browned and the top is beginning to color. Remove from the oven and allow to cool for at least 15 minutes before serving. Serve warm or at room temperature, cut into squares or wedges

Nutrition Information

- 198: calories;
- 2 grams: saturated fat;
- 0 grams: trans fat;
- 4 grams: dietary fiber;
- 1 gram: polyunsaturated fat;
- 24 grams: carbohydrates;
- 6 grams: sugars;
- 7 grams: fat;
- 10 grams: protein;
- 575 milligrams: sodium;

46. Caesar Salad

Serving: Six to eight servings | Prep: | Cook: |Ready in: 10mins

Ingredients

- The croutons:
- 1 cup cubed French bread pieces
- Olive oil
- The dressing:
- 2 ounces anchovy fillets
- 1 egg yolk (see note)
- 1 teaspoon finely chopped parsley
- 1 tablespoon finely chopped garlic (or less to taste)
- 1 cup extra-virgin olive oil
- ¼ cup grated Parmesan cheese
- ¼ cup red-wine vinegar
- The lettuce:
- 1 head romaine lettuce, cut, washed and drained

Direction

- Preheat the oven to 300 degrees. Spread the bread on a baking sheet, drizzle with olive oil

and bake 4 to 5 minutes, stirring once or twice, until golden. Set aside.
- In a stainless-steel bowl, crush the anchovy fillets with a fork until they are well mashed. Add the egg yolk and stir with a wire whisk for 2 to 3 minutes. Stir in the parsley and garlic. Slowly add the olive oil in a steady stream while whisking to incorporate. Add the vinegar and 2 tablespoons of the Parmesan and stir briskly with the whisk.
- In a large bowl, toss the lettuce with the dressing and the croutons. Sprinkle remaining cheese on top.

Nutrition Information

- 322: calories;
- 0 grams: trans fat;
- 22 grams: monounsaturated fat;
- 3 grams: polyunsaturated fat;
- 6 grams: carbohydrates;
- 2 grams: dietary fiber;
- 1 gram: sugars;
- 355 milligrams: sodium;
- 31 grams: fat;
- 5 grams: protein;

47. California Sandwiches

Serving: 6 servings | Prep: | Cook: | Ready in: 20mins

Ingredients

- 1 tablespoon extra-virgin olive oil
- 1 teaspoon soy sauce
- Juice of 1 lime
- 1 pound skinless and boneless chicken breasts
- 1 ripe Haas avocado
- 2 teaspoons chili powder
- ¾ cup plain nonfat yogurt
- 1 cup radish sprouts
- ¼ cup grated carrot
- 12 slices multigrain bread

Direction

- Preheat a grill or broiler. Mix the olive oil with the soy sauce and one tablespoon of the lime juice. Brush this mixture on the chicken and grill or broil the chicken until it is lightly browned and cooked through. Set aside.
- Halve the avocado, remove the pit and peel off the skin. Cut the avocado into slices and gently toss them with the remaining lime juice and the chili powder.
- Mix the yogurt with the sprouts and the grated carrot. Spoon this mixture on the slices of bread. Top six of the slices of bread with the avocado slices. Slice the chicken one-half inch thick against the grain and arrange the slices of chicken on the avocado. Cover with the remaining slices of bread, yogurt-side down. Cut the sandwiches in half and serve.

Nutrition Information

- 386: calories;
- 27 grams: protein;
- 17 grams: fat;
- 4 grams: polyunsaturated fat;
- 0 grams: trans fat;
- 33 grams: carbohydrates;
- 7 grams: sugars;
- 8 grams: monounsaturated fat;
- 376 milligrams: sodium;

48. Caraway Pork Sausages With Red Wine

Serving: about 20 3-inch links | Prep: | Cook: | Ready in: 30mins

Ingredients

- 3 pounds pork shoulder or butt, put through medium or coarse grinder
- 1 tablespoon caraway seeds
- ¾ cup dry red wine, like a cabernet sauvignon

- 1 tablespoon chopped parsley
- Salt and coarsely ground black pepper to taste
- 3 large cloves garlic, minced

Direction

- Combine all ingredients, and using sausage stuffer, stuff into casing, twisting and tying at 3- or 4-inch intervals. Prick with fork.
- Place in boiling water; reduce heat and blanch for 5 minutes after water returns to a boil.
- To serve, broil or grill. Serve with coarse-grained mustard.

Nutrition Information

- 171: calories;
- 5 grams: monounsaturated fat;
- 1 gram: carbohydrates;
- 0 grams: sugars;
- 182 milligrams: sodium;
- 12 grams: protein;
- 4 grams: saturated fat;

49. Champagne Granita With Strawberries

Serving: Six servings | Prep: | Cook: | Ready in: 6hours15mins

Ingredients

- ¾ cup, plus 2 tablespoons, sugar
- 6 tablespoons water
- 1 pint ripe strawberries, hulled and sliced in thick rounds
- 1 tablespoon plus 4 1/2 teaspoons fresh lemon juice
- 2 tablespoons thinly sliced mint leaves, plus 6 sprigs for garnish
- 2 tablespoons Grand Marnier (optional)
- 2 ½ cups dry Champagne or other sparkling wine
- ½ cup fresh orange juice

Direction

- Mix the 3/4 cup of sugar and water in a small saucepan. Bring to a boil over medium heat and boil until the sugar dissolves, about 1 minute. Let cool. Meanwhile, in a medium-size bowl, combine the berries, 2 tablespoons of sugar, 1 tablespoon of lemon juice, sliced mint and Grand Marnier, if using. Cover and let stand for at least 2 hours.
- In a shallow nonreactive pan, combine the sugar syrup, Champagne, orange juice and 4 1/2 teaspoons of lemon juice. Cover with plastic wrap and freeze for at least 6 hours.
- To serve, scrape the granita with a fork into large crystals. Spoon into chilled martini or other wide-mouthed glasses. Surround with berries and garnish with mint. Serve immediately.

Nutrition Information

- 113: calories;
- 1 gram: protein;
- 7 grams: sugars;
- 6 milligrams: sodium;
- 0 grams: polyunsaturated fat;
- 11 grams: carbohydrates;

50. Chard And Sweet Corn Tacos

Serving: 8 tacos, serving 4 | Prep: | Cook: | Ready in: 15mins

Ingredients

- 1 generous bunch Swiss chard (about 3/4 pound)
- Salt to taste
- 1 medium white, red or yellow onion, sliced
- 3 large garlic cloves, minced
- Kernels from 2 ears sweet corn
- Freshly ground pepper
- 8 warm corn tortillas

- ½ cup crumbled queso fresco or feta (but not too salty a feta)
- Salsa of your choice

Direction

- Bring a large pot of water to a boil while you stem chard and wash leaves in 2 rinses of water. Rinse stalks and dice them if they are wide and not stringy.
- When water in pot comes to a boil, salt generously and add chard leaves. Blanch for a minute, then transfer to a bowl of cold water and drain. Take chard up by the handful and squeeze out excess water, then cut into 1/2-inch wide strips. Set aside.
- Heat oil over medium heat in a large, heavy skillet and add onion. Cook, stirring often, until onions are tender and beginning to color, about 8 minutes, and add a generous pinch of salt, the garlic, diced chard stalks and corn kernels. Continue to cook, stirring often, until corn is just tender, about 4 minutes. Stir in chard and cook, stirring, for another minute or two, until ingredients are combined nicely and chard is tender but still bright. Season to taste with salt and pepper. Remove from heat.
- Heat tortillas. Top with vegetables, a sprinkling of cheese and a spoonful of salsa.

51. Chermoula

Serving: Makes 1 cup, about | Prep: | Cook: | Ready in: 10mins

Ingredients

- 2 cups cilantro leaves (2 large bunches)
- 1 ½ cups parsley leaves (1 large bunch)
- 3 to 4 garlic cloves (to taste), halved, green shoots removed
- ½ to ¾ teaspoon salt (to taste)
- 2 teaspoons cumin seeds, lightly toasted and ground
- 1 teaspoon sweet paprika
- ½ teaspoon coriander seeds, lightly toasted and ground
- ⅛ teaspoon cayenne (more to taste)
- ⅓ to ½ cup extra virgin olive oil, to taste
- ¼ cup freshly squeezed lemon juice

Direction

- Coarsely chop the cilantro and parsley. A scissors is a good tool for this; point it tip down in the measuring cup and cut the leaves. Then place them in a food processor and chop very fine, or chop on a cutting board. You should have 1 cup finely chopped herbs.
- Place the garlic and salt in a mortar and puree. Add a small handful of the chopped herbs, and gently but firmly grind until the herbs begin to dissolve. Add another handful. When all of the herbs have been mashed, work in the spices, 1/3 cup olive oil and lemon juice. Taste and adjust seasoning. Add more olive oil or salt if desired. Serve with grilled fish and/or vegetables, or with chicken.

Nutrition Information

- 225: calories;
- 17 grams: monounsaturated fat;
- 2 grams: protein;
- 5 grams: carbohydrates;
- 1 gram: sugars;
- 200 milligrams: sodium;
- 23 grams: fat;
- 3 grams: saturated fat;

52. Cherry Clafouti

Serving: Six servings | Prep: | Cook: | Ready in: 1hours

Ingredients

- 1 quart Bing or Queen Anne cherries, about 1 pound, stemmed and pitted
- ¼ pound, plus 1 tablespoon, unsalted butter

- 3 eggs
- ¾ cup sugar
- ¾ cup all-purpose flour, sifted
- ½ teaspoon vanilla extract
- ½ pint heavy cream, lightly whipped (optional)

Direction

- Preheat the oven to 350 degrees.
- Evenly coat a glass or porcelain 10-inch pie pan with one tablespoon of butter. Melt the remaining butter in a saucepan and reserve.
- In a medium-sized bowl, beat the eggs with the sugar until the mixture is thickened and a light lemon color. Add the butter, flour and vanilla and beat until thoroughly blended. Set aside for 15 minutes.
- Place the cherries over the bottom of the buttered pan. Pour the batter evenly over the cherries and bake for 40 minutes or until golden and puffy. Serve warm with the lightly whipped cream.

Nutrition Information

- 248: calories;
- 37 grams: sugars;
- 5 grams: protein;
- 0 grams: trans fat;
- 52 grams: carbohydrates;
- 31 milligrams: sodium;
- 3 grams: fat;
- 1 gram: polyunsaturated fat;
- 2 grams: dietary fiber;

53. Chicken Breasts With Olives And Tomatoes

Serving: 6 servings | Prep: | Cook: | Ready in: 1hours

Ingredients

- 4 tablespoons extra-virgin olive oil
- 2 cloves garlic, minced
- Juice of 1 lemon
- Salt and freshly ground black pepper
- 2 ¼ pounds skinless and boneless chicken breasts
- 1 medium onion, chopped
- 1 pound canned plum tomatoes, very well drained and chopped
- 18 Nicoise olives, pitted and coarsely chopped
- 1 tablespoon chopped fresh parsley
- 1 teaspoon fresh thyme leaves or 1/2 teaspoon dried

Direction

- In a shallow baking dish combine two tablespoons of the olive oil with half the garlic, the lemon juice and salt and pepper to taste. Add chicken breasts, turning them in the dish so they are coated with the marinade. Arrange them in a single layer in the dish, cover with plastic wrap and allow them to marinate at room temperature for 30 minutes.
- Preheat oven to 375 degrees.
- Heat the remaining oil in a skillet. Add onion and remaining garlic and saute until tender but not brown. Add tomatoes and olives and allow to cook about 15 minutes, until the mixture begins to thicken. Stir in half the parsley and the thyme and season to taste with salt and pepper.
- Spread the tomato mixture over the marinated chicken breasts. Place in oven and bake about 20 minutes, until the chicken is done. Remove from oven and baste to combine juices in bottom of the pan with the tomato mixture on top. Sprinkle with the remaining parsley and serve.

Nutrition Information

- 411: calories;
- 37 grams: protein;
- 14 grams: monounsaturated fat;
- 7 grams: carbohydrates;
- 2 grams: dietary fiber;
- 3 grams: sugars;

- 4 grams: polyunsaturated fat;
- 686 milligrams: sodium;
- 26 grams: fat;
- 6 grams: saturated fat;
- 0 grams: trans fat;

54. Chicken Breasts With Sweet Red Peppers And Snow Peas

Serving: 4 servings | Prep: | Cook: | Ready in: 15mins

Ingredients

- 4 chicken breast halves, skinless and boneless, about 1 1/4 pounds
- 1 tablespoon cornstarch
- 2 tablespoons light soy sauce
- 2 tablespoons dry white wine or water
- 3 tablespoons olive oil
- ½ teaspoon red pepper flakes (optional)
- Salt and freshly ground pepper
- 2 large sweet red peppers, cored, seeded and cut into 1/2-inch cubes
- ¼ pound snow peas, trimmed and washed
- ½ cup sliced water chestnuts or bamboo shoots
- ¼ cup coarsely chopped red onion
- 1 tablespoon sesame seeds
- 1 tablespoon finely chopped garlic
- 1 tablespoon grated fresh ginger
- ¾ cup fresh or canned chicken broth
- 4 tablespoons coarsely chopped fresh coriander

Direction

- Using a sharp knife, cut chicken breasts in half lengthwise then crosswise into slices 1/2 inch thick.
- In a small mixing bowl, combine the cornstarch, soy sauce and white wine or water, blend well and set aside.
- In a wok or a large nonstick skillet, add oil over high heat. Add chicken, pepper flakes and salt and pepper. Cook and stir about 1 minute. Scoop out the chicken pieces, leaving the oil. Set aside.
- Add red peppers, snow peas, water chestnuts or bamboo shoots, onions and sesame seeds and cook over high heat, stirring, about 1 minute or until crisp and tender. Add garlic and ginger. Cook briefly over high heat. Add chicken and chicken broth. Cook stirring and tossing for 1 more minute.
- Add cornstarch mixture, cook and stir for 15 seconds. Sprinkle with coriander and serve immediately.

Nutrition Information

- 336: calories;
- 4 grams: dietary fiber;
- 0 grams: trans fat;
- 11 grams: monounsaturated fat;
- 17 grams: carbohydrates;
- 6 grams: sugars;
- 22 grams: protein;
- 711 milligrams: sodium;
- 20 grams: fat;
- 3 grams: polyunsaturated fat;

55. Chicken Cacciatore

Serving: 4 to 5 servings. | Prep: | Cook: | Ready in: 1hours45mins

Ingredients

- ½ ounce dried mushrooms, like porcini (1/2 cup)
- 2 tablespoons olive oil
- Salt and freshly ground pepper
- 6 to 8 skinless chicken legs and/or thighs (thighs can be boneless)
- 1 small onion, minced
- 1 small carrot, minced
- 3 ribs celery, minced
- 2 large garlic cloves, minced

- 2 tablespoons fresh minced Italian parsley
- 1 heaped teaspoon minced fresh rosemary, or 1/2 teaspoon crumbled dried rosemary
- ¼ teaspoon red pepper flakes
- ½ pound mushrooms, trimmed and sliced
- ½ cup red wine
- 1 28-ounce can chopped tomatoes in juice, pulsed in a food processor

Direction

- Place the dried mushrooms in a bowl or heat-proof glass measuring cup and pour on 2 cups boiling water. Let sit 15 to 30 minutes, until mushrooms are softened. Drain through a strainer lined with cheesecloth or a paper towel and set over a bowl. Rinse the mushrooms in several changes of water, squeeze out excess water and chop coarsely. Set aside. Measure out 1 cup of the soaking liquid and set aside.
- Heat 1 tablespoon of the olive oil over medium-high heat in a large, heavy nonstick skillet. Season the chicken with salt and pepper and brown, in batches, for 5 minutes on each side. Transfer the chicken pieces to a bowl as they are done. Pour the fat off from the pan and discard.
- Turn the heat down to medium, add the remaining oil and the onion, carrot and celery, as well as a pinch of salt. Cook, stirring, until the vegetables begin to soften, about 5 minutes. Add the garlic, parsley, rosemary, red pepper flakes and salt to taste. Cover, turn the heat to low and cook, stirring often, for 5 minutes, until the mixture is soft and aromatic. Stir in the fresh and dried mushrooms, turn the heat back up to medium, and cook, stirring, until the mushrooms are just tender, about 5 minutes. Season with salt and pepper. Stir in the wine and bring to a boil. Cook, stirring, for a few minutes, until the wine has reduced by about half. Add the tomatoes and salt and pepper to taste. Cook over medium heat for 5 to 10 minutes, stirring often, until the tomatoes have cooked down a little and smell fragrant. Stir in the mushroom soaking liquid that you set aside.
- Return the chicken pieces to the pan and stir so that they are well submerged in the tomato mixture. Cover and simmer over medium heat for 30 minutes, until the chicken is tender. Taste, adjust seasoning and serve with pasta or rice.

Nutrition Information

- 629: calories;
- 19 grams: monounsaturated fat;
- 8 grams: polyunsaturated fat;
- 24 grams: carbohydrates;
- 39 grams: protein;
- 41 grams: fat;
- 10 grams: saturated fat;
- 0 grams: trans fat;
- 7 grams: sugars;
- 1184 milligrams: sodium;

56. Chicken Cacciatore, New Version

Serving: 4 servings | Prep: | Cook: | Ready in: 1hours15mins

Ingredients

- 1 3 1/2-pound chicken, quartered
- 2 tablespoons extra-virgin olive oil
- 1 cup onion, sliced very thin
- 2 cloves garlic, sliced very thin
- Salt and freshly ground black pepper to taste
- ¼ cup dry white wine
- 1 ½ cups fresh ripe tomatoes, skinned with a peeler and chopped, or canned Italian plum tomatoes, cut up, with their juice

Direction

- Rinse chicken in cold water and pat dry.

- Put olive oil and onion in a saute pan large enough to hold the chicken without crowding. Place over medium heat and cook, stirring occasionally, until onion is translucent. Add garlic. Add chicken, skin side down, and saute until skin turns golden. Turn and cook chicken on the other side.
- Add salt and pepper and turn the chicken a few times. Add the wine, and simmer until it is reduced by half.
- Add the tomatoes, reduce the heat to a very slow simmer, partly cover the pan, and cook the chicken about 40 minutes, until it is very tender and comes away from the bone easily. Turn and baste it from time to time during cooking. If necessary add a little water.
- Transfer the chicken to a warm dish and serve. If desired, it can be prepared in advance and reheated.

Nutrition Information

- 684: calories;
- 8 grams: carbohydrates;
- 3 grams: sugars;
- 1202 milligrams: sodium;
- 48 grams: fat;
- 22 grams: monounsaturated fat;
- 2 grams: dietary fiber;
- 51 grams: protein;
- 13 grams: saturated fat;
- 0 grams: trans fat;
- 10 grams: polyunsaturated fat;

57. Chicken Noodle Salad With Creamy Sesame Dressing

Serving: Serves 6 | Prep: | Cook: | Ready in: 40mins

Ingredients

- 2 cups shredded poached chicken breast (1 whole breast on the bone; see below)
- 9 ounces udon or soba
- 1 tablespoon dark sesame oil
- ½ pound baby bok choy ---blanch until water comes back to boil then slice
- 1 Persian cucumber or 1/3 European cucumber, cut in 2-inch julienne
- 1 stalk celery, cut in 2-inch julienne
- ½ to 1 cup chopped cilantro
- ¼ cup chopped scallions
- 1-2 serrano peppers, minced (optional)
- For the dressing
- 3 tablespoons tahini (a runny variety if possible, available in Middle Eastern markets)
- 1 tablespoon soy sauce
- ¼ cup seasoned rice wine vinegar
- 1 to 2 teaspoons hot red pepper oil (to taste)
- Pinch of cayenne
- 2 teaspoons finely minced fresh ginger or 1 teaspoon ginger juice
- Salt and freshly ground pepper to taste
- 1 tablespoon sesame oil
- ¼ cup vegetable or chicken broth or water (more to taste)

Direction

- To poach the chicken breast, combine 1 quart water with 1 quartered onion, 4 thick slices of ginger, 2 crushed whole garlic cloves and salt to taste in a 2-quart saucepan, and bring to a simmer over medium heat. Add the chicken breasts, and bring back to a simmer. Skim off any foam that rises. Cover partially, reduce the heat to low and simmer 15 to 20 minutes, until the chicken is cooked through (it should register 160 on a meat thermometer at the thickest section). Allow the chicken to cool in the broth if there is time. Remove the chicken from the broth when cool enough to handle. Remove and discard the skin. Remove from the bone and shred, pulling strips of chicken off the top of the breast. Pull with the grain and the meat will come apart naturally. Strain the chicken broth, and refrigerate overnight. The next morning, skim off and discard the fat, and freeze the broth in smaller containers or freezer bags.

- Cook the noodles. Drain, rinse with cold water and drain well. Toss in a bowl with 1 tablespoon sesame oil and refrigerate while you prepare the other ingredients.
- Bring a medium pot of water to a boil, add salt if desired and add the bok choy. Blanch for 1 minute and transfer to a bowl of cold water. Drain and squeeze out excess water. Slice crosswise and add to the noodles. Add the remaining ingredients. Season if desired with salt and pepper.
- Whisk together all of the ingredients for the dressing. Toss with the salad and serve, or refrigerate until ready to serve.

Nutrition Information

- 395: calories;
- 36 grams: carbohydrates;
- 2 grams: sugars;
- 23 grams: protein;
- 499 milligrams: sodium;
- 17 grams: fat;
- 3 grams: dietary fiber;
- 0 grams: trans fat;
- 7 grams: monounsaturated fat;
- 6 grams: polyunsaturated fat;

58. Chicken Paprikash

Serving: 6 servings | Prep: | Cook: | Ready in: 35mins

Ingredients

- 6 leg-thigh pieces of chicken, skinned and cut apart
- 5 scallions, chopped
- 1 teaspoon salt, or to taste
- 5 cloves garlic, crushed
- 1 tablespoon dill weed
- 1 cup chicken stock or water
- ½ cup dry white wine
- 4 tablespoons sweet paprika, preferably Hungarian
- ¼ cup tomato sauce
- ¾ cup sour cream

Direction

- Put chicken, scallions, salt, garlic, dill weed, chicken stock and wine into a pot, bring to a boil, cover and simmer over low heat for 20 to 25 minutes. Remove chicken pieces to a warm place.
- Boil the liquid in the pot until it is slightly reduced. Stir in paprika and tomato sauce and mix well. Add sour cream and heat to just below boiling. Return chicken pieces to the pot to reheat, but do not allow to boil. Serve with buttered noodles.

Nutrition Information

- 301: calories;
- 19 grams: protein;
- 4 grams: polyunsaturated fat;
- 2 grams: dietary fiber;
- 7 grams: carbohydrates;
- 0 grams: trans fat;
- 3 grams: sugars;
- 482 milligrams: sodium;
- 20 grams: fat;

59. Chicken Soup With Lime And Avocado

Serving: Serves four | Prep: | Cook: | Ready in: 30mins

Ingredients

- 2 quarts chicken stock, preferably homemade, or 1 quart commercial chicken broth and 1 quart water
- 1 medium onion, finely chopped
- 1 garlic clove, minced
- 1 serrano or jalapeño chile, seeded if desired and minced

- 1 pound tomatoes, peeled, seeded and diced, or 1 (14-ounce) can, drained
- 1 cup shredded cooked chicken breast
- ¼ cup chopped cilantro
- 1 to 2 tablespoons freshly squeezed lime juice (to taste), plus thin slices of lime for garnish
- 1 avocado, cut in small dice or thinly sliced
- Corn tortilla crisps for garnish

Direction

- Bring the chicken stock to a simmer, add the onion, garlic and chile, and simmer 15 minutes.
- Add the tomatoes, and simmer for another five minutes. Taste and adjust salt, then stir in the chicken breast and chopped cilantro. Cover and let sit for five minutes. Add the lime juice.
- Divide the avocado between four soup bowls. Ladle in the soup, place a slice of lime on each bowl, and serve with crisp corn tortillas.

Nutrition Information

- 342: calories;
- 3 grams: saturated fat;
- 2 grams: polyunsaturated fat;
- 28 grams: carbohydrates;
- 5 grams: dietary fiber;
- 15 grams: fat;
- 8 grams: monounsaturated fat;
- 12 grams: sugars;
- 25 grams: protein;
- 732 milligrams: sodium;

60. Chicken With Apples And Ginger

Serving: 4 servings | Prep: | Cook: | Ready in: 30mins

Ingredients

- 1 3- to 4-pound chicken, cut into 16 pieces
- 1 to 2 tablespoons corn or canola oil
- 1 large onion, chopped
- 1 clove garlic, minced
- ¼ cup dry white wine
- 1 cup apple juice
- 1 tablespoon fresh ginger, finely chopped
- 1 tablespoon cornstarch
- 1 cup plain low-fat or nonfat yogurt
- 2 well-flavored apples, cored and cut into small chunks
- Freshly ground black pepper to taste
- 8 ounces medium egg noodles, cooked and drained

Direction

- Remove as much skin and external fat as possible from chicken. Heat 1 tablespoon oil in nonstick skillet or 2 tablespoons oil in regular skillet large enough to hold chicken pieces in single layer. Brown chicken on both sides in hot oil over medium heat; remove and set aside.
- Saute onion and garlic in same pan until onion is soft. Add wine, apple juice and ginger to pan and cook over medium-high heat until liquid is reduced to 1 cup.
- Stir cornstarch into yogurt. Add to pan with apples and chicken and season with pepper. Cook, covered, for about 20 minutes, until chicken is cooked through.
- Arrange noodles on each of 4 plates. Spoon chicken and sauce over noodles.

Nutrition Information

- 997: calories;
- 255 milligrams: sodium;
- 49 grams: fat;
- 13 grams: saturated fat;
- 0 grams: trans fat;
- 72 grams: carbohydrates;
- 5 grams: dietary fiber;
- 63 grams: protein;
- 21 grams: monounsaturated fat;
- 11 grams: polyunsaturated fat;

- 23 grams: sugars;

61. Chicken With Olives, Prunes And Capers

Serving: Twelve to fourteen servings | Prep: | Cook: | Ready in: 1hours10mins

Ingredients

- 12 chicken breasts and thighs, trimmed of fat and skin
- 2 cups pitted prunes (or dried apricots or dried pears)
- 1 ¼ cups white wine
- ¾ cup dark brown sugar
- ¾ cup olive oil
- ¾ cup red-wine vinegar
- ¾ cup green olives, pitted
- ¾ cup capers
- 4 tablespoons oregano
- 1 teaspoon freshly ground pepper
- 1 teaspoon salt
- ½ teaspoon crushed red pepper
- 6 medium-size bay leaves
- 1 small garlic head, minced
- 3 tablespoons chopped cilantro

Direction

- In two or three baking pans, arrange the chicken pieces in one layer.
- Combine all the ingredients except the cilantro and one-half cup of the brown sugar. Pour over the chicken so that the prunes, olives and capers are evenly distributed. Cover and refrigerate overnight.
- Preheat the oven to 350 degrees.
- Sprinkle the remaining brown sugar over the chicken and bake for about one hour, basting often.
- To serve, arrange the chicken pieces with the sauce on a platter. Sprinkle with the cilantro.

Nutrition Information

- 514: calories;
- 8 grams: saturated fat;
- 18 grams: monounsaturated fat;
- 6 grams: polyunsaturated fat;
- 27 grams: carbohydrates;
- 3 grams: dietary fiber;
- 22 grams: protein;
- 34 grams: fat;
- 0 grams: trans fat;
- 17 grams: sugars;
- 519 milligrams: sodium;

62. Chicken And Sausage Jambalaya

Serving: 2 servings | Prep: | Cook: | Ready in: 35mins

Ingredients

- ¾ cup long-grain rice
- 4 ounces skinless, boneless chicken breasts
- 4 ounces low-fat spicy chicken or turkey sausage
- 16 ounces mixed whole red and green bell peppers, or 14 ounces chopped ready-cut peppers (4 cups)
- 8 ounces whole onion or 7 ounces ready-cut (1 2/3 cups)
- 2 cloves garlic
- 2 or 3 sprigs thyme (to make 1 1/2 tablespoons chopped)
- ⅔ cup no-salt-added tomato puree
- ⅓ cup dry white wine
- 1 cup no-salt-added chicken stock or broth
- ¼ teaspoon hot pepper flakes
- ⅛ teaspoon salt
- Freshly ground black pepper to taste

Direction

- Combine rice and 1 1/2 cups water in a heavy-bottomed pot; bring to a boil. Reduce heat and

simmer, covered, until liquid has been absorbed (17 minutes total).
- Wash and dry chicken and cut chicken into bite-size pieces. Slice sausage thin. Saute chicken and sausage in the sausage's own fat until chicken is brown on both sides; remove and set aside.
- Chop whole peppers and onion.
- Wipe out all but a thin coating of fat from the pot. Saute the peppers and onions until onions begin to soften.
- Meanwhile, mince garlic and add to pot. Wash, dry and chop thyme.
- When onion has softened, add the tomato puree, wine, chicken stock, hot pepper flakes and thyme along with chicken and sausage. Reduce heat to simmer, cover and continue to cook until flavors are completely blended, just a few minutes.
- When rice is cooked, add to pot and stir in. Season with salt and pepper and serve with some crusty bread.

Nutrition Information

- 666: calories;
- 11 grams: dietary fiber;
- 19 grams: sugars;
- 860 milligrams: sodium;
- 0 grams: trans fat;
- 5 grams: monounsaturated fat;
- 3 grams: polyunsaturated fat;
- 97 grams: carbohydrates;
- 36 grams: protein;
- 13 grams: fat;

63. Chili Lime Bluefish Grilled With Red Peppers And Corn

Serving: Four servings | Prep: | Cook: | Ready in: 3hours

Ingredients

- 6 tablespoons fresh lime juice
- 2 jalapenos, seeded and minced
- 1 teaspoon olive oil
- ½ teaspoon salt, plus more to taste
- Freshly ground pepper to taste
- 1 bluefish fillet (about 1 1/2 pounds)
- 4 ears corn
- 2 red bell peppers, stemmed, cored and quartered

Direction

- Combine the the lime juice, jalapenos, olive oil, 1/2 teaspoon salt and pepper to taste in a large, shallow glass or ceramic dish. Cut diagonal slashes in the skin of the bluefish and place, skin side up, in the marinade. Spoon some of the marinade over the skin. Cover and refrigerate for 2 hours.
- Preheat a charcoal grill. Pull back the husks of the corn, remove the silk and cover the corn with the husks again. Soak in water for 10 minutes. Place the corn on the grill for 10 minutes, turning them one-quarter turn after 5 minutes.
- Place the fish, skin side up, on the grill with the corn. Place the peppers on the grill. Grill the fish for 7 minutes. Turn it over carefully and grill until just cooked through, about 5 minutes more.
- Grill the peppers until charred, about 5 minutes per side. Grill the corn until tender, about 10 minutes longer, turning twice.
- Cut the fish in half lengthwise. Cut again crosswise, making roughly equal pieces. Season with salt to taste. Place 1 piece of fish, 1 ear of corn and 2 pieces of red pepper on each of 4 plates and serve immediately, with hot corn bread.

Nutrition Information

- 338: calories;
- 38 grams: protein;
- 411 milligrams: sodium;
- 10 grams: sugars;
- 2 grams: polyunsaturated fat;
- 0 grams: trans fat;

- 4 grams: dietary fiber;
- 26 grams: carbohydrates;

64. Chinese Fried Rice With Shrimp And Peas

Serving: Serves four to six | Prep: | Cook: | Ready in: 15mins

Ingredients

- 3 large eggs
- 2 tablespoons vegetable or canola oil
- 2 garlic cloves, minced
- 2 teaspoons minced fresh ginger
- ½ pound medium shrimp, peeled, deveined and cut in 3/4-inch pieces
- 1 tablespoon dry sherry
- 5 to 6 cups cooked and cooled basmati or long-grain rice
- 1 bunch scallions, thinly sliced, white and green parts separated
- ½ cup cooked fresh or thawed frozen peas
- 2 tablespoons soy sauce
- ¼ cup chopped cilantro

Direction

- Beat one of the eggs in a small bowl and salt lightly. Heat 1 teaspoon of the oil over medium-high heat in a small nonstick frying pan, and add the beaten egg. Swirl in the pan until the egg forms an even coat, like a thin pancake. When the egg is cooked through, roll up and slide onto a plate. Cut in thin strips (you can use a scissors or a knife). Set aside.
- Heat a wok or large, heavy nonstick skillet over medium-high heat until a drop of water evaporates upon contact. Add the remaining oil and swirl around the pan, then add the shrimp and cook about one minute, stirring and tossing with a spatula or wok scoop until just about cooked through and pink. Add the garlic and ginger, and stir-fry for 30 seconds. Add the sherry, and stir everything together. When the sizzling stops, pour in the remaining beaten egg. Stir-fry until scrambled, and add the rice. Cook the rice — scooping it up, then pressing it into the pan and scooping it up again — for about two minutes. Stir in white and lighter green parts of the scallions, the peas and the soy sauce. Stir together for about half a minute, and transfer to a warm serving platter. Sprinkle the egg strips, scallion greens and cilantro over the top. Serve hot.

Nutrition Information

- 315: calories;
- 8 grams: fat;
- 2 grams: dietary fiber;
- 45 grams: carbohydrates;
- 560 milligrams: sodium;
- 1 gram: sugars;
- 0 grams: trans fat;
- 4 grams: monounsaturated fat;
- 14 grams: protein;

65. Chunky Avocado Papaya Salsa

Serving: Serves 6 to 8 | Prep: | Cook: | Ready in: 20mins

Ingredients

- 2 medium-size ripe Hass avocados, halved, pitted and cut in small dice
- 1 small ripe papaya, halved, seeded, peeled and cut in small dice (about 2 cups dice)
- 1 tart apple, unpeeled, or Asian pear, peeled if desired, cored and cut in small dice
- ¼ cup freshly squeezed lime juice
- 1 fresh red or green serrano chile, seeded and thinly sliced or minced, or more to taste
- ¼ cup chopped cilantro
- 2 tablespoons chopped fresh mint
- ½ small red onion, diced small, soaked for 5 minutes in water to cover, drained and rinsed (optional)
- Salt to taste

Direction

- Combine diced avocados and papaya in a medium bowl. Add remaining ingredients and toss together. Season to taste with salt. Serve as a salad or a salsa.

Nutrition Information

- 105: calories;
- 7 grams: fat;
- 1 gram: protein;
- 5 grams: dietary fiber;
- 11 grams: carbohydrates;
- 4 grams: sugars;
- 241 milligrams: sodium;

66. Cinnamon Curry Rice

Serving: 6 servings | Prep: | Cook: | Ready in: 1hours30mins

Ingredients

- 4 sticks cinnamon or Chinese cinnamon bark, about 1/2 ounce
- 2 cups water
- 3 tablespoons corn or safflower oil
- 2 tablespoons curry powder
- 1 medium onion, diced, about 1 3/4 cups
- 1 ½ tablespoons flour
- 4 cups canned or homemade chicken broth
- 3 carrots, diced, about 1 1/2 cups
- 1 large apple, peeled, cored, and diced, about 1 cup
- 2 medium potatoes, diced, about 2 cups
- 1 ½ tablespoons minced garlic
- ½ pound boneless center-cut pork loin, trimmed of fat and diced
- 1 teaspoon salt
- ¼ teaspoon freshly ground black pepper
- 6 servings cooked white rice

Direction

- In a saucepan, bring the cinnamon and water to a boil. Simmer, partly covered, until the liquid is reduced to 1 cup, about 30 minutes. Strain the cinnamon, and reserve the liquid.
- In a heavy casserole or Dutch oven, heat 2 tablespoons of oil until hot, add the curry powder and the onion, and cook over medium heat for about 1 minute. Add the flour, and cook for another minute, stirring constantly. Add the chicken broth, heat until boiling, and add the carrot, apple and potatoes. Partly cover, and simmer over low heat for 30 minutes.
- Heat a wok or a saute pan, add the remaining oil, and heat until hot. Add the garlic and pork, and cook over high heat, stirring until pork changes color. Remove garlic and pork with a slotted spoon.
- When the vegetables are tender, add the pork and cinnamon liquid. Turn up the heat, and cook for 20 minutes. Add salt and pepper, and serve over hot rice.

Nutrition Information

- 503: calories;
- 3 grams: saturated fat;
- 6 grams: dietary fiber;
- 14 grams: fat;
- 4 grams: monounsaturated fat;
- 76 grams: carbohydrates;
- 9 grams: sugars;
- 18 grams: protein;
- 667 milligrams: sodium;

67. Classic Irish Salad

Serving: 6 servings | Prep: | Cook: | Ready in: 1hours10mins

Ingredients

- 2 medium beets
- 2 small heads bibb lettuce

- 2 bunches watercress
- 2 tablespoons creme fraiche
- 1 tablespoon chopped parsley
- 5 tablespoons extra-virgin olive oil
- 3 tablespoons herb infused white vinegar (or to taste)
- Coarse salt and freshly ground pepper to taste
- 1 dozen quail eggs, boiled for two minutes
- ½ cup chopped chervil leaves

Direction

- Place the beets in a saucepan with water to cover and simmer for one hour or until tender. Remove from heat and allow to cool in the liquid. Peel and julienne.
- Break up the heads of bibb lettuce, leaving the leaves whole. Wash and dry. Cut the stems from the watercress; wash and dry the leaves.
- Make the dressing. Mix the creme fraiche, parsley, olive oil and vinegar together and season to taste with salt and pepper.
- To assemble, put whole leaves of lettuce around the outer edges of six individual plates. Place watercress in the middle of the plate and sprinkle the beets on top. Peel the quail eggs and cut them in half. Place the eggs on top and sprinkle with chervil. Drizzle dressing over and serve.

Nutrition Information

- 162: calories;
- 2 grams: dietary fiber;
- 5 grams: carbohydrates;
- 4 grams: protein;
- 346 milligrams: sodium;
- 14 grams: fat;
- 3 grams: sugars;
- 9 grams: monounsaturated fat;

68. Classic Oatmeal Raisin Cookies

Serving: 3 dozen cookies | Prep: | Cook: | Ready in: 45mins

Ingredients

- 1 cup/227 grams (2 sticks) unsalted butter, softened, more for pans
- 1 cup/200 grams dark brown sugar, packed
- ⅓ cup/66 grams granulated sugar
- 2 large eggs
- 1 tablespoon/15 milliliters vanilla extract
- 1 ½ cups/187 grams all-purpose flour
- ¾ teaspoon salt
- 1 teaspoon baking soda
- 1 teaspoon ground cinnamon
- ¼ teaspoon freshly grated nutmeg
- ¼ teaspoon ground cardamom or ground ginger
- 3 cups/270 grams rolled oats (not instant)
- 1 ½ cups/225 grams raisins

Direction

- Heat oven to 350 degrees. Butter two large cookie sheets, or line them with parchment paper or reusable silicone liners.
- Using an electric mixer, beat butter in a large bowl until creamy. Add brown and granulated sugars, then beat until fluffy, about 2 minutes. Beat in eggs, one at a time, until fully incorporated. Then, beat in vanilla extract.
- In a separate bowl, use a wooden spoon or spatula to mix together the flour, salt, baking soda, cinnamon, nutmeg and cardamom. Set mixer on low speed, and beat flour mixture into the butter mixture. Stir in oats and raisins.
- Spoon out dough by large tablespoonfuls onto prepared cookie sheets, leaving at least 2 inches between each cookie.
- Bake until cookie edges turn golden brown, about 9 to 13 minutes. Centers will still be quite soft, but they will firm up as the cookies cool. Cool completely on a wire rack. Store in an airtight container at room temperature.

Nutrition Information

- 144: calories;
- 21 grams: carbohydrates;
- 84 milligrams: sodium;
- 0 grams: polyunsaturated fat;
- 6 grams: fat;
- 3 grams: saturated fat;
- 2 grams: protein;
- 1 gram: dietary fiber;
- 11 grams: sugars;

69. Cocoa Brownies

Serving: 16 squares | Prep: | Cook: | Ready in: 50mins

Ingredients

- ¾ cup cake flour
- ⅔ cup sugar
- ⅓ cup European-style cocoa powder
- ⅓ cup cornstarch
- 1 teaspoon baking powder
- ½ teaspoon baking soda
- ½ teaspoon salt
- 1 egg white
- ½ cup evaporated skim milk
- ¾ cup applesauce
- ½ cup light corn syrup
- 1 teaspoon pure vanilla extract

Direction

- Preheat oven to 350 degrees.
- Spray an 8-by-8 or 9-by-9-inch square pan with nonstick cooking spray.
- Thoroughly mix flour, sugar, cocoa, cornstarch, baking powder, baking soda and salt.
- In another bowl, whisk the egg white and milk and then stir in applesauce, corn syrup and vanilla. Stir in dry mixture until blended.
- Pour batter into prepared pan and bake 35 to 40 minutes, or until knife inserted in center comes out clean. Cool in pan and cut into squares.

Nutrition Information

- 109: calories;
- 0 grams: polyunsaturated fat;
- 27 grams: carbohydrates;
- 1 gram: protein;
- 18 grams: sugars;
- 119 milligrams: sodium;

70. Cod Ceviche

Serving: Serves 4 to 6 | Prep: | Cook: | Ready in: 8hours

Ingredients

- 1 ½ pounds Alaskan cod fillets
- 1 ½ cups freshly squeezed lime juice
- Salt and freshly ground pepper
- 1 small white or red onion, sliced
- 1 garlic clove, minced
- 1 or 2 serrano or jalapeño chiles, minced
- 2 medium tomatoes (in season only), diced
- ¼ cup extra virgin olive oil
- 1 ripe but firm avocado, diced
- ¼ to ½ cup chopped cilantro (to taste)
- 1 6-ounce bag baby spinach

Direction

- Cut the fish into 1/2-inch cubes. Make sure to pull out any bones and discard. Place in a large bowl, add the lime juice and stir together. Make sure that the fish is covered with lime juice. Cover and refrigerate for 6 to 7 hours, stirring every once in awhile.
- Add salt and pepper to taste, and toss together. Add the onion, garlic, chiles, tomatoes if using, and olive oil, and toss together. Cover and refrigerate for another hour. Stir in the avocado and cilantro and gently toss together.

- Line plates or wide bowls, or a platter with the spinach leaves. Taste the ceviche and adjust seasoning. Using a slotted spoon so that your plate doesn't become flooded with lime juice, top the spinach with the ceviche and serve.

Nutrition Information

- 268: calories;
- 23 grams: protein;
- 14 grams: carbohydrates;
- 4 grams: dietary fiber;
- 3 grams: sugars;
- 15 grams: fat;
- 2 grams: polyunsaturated fat;
- 10 grams: monounsaturated fat;
- 727 milligrams: sodium;

71. Cod Fillets With Cilantro Yogurt Sauce

Serving: 4 servings (you'll have sauce left over) | Prep: | Cook: | Ready in: 40mins

Ingredients

- 2 cups cilantro leaves (some stems are O.K. – you don't have to pick off each leaf the way you do with parsley)
- ½ cup flat-leaf parsley leaves
- 2 garlic cloves
- Salt and freshly ground pepper
- 2 tablespoons fresh lemon juice
- 2 tablespoons extra virgin olive oil
- 1 cup plain Greek yogurt (low-fat or whole)
- 1 ½ pounds Alaskan cod fillets
- Lemon wedges for garnish

Direction

- To make the sauce, coarsely chop the cilantro and the parsley leaves. In a mortar and pestle, mash the garlic with a pinch of salt. Place the cilantro and parsley in a food processor fitted with the steel blade and process until finely chopped. Add the garlic, lemon juice, olive oil, about 1/2 teaspoon salt (or to taste), and the yogurt and process until the mixture is smooth and green. Transfer to a bowl.
- Preheat the oven to 300 degrees. Line a sheet pan with foil and oil the foil. Season the fish fillets with salt and pepper and lay on the foil. Place a pan of just boiled water on the floor of your oven and place the baking sheet with the fish in the oven on the middle rack. Bake 10 to 20 minutes, depending on the thickness of the fillets, until the fish is opaque on the surface and you can pull it apart with a fork.
- Remove the fish from the oven, transfer to plates or a platter, and spoon on the sauce. Garnish with lemon wedges and serve.

Nutrition Information

- 272: calories;
- 5 grams: carbohydrates;
- 1 gram: dietary fiber;
- 3 grams: sugars;
- 36 grams: protein;
- 636 milligrams: sodium;
- 12 grams: fat;
- 4 grams: saturated fat;

72. Cold Baked Salmon With Green Mayonnaise

Serving: 10 to 12 servings | Prep: | Cook: | Ready in: 1hours

Ingredients

- 1 whole salmon, scaled, with head on, about 5 to 6 pounds
- 1 onion, sliced
- 1 lemon, cut in half
- 6 sticks rosemary
- Coarse salt and freshly ground pepper to taste
- 3 tablespoons olive oil

Direction

- Preheat the oven to 375 degrees.
- Place the salmon on a roasting pan, on a piece of foil if the pan is too short for the fish. Place slices of onion inside the cavity and squeeze the lemon inside and over the top. Place two to three whole sticks of rosemary inside the cavity and sprinkle the leaves from the remaining sticks on top. Season with salt and pepper and brush the fish with olive oil.
- Cover the salmon lightly with foil, turning up the ends of the piece underneath so that the juices do not run out while it is cooking. Roast for 30 minutes, then remove the foil. Roast for 15 to 20 more minutes or until the salmon is cooked (test by inserting a knife into the flesh to check; it is better to undercook than overcook salmon. When overcooked it becomes dry).
- Place the salmon on a serving platter. It can be served hot or cold. If serving the salmon hot, decorate it with lime or lemon slices and sprinkle it with chives. Serve it immediately. If serving it cold, allow the salmon to cool to room temperature (you can refrigerate it overnight or serve on the day a few hours after it has been cooked, without refrigerating it). Remove the skin from the top side of the salmon. Decorate the fish with slices of lime and lemon and chopped chives.

Nutrition Information

- 108: calories;
- 1 gram: sugars;
- 7 grams: protein;
- 126 milligrams: sodium;
- 8 grams: fat;
- 2 grams: carbohydrates;
- 4 grams: monounsaturated fat;

73. Cold Tomato Soup With Rosemary

Serving: 4 servings | Prep: | Cook: | Ready in: 15mins

Ingredients

- 2 slices stale French or Italian white bread, crusts removed
- 3 pounds ripe tomatoes, peeled, seeded and roughly chopped
- 1 teaspoon fresh rosemary leaves
- 1 small clove garlic, peeled
- 1 cup chicken stock or ice cubes
- Salt and freshly ground black pepper to taste
- The juice of 1 lemon, or more to taste

Direction

- Soak bread in cold water briefly; squeeze dry, and combine in a blender with tomatoes, rosemary and garlic (you may have to do this in two batches). If using stock, turn on machine and drizzle in the stock; blend until smooth. If using ice cubes, place them in the blender and blend until mixture is smooth. Pour the mixture into a bowl.
- Season with salt and pepper, then add lemon juice to taste. Chill and serve.

Nutrition Information

- 130: calories;
- 0 grams: trans fat;
- 25 grams: carbohydrates;
- 11 grams: sugars;
- 6 grams: protein;
- 1003 milligrams: sodium;
- 2 grams: fat;
- 1 gram: polyunsaturated fat;
- 5 grams: dietary fiber;

74. Cole Slaw

Serving: About 10 cups | Prep: | Cook: | Ready in: 1hours10mins

Ingredients

- 2 carrots, trimmed, peeled and chopped coarsely
- 1 medium sweet onion such as a Vidalia, peeled and chopped coarsely
- ½ each red bell pepper and green bell pepper, seeded, chopped coarsely
- 1 head cabbage (about 2 pounds), outer leaves discarded, cored and shredded
- 2 tablespoons sugar
- 2 tablespoons distilled white vinegar
- 1 ½ cups Hellmann's mayonnaise, or more to taste
- 1 teaspoon celery seed or caraway seed
- Kosher salt

Direction

- In batches, pulse carrots, onion, peppers and cabbage separately, until each is finely chopped. Do not overprocess! Combine ingredients in a bowl.
- Combine sugar and vinegar in a pan and stir over low heat until sugar melts. Pour over vegetables and mix. Add 1 1/2 cups mayonnaise and caraway or celery seeds, stir to combine and season with salt to taste. Add more mayonnaise, if desired. Chill for an hour and serve.

Nutrition Information

- 291: calories;
- 12 grams: carbohydrates;
- 3 grams: dietary fiber;
- 16 grams: polyunsaturated fat;
- 8 grams: sugars;
- 2 grams: protein;
- 424 milligrams: sodium;
- 27 grams: fat;
- 4 grams: saturated fat;
- 7 grams: monounsaturated fat;

75. Connemara Lamb Stew

Serving: Four servings | Prep: | Cook: | Ready in: 45mins

Ingredients

- ½ cup flour
- ½ teaspoon salt
- 1 teaspoon freshly ground pepper
- 1 ½ pounds lamb shoulder or stewing meat, cut into 1/2-inch chunks
- 1 tablespoon olive oil
- 3 tablespoons minced fresh mint leaves
- Salt and freshly ground pepper
- 1 cup dry white wine
- 2 ½ cups chicken broth
- 2 tablespoons lemon juice
- 4 raw, fresh artichoke hearts, trimmed, cleaned and cut into quarters
- 3 tablespoons minced parsley
- 1 tablespoon minced lemon zest
- 8 fresh oysters, shucked

Direction

- Season the flour with the salt and pepper. Lightly dust the lamb with the flour and shake off the excess. Heat the olive oil in a heavy-bottom pot over medium heat until hot. Add the lamb in one layer and saute until golden brown on all sides, about 6 to 10 minutes. Add 1 tablespoon of the mint and season lightly with salt and pepper. Add the white wine, stir well and simmer for 5 minutes. Add the chicken broth, lemon juice and artichoke hearts, lower the heat, cover the pot and simmer gently until the lamb is tender, about 30 minutes.
- Meanwhile, mix the remaining 2 tablespoons mint, the parsley and the lemon zest. When the lamb is tender, gently slide the oysters into the stew and simmer for an additional 3

minutes. Sprinkle with the mint mixture, divide among heated bowls and serve.

Nutrition Information

- 748: calories;
- 5 grams: polyunsaturated fat;
- 31 grams: carbohydrates;
- 19 grams: monounsaturated fat;
- 44 grams: fat;
- 17 grams: saturated fat;
- 4 grams: sugars;
- 45 grams: protein;
- 1294 milligrams: sodium;

76. Corn And Lobster Pie In A Chili Polenta Crust

Serving: Six servings | Prep: | Cook: |Ready in: 2hours30mins

Ingredients

- The polenta:
- 2 ⅔ cups water
- ⅔ cup yellow cornmeal
- 1 teaspoon chili powder
- ¾ teaspoon salt
- Freshly ground pepper to taste
- Olive oil spray
- The custard:
- 3 large cloves garlic, unpeeled
- 2 eggs
- 1 cup milk
- 1 teaspoon salt
- Freshly ground pepper to taste
- Kernels from 2 large ears of corn
- The lobster mix:
- Kernels from 1 large ear of corn
- 2 lobsters, steamed, tail and claw meat removed and cut into 1/2-inch dice
- 1 red and 1 yellow bell pepper, stemmed, cored, deribbed and cut into 1/4-inch dice
- 1 jalapeno pepper, seeded and minced
- 1 tablespoon chopped cilantro
- 2 scallions, chopped
- 1 tablespoon fresh lime juice
- ½ teaspoon salt, plus more to taste
- Freshly ground pepper to taste

Direction

-
-
-

Nutrition Information

- 178: calories;
- 2 grams: dietary fiber;
- 0 grams: trans fat;
- 640 milligrams: sodium;
- 4 grams: fat;
- 1 gram: polyunsaturated fat;
- 21 grams: carbohydrates;
- 3 grams: sugars;
- 14 grams: protein;

77. Couscous Risotto

Serving: 8 cups | Prep: | Cook: |Ready in: 25mins

Ingredients

- ½ cup olive oil
- 1 medium-size onion, minced
- 10 medium-size garlic cloves, smashed, peeled and minced
- 3 tablespoons ground cumin, preferably freshly ground
- 1 tablespoon curry powder
- 2 cups couscous
- 4 cups chicken broth or vegetarian broth (see Micro-Tip)
- 1 ½ teaspoons kosher salt
- Freshly ground black pepper

Direction

- Place oil in a 14- by 9- by 2-inch oval dish. Cook, uncovered, at 100 percent in a high-power oven for 2 minutes. Stir in onion and garlic. Cook for 2 minutes. Stir in spices and cook for 3 minutes.
- Stir in couscous and pour broth over mixture. Cook for 10 minutes.
- Remove from oven. Stir in salt and pepper.

Nutrition Information

- 245: calories;
- 2 grams: saturated fat;
- 8 grams: monounsaturated fat;
- 3 grams: dietary fiber;
- 305 milligrams: sodium;
- 12 grams: fat;
- 1 gram: sugars;
- 30 grams: carbohydrates;
- 5 grams: protein;

78. Couscous With Tomatoes, Okra And Chickpeas

Serving: 6 to 8 servings | Prep: | Cook: | Ready in: 30mins

Ingredients

- 1 pound okra
- Salt to taste
- ½ cup red wine vinegar or cider vinegar
- 2 tablespoons olive oil
- 1 large onion, chopped
- 2 to 4 large garlic cloves (to taste), minced
- Salt, preferably kosher, to taste
- 1 ½ teaspoons paprika
- ½ teaspoon cayenne (more to taste)
- 1 pound tomatoes, grated, or peeled, seeded and chopped
- 2 cups chickpeas, soaked for 6 hours or overnight and drained
- A bouquet garni consisting of 8 sprigs each parsley
- A bouquet garni consisting of 8 sprigs cilantro
- 1 large sweet red pepper, seeded and cut in large dice
- 2 tablespoons tomato paste
- 1 tablespoon harissa (more to taste), plus additional for serving (optional)
- ½ cup chopped fresh parsley, or a mixture of parsley and cilantro or mint
- 2 to 2 ⅔ cups couscous (1/3 cup per serving)

Direction

- Heat 1 tablespoon of the olive oil in a large, heavy soup pot or Dutch oven over medium heat and add the onion. Cook, stirring, until it is tender, about 5 minutes, and stir in the garlic, 1/2 teaspoon salt and the spices. Stir together for about 1 minute and add the tomatoes. Cook, stirring often, until the tomatoes have cooked down slightly, 5 to 10 minutes. Add the chickpeas, 2 quarts water and the bouquet garni. Bring to a gentle boil, reduce the heat, cover and simmer 1 1/2 hours.
- Meanwhile, trim the stems off the okra and place in a large bowl. Salt generously, douse with the vinegar and let sit for 30 minutes to an hour. Drain the okra and rinse thoroughly. Set aside.
- After 1 1/2 hours, season the chickpeas with salt to taste and add the harissa, tomato paste, red pepper and okra. Bring back to a simmer and simmer 30 to 45 minutes, or until okra and beans are tender. Remove a cup of broth to use for flavoring the couscous. Stir in the chopped fresh herbs and simmer another few minutes. Taste and adjust salt. The stew should be spicy and flavorful.
- Reconstitute and steam the couscous (see recipe). Serve the couscous in wide bowls or mound onto plates and top with the stew. Pass more harissa at the table.

Nutrition Information

- 463: calories;
- 7 grams: fat;
- 3 grams: monounsaturated fat;
- 2 grams: polyunsaturated fat;
- 10 grams: sugars;
- 655 milligrams: sodium;
- 1 gram: saturated fat;
- 82 grams: carbohydrates;
- 12 grams: dietary fiber;
- 19 grams: protein;

79. Couscous With Raisins

Serving: 4 servings | Prep: | Cook: | Ready in: 30mins

Ingredients

- ¼ cup raisins
- 2 tablespoons butter
- ½ cup chopped onion
- 1 ½ cups boiling water
- 2 teaspoons lemon juice
- ¼ teaspoon ground cumin
- 1 cup quick-cooking couscous
- Salt to taste

Direction

- Put the raisins in a small bowl and cover with lukewarm water. Soak for about 20 minutes. Drain.
- Melt the butter in a saucepan over low heat and add the onion. Cook and stir until wilted but not brown. Add the boiling water, raisins, lemon juice and cumin. Bring to a boil, remove from the heat and add the couscous. Add salt. Cover and let stand for 5 minutes. Uncover and fluff the couscous with a fork.

Nutrition Information

- 250: calories;
- 398 milligrams: sodium;
- 6 grams: protein;

- 4 grams: saturated fat;
- 0 grams: polyunsaturated fat;
- 2 grams: monounsaturated fat;
- 43 grams: carbohydrates;
- 3 grams: dietary fiber;

80. Creamy Basil Sauce For Rigatoni

Serving: 2 servings | Prep: | Cook: | Ready in: 15mins

Ingredients

- 6 ounces rigatoni or other spiral pasta
- 1 large clove garlic, peeled
- ¾ cup low-fat cottage cheese
- 1 ounce Gorgonzola
- 1 ¼ cups lightly packed fresh basil leaves
- 5 ounces ripe tomato, cut in large chunks
- Freshly ground black pepper to taste
- 2 tablespons pine nuts (optional)

Direction

- Bring 3 quarts of water to boil and cook rigatoni according to package directions.
- Meanwhile, chop garlic in food processor. Add cottage cheese, Gorgonzola and basil, and process until smooth. Add tomato and process into tiny chunks. Stir in pepper and, if you like, the pine nuts.
- Drain rigatoni, stir into sauce and serve.

Nutrition Information

- 456: calories;
- 4 grams: dietary fiber;
- 2 grams: monounsaturated fat;
- 1 gram: polyunsaturated fat;
- 8 grams: sugars;
- 0 grams: trans fat;
- 72 grams: carbohydrates;
- 24 grams: protein;
- 433 milligrams: sodium;

81. Croutons (Toasted French Bread Slices)

Serving: Twenty-eight croutons | Prep: | Cook: | Ready in: 15mins

Ingredients

- 1 loaf French bread, about 14 inches long
- 1 large clove garlic, peeled
- 3 tablespoons melted butter

Direction

- Preheat the oven to 450 degrees.
- Rub the crust of the bread all over and generously with the garlic clove. Cut the bread crosswise into 28 slices of equal width. Arrange the slices on a baking sheet. Brush each slice with butter.
- Place the baking sheet in the oven and bake six minutes or until the slices are nicely toasted.

Nutrition Information

- 188: calories;
- 302 milligrams: sodium;
- 4 grams: saturated fat;
- 0 grams: trans fat;
- 2 grams: sugars;
- 5 grams: protein;
- 7 grams: fat;
- 1 gram: dietary fiber;
- 26 grams: carbohydrates;

82. Crêpes With Grilled Peaches And Apricots

Serving: 6 servings | Prep: | Cook: | Ready in: 1hours30mins

Ingredients

- For the crêpes
- ¾ cup / 175 milliliters milk
- ½ cup / 125 milliliters water
- 2 large eggs
- ¼ teaspoon / 2 grams salt
- 1 tablespoon / 15 grams sugar
- ⅓ cup plus 1 tablespoon / 55 grams whole-wheat flour, sifted
- 3 tablespoons unsalted butter, melted, plus butter for the pan
- ⅓ cup plus 1 tablespoon / 55 grams unbleached all-purpose flour, sifted
- For the Fruit
- 2 ½ pounds mixed peaches and apricots
- Grape seed oil (or another neutral oil like canola oil) or extra-virgin olive oil as needed, about 2 tablespoons
- ¼ cup mild honey, such as clover
- 1 tablespoon butter
- Finely chopped or grated zest of 1 lemon
- Powdered sugar for dusting the crêpes (optional)

Direction

-
-

Nutrition Information

- 554: calories;
- 1 gram: trans fat;
- 6 grams: polyunsaturated fat;
- 79 grams: carbohydrates;
- 9 grams: dietary fiber;
- 49 grams: sugars;
- 11 grams: protein;
- 172 milligrams: sodium;
- 25 grams: fat;
- 10 grams: saturated fat;

83. Cucumber Mint Soup

Serving: 6 servings (8 cups) | Prep: | Cook: | Ready in: 20mins

Ingredients

- 3 cucumbers (3 pounds total), peeled, seeded and coarsely sliced
- 1 cup (loose) mint leaves
- 5 cloves garlic, peeled
- 2 cups yogurt
- 3 tablespoons virgin olive oil
- 3 tablespoons cider vinegar
- 2 ½ teaspoons salt
- 12 drops Tabasco sauce
- 2 cups water

Direction

- Place the sliced cucumbers in the bowl of a food processor with the mint, garlic and 1/2 cup cold water. Process until pureed (the mixture will be granular).
- Transfer the puree to a bowl and mix in the yogurt, olive oil, vinegar, salt and Tabasco, with 1 1/2 cups cold water. Chill.
- Stir before serving.

Nutrition Information

- 144: calories;
- 6 grams: sugars;
- 1 gram: polyunsaturated fat;
- 11 grams: carbohydrates;
- 2 grams: dietary fiber;
- 4 grams: protein;
- 10 grams: fat;
- 3 grams: saturated fat;
- 798 milligrams: sodium;

84. Cucumber Raita

Serving: Serves 4 as a side dish | Prep: | Cook: | Ready in: 20mins

Ingredients

- 1 large cucumber (about 1/2 pound), peeled if waxy, seeds removed if you can't get a seedless cucumber (like a Japanese, Persian, or hothouse)
- Salt
- 1 cup plain Greek style yogurt
- ⅛ teaspoon cayenne (more to taste)
- 2 tablespoons chopped cilantro
- ½ teaspoon garam masala (more to taste)
- 1 small serrano or Thai chile, minced (optional)

Direction

- Cut the cucumber into very small dice or grate on the large holes of a grater. Sprinkle with a generous amount of salt, toss and let sit in a colander in the sink for 15 minutes. Rinse briefly and squeeze dry in a kitchen towel. Transfer to a bowl.
- Beat the yogurt with a fork or a whisk and add the cayenne and garam masala. Toss with the cucumbers. Add the cilantro and chile and toss again. Taste and adjust salt. Chill until ready to serve.

Nutrition Information

- 72: calories;
- 6 grams: protein;
- 303 milligrams: sodium;
- 4 grams: fat;
- 2 grams: saturated fat;
- 0 grams: dietary fiber;
- 5 grams: carbohydrates;
- 3 grams: sugars;

85. Cucumber, Melon And Watermelon Salad

Serving: 4 servings | Prep: | Cook: | Ready in: 2mins

Ingredients

- 4 cups mixed diced watermelon, honeydew and cantaloupe
- 2 cups diced cucumber, seeded if there are seeds
- Salt to taste
- 1 teaspoon lemon or lime zest
- 2 tablespoons freshly squeezed lemon or lime juice
- 1 to 2 tablespoons chopped fresh mint
- 1 ounce feta cheese, crumbled
- ¼ to ½ teaspoon Aleppo pepper or mild chili powder (to taste), or 1 serrano chile, minced
- 2 tablespoons extra virgin olive oil

Direction

-

Nutrition Information

- 259: calories;
- 5 grams: protein;
- 2 grams: saturated fat;
- 1 gram: polyunsaturated fat;
- 45 grams: carbohydrates;
- 4 grams: dietary fiber;
- 39 grams: sugars;
- 1359 milligrams: sodium;
- 9 grams: fat;

86. Cupid's Coupe

Serving: Four servings | Prep: | Cook: | Ready in: 20mins

Ingredients

- 1 sheet phyllo dough
- 1 tablespoon melted butter
- 1 tablespoon confectioners' sugar
- 2 pints fresh strawberries, hulled
- 1 cup heavy cream
- ¼ cup granulated sugar
- Grated zest of 1 lime

Direction

- Preheat oven to 350 degrees. Brush the phyllo sheet with butter and sprinkle with confectioners' sugar. Cut the sheet in half crosswise and then lengthwise to make 4 rectangles. Make a fan by taking the short side of 1 of the rectangles and gathering it together like pleats on a skirt, pinching the pleats together to make them stick. Place on a parchment-lined baking sheet. Repeat with remaining rectangles. Bake until light brown, about 5 minutes. Set aside.
- Place a scant pint of the strawberries in a blender and puree, stopping as necessary to scrape sides of jar. Pass the puree through a fine sieve so you are left with only a thick liquid. Set aside. Whip cream to soft peaks. Add the sugar and the lime zest. Whip to stiff peaks. Coarsely chop enough of the remaining strawberries to make 1/2 cup. Stir them into the cream mixture. Stir in the strawberry puree.
- Thinly slice the remaining strawberries. Either use a small heart-shaped cutter to cut hearts out of the strawberry slices or trim them into heart shapes with a small knife. Press several of the strawberry hearts in a decorative, asymmetrical pattern against the inside of each of 4 wineglasses. Spoon in the mousse. Top with a layer of strawberry hearts. Place the narrow end of each fan into the mousse. Serve immediately.

Nutrition Information

- 363: calories;
- 7 grams: monounsaturated fat;
- 34 grams: carbohydrates;
- 48 milligrams: sodium;

- 0 grams: trans fat;
- 1 gram: polyunsaturated fat;
- 4 grams: dietary fiber;
- 25 grams: sugars;
- 3 grams: protein;
- 26 grams: fat;
- 16 grams: saturated fat;

87. Curried Grilled Jumbo Shrimp

Serving: Four servings | Prep: | Cook: |Ready in: 2hours30mins

Ingredients

- 1 ½ pounds jumbo shrimp
- 4 cloves garlic
- 2 small red chilies, chopped
- 2 teaspoons sugar
- ¾ teaspoon salt
- ½ cup finely chopped coriander leaves
- 1 teaspoon curry paste or powder
- 1 tablespoon vegetable oil
- 4 cups cooked white rice, warm

Direction

- Use scissors to cut down the back of the shrimp, through the shell, to remove the vein. Gently loosen the shell around the shrimp, but keep it in place. Set aside. In a mortar, pound the garlic and chilies to a coarse paste (or use a mini food processor or chop to a paste with a knife). Add the sugar and salt and pound or chop to a finer paste. Stir in the coriander, curry and oil.
- Gently pull open the shell of each shrimp and, dividing the coriander paste evenly, push some of it down the back of the shrimp where the vein was and under the shell a bit. Close up the shell around the shrimp. Marinate at room temperature at least 2 hours or, covered, in the refrigerator up to 4 hours.
- Preheat a grill or broiler. Grill or broil the shrimp until the shells are charred on one side and the shrimp is cooked halfway through, about 3 minutes. Turn and cook on the other side for 1 to 3 minutes. Serve immediately with the rice.

Nutrition Information

- 415: calories;
- 28 grams: protein;
- 972 milligrams: sodium;
- 6 grams: fat;
- 1 gram: dietary fiber;
- 0 grams: trans fat;
- 3 grams: sugars;
- 60 grams: carbohydrates;

88. Curried Lentil And Grilled Chicken Casserole

Serving: 6 to 8 servings | Prep: | Cook: |Ready in: 55mins

Ingredients

- 2 skinless and boneless chicken breasts (about 1 1/4 pounds)
- 3 tablespoons olive oil or vegetable oil
- 1 cup finely chopped onion
- 1 medium sweet red pepper, cored, seeded and chopped
- 1 fresh hot green chili, seeded and minced
- 2 cloves garlic, minced
- 1 teaspoon minced fresh ginger
- 2 teaspoons ground cumin
- 4 cups chicken stock
- 2 cups lentils
- Salt and freshly ground black pepper
- Plain yogurt

Direction

- Preheat a grill or broiler. Brush the chicken with one tablespoon of the oil and sear the

chicken, turning it once, until it is brown and just cooked through, about 10 minutes.
- Meanwhile heat the remaining oil in a large, heavy ovenproof casserole. Add the onion, sweet and hot peppers, garlic and ginger and saute until lightly browned. Stir in the cumin. Pare or cut the cooked chicken into chunks and add to the casserole.
- Preheat oven to 350 degrees.
- Stir in the broth. Pick over the lentlis and add them. Bring to a simmer, cover and bake for about 30 minutes, until the lentils are tender. Season to taste with salt and pepper. Serve with yogurt on the side.

Nutrition Information

- 375: calories;
- 2 grams: polyunsaturated fat;
- 5 grams: sugars;
- 27 grams: protein;
- 667 milligrams: sodium;
- 12 grams: fat;
- 3 grams: saturated fat;
- 0 grams: trans fat;
- 7 grams: monounsaturated fat;
- 39 grams: carbohydrates;
- 6 grams: dietary fiber;

89. Curry Laced Moules À La Marinière With Fresh Peas

Serving: 4 main-course servings | Prep: | Cook: | Ready in: 45mins

Ingredients

- 3 ½ pounds black mussels
- 1 to 1 ½ cups freshly shelled peas
- 2 tablespoons unsalted butter
- 1 small onion or 2 to 4 shallots, minced
- 1 ½ teaspoons curry powder (more to taste)
- 2 cups dry white wine
- 2 to 3 garlic cloves, peeled and crushed
- 4 sprigs fresh parsley
- 2 sprigs fresh thyme
- 1 small bay leaf
- 6 whole peppercorns
- 3 tablespoons finely chopped fresh parsley

Direction

- Clean the mussels. Inspect each one carefully and discard any that have opened (if some are partly open, tap them with your finger, and if they close back up they are O.K.) or have cracked shells. Place in a large bowl, fill the bowl with cold water and rinse several times, swishing the mussels around in the water, pouring out the water and refilling. Clean the shells, if necessary, with a brush or the end of one of the mussels, and pull out the beards – the hairy attachments emerging from the shells. Do not do this until just before cooking, or the mussels will die and spoil.
- Steam the peas or cook them in lightly salted boiling water until tender, 4 to 10 minutes, depending on the size and age of the peas. Drain and set aside.
- Heat 1 tablespoon of the butter over medium heat in a large Dutch oven or pot and add the onion or shallots. Cook, stirring occasionally, until they begin to soften, 2 to 3 minutes, and add the curry powder. Stir together for a minute, until fragrant, and add the wine, garlic, bay leaf, sprigs of parsley and thyme, and the peppercorns. Bring to a boil over high heat, reduce the heat to medium and boil for 2 minutes.
- Add the mussels and cover tightly. Cook 2 minutes, shake the pot vigorously and cook another 2 minutes. Uncover and use tongs to transfer all of the mussels that have opened to wide soup bowls. Cover the pot and cook for another minute, or until all of the mussels have opened. Transfer them to the bowls with the other mussels. Discard any mussels that have not opened. Cover the mussels to keep warm.
- Line a strainer with a few thicknesses of damp cheesecloth and place over a bowl. Strain the

liquid from the pot into the bowl, return to the pot and bring to a boil. Stir in the remaining tablespoon of butter and simmer until it melts. Stir in the peas. Taste and adjust seasoning. You may want to add more pepper or curry powder. Spoon the broth and peas over the mussels, sprinkle with parsley and serve.

Nutrition Information

- 542: calories;
- 29 grams: carbohydrates;
- 15 grams: fat;
- 0 grams: trans fat;
- 4 grams: dietary fiber;
- 3 grams: polyunsaturated fat;
- 5 grams: sugars;
- 51 grams: protein;
- 1149 milligrams: sodium;

90. Dandelion Greens With Crispy Onions

Serving: Four servings | Prep: | Cook: | Ready in: 30mins

Ingredients

- 3 tablespoons olive oil
- 2 medium-size onions, peeled and sliced thin
- 1 ½ pounds fresh dandelions, washed and stemmed
- 1 clove garlic, peeled and crushed
- 2 tablespoons fresh lemon juice
- Coarse sea salt, to taste
- 4 lemon wedges

Direction

- Heat the olive oil in a 9- or 10-inch skillet over medium heat. Pat the onions dry between paper towels. Add the onions to the skillet and cook, stirring often, until golden, about 10 minutes. Using a slotted spoon, remove half of the onions from the skillet and set them aside to cool. Raise the heat and continue cooking the remaining onions until crisp and golden brown, about 5 minutes. Transfer the fried onions with a slotted spoon to paper toweling to drain.
- Blanch the dandelions in lightly salted boiling water until just tender, about 3 minutes. Drain, refresh under cold running water and squeeze out the excess water. Shred the dandelions and chop the reserved half-cooked onions. Heat the oil that remains in the skillet over medium heat. Add the dandelions, chopped onions and garlic and, stirring often, cook until mixture is thick and dandelions are soft to the bite (about 5 minutes). Stir in the lemon juice and season with salt to taste. Serve warm, sprinkled with the crisp onions and surrounded with lemon wedges.

Nutrition Information

- 182: calories;
- 11 grams: fat;
- 2 grams: polyunsaturated fat;
- 7 grams: dietary fiber;
- 20 grams: carbohydrates;
- 3 grams: sugars;
- 5 grams: protein;
- 517 milligrams: sodium;

91. Dark Chocolate And Pomegranate Bark

Serving: About 3/4 pound of bark (8 servings) | Prep: | Cook: | Ready in: 10mins

Ingredients

- 140 grams dark (bittersweet) chocolate pieces (5 ounces)
- 20 grams minced crystallized ginger (2 tablespoons)
- 140 grams fresh pomegranate seeds (1 cup)
- 6 grams flaky sea salt (1 teaspoon)

Direction

- Fit a heatproof bowl over a pot of simmering water, making sure the water doesn't touch the bottom of the bowl. Place the chocolate in the bowl and stir until fully melted, about 5 minutes. Remove the bowl from the pot and stir the crystallized ginger and half of the pomegranate seeds into the melted chocolate.
- Line a small baking sheet with parchment paper. Pour melted chocolate mixture onto the sheet. Use a spatula to smooth the chocolate into one even layer about 1/4 inch thick (it does not need to fill the entire sheet). Sprinkle chocolate with remaining pomegranate seeds and sea salt.
- Chill for 20 to 30 minutes or until firm. Break or cut into pieces and store in an airtight container, separating the layers with wax paper. This is best served the same day it's made, otherwise condensation may form on the surface.

Nutrition Information

- 115: calories;
- 3 grams: saturated fat;
- 2 grams: dietary fiber;
- 0 grams: polyunsaturated fat;
- 18 grams: carbohydrates;
- 16 grams: sugars;
- 1 gram: protein;
- 101 milligrams: sodium;
- 6 grams: fat;

92. Dried Fruit Compote With Fresh Apple And Pear

Serving: Serves 6 to 8 | Prep: | Cook: | Ready in: 10mins

Ingredients

- 2 cups mixed dried fruit, such as raisins (several types), apples, pears, peaches, cranberries, chopped apricots (about 1/2 pound)
- 2 ½ cups water
- 3 tablespoons mild honey, such as clover (more to taste)
- 1 cinnamon stick
- 1 teaspoon vanilla extract
- 2 strips orange zest
- 1 strip lemon zest
- 1 firm but ripe pear, peeled, cored and diced (optional)
- 1 apple, preferably a slightly tart variety like Pink Lady, peeled, cored and diced (optional)
- Whipped cream or plain yogurt for serving, if desired

Direction

- Cut large pieces of dried fruit into smaller pieces.
- Combine all of the ingredients in a saucepan and bring to a boil. Reduce heat, cover and simmer 5 minutes. Turn off heat and allow fruit to steep for 30 minutes or longer. Remove cinnamon stick and orange and lemon zest. Serve topped with whipped cream or yogurt if desired, or stir into your morning yogurt.

Nutrition Information

- 39: calories;
- 10 grams: carbohydrates;
- 2 grams: dietary fiber;
- 8 grams: sugars;
- 4 milligrams: sodium;
- 0 grams: protein;

93. Duck In Red Wine Currant Sauce With Cracklings And Bacon

Serving: Four servings | Prep: | Cook: | Ready in: 30mins

Ingredients

- 2 small boneless duck breasts, skin removed and reserved
- 2 slices bacon, cut across into thin strips
- ½ teaspoon salt
- Freshly ground pepper to taste
- 3 tablespoons finely chopped shallots
- 1 cup red wine
- ½ cup chicken broth, homemade or low-sodium canned
- 1 tablespoon sherry vinegar
- 3 tablespoons currants
- 2 teaspoons unsalted butter

Direction

- Julienne half of the duck skin and discard the rest. Heat a large heavy skillet over medium-high heat. Add the duck skin and bacon and cook, stirring constantly, pouring off and reserving rendered fat as it accumulates, until skin and bacon are well browned, about 6 to 7 minutes. Remove with a slotted spoon, drain on paper towels and set aside. Save 2 teaspoons of fat and discard the rest.
- Season the duck with salt and pepper to taste. Place 1 teaspoon of the fat in the skillet. Sear duck until browned on the outside and medium rare inside, about 2 minutes per side. Set aside and keep warm.
- Add the remaining fat and the shallots to the skillet and cook for 30 seconds. Stir in the wine, broth, vinegar and currants and simmer until reduced to 1/2 cup, about 10 minutes.
- Remove pan from heat and whisk in butter. Season with 1/2 teaspoon of salt and pepper to taste. Cut the duck on the diagonal into thin strips and fan out onto 4 plates. Spoon the sauce over the duck, sprinkle with the reserved duck skin and bacon and serve immediately.

Nutrition Information

- 239: calories;
- 6 grams: sugars;
- 16 grams: protein;
- 428 milligrams: sodium;
- 9 grams: carbohydrates;
- 0 grams: trans fat;
- 1 gram: dietary fiber;
- 11 grams: fat;
- 4 grams: monounsaturated fat;

94. Duck, Wilted Spinach And White Bean Salad

Serving: Four servings | Prep: | Cook: | Ready in: 25mins

Ingredients

- 2 small duck breasts (1 1/4 pounds), skinned and boned
- 1 teaspoon salt, plus more to taste
- Freshly ground pepper to taste
- 3 teaspoons canola oil
- 20 cups fresh spinach (about 3 pounds)
- 2 cups cooked cannellini beans
- ¼ cup balsamic vinegar

Direction

- Season the duck breasts with the salt and pepper to taste. Heat the oil in a large cast-iron skillet over medium heat until almost smoking. Add the duck and cook for 3 minutes. Turn and cook until crisp and brown on the outside and still rare in the center, about 3 minutes longer. Remove the duck from the pan and set aside; keep warm.
- Gradually place the spinach in the skillet, and stir-fry until barely wilted, adding more as room allows. Place in a bowl and toss with the beans. Add the vinegar to the skillet and cook, stirring with a wooden spoon and scraping up any browned bits stuck to the bottom of the pan. Add to the spinach mixture and toss to combine. Season with salt and pepper to taste.
- Cut the duck on the diagonal into thin slices. Divide the spinach mixture among 4 plates and drape the duck slices over it. Serve immediately.

Nutrition Information

- 345: calories;
- 14 grams: dietary fiber;
- 4 grams: sugars;
- 903 milligrams: sodium;
- 8 grams: fat;
- 39 grams: carbohydrates;
- 34 grams: protein;
- 2 grams: polyunsaturated fat;
- 0 grams: trans fat;
- 3 grams: monounsaturated fat;

95. Egg And Herb Salad

Serving: Serves four to six | Prep: | Cook: | Ready in: 30mins

Ingredients

- 8 large eggs, hard-boiled (see below) and finely chopped
- 1 cup finely chopped fresh herbs, such as parsley, dill, tarragon, chervil or chives
- 2 celery stalks, finely chopped
- 1 small red onion, finely chopped, soaked for five minutes in cold water, drained and rinsed
- Salt
- freshly ground pepper to taste
- 1 tablespoon white wine vinegar or sherry vinegar
- 2 tablespoons freshly squeezed lemon juice
- ⅓ cup plain low-fat yogurt or buttermilk
- 1 tablespoon Hellmann's or Best Foods mayonnaise
- 1 garlic clove, green shoot removed, minced
- 1 teaspoon Dijon mustard
- 2 tablespoons extra virgin olive oil
- 1 6-ounce bag baby arugula

Direction

- To hard-boil the eggs, place in a saucepan, cover with cold water and bring to a boil. Cover the pan tightly, and turn off the heat. Let sit for 12 minutes. Fill a bowl with ice water, drain the eggs and chill immediately in the ice water.
- Combine the chopped eggs, herbs, celery and red onion in a large bowl, and season to taste with salt and pepper.
- Whisk together the vinegar, lemon juice, yogurt, mayonnaise, mustard and olive oil. Season to taste with salt and pepper. Toss with the egg mixture.
- Line plates or a platter with arugula, top with the egg salad and serve.

Nutrition Information

- 182: calories;
- 13 grams: fat;
- 3 grams: sugars;
- 6 grams: monounsaturated fat;
- 5 grams: carbohydrates;
- 1 gram: dietary fiber;
- 371 milligrams: sodium;
- 0 grams: trans fat;
- 10 grams: protein;

96. Enfrijoladas

Serving: Serves 4 | Prep: | Cook: | Ready in: 2hours30mins

Ingredients

- ½ pound (1 1/8 cups) black beans, washed, picked over and soaked for 4 to 6 hours or overnight in 1 quart water
- 1 onion, cut in half
- 2 plump garlic cloves, minced
- 1 to 2 sprigs epazote or 2 tablespoons chopped cilantro, plus additional for garnish (optional)
- 1 to 2 teaspoons ground cumin, to taste
- ½ to 1 teaspoon ground mild chili powder (more to taste)
- Salt to taste
- 12 corn tortillas

- ¼ cup chopped walnuts (optional)

Direction

- In a large soup pot or Dutch oven combine the black beans with their soaking water (they should be submerged by at least 1 1/2 inches of water; add if necessary), one half of the onion, and half the garlic and bring to a boil. Reduce the heat, cover and simmer gently for 1 hour. Add the remaining garlic, epazote or cilantro if using, cumin, chili powder, and salt to taste and simmer for another hour, until the beans are very soft and the broth thick, soupy and aromatic. Remove from the heat. Remove and discard the onion.
- Using an immersion blender or a food processor fitted with the steel blade coarsely puree the beans. The mixture should retain some texture and the consistency should be thick and creamy. Heat through, stirring the bottom of the pot so the beans don't stick. Taste and adjust salt. Keep warm.
- Slice the remaining onion half crosswise into thin half-moons and cover with cold water while you assemble the enfrijoladas. Heat the corn tortillas: either wrap them in a damp dish towel and heat them, 4 at a time, in the microwave for about 30 seconds at 100 percent power, or wrap in a dish towel and steam for 1 minute, then let rest for 5 minutes.
- Assemble the enfrijoladas just before serving them. Spoon about 1/2 cup of the hot, thick beans over the bottom of a large lightly oiled baking dish or serving platter. Using tongs, dip a softened tortilla into the beans and flip over to coat both sides with black beans. Remove from the beans and place on the baking dish or platter (this is messy; have the serving dish right next to the pot.) Fold into quarters. Use the tongs to do this, and if you find that the tortilla tears too much, then just coat one side with the black beans, transfer to the baking dish and spoon some of the black beans over the other side, then fold into quarters. Continue with the remaining tortillas, arranging the quartered bean-coated tortillas in overlapping rows. When all of the tortillas are in the dish, spoon the remaining black bean sauce over the top. Drain and rinse the onions, dry briefly on paper towels and sprinkle over the bean sauce. Garnish with cilantro and chopped walnuts if desired and serve at once.

Nutrition Information

- 369: calories;
- 3 grams: sugars;
- 1 gram: polyunsaturated fat;
- 72 grams: carbohydrates;
- 14 grams: dietary fiber;
- 17 grams: protein;
- 378 milligrams: sodium;

97. Farfalle With Artichokes, Peas, Favas And Onions

Serving: 6 servings | Prep: | Cook: | Ready in: 1hours

Ingredients

- Juice of 1 lemon
- 4 medium or 2 large artichokes, or 8 baby artichokes
- 2 tablespoons extra virgin olive oil
- ½ pound spring onions or scallions, white and light green parts only, finely chopped
- Salt and freshly ground black pepper to taste
- 2 pounds fava beans, shelled and skinned
- 2 cups shelled peas (about 2 1/2 pounds fresh peas in the pod)
- 2 teaspoons chopped mint
- ¾ pound farfalle
- Freshly grated Parmesan or Pecorino (or a combination) for serving

Direction

- Fill a bowl with water and add the lemon juice. Cut away the stem and the top third of each artichoke, break off the leaves and trim them down to the bottoms, placing them in the water as you go along. Quarter them and slice large quarters about 1/4 inch thick. Save the leaves and steam them; serve them as a first course or a side dish.

- Drain the artichoke hearts and dry on a clean dish towel. Heat the oil over medium-high heat in a large, heavy lidded skillet or Dutch oven. Add the sliced artichoke hearts and cook, stirring, until lightly browned, about 5 minutes. Turn the heat down to medium, add the onions (or scallions) and cook, stirring, until the onions are tender, 3 to 5 minutes. Add the peas and favas, 2/3 cup water and salt to taste and bring to a boil. Reduce the heat to low, cover and simmer for 20 minutes, until all of the vegetables are tender. Taste, adjust salt and add pepper to taste. Stir in the mint and remove from the heat, but keep warm while you cook the pasta.
- Bring a large pot of water to a boil, add salt to taste and the pasta. Cook al dente, usually 10 to 11 minutes for farfalle. Add a ladleful of the cooking water from the pasta to the vegetable mixture and drain the pasta. Toss with the vegetables and serve, with Parmesan or Pecorino, or both.

Nutrition Information

- 488: calories;
- 91 grams: carbohydrates;
- 20 grams: sugars;
- 26 grams: protein;
- 7 grams: fat;
- 4 grams: monounsaturated fat;
- 2 grams: polyunsaturated fat;
- 1 gram: saturated fat;
- 23 grams: dietary fiber;
- 954 milligrams: sodium;

98. Farfalle With Cabbage And Black Kale

Serving: 4 servings | Prep: | Cook: | Ready in: 45mins

Ingredients

- 1 bunch black kale cavolo nero, stemmed and washed
- ¼ medium head of cabbage about 1/2 pound, kept intact on the core
- 2 tablespoons extra virgin olive oil
- 1 small shallot, minced
- 2 large garlic cloves, minced
- ½ teaspoon chili flakes
- Salt to taste
- ¾ pound farfalle
- 1 to 2 ounces Parmesan, grated 1/4 to 1/2 cup

Direction

- Bring a large pot of water to a boil; you'll use it first to blanch the kale and cabbage and then to cook the pasta. Fill a large bowl with ice water. When the water comes to a boil, salt generously and add the kale. Blanch 3 minutes and, using a skimmer or a slotted spoon, transfer kale to the bowl of ice water, then drain and squeeze out excess water. Place on a cutting board and cut into thin ribbons. Add the wedge of cabbage to the pot and blanch for 3 minutes. Transfer to the ice water, then drain and squeeze out excess water. Cut away the core and cut crosswise into thin ribbons. Cover the pot and keep the water at a simmer for cooking the pasta.
- Heat the oil over medium heat in a large, wide skillet and add the shallot. Cook, stirring until tender, about 3 minutes, and add the garlic and chili flakes. Cook, stirring, until the garlic is fragrant, 30 seconds to a minute, and add the kale and cabbage to the pan. Stir together for a couple of minutes, then add 1/2 cup of the blanching water to the pan. Cook uncovered, stirring often, for 5 minutes, then add another 1/2 cup of the blanching water to the pan and cook for another 5 minutes. Cover

the pan and turn the heat to medium-low. Simmer for another 5 minutes. Taste and adjust seasonings.
- Meanwhile, bring the remaining water in the pasta pot back to a boil and add the farfalle. Cook al dente, about 10 minutes. If desired, add another 1/4 to 1/2 cup of the pasta water to the kale and cabbage, then drain the pasta and add to the pan. Toss together and transfer to a platter, a wide pasta bowl or plates. Top with the Parmesan, and serve.

Nutrition Information

- 467: calories;
- 11 grams: fat;
- 3 grams: saturated fat;
- 6 grams: sugars;
- 1 gram: polyunsaturated fat;
- 74 grams: carbohydrates;
- 18 grams: protein;
- 517 milligrams: sodium;

99. Farofias (Poached Meringues In Lemon Custard With Cinnamon)

Serving: 4 to 6 servings | Prep: | Cook: | Ready in: 45mins

Ingredients

- 3 ¼ cups milk
- Zest of 1 lemon, cut in long strips
- 4 extra-large eggs, separated
- 1 cup sugar
- 1 tablespoon cornstarch
- ¼ teaspoon ground cinnamon

Direction

- In a deep 10- or 11-inch skillet set over moderately low heat, bring 3 cups of the milk and the lemon zest to a simmer; remove from the heat and let steep 5 minutes. Strain the milk and return to the skillet.
- Beat the egg whites to soft peaks, then add 1/2 cup of the sugar, 1 tablespoon at a time, beating all the while; continue until stiff glossy peaks form.
- Return the milk to low heat and when steam rises from the surface, drop meringue in by rounded tablespoons. (To keep meringue from sticking, dip the spoon often in hot water).
- Poach the meringues about 2 minutes in the milk, turn and poach the other side 2 minutes. With a slotted spoon, carefully transfer them to a large wet plate and reserve.
- As soon as all meringues are poached, strain the milk into a medium-size heavy saucepan and mix in the remaining sugar. Combine the remaining 1/4 cup milk with the cornstarch, whisk a little of the hot milk into this mixture, then blend into the pan and cook, stirring constantly, over moderately low heat 3 minutes or until slightly thickened.
- Beat the egg yolks lightly, whisk in a little of the hot sauce, stir back into pan and cook, stirring constantly, over low heat 2 to 3 minutes until no raw egg taste remains (do not boil or the mixture may curdle).
- Pour the hot custard into a large shallow heatproof bowl, cool 10 minutes, then float the meringues on top.
- Serve warm or well chilled, dusting the meringues with cinnamon at the last minute.

Nutrition Information

- 271: calories;
- 0 grams: dietary fiber;
- 42 grams: carbohydrates;
- 40 grams: sugars;
- 9 grams: protein;
- 4 grams: saturated fat;
- 8 grams: fat;
- 2 grams: monounsaturated fat;
- 1 gram: polyunsaturated fat;
- 111 milligrams: sodium;

100. Farro Or Bulgur With Black Eyed Peas, Chard And Feta

Serving: Serves 6 | Prep: | Cook: | Ready in: 1hours

Ingredients

- 1 pound black-eyed peas
- 2 tablespoons extra virgin olive oil
- 1 large onion, chopped
- 3 large garlic cloves, minced
- 1 to 2 serrano peppers, minced (optional)
- 1 bay leaf
- Salt to taste
- 1 bunch Swiss chard (about 1 pound), stemmed, leaves washed in two changes of water, stems diced if wide and fleshy, discarded if thin and stringy
- ¼ cup chopped fresh dill or cilantro
- Freshly ground pepper to taste
- 3 cups cooked farro or bulgur
- 1 red pepper, cut in small dice, for topping
- 2 ounces feta, crumbled

Direction

- Rinse the beans and pick over to check for stones. Heat 1 tablespoon of the oil over medium heat in a large, heavy soup pot or Dutch oven and add the onion. Cook, stirring, until tender, about 5 minutes, and add half the garlic and the chiles. Cook, stirring, until fragrant, 30 seconds to a minute, and add the black-eyed peas, 2 quarts water and the bay leaf. Bring to a boil, reduce the heat to low, and skim off any foam that rises. Cover and simmer 30 minutes.
- Add salt to taste and the remaining garlic. A handful at a time, stir in the chard. As the greens wilt, stir in another handful, until all the greens have been added. Bring back to a simmer, cover and simmer over low heat for 15 to 20 minutes, or until the greens and beans are tender.
- Stir in the remaining tablespoon of olive oil and the dill or cilantro, cover and continue to simmer for another 5 minutes. Add salt and freshly ground pepper to taste.
- Spoon farro or bulgur into bowls or onto plates. Top with the beans. Top the beans with diced red pepper and crumbled feta, and serve.

Nutrition Information

- 287: calories;
- 8 grams: fat;
- 2 grams: saturated fat;
- 1 gram: polyunsaturated fat;
- 11 grams: protein;
- 677 milligrams: sodium;
- 4 grams: monounsaturated fat;
- 47 grams: carbohydrates;
- 10 grams: dietary fiber;
- 5 grams: sugars;

101. Fava Bean And Asparagus Salad

Serving: 4 servings. | Prep: | Cook: | Ready in: 45mins

Ingredients

- 2 pounds fava beans, shelled and skinned
- 1 pound trimmed asparagus, preferably fat spears
- 2 tablespoons chopped fresh mint, dill or tarragon
- 2 tablespoons minced chives
- 1 to 2 teaspoons lemon zest (to taste)
- 1 tablespoon fresh lemon juice
- 2 tablespoons red or white wine vinegar or sherry vinegar
- Salt to taste
- 1 small garlic clove, minced or puréed, or 2 tablespoons minced shallots
- 3 tablespoons extra virgin olive oil
- 2 tablespoons low-fat plain yogurt

- 1 ounce Parmesan, shaved
- 1 15-ounce can chickpeas, drained and rinsed

Direction

- Blanch and skin the fava beans and place them in a bowl. Use the blanching water to blanch the asparagus, or steam the asparagus if you prefer. If blanching, bring the water in the pot to a boil, salt generously and add the asparagus spears. Blanch 1 to 4 minutes, depending on how thick the asparagus is; fat spears (recommended) will take up to 4 minutes, but thin ones are ready in 1 minute. You can steam the asparagus over 1 inch boiling water for the same amount of time if you prefer. Transfer the lightly cooked asparagus to a bowl of cold water, then drain and dry on paper towels. Cut into 1-inch lengths. Add to the bowl with the fava beans. Add the herbs, and the chickpeas if using.
- Combine the lemon zest and juice, vinegar, garlic or shallots, and salt to taste in a bowl. Whisk in the oil and yogurt. Toss with the favas and asparagus. Add the shaved Parmesan, toss again and serve, or allow to marinate for 30 minutes, then serve.

Nutrition Information

- 507: calories;
- 27 grams: dietary fiber;
- 29 grams: sugars;
- 1168 milligrams: sodium;
- 3 grams: polyunsaturated fat;
- 72 grams: carbohydrates;
- 31 grams: protein;
- 17 grams: fat;
- 9 grams: monounsaturated fat;

102. Fennel And Orange Bluefish Grilled With Tomatoes, Potatoes And Fennel

Serving: Four servings | Prep: | Cook: | Ready in: 1hours

Ingredients

- 4 medium-size red potatoes
- 2 fennel bulbs, trimmed and halved lengthwise
- 1 bluefish fillet (about 1 1/2 pounds)
- 1 teaspoon roasted garlic oil
- 1 teaspoon grated orange zest
- 2 teaspoons crushed fennel seeds
- 1 teaspoon black mustard seeds
- ½ teaspoon salt
- Freshly ground pepper to taste
- 2 large tomatoes, halved horizontally

Direction

- Start a charcoal grill. Meanwhile, bring a large pot of water to the boil. Add the potatoes and cook for 15 minutes. Add the fennel and cook for 5 minutes longer. Drain. Cut the potatoes in half.
- Rub the flesh of the bluefish with the garlic oil. Sprinkle with the orange zest, then the fennel seeds, mustard seeds, 1/2 teaspoon salt and pepper to taste. Let the coals burn down so that the fire is quite low.
- Place the fish on the grill, skin side down. Place the potatoes, fennel and tomatoes on the grill, cut side down. Cover the grill and cook for 25 minutes, or until the fish is cooked through and the vegetables are tender.
- Cut the fish in half lengthwise. Cut again crosswise, making roughly equal pieces. Place 1 piece of fish, 1/2 tomato, 1 piece of fennel and 2 pieces of potato on each of 4 plates and serve immediately.

Nutrition Information

- 431: calories;
- 9 grams: sugars;

- 0 grams: trans fat;
- 47 grams: carbohydrates;
- 41 grams: protein;
- 497 milligrams: sodium;
- 2 grams: saturated fat;
- 4 grams: monounsaturated fat;
- 3 grams: polyunsaturated fat;

103. Fennel And Orange Salad With Black Olives On A Bed Of Couscous

Serving: Serves 6 | Prep: | Cook: | Ready in: 20mins

Ingredients

- For the dressing
- 3 tablespoons fresh lemon juice
- Salt to taste
- 1 ½ teaspoons mild honey or sugar
- 1 teaspoon crushed cumin seeds
- 6 tablespoons extra virgin olive oil
- Pinch of cayenne (optional)
- For the salad
- 1 cup couscous
- Salt to taste
- 2 medium fennel bulbs (about 1 1/4 pounds), quartered and cored
- 2 tablespoons chopped imported black olives (about 1/2 ounce), plus 12 imported black olives, pitted and halved
- 4 navel oranges or 6 to 8 Valencia oranges (depending on the size)
- Chopped fresh parsley or fennel fronds for garnish

Direction

- Reconstitute the couscous. Place it in a bowl, add salt to taste and cover by 1/2 inch with hot water. Let sit until all of the water has been absorbed by the couscous, stirring every once in a while. Cover the bowl with a plate and place in the microwave. Microwave for 3 minutes. Carefully remove from the microwave (the bowl will be hot). Uncover and fluff with forks. Set aside.
- In a small bowl or measuring cup, whisk together the ingredients for the dressing.
- Remove tough outer layers of the fennel bulb and discard. Using a sharp knife or a mandolin, slice the fennel quarters as thin as you can. Place in a bowl and toss with half the dressing and the chopped olives.
- Spoon the couscous into a wide bowl or onto a platter and smooth to make an even layer. Arrange the fennel on top, making sure to tip out any dressing from the bottom of the bowl over the fennel and couscous.
- Cut away the peel and pith from the oranges and slice into thin rounds. Tip any juice that runs out of the oranges as you are working with them over the fennel. Arrange the orange slices over the fennel.
- Drizzle the remaining dressing over the oranges. Arrange the halved olives on top, sprinkle with chopped parsley or fennel fronds and serve, or refrigerate until ready to serve.

Nutrition Information

- 315: calories;
- 15 grams: fat;
- 41 grams: carbohydrates;
- 7 grams: dietary fiber;
- 6 grams: protein;
- 2 grams: polyunsaturated fat;
- 11 grams: monounsaturated fat;
- 5 grams: sugars;
- 547 milligrams: sodium;

104. Fig Sorbet

Serving: 4 to 6 servings | Prep: | Cook: | Ready in: 4hours45mins

Ingredients

- 125 grams (1/2 cup) water or red wine
- 75 grams (about 1/3 cup) sugar
- 1 sprig rose geranium (optional) or 1/2 teaspoon rose water (optional)
- 33 grams (about 1 tablespoon plus 2 teaspoons) corn syrup
- 20 grams (1 tablespoon) clover honey
- 60 grams (1/4 cup) freshly squeezed orange juice
- 750 grams (1 pound 10 ounces) ripe figs, stems removed

Direction

- Combine the water or wine and sugar in a saucepan and bring to a boil. Reduce the heat and simmer until the sugar has dissolved. Add the rose geranium or rose water, remove from the heat and allow to cool. Strain if you steeped the rose geranium sprig.
- Combine all of the ingredients in a blender and purée until smooth. You may have to do this in two batches. Chill in the refrigerator for 2 hours or overnight.
- Chill a container in the freezer. Blend the mixture with an immersion blender for 30 seconds, then freeze in an ice cream maker following the manufacturer's instructions. Transfer to the chilled container and place in the freezer for 2 hours to pack. Allow to soften in the refrigerator for 15 to 30 minutes before serving.

Nutrition Information

- 189: calories;
- 1 gram: protein;
- 6 milligrams: sodium;
- 0 grams: polyunsaturated fat;
- 45 grams: carbohydrates;
- 4 grams: dietary fiber;
- 41 grams: sugars;

105. Filet Mignon Of Beef With Roganjosh Spices

Serving: Four servings | Prep: | Cook: | Ready in: 6hours15mins

Ingredients

- The meat:
- 2 teaspoons ground coriander
- ½ teaspoon ground cumin
- ½ teaspoon ground turmeric
- ¼ teaspoon ground fenugreek
- 1 teaspoon red chili-powder
- 1 large clove garlic, peeled and smashed to a paste
- 2 tablespoons fresh grated ginger
- 2 tablespoons grape-seed oil
- 4 6-ounce tournedos
- 1 teaspoon vegetable oil
- The salad:
- ½ cup fresh lime juice
- 1 tablespoon apple-cider vinegar
- ½ teaspoon salt
- 1 teaspoon minced jalapeno chili pepper
- 2 tablespoons olive oil
- 1 medium celery root, peeled and grated
- 1 large red delicious apple, peeled and grated
- 1 small jicama, peeled and grated
- ½ cup minced mint leaves
- ½ cup minced coriander leaves
- The vinaigrette:
- ¼ cup fresh lime juice
- 1 teaspoon grated orange rind
- ¼ teaspoon salt
- ½ teaspoon freshly ground pepper
- 1 tablespoon olive oil

Direction

- Combine all of the spices, garlic, ginger and grape-seed oil in a blender. Puree until smooth. Place tournedos with marinade in a large glass or ceramic bowl. Marinate in the refrigerator for 6 hours.
- To make the salad: Combine lime juice, cider vinegar, salt and minced jalapeno in a large

glass or ceramic bowl. Whisk in 2 tablespoons of olive oil. Add celery root, apple and jicama. Toss. Refrigerate for 4 hours.
- To make the vinaigrette: Combine lime juice, orange rind, salt and pepper in a small glass or ceramic bowl. Whisk in 1 tablespoon olive oil. Set aside.
- Heat the vegetable oil in a seasoned cast-iron skillet. Add the tournedos and cook over medium-high heat until medium rare, about 5 minutes per side. Set aside to rest for 5 minutes.
- Add mint and coriander to the salad and toss. Divide among four plates. Cut the meat into thin strips. Drape the meat around the salad. Drizzle with the vinaigrette. Serve immediately.

106. Fluke Crudo With Lime, Sea Salt And Olive Oil

Serving: 4 appetizer servings | Prep: | Cook: |Ready in: 10mins

Ingredients

- 1 pound fresh fluke fillet, skinned and chilled
- 1 to 2 limes
- Coarse sea salt
- Extra virgin olive oil

Direction

- Slice the fillet in half lengthwise at its natural seam. Then slice the fillet horizontally from end to end at an angle like lox. The slices should be about 1/8-inch thick and 2 inches wide. Divide among 4 small plates. Cover and chill for at least 10 minutes.
- When ready to serve, juice the lime over the fish; be generous. Season with sea salt and sprinkle with olive oil. Serve.

Nutrition Information

- 104: calories;
- 4 grams: fat;
- 1 gram: dietary fiber;
- 0 grams: sugars;
- 2 grams: monounsaturated fat;
- 3 grams: carbohydrates;
- 14 grams: protein;
- 336 milligrams: sodium;

107. Focaccia With Duck And Green Olive Ragout

Serving: 4 main-course servings | Prep: | Cook: |Ready in: 2hours25mins

Ingredients

- Basic dough (see recipe)
- 4 teaspoons olive oil
- 2 boneless, skinless duck breasts, halved lengthwise and cut across into slices 1/4 inch thick
- 4 tablespoons minced shallots
- 2 teaspoons minced garlic
- ½ cup sweet sherry
- 1 cup chicken broth, homemade or low-sodium canned
- 1 cup green olives, pitted and coarsely chopped
- 2 teaspoons cornstarch mixed with 2 tablespoons water
- Freshly ground pepper to taste

Direction

- Prepare the dough. While it is rising, heat 3 teaspoons of the olive oil in a large skillet over medium-high heat. Add the duck slices, and stir-fry until browned on the outside but still rare in the center, about 2 minutes. Remove with a slotted spoon and set aside. Add the remaining 1 teaspoon olive oil. Add the shallots and garlic and saute for 2 minutes.
- Stir in the sherry, chicken broth, any juices accumulated from the duck, and the olives.

Cook, stirring often, until reduced by half, about 10 minutes. Stir in the cornstarch mixture and cook, stirring constantly, for 1 minute. Remove from heat, and season with pepper. Set aside.
- Preheat oven to 425 degrees. When the dough is rolled out, stir the duck into the sauce and spread the mixture over the dough, leaving a 1-inch border around the circumference. Bake until crust is golden brown, about 20 minutes. Cut into wedges, and serve hot.

Nutrition Information

- 242: calories;
- 8 grams: carbohydrates;
- 1 gram: polyunsaturated fat;
- 2 grams: sugars;
- 19 grams: protein;
- 603 milligrams: sodium;
- 13 grams: fat;
- 3 grams: saturated fat;

108. French Grated Carrot Salad

Serving: 4 to 6 servings | Prep: | Cook: |Ready in: 20mins

Ingredients

- 6 tablespoons extra-virgin olive oil or canola oil (or a mix of the two), or use 2 tablespoons plain low-fat yogurt or buttermilk and 4 tablespoons oil
- 1 tablespoon freshly squeezed lemon juice
- 1 tablespoon sherry vinegar or white-wine vinegar
- 1 teaspoon Dijon mustard
- Salt and black pepper
- 1 pound carrots, peeled and grated
- ¼ cup finely chopped flat-leaf parsley

Direction

- Whisk together the oil, lemon juice, vinegar, and mustard in a large bowl; season with salt and pepper. Add the carrots and parsley and toss to coat. Season to taste with salt and pepper. Refrigerate before serving (I recommend making this 30 minutes to 1 hour ahead, then tossing again).

Nutrition Information

- 153: calories;
- 14 grams: fat;
- 1 gram: protein;
- 227 milligrams: sodium;
- 2 grams: dietary fiber;
- 0 grams: trans fat;
- 10 grams: monounsaturated fat;
- 8 grams: carbohydrates;
- 4 grams: sugars;

109. Fried Green Beans, Scallions And Brussels Sprouts With Buttermilk Cornmeal Coating

Serving: Serves 8 | Prep: | Cook: |Ready in: 30mins

Ingredients

- ½ cup cornstarch
- 2 tablespoons fine polenta or cornmeal
- ½ teaspoon salt, plus additional for sprinkling
- ½ teaspoon baking powder
- 1 cup less 2 tablespoons buttermilk or yogurt thinned with milk
- 3 tablespoons cold sparkling water
- ½ pound green beans
- ½ pound brussels sprouts
- 2 bunches scallions
- Canola or grapeseed oil for frying

Direction

- Combine cornstarch, polenta or cornmeal, salt and baking powder in a bowl and whisk together. Add buttermilk and sparkling water and whisk together until mixture is blended and has the consistency of thick cream.
- Top and tail beans. Trim brussels sprouts and quarter. Trim root end off the scallions and cut away dark green ends.
- Pour oil into a wok or wide saucepan to a depth of 3 inches and heat over medium-high heat to 360 to 375 degrees. Set up a sheet pan with a rack on it next to the pan. Cover rack with a few layers of paper towels. Have a spider or deep fry skimmer handy for removing vegetables from the oil.
- Using tongs, dip vegetables into batter a few at a time, making sure to coat thoroughly. Transfer to hot oil and fry until golden brown, which should not take more than a couple of minutes. Flip over halfway through with the spider to make sure the coating is evenly fried. It is important not to crowd pan and to let oil come back up to temperature between batches.
- Using the spider, remove vegetables from oil, allowing excess oil to drip back into pan, and drain on towel-covered rack. Sprinkle with salt right away if desired. Allow to cool slightly and serve.

Nutrition Information

- 207: calories;
- 3 grams: dietary fiber;
- 2 grams: protein;
- 41 milligrams: sodium;
- 16 grams: carbohydrates;
- 0 grams: trans fat;
- 10 grams: monounsaturated fat;
- 4 grams: polyunsaturated fat;
- 1 gram: saturated fat;

110. Game Chips

Serving: Eight to 10 servings | Prep: | Cook: | Ready in: 20mins

Ingredients

- 4 cups vegetable oil
- 12 medium baking potatoes, peeled and sliced 1/16 inch thick, submerged in cold water
- 2 teaspoons salt
- 1 tablespoon dried basil
- 1 tablespoon dried parsley
- 1 tablespoon dried rosemary
- 1 teaspoon saffron

Direction

- Heat the oil in a heavy skillet to 360 degrees or until the oil begins to ripple on the surface.
- When ready, drain the potatoes and pat thoroughly dry.
- Place approximately a half cup of potatoes at a time into hot oil. Fry for two to three minutes, or until golden.
- Remove the potatoes from the oil with a slotted spoon and drain in a single layer on a paper bag.
- Sprinkle with salt and herbs.

Nutrition Information

- 996: calories;
- 6 grams: protein;
- 4 grams: dietary fiber;
- 2 grams: sugars;
- 479 milligrams: sodium;
- 90 grams: fat;
- 1 gram: trans fat;
- 65 grams: monounsaturated fat;
- 15 grams: polyunsaturated fat;
- 47 grams: carbohydrates;

111. Garden Vegetable Gratin

Serving: 8 servings | Prep: | Cook: | Ready in: 2hours30mins

Ingredients

- 3 pounds russet potatoes, peeled
- 2 tablespoons unsalted butter
- 4 ounces shallots, diced
- 1 medium carrot, diced
- 1 small zucchini, diced
- 1 cup frozen peas, thawed
- 2 cloves garlic, minced
- 2 tablespoons stemmed thyme
- 1 teaspoon salt
- ½ teaspoon freshly ground black pepper
- ¼ teaspoon grated or ground mace
- 3 cups reduced-sodium vegetable broth
- 1 cup low-fat or fat-free cream

Direction

- Position the rack in the center of the oven and preheat the oven to 350 degrees Fahrenheit. Peel and thinly slice the potatoes. Place the slices in a bowl, cover with cool water and set aside.
- Melt the butter in a large skillet over medium heat.
- Add the shallots, carrot, zucchini and peas. Cook, stirring often, until softened, about 3 minutes.
- Add the garlic, thyme, salt, pepper and mace. Stir well to warm through. Remove from the heat.
- Layer the potatoes and vegetable mixture in a 10-cup gratin or 9-by-13-inch baking dish by first blotting some potato slices on a paper towel, then layering them across the bottom of the dish. Add some of the vegetable mixture, spread it over the slices, then blot dry more slices and add them as another layer. Keep layering the casserole, like a lasagna, ending with a layer of potato slices.
- Whisk the broth and cream in a large bowl. Pour it over the contents of the baking dish.
- Bake, uncovered, basting occasionally, until it is golden and most of the liquid has been absorbed, about 2 hours.

Nutrition Information

- 296: calories;
- 4 grams: dietary fiber;
- 38 grams: carbohydrates;
- 351 milligrams: sodium;
- 14 grams: fat;
- 9 grams: saturated fat;
- 0 grams: trans fat;
- 1 gram: polyunsaturated fat;
- 5 grams: sugars;
- 6 grams: protein;

112. Garlic Spiedies

Serving: 6 to 8 servings | Prep: | Cook: | Ready in: 1hours

Ingredients

- 3 pounds lean beef, pork, lamb or venison suitable for grilling
- ½ cup red-wine vinegar
- 4 large cloves garlic, peeled
- ¾ cup olive oil
- ¼ cup brown sugar
- 1 teaspoon Dijon-style mustard
- 1 teaspoon Worcestershire sauce
- Salt and freshly ground black pepper
- 12 to 14 sprigs fresh herbs: parsley, oregano, dill, tarragon, and/ or thyme parsley, oregano, dill, tarragon, and/ or thyme (about 1/4 cup)
- ½ cup minced fresh chives
- 1 teaspoon plus 1 tablespoon lemon juice
- 1 large red bell pepper, seeded and cut in squares
- 1 large green bell pepper, seeded and cut in squares
- 1 pound small white onions, peeled and blanched
- 1 head elephant garlic, peeled and blanched

- 2 tablespoons finely chopped garlic
- 1 cup plain yogurt
- 12 pita breads, split and warmed (optional)
- :
- 2 tablespoons plus 1/4 cup minced fresh mint

Direction

- Trim meat of excess fat. Cut in 1- to 1 1/2-inch cubes so it can be threaded on skewers. Put meat in single layer in glass baking dish.
- Combine vinegar, garlic, oil, sugar, mustard and Worcestershire sauce in a food processor and process until smooth. Season to taste with salt and pepper. Add mixed herbs, chives, 2 tablespoons of the mint and 1 teaspoon of the lemon juice, and process briefly.
- Pour marinade over meat. Turn meat to coat it well, cover and refrigerate 24 hours to 3 days. Stir at least once every day.
- Preheat grill or broiler to hot. Thread meat on skewers, alternating the cubes with pieces of pepper, onions and elephant garlic.
- Puree the chopped garlic, the remaining tablespoon of lemon juice and a half cup of the yogurt together in a food processor. Stir into the remaining yogurt and add the remaining 1/4 cup of mint. Set aside.
- Grill or broil skewers, turning once, until meat is cooked to desired degree of doneness, 10 to 20 minutes.
- Remove meat and vegetables from skewers and serve with yogurt sauce, in pita bread if desired.

Nutrition Information

- 485: calories;
- 6 grams: saturated fat;
- 3 grams: dietary fiber;
- 10 grams: sugars;
- 840 milligrams: sodium;
- 28 grams: fat;
- 0 grams: trans fat;
- 19 grams: carbohydrates;
- 40 grams: protein;

113. Giant Limas With Winter Squash

Serving: 4 to 6 servings. | Prep: | Cook: | Ready in: 2hours

Ingredients

- 2 tablespoons extra virgin olive oil
- 1 medium onion, chopped
- 4 garlic cloves, minced
- 1 pound (about 2 1/2 cups) dried giant lima beans, rinsed
- 2 quarts plus 1 cup water
- A bouquet garni made with a bay leaf, a Parmesan rind and a sprig each of sage, thyme and parsley
- 1 pound winter squash, peeled and cut in small dice
- Salt to taste
- Freshly ground pepper
- 2 tablespoons slivered fresh sage leaves
- Freshly grated Parmesan for serving (optional)

Direction

- Preheat the oven to 325 degrees. Heat the olive oil over medium heat in a large, heavy ovenproof casserole or Dutch oven and add the onion. Cook, stirring often, until it is tender, about 5 minutes. Stir in half the garlic and cook, stirring, until it is fragrant, 30 seconds to a minute. Add the beans, water and bouquet garni and bring to a simmer. Cover and place in the oven for 45 minutes.
- Remove the casserole from the oven and stir in the remaining garlic, the winter squash, and salt to taste. If the mixture seems dry, add a little more water. Return to the oven and bake an hour longer, or until the beans and squash are very tender. Remove from the heat and remove the bouquet garni. Adjust salt, add pepper to taste and stir in the slivered sage.

Nutrition Information

- 344: calories;
- 18 grams: protein;
- 1 gram: polyunsaturated fat;
- 3 grams: monounsaturated fat;
- 59 grams: carbohydrates;
- 17 grams: dietary fiber;
- 9 grams: sugars;
- 6 grams: fat;
- 1245 milligrams: sodium;

114. Ginger Vinaigrette

Serving: One cup | Prep: | Cook: | Ready in: 5mins

Ingredients

- ¼ cup grated ginger
- 1 cup flat-leaf parsley leaves
- ½ cup olive oil
- ½ cup rice-wine or cider vinegar
- 2 tablespoons fresh lemon juice
- 1 teaspoon Dijon mustard
- 1 teaspoon minced coriander leaves
- ¼ teaspoon minced shallot
- ¼ teaspoon salt
- ¼ teaspoon freshly ground pepper

Direction

- Combine all ingredients in a blender. Puree until smooth. Store in a covered container in the refrigerator for up to 3 days.

Nutrition Information

- 582: calories;
- 6 grams: polyunsaturated fat;
- 2 grams: protein;
- 54 grams: fat;
- 8 grams: carbohydrates;
- 0 grams: trans fat;
- 40 grams: monounsaturated fat;
- 1 gram: sugars;
- 339 milligrams: sodium;

115. Gluten Free Pumpkin Muffins With Crumble Topping

Serving: 12 muffins | Prep: | Cook: | Ready in: 45mins

Ingredients

- Topping
- ¼ cup store-bought gluten-free flour blend
- ¼ cup packed light brown sugar
- ¼ cup granulated sugar
- ½ teaspoon pumpkin pie spice
- 4 tablespoons all-vegetable shortening
- Confectioners' sugar, for sprinkling
- Muffins
- 1 ¾ cups store-bought gluten-free flour blend
- 2 teaspoons baking powder
- 2 teaspoons pumpkin pie spice
- ¾ teaspoon salt
- 2 large eggs, at room temperature
- 1 cup canned pure pumpkin puree
- 1 cup granulated sugar
- ½ cup vegetable oil
- 1 tablespoon pure vanilla extract

Direction

- Preheat oven to 350 degrees Fahrenheit. Line a 12-cup muffin pan with paper liners.
- Prepare the crumble topping. Whisk together the flour, brown sugar, granulated sugar and pumpkin pie spice in a medium bowl. Add the shortening and, using your fingers or a fork, blend together until coarse crumbs form.
- To make the muffins: Whisk together the flour, baking powder, pumpkin pie spice and salt in a large bowl.
- In a medium bowl, whisk together the eggs, pumpkin puree, granulated sugar, oil and vanilla until smooth. Add to the flour mixture; stir until just combined.

- Fill each muffin cup almost full; top each with crumble topping. Bake until the muffins are springy to the touch and a toothpick inserted into the center comes out clean, 20 to 25 minutes. Let cool in the pan, set on a wire rack. Using a sieve, sprinkle with confectioners' sugar.

116. Goat Cheese Salad With Pancetta, Garlic And Figs

Serving: Four servings | Prep: | Cook: | Ready in: 15mins

Ingredients

- ½ pound pancetta, cut into small dice
- 4 tablespoons olive oil
- 4 teaspoons minced garlic
- 2 teaspoons minced fresh thyme
- ¾ cup sherry vinegar
- ½ pound goat cheese
- 8 cups mixed wild greens, washed and stemmed
- 12 fresh or dried figs, stemmed and halved
- Salt and freshly ground pepper to taste

Direction

- Place the pancetta in a large skillet over low heat and cook until it has browned and released half of its fat. Remove the pancetta from the skillet with a slotted spoon. Add the olive oil to the skillet and increase the heat to medium. When the pancetta is hot but not smoking, return it to the pan and cook for a few seconds.
- Add the garlic and cook until lightly browned. Add the thyme and cook just until it makes a popping sound. Stir in the vinegar and simmer until reduced to 1/4 cup, about 5 minutes. Crumble the goat cheese into the skillet and cook just until it begins to weep. Toss in the greens and immediately remove the pan from the heat. Toss in the figs and season with salt and pepper to taste. Place the salad in a bowl and serve warm.

117. Grated Black Radish Relish

Serving: 1/2 cup | Prep: | Cook: | Ready in: 10mins

Ingredients

- 1 black radish, peeled and coarsely grated
- 1 teaspoon sugar
- ½ teaspoon coarse salt (or to taste)
- 1 tablespoon white wine vinegar
- 1 tablespoon olive oil
- Hot red pepper flakes to taste

Direction

- Combine all ingredients.
- Refrigerate until ready to serve.

118. Gratin Of Fennel And Potatoes

Serving: Eight servings | Prep: | Cook: | Ready in: 2hours

Ingredients

- ¾ pound fennel bulbs
- 3 to 4 cups chicken stock
- 4 large cloves garlic, peeled
- 2 teaspoons lemon juice
- Salt to taste
- 1 pound red potatoes
- ¼ cup freshly grated Parmesan cheese
- Freshly ground black pepper to taste
- ¾ cup fresh bread crumbs, preferably sourdough bread
- 1 tablespoon unsalted butter

Direction

- Cut the roots off the fennel. Discard the tough, stringy or discolored outer leaves. Chop the feathery leaves and set them aside to use as a garnish. Slice the bulbs lengthwise into 1/8-inch-thick pieces and place them in a 2-quart saucepan. Add 3 cups of stock and the garlic, lemon juice and salt (if desired). Bring the broth to a boil, then immediately reduce the heat and simmer for 15 minutes. Remove the fennel slices and set them aside.
- Peel the potatoes and slice them into 1/8-inch-thick rounds. Put them in the broth and, if necessary, add more stock or water if the broth has cooked down too far. Bring to a boil, then immediately reduce the heat and simmer for 5 to 8 minutes, or until the potatoes just lose their crunch. Do not allow them to soften beyond this point. Lift the potatoes out of the pot and set them aside.
- Cook the broth over medium-high heat until it is reduced by a little more than half, to approximately 1 1/4 cups. Force the broth through a medium sieve into a bowl, using a spatula to push through the garlic cloves.
- Preheat the oven to 350 degrees. Cover the bottom of an 8-inch baking dish or gratin dish with several spoonfuls of the strained broth. Make a layer of fennel and potatoes, arranging the slices so that fennel alternates with potato; use up all the fennel. Spoon on a little more broth and sprinkle with one-third of the Parmesan cheese and some freshly ground black pepper. Put the remaining potato slices on top - they should overlap slightly.
- Lightly press the potatoes with the palm of your hand so that the layer is even. Pour the remaining broth over the potatoes, grind pepper on top and sprinkle with the rest of the Parmesan cheese. Bake for an hour and 15 minutes.
- While the gratin is baking, saute the bread crumbs in the butter until they are golden-brown. Five minutes before the gratin is done, sprinkle the bread crumbs over the top with about a tablespoon of the chopped fennel leaves. Let the dish cool slightly before serving.

Nutrition Information

- 132: calories;
- 4 grams: sugars;
- 19 grams: carbohydrates;
- 3 grams: dietary fiber;
- 6 grams: protein;
- 2 grams: saturated fat;
- 0 grams: polyunsaturated fat;
- 1 gram: monounsaturated fat;
- 505 milligrams: sodium;

119. Greek Zucchini And Herb Pie

Serving: One 10- inch pie, serving eight to ten | Prep: | Cook: | Ready in: 3hours

Ingredients

- 2 ¼ to 2 ½ pounds zucchini, ends trimmed
- Salt to taste
- 2 tablespoons extra virgin olive oil, plus additional for brushing the phyllo dough
- 1 large onion, finely chopped
- 2 garlic cloves, minced
- 1 cup finely chopped dill
- ½ cup chopped fresh mint, or a combination of mint and parsley
- 1 cup crumbled feta
- 3 eggs, beaten
- Freshly ground pepper
- 12 sheets phyllo dough or 1 recipe whole wheat yeasted olive oil pie pastry

Direction

- Grate the zucchini using a food processor or a hand grater. Place in a large colander, salt generously, and let drain for 1 hour, pressing down on it occasionally to squeeze out liquid. After an hour, take up handfuls and squeeze out moisture (or wrap in a kitchen towel and

twist the towel to squeeze out the moisture). Place in a bowl.
- Heat 1 tablespoon of the oil over medium heat in a large, heavy nonstick skillet over medium heat, and add the onion. Cook, stirring, until tender, about five minutes, then add the garlic. Cook, stirring, until the garlic is fragrant, about one minute. Transfer to the bowl with the zucchini. Stir in the herbs, feta, eggs and pepper.
- Preheat the oven to 350 degrees. Oil a 10-inch pie or cake pan. If using phyllo, line the pie dish with seven pieces of phyllo, lightly brushing each piece with oil and turning the dish after each addition so that the edges of the phyllo drape evenly over the pan. Fill with the zucchini mixture. Fold the draped edges in over the filling, lightly brushing the folded in sheets of phyllo, then layer the remaining five pieces on top, brushing each piece with olive oil. Stuff the edges into the sides of the pan. If using the olive oil pastry, divide the dough into two equal pieces. Roll out the first ball to a circle 2 inches wider than the pan. Line the pan with the pastry, and brush with olive oil. Top with the filling. Roll out the remaining dough. Place over the filling. Press the edges of the top and bottom layers of dough together, and pinch to form an attractive lip around the edge.
- Make a few slashes in the top crust so that steam can escape as the pie bakes. Score in a few places with the tip of a knife, and brush with olive oil. Bake 50 to 60 minutes, until the pastry is golden brown. Remove from the heat, and allow to cool 15 to 30 minutes or to room temperature. Slice in wedges and serve.

Nutrition Information

- 167: calories;
- 0 grams: trans fat;
- 1 gram: polyunsaturated fat;
- 4 grams: sugars;
- 7 grams: protein;
- 432 milligrams: sodium;
- 6 grams: fat;
- 3 grams: saturated fat;
- 21 grams: carbohydrates;
- 2 grams: dietary fiber;

120. Green Bean Salad With Chickpeas And Mushrooms

Serving: Serves 4 | Prep: | Cook: | Ready in: 10mins

Ingredients

- ½ pound green beans
- 3 ounces mushrooms, cleaned, trimmed and sliced thin (about 1 1/4 cups)
- 2 cups cooked chickpeas, or 1 15-ounce can, drained and rinsed
- 1 ounce shaved Parmesan (about 1/4 cup)
- 3 tablespoons chopped fresh herbs, like chives, marjoram, parsley and tarragon
- 1 tablespoon freshly squeezed lemon juice
- 1 tablespoon sherry vinegar
- Salt to taste
- 1 teaspoon Dijon mustard
- 1 small garlic clove, green shoot removed, finely minced or put through a press
- 6 tablespoons extra virgin olive oil
- Freshly ground pepper
- Optional: 1/4 red pepper, sliced

Direction

- Steam or blanch the green beans for five minutes, then cool in a bowl of ice water. Drain and trim the stems. If the beans are very long, break in half.
- Combine the beans, mushrooms, chickpeas, Parmesan and herbs in a salad bowl. In a small bowl or measuring cup, whisk together the lemon juice, vinegar, salt, mustard and garlic. Whisk in the olive oil.
- Toss the dressing with the bean mixture shortly before serving. If desired, garnish with red pepper slices or toss them with the salad.

Nutrition Information

- 582: calories;
- 17 grams: monounsaturated fat;
- 18 grams: dietary fiber;
- 23 grams: protein;
- 745 milligrams: sodium;
- 28 grams: fat;
- 5 grams: polyunsaturated fat;
- 0 grams: trans fat;
- 64 grams: carbohydrates;
- 12 grams: sugars;

121. Green Mole With Chicken

Serving: 6 to 8 servings | Prep: | Cook: | Ready in: 2hours

Ingredients

- For the chicken and stock
- 2 quarts water
- ½ medium onion, sliced
- 2 large garlic cloves, roughly chopped
- 1 large carrot, sliced
- 2 bay leaves
- ¼ teaspoon dried thyme, or 1 sprig fresh
- ¼ teaspoon dried marjoram, or 1 sprig fresh
- Salt
- 2 whole chicken breasts on the bone, split, then cut in half crosswise for 8 pieces total
- For the mole
- ⅔ cup hulled pumpkin seeds
- 1 pound tomatillos, husked and rinsed, or 1 13-ounce can, drained
- 2 to 4 serrano or jalapeño chilies, to taste, seeded
- ½ medium onion, sliced, soaked in cold water for 5 minutes, drained and rinsed
- 2 garlic cloves, roughly chopped
- 6 large, dark romaine or leaf lettuce leaves, washed and dried, roughly chopped
- 12 large cilantro sprigs, plus additional for garnish
- 3 cups chicken stock (above) or vegetable stock
- 2 tablespoons rice bran oil or canola oil
- Salt to taste

Direction

- To poach the chicken, combine all of the ingredients except the chicken in a large pot and bring to a simmer. Simmer 20 minutes. Add the chicken breasts and skim off any foam when the liquid comes back to a simmer. Partly cover and simmer 15 minutes. Remove from the heat and allow to cool for 5 to 10 minutes, or longer if possible. Then, using tongs, remove the chicken breasts to a sheet tray or bowl. When they are cool enough to handle, remove the skin. Cover and set aside. Strain the stock through a cheesecloth-lined strainer and measure out 3 cups. Skim off the fat from the top. (If you do this step the day before, chill the stock first, then skim off the fat from the top. Chill any remaining stock, skim off the fat and freeze.)
- To make the mole, heat a heavy Dutch oven or saucepan over medium heat and add the pumpkin seeds. Wait until you hear one pop, then stir constantly until they have puffed and popped, and smell toasty. They should not get any darker than golden, or they will taste bitter. Transfer to a bowl or a baking sheet and allow to cool. Set aside 2 tablespoons of the seeds for garnish.
- If you're using fresh tomatillos, bring a medium pot of water to a simmer, add the tomatillos, and simmer for 10 minutes, flipping them over in the water halfway through, until soft. Drain and place in a blender. If using canned tomatillos, drain and place them in a blender. Add the cooled pumpkin seeds, the chilies, lettuce, onion, garlic, cilantro, and 1/2 cup of the stock. Cover the blender and blend the mixture until smooth, stopping the blender to stir if necessary. If necessary, do this in 2 batches.
- Heat the Dutch oven or heavy saucepan over medium-high heat until a drop of water evaporates immediately on contact. Add the oil, wait for a minute, then drizzle in a bit of

the pumpkin seed mixture; if it sizzles loudly, add the rest, holding the lid above the pan, as the mixture will spatter. Cook, stirring, until the mixture darkens and thickens, about 5 minutes. It will splutter, so be careful. Hold the lid of the pot above the pot to shield you and your stove from the splutters. Stir or whisk in the remaining stock, bring to a simmer, reduce the heat to medium-low and simmer uncovered, stirring often, until the sauce is thick and creamy, 15 to 20 minutes. Season to taste with salt.

- To serve, place the chicken breasts in the pot with the mole and warm on top of the stove, then remove the chicken pieces to a platter and nap with the warm sauce; or place in a large, attractive baking dish, pour on the sauce, cover and warm in a low oven (275 degrees) for 20 minutes. Garnish with cilantro sprigs and pumpkin seeds. Serve with rice.

Nutrition Information

- 199: calories;
- 13 grams: protein;
- 3 grams: dietary fiber;
- 0 grams: trans fat;
- 5 grams: polyunsaturated fat;
- 8 grams: carbohydrates;
- 4 grams: sugars;
- 1093 milligrams: sodium;

122. Green Pipian

Serving: Makes about 1 3/4 cups | Prep: | Cook: | Ready in: 40mins

Ingredients

- ½ cup hulled untoasted pumpkin seeds
- ½ pound tomatillos, husked, rinsed, and coarsely chopped, or 2 13-ounce cans, drained
- 1 serrano chile or 1/2 jalapeño (more to taste), stemmed and roughly chopped
- 3 romaine lettuce leaves, torn into pieces
- ¼ small white onion, coarsely chopped, soaked for 5 minutes in cold water, drained and rinsed
- 2 garlic cloves, halved, green shoots removed
- ¼ cup loosely packed chopped cilantro
- 1 ½ cups chicken stock
- 1 tablespoon canola or extra virgin olive oil
- Salt, preferably kosher salt, to taste

Direction

- Heat a heavy Dutch oven or saucepan over medium heat and add the pumpkin seeds. Wait until you hear one pop, then stir constantly until they have puffed and popped, and smell toasty. They should not get any darker than golden or they will taste bitter. Transfer to a bowl and allow to cool.
- Place the cooled pumpkin seeds in a blender and add the tomatillos, chiles, lettuce, onion, garlic, cilantro, and 1/2 cup of the chicken stock. Cover the blender and blend the mixture until smooth, stopping the blender to stir if necessary.
- Heat the oil in the Dutch oven or heavy saucepan over medium-high heat. Drizzle in a bit of the pumpkin seed mixture and if it sizzles, add the rest. Cook, stirring, until the mixture darkens and thickens, 8 to 10 minutes. It will splutter, so be careful. Hold the lid of the pot above the pot to shield you and your stove from the splutters. Add the remaining chicken stock, bring to a simmer, reduce the heat to medium-low and simmer uncovered, stirring often, until the sauce is thick and creamy, 15 to 20 minutes. Season to taste with salt. For a silkier sauce, blend again in batches.

Nutrition Information

- 176: calories;
- 2 grams: dietary fiber;
- 0 grams: trans fat;
- 9 grams: carbohydrates;
- 416 milligrams: sodium;
- 13 grams: fat;

- 6 grams: monounsaturated fat;
- 4 grams: sugars;
- 8 grams: protein;

123. Green Tomato Salsa Verde

Serving: About 1 3/4 cups (more if thinned with water) | Prep: | Cook: | Ready in: 45mins

Ingredients

- 1 pound green tomatoes
- 2 to 3 jalapeño or serrano peppers (more to taste)
- ½ medium onion, preferably a white onion, chopped, soaked for five minutes in cold water, drained, rinsed and drained again on paper towels
- Salt to taste
- ½ cup roughly chopped cilantro
- ¼ to ½ cup water, as needed (optional)

Direction

- Preheat the broiler. Line a baking sheet with foil. Place the green tomatoes on the baking sheet, stem-side down, and place under the broiler about 2 inches from the heat. Broil two to five minutes, until charred. Using tongs, turn the tomatoes over, and grill on the other side for two to five minutes, until blackened. Remove from the heat. When cool enough to handle, core the tomatoes and remove the charred skin. Quarter and place in a blender or a food processor fitted with a steel blade (I prefer the blender).
- Add the remaining ingredients, except the water, to the blender or food processor, and blend to a coarse or a smooth puree (to your taste). Transfer to a bowl, taste and adjust seasonings, and thin out with water if desired. Allow to stand for 30 minutes or longer before serving to allow the flavors to develop. You may wish to thin out after it stands.

Nutrition Information

- 39: calories;
- 0 grams: polyunsaturated fat;
- 9 grams: carbohydrates;
- 2 grams: protein;
- 6 grams: sugars;
- 358 milligrams: sodium;

124. Grilled Chicken Wings With Provençal Flavors

Serving: 4 servings | Prep: | Cook: | Ready in: 45mins

Ingredients

- Salt and freshly ground black pepper
- 1 teaspoon fresh thyme, oregano or marjoram leaves
- 1 teaspoon chopped fresh rosemary leaves
- ½ teaspoon chopped fresh lavender leaves, optional
- ¼ cup roughly chopped parsley
- Extra virgin olive oil
- 8 chicken wings, cut into three sections, smallest section reserved for stock
- 8 bay leaves, cut in half
- Lemon wedges

Direction

- Start a gas or charcoal grill; fire should be moderately hot and rack about 6 inches from heat source. Keep part of grill cooler for indirect cooking.
- In a small bowl, combine a sprinkle of salt and pepper with herbs. Add enough olive oil to make a paste. Loosen skin of chicken and slide a bay leaf between skin and meat, then insert a portion of herb mixture. Push skin back onto flesh and sprinkle with a little more salt and pepper.

- Start chicken on cool side of grill. After some fat has been rendered, turn chicken; if it flares up, move it to an even cooler part of fire. When skin has lost its raw look and most fat has been rendered, no more than 15 minutes, move chicken directly over fire. Cook until both sides are nicely browned and flesh is firm and cooked through, another 5 to 10 minutes.
- Serve hot, warm or at room temperature, with lemon wedges. (Bay leaf is not edible.)

Nutrition Information

- 109: calories;
- 4 grams: monounsaturated fat;
- 1 gram: dietary fiber;
- 9 grams: protein;
- 135 milligrams: sodium;
- 8 grams: fat;
- 2 grams: polyunsaturated fat;
- 0 grams: sugars;

125. Grilled Fish With Tomato Cilantro Vinaigrette

Serving: 4 servings | Prep: | Cook: | Ready in: 15mins

Ingredients

- 1 ½ pounds tuna or swordfish
- 4 tablespoons extra-virgin olive oil
- 4 tablespoons rice vinegar
- ½ teaspoon dry mustard
- 4 scallions, chopped
- ½ cup chopped cilantro
- 4 medium-large ripe tomatoes, coarsely chopped
- Freshly ground black pepper to taste

Direction

- Either grill fish over medium-hot coals outdoors or broil it in the oven. Measure fish at thickest point and cook it 10 minutes to the inch.
- Whisk oil with vinegar and mustard. Stir in scallions, cilantro and tomatoes. Season with pepper.
- When fish is cooked, spoon some vinaigrette onto each of four dinner plates; arrange fish on top, and top with additional vinaigrette.

Nutrition Information

- 339: calories;
- 2 grams: dietary fiber;
- 0 grams: trans fat;
- 10 grams: monounsaturated fat;
- 87 milligrams: sodium;
- 15 grams: fat;
- 7 grams: carbohydrates;
- 4 grams: sugars;
- 43 grams: protein;

126. Grilled Gorgonzola And Beet Green Sandwich

Serving: Serves 1 | Prep: | Cook: | Ready in: 10mins

Ingredients

- 2 large slices whole-wheat country bread (3 ounces total)
- ½ garlic clove (optional)
- About 3/4 ounce (3 tablespoons crumbled) Gorgonzola or creamy blue cheese
- ⅓ cup chopped blanched beet greens
- Chopped fresh herbs such as parsley, thyme, rosemary, marjoram (optional)
- ½ teaspoon extra-virgin olive oil
- 1 small or 1/2 medium beet, sliced thin

Direction

- Rub surface of one slice of bread with the cut clove of garlic if desired. Spread blue cheese

over the bread. If you wish, save a little cheese for the top slice.
- Toss greens with herbs if desired. Spoon over cheese and press down onto the bread. Drizzle on 1/4 teaspoon olive oil. Arrange beet slices over the greens. If desired, add a little more cheese: either spread on the top slice of bread or sprinkle it over the beets. If desired, rub second piece of bread with the cut garlic clove before spreading with cheese. Place over beets and press down firmly. Drizzle remaining olive oil over the top slice.
- Toast in toaster oven for 3 to 4 minutes, until cheese has melted. Remove from toaster, press down firmly, cut in half and serve.

Nutrition Information

- 274: calories;
- 561 milligrams: sodium;
- 3 grams: monounsaturated fat;
- 1 gram: polyunsaturated fat;
- 40 grams: carbohydrates;
- 5 grams: dietary fiber;
- 7 grams: sugars;
- 11 grams: protein;
- 8 grams: fat;
- 0 grams: trans fat;

127. Grilled Leg Of Lamb With Mustard Seeds

Serving: 6 to 8 servings | Prep: | Cook: | Ready in: 3hours

Ingredients

- 1 8-pound leg of lamb, boned, butterflied and trimmed of fat, inside and out (ask butcher)
- Salt and freshly ground pepper to taste
- ¼ cup olive oil
- 5 tablespoons mustard seeds
- 1 teaspoon ground cumin
- 1 tablespoon finely chopped garlic
- 4 sprigs fresh thyme or 1 teaspoon dried
- 1 teaspoon fennel seeds
- 2 tablespoons chopped fresh rosemary or 1 tablespoon dried
- 2 bay leaves, crumbled
- 4 tablespoons fresh lemon juice
- 2 cups red wine
- 2 tablespoons butter, melted
- 4 tablespoons finely chopped parsley

Direction

- Lay lamb out flat, and sprinkle with salt and pepper on all sides.
- Put oil in baking dish large enough to hold lamb. Add lamb, and sprinkle on both sides with mustard seeds, cumin, garlic, thyme, fennel seeds, rosemary, bay leaves, lemon juice and red wine. Turn and rub lamb so it is evenly coated with the ingredients. Marinate in a cool place for 1 or 2 hours, or in a refrigerator up to 6 hours. If lamb is refrigerated, let it return to room temperature before cooking.
- Preheat a charcoal grill or oven broiler.
- Remove lamb from marinade and reserve marinade. If a grill is used, put lamb flat on grill. If broiler is used, place lamb under broiler 4 to 5 inches from heat. Cook lamb uncovered on grill or under broiler about 15 minutes. Turn and cook 10 to 15 minutes on second side. For medium or well-done meat, cook longer.
- Meanwhile, in a baking pan large enough to hold lamb, bring reserved marinade to a boil, stirring until the liquid is reduced by half. Remove from heat, and swirl in butter and parsley. Transfer lamb to marinade pan, cover loosely with foil and keep warm. Let meat rest 10 to 15 minutes before serving. Slice thinly and serve with pan gravy.

Nutrition Information

- 905: calories;
- 25 grams: saturated fat;
- 0 grams: trans fat;
- 28 grams: monounsaturated fat;

- 1252 milligrams: sodium;
- 62 grams: fat;
- 5 grams: carbohydrates;
- 1 gram: sugars;
- 67 grams: protein;

128. Grilled Pizza With Grilled Fennel And Parmesan

Serving: 3 10-inch pizzas | Prep: | Cook: | Ready in: 30mins

Ingredients

- 1 medium fennel bulb, trimmed, cut in half or quartered, cored, and sliced thin across the grain
- Extra virgin olive oil (about 2 tablespoons)
- Salt and freshly ground pepper
- 3 10-inch pizza crusts (1 recipe)
- 3/4¾ cup marinara sauce made with fresh or canned tomatoes
- 36 imported black olives (12 per pizza, optional)
- 1 tablespoon (or more, to taste) fresh thyme leaves
- 3 ounces freshly grated Parmesan
- Fresh basil leaves, torn or cut in slivers

Direction

- Prepare a hot grill. Place the sliced fennel in a bowl and toss with 1 tablespoon of the olive oil and salt and pepper to taste. Place a perforated grill pan on the grill and let it get hot, then add the fennel and cook, tossing in the pan or stirring with tongs, for about 5 minutes, just until it softens slightly and begins to char. Remove from the grill and return the fennel to the bowl.
- Oil the hot grill rack with olive oil, either by brushing with a grill brush or by dipping a folded wad of paper towels in olive oil and using tongs to rub the rack with it. Place a round of dough on a lightly dusted baker's peel or rimless baking sheet. Slide the pizza dough from the peel or baking sheet onto the grill rack. If the dough has just come from the freezer and is easy to handle, you can just place it on the rack without bothering with the peel. Close the lid of the grill – the vents should be closed —-- and set the timer for 2 minutes.
- Lift up the grill lid. The surface of the dough should display some big air bubbles. Using tongs, lift the dough to see if it is evenly browning on the bottom. Rotate the dough to assure even browning. Keep it on the grill, moving it around as necessary, until it is nicely browned, with grill marks. Watch closely so that it doesn't burn. When it is nicely browned on the bottom (it may be blackened in spots), use tongs or a spatula to slide the dough onto the baking sheet or peel, and remove from the grill. Cover the grill again.
- Make sure that there is still some flour on the peel or baking sheet and flip the dough over so that the uncooked side is now on the bottom. Brush the top lightly with oil, then top with a thin layer of marinara sauce (no more than 1/4¼ cup) and a layer of fennel. Arrange the olives, if using, here and there, and sprinkle with thyme and Parmesan. Drizzle on a little more olive oil. Slide the pizza back onto the grill. If using a gas grill, reduce the heat to medium-high. Close the lid and cook for 2 to 3 more minutes, until the bottom is brown. Open the grill and check the pizza. The top should be hot and the bottom nicely browned. If the bottom is getting too dark but the pizza still needs a little more time, move it to a cooler part of the grill and close the top. Use a spatula or tongs to remove the pizza to a cutting board. Sprinkle with torn or cut basil leaves. Cut into wedges and serve. Repeat with the other two crusts.

129. Grilled Polenta

Serving: Serves six to eight | Prep: | Cook: | Ready in: 1hours

Ingredients

- 1 ½ cups polenta
- 1 ½ teaspoons salt
- 1 ½ tablespoons unsalted butter
- Extra virgin olive oil for grilling

Direction

- Preheat the oven to 350 degrees. Combine the polenta, 1 1/2 quarts water and salt in a 2-quart baking dish, and stir together. Place the baking dish on top of a sheet pan (so that if water sloshes when you put it in the oven, it will just go onto the sheet pan), and place in the oven. Bake one hour. Remove from the oven, stir in the butter and return to the oven for 20 minutes. Remove from the oven, and stir again. Return to the oven for 10 to 20 minutes, until stiff. Remove from the oven and allow to cool, then chill for one hour or more.
- Prepare a medium grill or heat an electric griddle on medium. Cut the polenta into squares, and brush the squares on both sides with olive oil. Place on the grill or griddle. When grill marks appear or when nicely browned, usually in about two to three minutes, turn and brown the other side. Serve hot.

Nutrition Information

- 132: calories;
- 3 grams: fat;
- 1 gram: dietary fiber;
- 0 grams: sugars;
- 23 grams: carbohydrates;
- 2 grams: protein;
- 76 milligrams: sodium;

130. Grilled Porcini, Italian Style

Serving: 4 servings | Prep: | Cook: | Ready in: 15mins

Ingredients

- 8 to 12 fresh porcini or other flat-capped mushrooms such as shiitake, Lundy's yellow, cepes or Black Forest, about 1 pound
- 4 tablespoons olive oil
- 2 teaspoons dried oregano
- 2 teaspoons finely minced garlic
- Salt to taste if desired
- Freshly ground pepper to taste

Direction

- Preheat charcoal or gas-fired grill to high.
- Remove stems from mushrooms. Stems may be chopped and used for another purpose. Wipe caps with damp cloth.
- Blend olive oil, oregano, garlic, salt and pepper in small bowl. Blend. Brush mushroom caps with mixture.
- Place mushrooms, stem side up, on grill and cook 2 minutes. Turn and brush with remaining oil mixture. Cook 2 minutes longer.

Nutrition Information

- 130: calories;
- 14 grams: fat;
- 2 grams: carbohydrates;
- 10 grams: monounsaturated fat;
- 1 gram: protein;
- 0 grams: dietary fiber;
- 106 milligrams: sodium;

131. Grilled Watermelon And Feta Salad

Serving: Serves 4 | Prep: | Cook: | Ready in: 10mins

Ingredients

- 1 small red onion, sliced
- 3 large or 4 smaller 1-inch-thick slices watermelon
- 3 tablespoons extra-virgin olive oil
- 2 tablespoons sherry vinegar
- Salt to taste
- 2 tablespoons chopped fresh mint
- 2 ounces feta cheese, crumbled
- ¼ to ½ teaspoon Aleppo pepper or mild chili powder (to taste)

Direction

- Place sliced onion in a bowl and cover with water and 1 teaspoon of the vinegar. Soak 5 minutes, then drain and rinse. Drain on paper towels.
- Prepare a medium-hot grill. Use 1 tablespoon of the olive oil to brush the watermelon slices lightly. Grill for about 3 minutes per side, or until charred. Remove from heat and dice. Transfer, with juice, to a large salad bowl.
- Add onions and remaining ingredients and toss together. Let sit for a few minutes or for up to an hour before serving. Toss again just before serving.
-

132. Grilled Or Pan Cooked Albacore With Soy/Mirin Marinade

Serving: 4 servings. | Prep: | Cook: | Ready in: 2hours45mins

Ingredients

- ¼ cup low-sodium soy sauce
- 2 tablespoons mirin (sweet Japanese rice wine)
- 1 tablespoon seasoned rice vinegar
- 1 tablespoon minced or grated fresh ginger
- 1 teaspoon sugar
- 1 tablespoon plus 1 teaspoon dark sesame oil
- 1 ½ pounds albacore steaks

Direction

- Combine the soy sauce, mirin, vinegar, ginger and sugar in a bowl and whisk together well. Whisk in the sesame oil.
- Place the albacore steaks in a large bowl or baking dish and toss with the marinade. Cover the bowl, or transfer the fish and marinade to a large zip-top bag and refrigerate for 1 to 2 hours, or longer.
- Prepare a hot grill, or heat a heavy cast-iron or nonstick skillet over medium-high heat. Remove the fish from the marinade. Cook the steaks for 2 to 4 minutes on each side, depending on how well done you like the fish to be. Serve hot.

Nutrition Information

- 251: calories;
- 0 grams: dietary fiber;
- 2 grams: polyunsaturated fat;
- 3 grams: carbohydrates;
- 43 grams: protein;
- 651 milligrams: sodium;
- 5 grams: fat;
- 1 gram: sugars;

133. Grits

Serving: | Prep: | Cook: | Ready in: 8mins

Ingredients

- 4 cups water
- 1 cup yellow stone-ground cornmeal
- Salt and pepper to taste

Direction

- Bring water and salt to boil. Slowly add cornmeal, stirring to prevent lumping. Cook

over low heat until grits are cooked and mixture is thick. Season with pepper.
- Either serve grits from the pot or pour into 10-inch pie plate and chill.
- If chilled, cut into triangles and reheat in oven at 350 degrees for 10 minutes before serving.

Nutrition Information

- 112: calories;
- 1 gram: polyunsaturated fat;
- 0 grams: sugars;
- 24 grams: carbohydrates;
- 2 grams: dietary fiber;
- 3 grams: protein;
- 624 milligrams: sodium;

134. Guacamole

Serving: Makes about 1 1/2 cups | Prep: | Cook: | Ready in: 10mins

Ingredients

- ½ small red onion, minced optional
- 3 ripe Haas avocados
- 1 medium ripe tomato, chopped
- Juice of 1 to 2 limes, to taste
- 1 small garlic clove, minced
- ¼ teaspoon lightly toasted cumin seeds, ground
- 1 small serrano chile, seeded and minced optional
- Salt, preferably kosher salt, to taste

Direction

- If you are including onion in your guacamole, place the onion in a small bowl and cover with cold water. Soak for five minutes, then drain, rinse and dry on paper towels.
- Cut the avocados in half, remove the pits and scoop out the flesh. Mash in a mortar and pestle or with a fork. Do not use a food processor. Add the chopped tomatoes and lime juice, and continue to mash. Stir in the onion, garlic, cumin, chile and salt to taste. Taste and adjust seasonings. If not using right away, cover with plastic, placing it directly on top of the guacamole. Stir before serving to restore the green color.

Nutrition Information

- 170: calories;
- 15 grams: fat;
- 2 grams: protein;
- 10 grams: monounsaturated fat;
- 11 grams: carbohydrates;
- 7 grams: dietary fiber;
- 1 gram: sugars;
- 321 milligrams: sodium;

135. Habichuelas Rojas (Red Beans, Dominican Style)

Serving: Eight servings | Prep: | Cook: | Ready in: 2hours30mins

Ingredients

- 1 pound dried small red beans (do not use kidney beans)
- ½ teaspoon salt
- 14 cups water
- 1 tablespoon olive oil
- 4 strips bacon, cut into pieces
- 1 large onion, chopped
- 3 cloves garlic, chopped
- 1 green bell pepper, chopped
- 2 tomatoes, peeled and chopped
- 1 teaspoon tomato paste mixed with 1 teaspoon water
- 1 sprig each of cilantro and fresh parsley, tied together to make a bouquet garni
- Salt to taste
- ½ teaspoon white vinegar
- 1 teaspoon oregano

- 1 hot green pepper, chopped

Direction

- Rinse the beans thoroughly and pick out any foreign matter. Place in a bowl and cover with 6 cups of cold water; let sit overnight. (Alternatively, place the beans in a saucepan with 6 cups of cold water and boil for 2 minutes; set aside for 1 hour.)
- Drain the beans and place in a large saucepan with 1/2 teaspoon of salt and 8 cups of water. Bring to a boil and simmer at medium heat until the beans are tender, about 1 to 1 1/2 hours.
- Meanwhile, make a sofritoor paste. In a skillet, heat the olive oil and the bacon until the fat is rendered. Add the onion, garlic, bell pepper and tomatoes and cook for 10 to 15 minutes or until the vegetables are soft. Add the diluted tomato paste and the bouquet garni. Cook for 5 minutes.
- Add the paste to the beans and cook, stirring, for 15 minutes. Add salt to taste, vinegar, oregano and hot pepper and cook an additional 15 to 20 minutes, or until the beans are very creamy.

Nutrition Information

- 286: calories;
- 39 grams: carbohydrates;
- 15 grams: dietary fiber;
- 16 grams: protein;
- 8 grams: fat;
- 2 grams: saturated fat;
- 0 grams: trans fat;
- 1 gram: polyunsaturated fat;
- 4 grams: sugars;
- 1322 milligrams: sodium;

136. Harvest Corn Fritters

Serving: Fifty pieces | Prep: | Cook: | Ready in: 10mins

Ingredients

- 2 ½ cups flour
- 1 tablespoon baking powder, plus 2 teaspoons
- 1 ½ teaspoons salt
- 1 teaspoon freshly ground white pepper
- 8 eggs, separated
- 4 cups milk
- 2 cups corn kernels (frozen or canned)
- 1 large red pepper, diced
- 4 scallions, diced
- 1 quart vegetable oil for deep frying
- Pepper jelly (optional)

Direction

- Place the flour, baking powder, salt and pepper in a large mixing bowl. Add the egg yolks and combine well. Add the milk and stir to form a smooth batter.
- Stir in the corn, diced pepper and scallions. Beat the egg whites to a soft peak and fold into the batter.
- In a deep frying pan or pot, heat the oil to 350 degrees.
- Using a teaspoon, take spoonfuls of the batter and drop into the hot oil. Fry until golden brown, about three minutes. Remove from the oil and drain on paper towels. Serve immediately, with pepper jelly if desired.

Nutrition Information

- 212: calories;
- 19 grams: fat;
- 2 grams: protein;
- 0 grams: dietary fiber;
- 13 grams: monounsaturated fat;
- 3 grams: polyunsaturated fat;
- 8 grams: carbohydrates;
- 1 gram: sugars;
- 125 milligrams: sodium;

137. Herbed And Butterflied Leg Of Lamb

Serving: 6 servings | Prep: | Cook: | Ready in: 1hours

Ingredients

- 1 teaspoon black peppercorns
- 1 teaspoon whole coriander seed
- ⅓ cup olive oil (not extra-virgin)
- 1 teaspoon salt
- 2 to 3 unpeeled cloves garlic, slightly crushed
- 1 lemon
- 2 9-inch sprigs fresh rosemary (or the equivalent in shorter lengths)
- 1 4-pound leg of lamb, boned and butterflied (opened with meat scored slightly to flatten it)

Direction

- With a mortar and pestle, lightly crush peppercorns and coriander seeds. Transfer to a small bowl, and add olive oil, salt and garlic. Finely grate lemon peel, and add to mixture. Cut lemon into quarters, and squeeze juice into mixture, then add leftover lemon as well.
- Place lamb skin side down in a shallow dish, and press whole rosemary sprigs into scored meat. Pour marinade over meat, pressing lemon pieces into meat. Cover dish with plastic wrap; refrigerate overnight.
- When ready to cook, remove lamb from refrigerator, and allow to sit at room temperature while oven heats to 425 degrees. Place lamb skin side up in a roasting pan, keeping lemon pieces and rosemary pressed into underside.
- Roast 35 to 40 minutes, until an instant-read thermometer inserted into thickest part of lamb registers 145 degrees (for medium-well lamb), or adjust cooking time as desired. When cooked to taste, remove lamb from oven, and allow to rest in pan for 10 to 15 minutes before carving.

Nutrition Information

- 608: calories;
- 1 gram: dietary fiber;
- 44 grams: protein;
- 523 milligrams: sodium;
- 23 grams: monounsaturated fat;
- 4 grams: polyunsaturated fat;
- 2 grams: carbohydrates;
- 0 grams: sugars;
- 46 grams: fat;
- 16 grams: saturated fat;

138. Homemade Oreos

Serving: 24 two-inch sandwich cookies. | Prep: | Cook: | Ready in: 2hours

Ingredients

- FOR THE COOKIES
- 6 tablespoons unsalted butter, at room temperature
- 105 grams (1/2 cup) sugar
- 45 grams (3 tablespoons) brown sugar
- 1 ½ teaspoons salt
- ¼ teaspoon plus 1/8 teaspoon baking powder
- ¼ teaspoon baking soda
- 1 teaspoon instant coffee powder
- 1 ½ teaspoons vanilla extract
- 2 large egg yolks
- 15 grams (3/4 cup) sifted all-purpose flour or rice flour
- 85 grams (1 cup) sifted cocoa powder, plus more as needed
- FOR THE FILLING:
- 4 tablespoons shortening or unsalted butter, at room temperature
- 145 grams (1 1/4 cups) sifted confectioner's sugar
- 1 teaspoon vanilla extract
- ⅛ teaspoon salt.

Direction

- For the cookies: Using a mixer, cream together butter, sugar, brown sugar, salt, baking powder, baking soda, coffee powder and vanilla extract. With mixer still running, add egg yolks one at a time.

- Stop mixer and scrape bowl with a rubber spatula. Add flour and 1 cup cocoa, and resume mixing at low speed until the mixture is crumbly and uniformly blended. Scrape the bowl and knead the dough lightly to form a smooth ball. Transfer to a work surface and flatten into a disk. The dough may be rolled right away or wrapped in plastic and refrigerated for up to a week; bring to room temperature before rolling.
- Heat oven to 350 degrees. Lightly sift some cocoa powder onto a work surface, and roll the dough to .125-inch thickness. Slide a metal spatula under the dough to prevent it from sticking. Using a 2-inch round cookie cutter, cut out cookies and transfer to an ungreased baking sheet. The cookies will not spread during baking so may be placed close together. Knead and reroll the dough scraps to make more cookies.
- To add texture to the cookies, place any remaining dough in a mixing bowl. Mix with enough hot water until the dough has thinned into a paste. Transfer to a piping bag fitted with a very small tip, or a heavy duty Ziploc bag with a tiny hole poked in the corner. Pipe a design on each cookie; a tight cornelli lace design gives the impression of an Oreo.
- Bake the cookies until firm, about 12 minutes. Remove from heat and cool completely on a rack.
- For the filling: Using a mixer, cream together shortening or butter, confectioner's sugar, vanilla and salt. Beat on medium speed for 5 minutes, scraping the bowl periodically. The long mixing time smoothes, whitens and aerates the filling.
- For assembly: Using a pastry bag fitted with a plain tip or a spoon, place 1 teaspoon (or more if desired) of filling directly onto the center of the undersides of half the cookies. To finish, top with remaining wafers and press down with your fingers, applying very even pressure so the filling will spread uniformly across the cookie. Place cookies in an airtight container and refrigerate for several hours before serving.

Nutrition Information

- 106: calories;
- 6 grams: fat;
- 2 grams: monounsaturated fat;
- 1 gram: protein;
- 12 grams: sugars;
- 0 grams: polyunsaturated fat;
- 15 grams: carbohydrates;
- 57 milligrams: sodium;
- 3 grams: saturated fat;

139. Honey Gremolata

Serving: 1 1/2 cups | Prep: | Cook: | Ready in: 30mins

Ingredients

- 1 cup fresh flat-leaf parsley, chopped
- ½ cup fresh oregano, chopped
- 1 teaspoon minced garlic
- ¾ teaspoon grated lemon zest
- 1 tablespoon fresh lemon juice
- 1 tablespoon honey
- 1 cup extra virgin olive oil
- Salt
- freshly ground black pepper

Direction

- In a bowl, mix together 1/2 cup parsley and remaining ingredients. Season to taste. Cover and refrigerate for at least 30 minutes and up to 24 hours. Just before serving, mix in remaining 1/2 cup parsley.

Nutrition Information

- 267: calories;
- 27 grams: fat;

- 4 grams: saturated fat;
- 20 grams: monounsaturated fat;
- 3 grams: sugars;
- 7 grams: carbohydrates;
- 1 gram: protein;
- 106 milligrams: sodium;

140. Honey Mustard Salad

Serving: 2 servings | Prep: | Cook: | Ready in: 10mins

Ingredients

- 3 ounces assorted greens
- 1 tablespoon raspberry vinegar
- 1 teaspoon honey mustard

Direction

- Wash and dry greens.
- Mix vinegar and mustard in serving bowl. Toss with greens.

141. Hot Cajun Style Crab Boil

Serving: 6 servings | Prep: | Cook: | Ready in: 1hours15mins

Ingredients

- 2 bags (3 ounces each) commercial crab-boil seasoning, or equivalent amount of your own spice mixture (see article)
- Salt, to taste
- 2 pounds medium onions (about 8), peeled
- 3 pounds small potatoes (about 24), washed but not peeled
- 24 live medium blue crabs
- 2 pounds kielbasa, cut into 3-inch pieces
- 35 to 40 cloves garlic (3 heads), unpeeled
- 12 ears sweet corn, hulled

Direction

- Place 2 gallons of water and the crab-boil seasoning in a large stockpot, cover and bring to a boil. (Note: This can be done a few hours ahead, set aside and brought back to a boil at serving time to intensify the stock flavor.) Add salt to taste.
- Add the onions and potatoes to the boiling stock, cover and bring the stock back to a boil. Boil gently for 10 minutes.
- Meanwhile, rinse the crabs well in a sink filled with cold water. Using metal tongs, lift the crabs from the sink, and after discarding any dead or smelly crabs, add them to the stockpot with the sausage and garlic. Bring the mixture back to a boil, and boil gently for 5 minutes.
- Add the corn, and bring the mixture back to a boil. Then, turn off the heat, and let the pot sit (up to 1 hour) until serving time.
- At serving time, drain off the stock, and arrange crab boil ingredients separately on a large platter. Serve with the hot mayonnaise (see following recipe), if desired.

Nutrition Information

- 1075: calories;
- 8 grams: polyunsaturated fat;
- 123 grams: carbohydrates;
- 15 grams: dietary fiber;
- 24 grams: sugars;
- 2024 milligrams: sodium;
- 19 grams: monounsaturated fat;
- 48 grams: fat;
- 16 grams: saturated fat;
- 1 gram: trans fat;
- 51 grams: protein;

142. Hot Chocolate Souffle

Serving: 4 servings | Prep: | Cook: | Ready in: 1hours

Ingredients

- Butter for greasing

- 5 ounces semisweet chocolate, broken into pieces
- ⅓ cup sugar
- 1 teaspoon pure vanilla extract
- 5 eggs at room temperature, separated
- ¼ cup confectioners' sugar
- 1 ½ cups heavy cream, whipped (optional)

Direction

- Preheat the oven to 400 degrees.
- Butter a one-quart souffle dish or four eight-ounce souffle dishes.
- Melt the chocolate in a double boiler and add the sugar and vanilla. Allow the mixture to cool.
- Whisk the egg yolks until they are pale yellow. Gradually stir them into the warm (but not hot) chocolate. The recipe can be prepared ahead to this point.
- Beat the egg whites until they stand up in glossy peaks. Stir one-third of the egg whites into the chocolate mixture, then gradually fold in the rest.
- Bake souffle in center of oven for about 25 minutes for a large souffle, about 10 minutes for smaller ones. Remove from oven, dust with confectioners' sugar and serve. Pass whipped cream separately.

Nutrition Information

- 355: calories;
- 9 grams: saturated fat;
- 47 grams: carbohydrates;
- 81 milligrams: sodium;
- 17 grams: fat;
- 1 gram: polyunsaturated fat;
- 2 grams: dietary fiber;
- 44 grams: sugars;
- 8 grams: protein;
- 0 grams: trans fat;
- 6 grams: monounsaturated fat;

143. Hot Pepper Liquid

Serving: About 2 cups | Prep: | Cook: | Ready in: 15mins

Ingredients

- 4 tablespoons unsalted butter
- ½ cup peeled, chopped onion
- ½ cup chopped celery
- 6 tablespoons peeled, chopped garlic
- 1 jalapeño, chopped
- 2 cups chicken or beef broth
- 2 tablespoons white vinegar
- 1 tablespoon plus 1 teaspoon salt
- 1 tablespoon black pepper
- 1 tablespoon cayenne pepper

Direction

- Melt the butter in a saucepan over medium heat. Add the onion, celery, garlic and jalapeño, cover and cook until wilted, about 10 minutes. Add the remaining ingredients, stir well and heat to boiling. Simmer 5 minutes and strain into a bowl.

Nutrition Information

- 157: calories;
- 1 gram: polyunsaturated fat;
- 2 grams: sugars;
- 7 grams: saturated fat;
- 0 grams: trans fat;
- 3 grams: monounsaturated fat;
- 12 grams: fat;
- 10 grams: carbohydrates;
- 4 grams: protein;
- 450 milligrams: sodium;

144. Indian Style Pilaf

Serving: 6 small servings | Prep: | Cook: | Ready in: 1hours

Ingredients

- 1 cup long-grain rice
- 1 medium onion, chopped
- 2 tablespoons butter or vegetable oil
- 4 whole cardamom pods
- 1 piece stick cinnamon
- 5 whole cloves
- ½ teaspoon ground turmeric
- 4 bay leaves
- 2 cups water
- 1 teaspoon salt, or to taste

Direction

- If desired, wash rice and let stand in cold water for 30 minutes. Drain.
- Saute onion in butter in a pot until golden. Add cardamom pods, cinnamon, cloves, turmeric and bay leaves and saute two minutes. Add rice and saute two minutes, stirring to color all grains. Add water and salt, bring to a boil, cover and simmer over very low heat 15 to 20 minutes. Turn off heat and allow to stand, covered and undisturbed, until needed. Fluff before serving. (The whole spices are not meant to be eaten.)

Nutrition Information

- 165: calories;
- 3 grams: monounsaturated fat;
- 1 gram: sugars;
- 27 grams: carbohydrates;
- 2 grams: protein;
- 312 milligrams: sodium;
- 5 grams: fat;
- 0 grams: trans fat;

145. Irish Whisky Pots De Creme

Serving: 8 servings | Prep: | Cook: | Ready in: 2hours30mins

Ingredients

- 1 pint heavy cream
- ¼ cup vanilla sugar
- 2 teaspoons powdered espresso coffee
- 1 tablespoon unsweetened Dutch cocoa mixed with 2 tablespoons water
- 12 ounces semisweet chocolate, chopped
- 6 large egg yolks
- 4 tablespoons Irish whisky

Direction

- In a heavy saute pan, mix the cream, sugar and powdered espresso. Bring to a boil and remove from heat. Add the cocoa mixture and stir until blended. Add the chocolate and stir until completely melted. Pour a small amount of the mixture into the egg yolks and blend in. Pour the egg yolks into the saute pan.
- Place the pan over medium heat and cook, stirring constantly, until the mixture thickens (about 15 minutes). Do not boil. Remove from heat and add the Irish whisky.
- Pour into eight one-half cup ramekins and chill in the refrigerator until set (about two hours).

Nutrition Information

- 494: calories;
- 38 grams: fat;
- 12 grams: monounsaturated fat;
- 3 grams: dietary fiber;
- 31 grams: sugars;
- 5 grams: protein;
- 23 grams: saturated fat;
- 2 grams: polyunsaturated fat;
- 36 grams: carbohydrates;
- 34 milligrams: sodium;

146. Jerry Anne Cardamom Cake

Serving: Ten servings | Prep: | Cook: | Ready in: 1hours30mins

Ingredients

- 1 ½ cups unsalted butter, plus some for greasing the pan
- 2 ¾ cups sifted cake flour, plus some for dusting the pan
- 1 pound confectioners' sugar
- 6 large eggs
- ½ teaspoon hulled cardamom seed, crushed
- ½ teaspoon grated orange zest
- ½ teaspoon lemon zest
- 1 ½ teaspoons vanilla extract

Direction

- Preheat the oven to 300 degrees. Grease and flour a 10- to 12-cup tube pan.
- Beat the butter until creamy. Add the confectioners' sugar and beat until very fluffy. Beat in the eggs one at a time.
- Stir in the flour. Mix in the cardamom, orange and lemon zests and the vanilla. Pour the batter into the pan.
- Bake for about 1 hour or until the cake springs back to the touch and starts to pull from the sides. Cool 10 minutes. Unmold onto a serving plate. Serve warm or cold, cut into thin slices.

Nutrition Information

- 602: calories;
- 8 grams: monounsaturated fat;
- 7 grams: protein;
- 48 milligrams: sodium;
- 1 gram: dietary fiber;
- 2 grams: polyunsaturated fat;
- 75 grams: carbohydrates;
- 45 grams: sugars;
- 31 grams: fat;
- 18 grams: saturated fat;

147. Jicama Relish In Chilpotle Marinade

Serving: About six cups | Prep: | Cook: | Ready in: 25mins

Ingredients

- 1 medium jicama, about 1 pound (see note)
- 1 large carrot
- 1 medium zucchini
- 1 to 3 pickled chilpotle peppers in an adobo sauce with their liquid (see note)
- 1 cup finely chopped onion
- 4 garlic cloves, peeled and minced
- 1 bay leaf
- 6 whole black peppercorns
- ½ cup white vinegar
- ½ cup water
- ⅓ cup olive oil
- 2 tablespoons chopped cilantro
- 1 teaspoon good-quality dried oregano
- Salt to taste

Direction

- Using a knife, remove the skin from the jicama. Cut the flesh into half-inch dice. Place in a glass or earthenware bowl.
- Peel the carrot. Bring a pot of water to a rolling boil and drop the carrot in. Let the water return to the boil, then remove the carrot and discard the water. When the carrot is cool enough to handle, cut it into half-inch dice. Add to the bowl with the jicama.
- Scrub the zucchini well but do not peel it. Trim, then cut it into half-inch dice and add it to the bowl.
- Drain the chilpotles, reserving the pickling sauce (use one chili for a relatively mild marinade; three will be stinging hot). Cut the chilies open lengthwise and scrape out the seeds (if your fingers are sensitive, you may want to wear rubber gloves). Finely chop the chilies and place them in a separate, medium-sized bowl.

- Add the onion, garlic, bay leaf, peppercorns, vinegar, water, olive oil and cilantro to the chilpotle in the bowl. Blend in the reserved chilpotle sauce. Crumble the oregano between your fingers into the bowl. Whisk all the ingredients together, then pour the marinade over the jicama mixture. Toss the vegetables with the marinade to coat them completely. Add salt to taste.
- Cover the relish and refrigerate for at least four hours, preferably overnight. Serve as an accompaniment to grilled meats or fish.

148. Kale And Quinoa Salad With Plums And Herbs

Serving: Serves 4 to 6 | Prep: | Cook: | Ready in: 45mins

Ingredients

- ½ cup quinoa
- Salt to taste
- 3 cups stemmed, slivered kale
- 1 serrano or Thai chiles, minced (optional)
- 1 to 2 ripe but firm plums or pluots, cut in thin slices
- ½ cup basil leaves, chopped, torn or cut in slivers
- 2 to 4 tablespoons chopped chives
- 1 tablespoon chopped cilantro (optional)
- 2 tablespoons seasoned rice vinegar
- Grated zest of 1 lime
- 2 tablespoons fresh lime juice
- 1 garlic clove, minced or puréed
- 3 tablespoons sunflower or grapeseed oil

Direction

- Rinse the quinoa and cook in a pot of rapidly boiling, generously salted water for 15 minutes. Drain, return to pot, place a towel across the top and replace the lid. Let sit for 15 minutes. Transfer to a sheet pan lined with paper towels and allow to cool completely.
- To cut the kale, stem, wash and spin dry the leaves, then stack several at a time and cut crosswise into thin slivers. Toss in a large bowl with the quinoa, chile, herbs, and half the plums.
- Whisk together the vinegar, lime zest and juice, salt to taste, garlic and sunflower or grapeseed oil. Toss with the salad. Garnish with the remaining plums and serve.

Nutrition Information

- 131: calories;
- 14 grams: carbohydrates;
- 2 grams: sugars;
- 3 grams: protein;
- 164 milligrams: sodium;
- 8 grams: fat;
- 1 gram: monounsaturated fat;
- 5 grams: polyunsaturated fat;

149. King Arthur Flour's Banana Crumb Muffins

Serving: 12 muffins | Prep: | Cook: | Ready in: 40mins

Ingredients

- TOPPING
- ½ cup King Arthur unbleached all-purpose flour
- ¼ cup sugar
- 1 teaspoon cinnamon
- 4 tablespoons (1/2 stick) butter or margarine, room temperature
- MUFFINS
- 1 ½ cups King Arthur unbleached all-purpose flour
- 1 teaspoon baking soda
- 1 teaspoon baking powder
- ½ teaspoon salt
- 3 large, ripe bananas, mashed
- ¾ cup sugar
- 1 egg, slightly beaten

- ⅓ cup butter or margarine, melted

Direction

- For the topping, in a medium bowl, mix flour, sugar and cinnamon. Add butter or margarine and mix with a fork or pastry cutter until crumbly. Put aside while preparing muffin batter.
- For the muffins, in large bowl, combine dry ingredients. Set aside.
- In another bowl, combine mashed bananas, sugar, slightly beaten egg and melted butter or margarine. Mix well. Stir into dry ingredients just until moistened.
- Fill greased muffin cups two-thirds full. (Do not use paper muffin cups!) Using hands, arrange coarse, pea-sized crumbs over muffin batter.
- Bake at 375 degrees for 18 to 20 minutes or until muffins test done with a cake tester. Cool in pan 10 minutes before removing to a wire rack.

150. Kohlrabi Home Fries

Serving: 4 to 6 servings | Prep: | Cook: |Ready in: 30mins

Ingredients

- 1 ½ to 2 pounds kohlrabi
- 1 tablespoon rice flour, chickpea flour or semolina (more as needed)
- Salt to taste
- 2 to 4 tablespoons canola oil or grapeseed oil, as needed
- Chili powder, ground cumin, curry powder or paprika to taste

Direction

- Peel the kohlrabi and cut into thick sticks, about 1/3 to 1/2 inch wide and about 2 inches long.
- Heat the oil over medium-high heat in a heavy skillet (cast iron is good). Meanwhile, place the flour in a large bowl, season with salt if desired and quickly toss the kohlrabi sticks in the flour so that they are lightly coated.
- When the oil is rippling, carefully add the kohlrabi to the pan in batches so that the pan isn't crowded. Cook on one side until browned, about 2 to 3 minutes. Then, using tongs, turn the pieces over to brown on the other side for another 2 to 3 minutes. The procedure should take only about 5 minutes if there is enough oil in the pan. Drain on paper towels, then sprinkle right away with the seasoning of your choice. Serve hot.

151. Kohlrabi Risotto

Serving: 4 to 6 servings. | Prep: | Cook: |Ready in: 1hours

Ingredients

- 1 pound kohlrabi, preferably with some greens attached
- 7 to 8 cups well-seasoned chicken or vegetable stock
- 1 tablespoon extra virgin olive oil
- ½ cup minced onion
- 1 ½ cups arborio rice
- 1 to 2 garlic cloves (to taste), minced
- Salt and freshly ground pepper to taste
- ½ cup dry white wine, like pinot grigio or sauvignon blanc
- ¼ to ½ cup freshly grated Parmesan cheese (1 to 2 ounces)
- 2 to 3 tablespoons chopped flat-leaf parsley

Direction

- Peel the kohlrabi, making sure to remove the fibrous layer just under the skin, and cut into .5-inch dice. If there are greens attached, wash, stem and blanch them for 1 minute in salted boiling water. Transfer to a bowl of cold water,

drain, squeeze out water and chop coarsely. Set aside.
- Put your stock or broth into a saucepan and bring it to a simmer over medium heat, with a ladle nearby or in the pot. Make sure that it is well seasoned. Turn the heat down to low.
- Heat the olive oil over medium heat in a wide, heavy nonstick skillet or a wide, heavy saucepan. Add the onion and a pinch of salt, and cook gently until it is just tender, about 3 minutes. Do not brown. Add the diced kohlrabi and the garlic and cook, stirring, until the kohlrabi is crisp-tender, about 5 minutes.
- Add the rice and stir until the grains separate and begin to crackle. Add the wine and stir until it has evaporated and been absorbed by the rice. Begin adding the simmering stock, a couple of ladlefuls (about .5 cup) at a time. The stock should just cover the rice, and should be bubbling, not too slowly but not too quickly. Cook, stirring often, until it is just about absorbed. Add another ladleful or two of the stock and continue to cook in this fashion, adding more stock and stirring when the rice is almost dry. You do not have to stir constantly, but stir often. After 15 minutes, stir in the greens from the kohlrabi. When the rice is just tender all the way through but still chewy, in 20 to 25 minutes, it is done. Taste now, add pepper and adjust salt.
- Add another ladleful of stock to the rice. Stir in the Parmesan and the parsley and remove from the heat. The mixture should be creamy (add more stock if it isn't). Serve right away in wide soup bowls or on plates, spreading the risotto in a thin layer rather than a mound.

Nutrition Information

- 381: calories;
- 4 grams: monounsaturated fat;
- 15 grams: protein;
- 1097 milligrams: sodium;
- 8 grams: fat;
- 3 grams: saturated fat;
- 1 gram: polyunsaturated fat;
- 58 grams: carbohydrates;
- 5 grams: dietary fiber;
- 7 grams: sugars;

152. Korean Chilled Buckwheat Noodles With Chilled Broth And Kimchi

Serving: Serves 4 | Prep: | Cook: | Ready in: 40mins

Ingredients

- For the broth
- 6 dried shiitake mushrooms or a small handful of dried porcinis or other dried mushrooms
- 1 bunch scallions, sliced, or 1/2 cup chopped chives
- 1 4- to 6-inch stick of kombu
- 1 medium carrot, sliced thin
- A handful of mushroom stems, or a couple of dried shiitakes
- 5 cups water
- Soy sauce to taste
- Salt and sugar to taste
- For the soup
- 9 ounces soba noodles (1 package imported)
- 2 tablespoons dark sesame oil
- 1 cup, tightly packed, cabbage kimchi, cut in thin strips (more to taste; we love it)
- 6 ounces firm tofu, cut in small cubes
- 1 bunch scallions, cut lengthwise into threads
- ½ European cucumber (about 6 ounces), cut into fine 4-inch long julienne
- ½ Asian pear or firm, ripe plum or pluot, peeled (pear only), seeded and cut into 2- or 3-inch long julienne
- 2 hardboiled eggs, cut into quarters
- 2 tablespoons seasoned rice vinegar
- Korean chili powder to taste (optional)
- Chopped cilantro or sprigs for garnish

Direction

- Make the broth. Combine all the ingredients for the broth except the salt and sugar in a saucepan and bring to a simmer. Cover and simmer 20 minutes. Strain. Season to taste with salt and sugar if desired. Place in the refrigerator until cold.
- Cook the soba noodles. Drain well and toss with 1 tablespoon of the sesame oil. Place in the refrigerator and chill while you prepare the other ingredients.
- Toss the kimchi with the remaining sesame oil and refrigerate. Chill all of the other ingredients.
- Divide the noodles among 4 wide bowls. Arrange the tofu, pear or plum and vegetables on top of and around the noodles and top with wedges of boiled egg. Stir the vinegar into the cold broth. Taste and adjust salt and sugar. Ladle into the bowls. Garnish with Korean chili powder and cilantro if desired, and serve. Guests should stir the mixture so that the kimchi flavors the broth and noodles.

Nutrition Information

- 18: calories;
- 3 grams: carbohydrates;
- 93 milligrams: sodium;
- 1 gram: protein;
- 0 grams: sugars;

153. Lamb Patties Moroccan Style With Harissa Sauce

Serving: 4 servings | Prep: | Cook: | Ready in: 25mins

Ingredients

- 1 ½ pounds ground lean lamb
- 1 teaspoon paprika
- ¼ teaspoon crushed dried red hot pepper flakes
- ¼ teaspoon freshly ground black pepper
- 1 teaspoon ground cumin
- 2 teaspoons finely chopped garlic
- 2 tablespoons grated onion
- 4 tablespoons finely chopped parsley
- Salt to taste
- 1 tablespoon vegetable oil
- Harissa sauce (see recipe)

Direction

- Put the lamb in a mixing bowl and add all of the ingredients except the vegetable oil and harissa sauce. Blend the mixture thoroughly by hand.
- Shape the mixture into 8 equal-size patties similar to hamburgers.
- Heat the oil in a nonstick skillet large enough to hold all of the patties. Two pans may be necessary.
- Add the patties to the skillet. Cook them over medium-high heat about 3 to 4 minutes on each side, depending on the degree of doneness desired. Drain on paper towels and serve with the harissa sauce on the side.

Nutrition Information

- 1143: calories;
- 121 grams: fat;
- 60 grams: saturated fat;
- 2 grams: carbohydrates;
- 11 grams: protein;
- 431 milligrams: sodium;
- 0 grams: sugars;
- 50 grams: monounsaturated fat;
- 6 grams: polyunsaturated fat;
- 1 gram: dietary fiber;

154. Lasagna With Roasted Beets And Herb Béchamel

Serving: 8 servings | Prep: | Cook: | Ready in: 2hours30mins

Ingredients

- 6 medium-size red beets
- 3 tablespoons extra virgin olive oil
- 3 tablespoons minced shallot or onion
- 3 tablespoons sifted all-purpose flour
- 3 cups low-fat (1 percent) milk
- Salt and freshly ground pepper
- Pinch of freshly grated nutmeg
- ¼ cup finely chopped fresh herbs, like parsley, tarragon and chives
- ½ pound no-boil lasagna noodles
- 4 ounces (1 cup) freshly grated Parmesan

Direction

- Preheat the oven to 425 degrees. Cut the greens away from the beets, leaving about 1/4 inch of stems. Scrub the beets and place in a baking dish or lidded ovenproof casserole. Add 1/4 inch water to the dish. Cover tightly. Place in the oven and roast 40 to 45 minutes, until the beets are easily penetrated with the tip of a knife. Remove from the oven and allow to cool in the dish. Cut away the ends and slip off the skins. Slice crosswise into 1/4-inch-thick rounds and set aside.
- Meanwhile, make the béchamel. Heat the oil over medium heat in a heavy medium saucepan. Add the shallot or onion and cook, stirring, until softened, about 3 minutes. Stir in the flour and cook, stirring, for about 3 minutes, until the mixture is smooth and bubbling, but not browned. It should have the texture of wet sand. Whisk in the milk all at once and bring to a simmer, whisking all the while, until the mixture begins to thicken. Turn the heat to very low and simmer, stirring often with a whisk and scraping the bottom and edges of the pan with a rubber spatula, for 10 to 15 minutes, until the sauce is thick and has lost its raw flour taste. Season with salt, pepper and nutmeg. Strain while hot into a large measuring cup or a medium bowl and stir in the chopped herbs and 1/4 cup of the Parmesan.
- Preheat the oven to 350 degrees. Oil a rectangular baking dish. Spread a spoonful of béchamel over the bottom. Top with a layer of lasagna noodles. Spoon a thin layer of the béchamel over the noodles. Top with a layer of beets and sprinkle with Parmesan. Repeat the layers, ending with a layer of lasagna noodles topped with béchamel and Parmesan. Make sure the noodles are well coated with béchamel so they will be sure to soften during baking.
- Cover the baking dish tightly with foil and place in the oven. Bake 40 minutes, until the noodles are tender and the mixture is bubbling. Uncover and, if you wish, bake another 5 to 10 minutes, until the top begins to brown. Remove from the heat and allow to sit for 5 minutes before serving.

Nutrition Information

- 289: calories;
- 4 grams: saturated fat;
- 14 grams: protein;
- 486 milligrams: sodium;
- 10 grams: sugars;
- 5 grams: monounsaturated fat;
- 1 gram: polyunsaturated fat;
- 36 grams: carbohydrates;
- 3 grams: dietary fiber;

155. Lasagna With Roasted Kabocha Squash And Béchamel

Serving: 6 to 8 servings | Prep: | Cook: | Ready in: 2hours

Ingredients

- 3 pounds kabocha squash
- 3 tablespoons extra virgin olive oil
- 3 tablespoons minced shallot or onion
- 3 tablespoons sifted all-purpose flour
- 3 cups low-fat milk (1 percent)
- Salt and freshly ground pepper
- Pinch of freshly grated nutmeg
- 2 tablespoons chopped fresh sage

- ½ pound no-boil lasagna noodles (or a little more, depending on the size of your lasagna pan)
- 4 ounces Parmesan cheese, grated (1 cup)

Direction

- Preheat the oven to 425 degrees. Line a baking sheet with foil. Cut the squash into big chunks, brush the exposed flesh with 1 tablespoon of the olive oil and place on the baking sheet. Bake 45 minutes or until squash is tender enough to be pierced through to the skin with a paring knife. Remove from the heat and allow to cool until you can handle it, then cut away the skin and cut in thin slices. Turn the oven down to 350 degrees
- While the squash is in the oven, make the béchamel. Heat the remaining oil over medium heat in a heavy medium saucepan. Add the shallot or onion and cook, stirring, until it has softened, about 3 minutes. Stir in the flour and cook, stirring, for about 3 minutes, until the mixture is smooth and bubbling, but not browned. It should have the texture of wet sand. Whisk in the milk all at once and bring to a simmer, whisking all the while, until the mixture begins to thicken. Turn the heat to very low and simmer, stirring often with a whisk and scraping the bottom and edges of the pan with a rubber spatula, for 10 to 15 minutes, until the sauce is thick and has lost its raw flour taste. Season with salt, pepper and nutmeg. Strain while hot into a large measuring cup or a medium bowl and stir in 1/4 cup of the Parmesan and 1 tablespoon of the sage
- Preheat the oven to 350 degrees. Oil a rectangular baking dish. Spread a spoonful of béchamel over the bottom. Top with a layer of lasagna noodles. Spread a thin layer of the béchamel over the noodles. Top with half the squash. Season the squash with salt and pepper and sprinkle with Parmesan. Repeat the layers, ending with a layer of lasagna noodles topped with béchamel and Parmesan. Sprinkle the remaining sage over the top.

Make sure the noodles are well coated with béchamel so they will soften during baking
- Cover the baking dish tightly with foil and place in the oven. Bake 40 minutes, until the noodles are tender and the mixture is bubbling. Uncover and, if you wish, bake another 5 to 10 minutes until the top begins to brown. Remove from the heat and allow to sit for 5 minutes before serving

Nutrition Information

- 324: calories;
- 741 milligrams: sodium;
- 4 grams: saturated fat;
- 5 grams: dietary fiber;
- 1 gram: polyunsaturated fat;
- 11 grams: fat;
- 45 grams: carbohydrates;
- 10 grams: sugars;
- 14 grams: protein;

156. Lasagna With Spicy Roasted Cauliflower

Serving: 6 servings | Prep: | Cook: | Ready in: 1hours30mins

Ingredients

- 1 ½ pounds cauliflower (3/4 of a medium head)
- 2 tablespoons extra virgin olive oil
- Salt and freshly ground pepper
- ¼ to ½ teaspoon red pepper flakes
- 3 cups marinara sauce, preferably homemade from fresh or canned tomatoes
- 7 to 8 ounces no-boil lasagna
- 8 ounces ricotta cheese
- 2 tablespoons water, vegetable stock or chicken stock
- Pinch of cinnamon
- 4 ounces (1 cup) freshly grated Parmesan

Direction

- Preheat the oven to 450 degrees. Line a baking sheet with parchment paper. Cut away the bottom of the cauliflower stem and trim off the leaves. Cut the cauliflower into slices 1/3 inch thick, letting the florets on the edges fall off. Toss all of it, including the bits that have fallen away, with the olive oil, salt and pepper. Place on the baking sheet in an even layer. Roast for about 15 minutes, stirring and flipping over the big slices after 8 minutes, until the slices are tender when pierced with a paring knife and the small florets are nicely browned. Remove from the oven, toss with the red pepper flakes and set aside. Turn the oven down to 350 degrees.
- Blend the ricotta cheese, water or stock, cinnamon, salt and pepper. Set aside.
- Oil a rectangular baking dish and spread a spoonful of tomato sauce over the bottom. Top with a layer of lasagna noodles. Spoon a thin layer of the ricotta mixture over the noodles. Top with a layer of cauliflower, then a layer of tomato sauce and a layer of Parmesan. Repeat the layers, ending with a layer of lasagna noodles topped with tomato sauce and Parmesan.
- Cover the baking dish tightly with foil and place in the oven. Bake 40 minutes, until the noodles are tender and the mixture is bubbling. Uncover and, if you wish, bake another 10 minutes, until the top begins to brown. Remove from the heat and allow to sit for 5 minutes before serving.

Nutrition Information

- 361: calories;
- 15 grams: fat;
- 7 grams: saturated fat;
- 6 grams: sugars;
- 1 gram: polyunsaturated fat;
- 39 grams: carbohydrates;
- 19 grams: protein;
- 781 milligrams: sodium;

157. Leek Quiche

Serving: Serves 6 | Prep: | Cook: | Ready in: 1hours30mins

Ingredients

- 3 large leeks, about 1 1/2 to 1 3/4 pounds, white and light green part only
- 2 tablespoons extra virgin olive oil or 1 tablespoon each olive oil and butter
- Salt to taste
- 1 garlic clove, minced (optional)
- 2 egg yolks
- 1 whole egg
- 1 Mediterranean pie crust (see recipe) or whole wheat yeasted olive oil crust
- Freshly ground pepper to taste
- ¾ cup milk (2% or regular)
- 3 ounces Gruyère, grated (3/4 cup tightly packed)

Direction

- Cut away the root and dark green leaves from the leeks and cut in half lengthwise. Run under cold water to remove sand. If the leeks are very sandy soak them for 15 minutes or so, then run under cold water again. Drain on paper towels. If the leeks are very fat, cut the halves in half again lengthwise, then cut in thin slices.
- Preheat the oven to 350 degrees. Heat the oil or oil and butter over medium heat in a lidded skillet or saucepan and add the leeks and a pinch of salt. Cook gently, stirring, until they begin to soften. Turn the heat to medium-low, cover and cook gently until the leeks are very soft but not browned, stirring often, 10 to 15 minutes. If they begin to stick or brown, add a little more salt and/or a spoonful of water or wine. Stir in the garlic if using and cook for another 30 seconds to a minute, until fragrant.
- Beat together the egg yolks and egg in a medium bowl. Set the tart pan on a baking sheet to allow for easy handling. Using a

- pastry brush lightly brush the bottom of the crust and place in the oven for 10 minutes. Remove from the oven and set aside.
- Add salt (about 1/2 teaspoon), pepper and the milk to the eggs and whisk together. Spread the leeks in an even layer in the crust. Sprinkle the cheese in an even layer on top. Pour in the custard filling. Place in the oven and bake for 30 minutes, or until set and just beginning to color on the top.
- Remove from the oven and allow to sit for at least 15 minutes before serving.

Nutrition Information

- 177: calories;
- 0 grams: trans fat;
- 6 grams: monounsaturated fat;
- 1 gram: dietary fiber;
- 4 grams: sugars;
- 8 grams: protein;
- 430 milligrams: sodium;
- 12 grams: fat;
- 5 grams: saturated fat;
- 10 grams: carbohydrates;

158. Leek And Pumpkin Soup

Serving: 4 servings | Prep: | Cook: | Ready in: 55mins

Ingredients

- 2 tablespoons butter
- 4 large leeks, white part only, well rinsed and chopped, about 2 cups
- 2 cloves garlic, minced
- 3 cups cubed pumpkin
- 3 cups water
- 1 cup milk or half-and-half
- Salt and freshly ground black pepper
- 1 tablespoon minced fresh chives

Direction

- Melt butter in a heavy casserole. Add the leeks and saute slowly, over low heat, until they are tender but not brown. Stir in the garlic.
- Add the pumpkin and water, cover and simmer until the pumpkin is tender, 35 to 40 minutes. Allow the mixture to cool for 15 minutes, then puree in one or two batches in a food processor.
- Return the puree to the casserole, add the milk and season to taste with salt and pepper. Reheat before serving. Sprinkle each serving with chives.

Nutrition Information

- 226: calories;
- 4 grams: monounsaturated fat;
- 1 gram: polyunsaturated fat;
- 9 grams: sugars;
- 1040 milligrams: sodium;
- 13 grams: fat;
- 8 grams: saturated fat;
- 0 grams: trans fat;
- 25 grams: carbohydrates;
- 3 grams: dietary fiber;
- 5 grams: protein;

159. Lemon Poundcake

Serving: 8 servings | Prep: | Cook: | Ready in: 1hours30mins

Ingredients

- ½ cup unsalted butter, at room temperature, plus additional for greasing pan
- 2 cups all-purpose flour, plus additional for pan
- 1 ¼ cups sugar
- 4 teaspoons grated lemon zest
- 3 eggs
- 1 teaspoon vanilla extract
- ½ teaspoon baking soda
- 1 teaspoon baking powder

- ½ teaspoon kosher salt
- ¾ cup sour cream
- ½ cup confectioners' sugar
- ½ cup fresh lemon juice

Direction

- Preheat the oven to 350 degrees. Butter and flour a 9-by-5-by-3-inch loaf pan. Using an electric mixer, cream together the butter and sugar until light. Add the lemon zest, then the eggs, one at a time, mixing until light and fluffy. Mix in the vanilla.
- Sift together the flour, baking soda, baking powder and salt. Add the dry ingredients alternately with the sour cream, mixing just to combine. Spoon the batter into the prepared pan. Bake until a toothpick inserted into the cake's center comes out clean, about 1 hour. Place on a rack.
- Put the confectioners' sugar in a bowl and gradually whisk in the lemon juice. Brush some of the mixture over the top of the cake. Let stand for 10 minutes. Turn the cake out of the pan and brush the cake top, sides and bottom well with the lemon mixture. Repeat after 10 minutes. Slice and serve.

Nutrition Information

- 436: calories;
- 10 grams: saturated fat;
- 0 grams: trans fat;
- 5 grams: monounsaturated fat;
- 1 gram: dietary fiber;
- 65 grams: carbohydrates;
- 278 milligrams: sodium;
- 40 grams: sugars;
- 6 grams: protein;
- 18 grams: fat;

160. Lemon And Garlic Chicken With Cherry Tomatoes

Serving: Serves 4 | Prep: | Cook: | Ready in: 30mins

Ingredients

- 2 tablespoons extra-virgin olive oil
- 3 tablespoons fresh lemon juice
- 2 garlic cloves, minced or pureed
- 1 teaspoon chopped fresh rosemary
- Salt and freshly ground pepper to taste
- 2 boneless skinless chicken breasts (most weight 8 to 10 ounces)
- ¼ cup dry white wine
- 2 heaped cups cherry tomatoes, – about 3/4 pound
- Pinch of sugar
- 2 tablespoons all-purpose flour or a gluten-free flour such as rice flour or corn flour
- 2 tablespoons grapeseed, sunflower or canola oil
- 1 tablespoon chopped flat-leaf parsley
- ¼ cup freshly grated Parmesan (optional)

Direction

- Stir together the olive oil, lemon juice, garlic, rosemary, and salt and pepper in a large bowl. Cut each chicken breast into 2 equal pieces (3 if they weigh 12 ounces or more) and place in the bowl. Stir together and refrigerate 15 to 30 minutes.
- Remove chicken from marinade and pat dry with paper towels (discard marinade). Place two sheets of plastic wrap (1 large sheet if you have extra-wide wrap) on your work surface, overlapping slightly, to make 1 wide sheet, and brush lightly with olive oil. Place a piece of chicken in the middle of plastic sheet and brush lightly with oil. Cover the chicken with another wide layer of plastic wrap. Working from the center to the outside, pound chicken breast with the flat side of a meat tenderizer until about 1/4 inch thick. (Don't pound too hard or you'll tear the meat. If that happens it won't be the end of the world, you'll just

have a few pieces to cook.) Repeat with the remaining chicken breast pieces.
- Season the pounded chicken breasts with salt and pepper on one side only. Dredge lightly in the flour (you will not use all of it) and tap the breasts to remove excess.
- Turn oven on low. Heat a wide, heavy skillet over high heat and add oil. When oil is hot, place one or two pieces of chicken in the pan – however many will fit without crowding. Cook for 1 1/2 minutes, until bottom is browned in spots. Turn over and brown other side, about 1 1/2 minutes. (Do not overcook or chicken will be dry.) Transfer to a platter or sheet pan and keep warm in the oven. If there is more than a tablespoon of fat in the pan, pour some off into a jar or bowl.
- Turn heat on burner down to medium-high. Add wine to pan and stir with a wooden spoon to deglaze. Add cherry tomatoes and cook, stirring often or tossing in the pan, until they begin to shrivel and burst. Add sugar and salt and pepper to taste and continue to cook, tossing the tomatoes in the pan and stirring often, for 5 to 10 minutes, until tomatoes have collapsed but are still intact. Top chicken breasts with the tomatoes, sprinkle with parsley and with Parmesan if using, and serve.

Nutrition Information

- 338: calories;
- 18 grams: fat;
- 2 grams: saturated fat;
- 3 grams: sugars;
- 32 grams: protein;
- 0 grams: trans fat;
- 10 grams: carbohydrates;
- 1 gram: dietary fiber;
- 629 milligrams: sodium;

161. Lemon Poppy Seed Drops

Serving: 2 1/2 dozen | Prep: | Cook: | Ready in: 40mins

Ingredients

- 1 ½ cups flour
- ¼ cup poppy seeds
- ¼ teaspoon salt
- 16 tablespoons butter, softened
- ¾ cup sugar
- 2 large egg yolks
- 2 teaspoons vanilla extract
- Zest of 3 large lemons

Direction

- Preheat the oven to 350 degrees.
- In a small bowl, combine the flour, poppy seeds and salt. Set aside. In a large bowl, cream together the butter and the sugar until fluffy. Add the egg yolks, vanilla extract and lemon zest. Stir until well mixed. Add the dry ingredients, and stir only until they are incorporated and dough pulls together into a ball. Do not overmix.
- Drop the dough from a teaspoon onto ungreased cookie sheets, leaving an inch between the cookies. Bake for 15 minutes, or until the cookies are lightly browned around the edges.

Nutrition Information

- 109: calories;
- 11 grams: carbohydrates;
- 0 grams: trans fat;
- 2 grams: monounsaturated fat;
- 1 gram: protein;
- 5 grams: sugars;
- 21 milligrams: sodium;
- 7 grams: fat;
- 4 grams: saturated fat;

162. Lentil Salad With Fresh Favas

Serving: 4 servings | Prep: | Cook: | Ready in: 2hours

Ingredients

- 1 cup lentils, rinsed and picked over
- 3 large garlic cloves, 2 of them crushed and left in the skin, 1 of them minced
- ½ onion, intact
- 1 bay leaf
- Salt to taste
- 1 tablespoon fresh lemon juice
- 2 tablespoons red wine vinegar or cider vinegar
- 3 tablespoons extra virgin olive oil
- 1 teaspoon cumin seeds, lightly toasted and ground
- ½ teaspoon mild chili powder or Aleppo pepper
- Freshly ground black pepper to taste
- ½ pound fresh fava beans, shelled and skinned
- 2 medium tomatoes, in season only, diced
- ¼ cup diced celery
- ¼ cup chopped flat-leaf parsley
- ¼ cup chopped fresh mint
- 1 bunch scallions, chopped

Direction

- Place the lentils, whole crushed garlic cloves, onion half and bay leaf in a large, heavy saucepan and cover by 1 inch with water. Bring to a boil, add salt to taste, reduce the heat, cover and simmer until lentils are tender but still firm, about 30 minutes. Remove from the heat, remove the lid and allow the lentils to cool for 30 minutes. Remove and discard the onion. Remove the garlic cloves and squeeze the cooked garlic out of the skins and back into the lentils. Drain off any liquid remaining in the pot.
- Transfer the lentils to a large bowl. Whisk together the lemon juice, vinegar, salt to taste, cumin, chili powder or Aleppo pepper, freshly ground pepper and olive oil. Toss with the lentils. Add the remaining ingredients and toss together. Let marinate in the refrigerator for at least 30 minutes before serving.

Nutrition Information

- 353: calories;
- 50 grams: carbohydrates;
- 9 grams: sugars;
- 18 grams: protein;
- 587 milligrams: sodium;
- 12 grams: dietary fiber;
- 2 grams: polyunsaturated fat;
- 8 grams: monounsaturated fat;

163. Lentil Soup With Cilantro (Lots Of It)

Serving: Serves four | Prep: | Cook: | Ready in: 1hours

Ingredients

- 1 tablespoon extra virgin olive oil
- 2 garlic cloves, minced
- 1 ¼ teaspoons cumin seeds, lightly toasted and ground
- Pinch of cayenne
- ½ pound brown lentils (about 1 1/8 cups), picked over and rinsed
- 1 small onion, cut in half
- 1 bay leaf
- 1 ½ quarts water
- Salt, preferably kosher salt, to taste
- Freshly ground pepper
- 1 cup chopped cilantro (from 1 large bunch)
- Plain low-fat yogurt for garnish

Direction

- Heat the oil in a large, heavy soup pot over medium heat, and add the garlic. Stir until fragrant, about a minute, and stir in the cumin and cayenne. Add the lentils, onion, bay leaf, water and salt. Bring to a boil, reduce the heat

and simmer 40 minutes, until the lentils are tender and the broth aromatic. Add pepper, taste and adjust salt. Remove the halved onion and the bay leaf.
- Coarsely puree the soup in an immersion blender or food mill. Alternatively, puree half the soup in blender, 1 1/2 cups at time, being careful to cover the top of the blender with a towel to avoid hot splashes, then stir back into the soup. Heat through.
- Chop the cilantro, discarding the stems. Stir into the soup just before serving. Taste, adjust seasoning and serve, topping each bowl with a dollop of yogurt.

Nutrition Information

- 237: calories;
- 4 grams: fat;
- 38 grams: carbohydrates;
- 7 grams: dietary fiber;
- 2 grams: sugars;
- 1017 milligrams: sodium;
- 1 gram: polyunsaturated fat;
- 3 grams: monounsaturated fat;
- 14 grams: protein;

164. Lentil And Pumpkin Tagine

Serving: 6 servings | Prep: | Cook: | Ready in: 1hours

Ingredients

- 2 tablespoons unsalted butter or olive oil
- 2 onions, diced
- 3 fresh chili peppers, thinly sliced
- 1 tablespoon paprika
- ½ teaspoon Cayenne pepper
- 1 teaspoon ground cumin
- 1 cup lentils
- 4 tomatoes, peeled, seeded and chopped
- ¼ cup tomato puree
- 1 piece pumpkin squash, two pounds, peeled and cut into 1-inch cubes
- 1 pound of greens like Swiss chard, dandelion or kale, blanched 3 to 5 minutes, drained well and coarsely chopped

Direction

- In a saucepan over medium heat, warm the butter or oil.
- Add the onions and chilies and cook until the onions begin to soften, about 10 minutes.
- Add the paprika, cayenne and cumin and continue to saute until the onions are tender, a few minutes longer. Add the lentils, tomatoes and tomato puree and water just to cover. Simmer for about 20 minutes.
- Add the squash and simmer until tender, about 20 minutes. Add the greens during the last five minutes of cooking. Transfer to a warm serving dish and serve immediately.

Nutrition Information

- 238: calories;
- 5 grams: fat;
- 3 grams: saturated fat;
- 0 grams: trans fat;
- 41 grams: carbohydrates;
- 8 grams: dietary fiber;
- 1 gram: polyunsaturated fat;
- 7 grams: sugars;
- 12 grams: protein;
- 194 milligrams: sodium;

165. Lime Marinated Chicken Over 'Creamed' Corn

Serving: Four servings | Prep: | Cook: | Ready in: 1hours30mins

Ingredients

- 5 tablespoons fresh lime juice

- 2 boneless, skinless chicken breasts (about 8 ounces each), split
- Kernels from 6 large ears of corn
- ½ cup low-fat milk
- 1 ¼ teaspoons salt
- Freshly ground pepper to taste
- 4 teaspoons chopped fresh cilantro
- 1 teaspoon minced jalapeno pepper
- ½ teaspoon grated lime zest
- 1 teaspoon olive oil

Direction

- Place 4 tablespoons of the lime juice in a small, shallow dish. Add chicken and turn to coat on both sides. Marinate for 1 hour.
- Meanwhile, place half of the corn in a food processor and pulse just enough to chop coarsely. Scrape into a medium saucepan. Put the remaining corn in the food processor with the milk. Process until pureed. Add to the saucepan.
- Place the pan over medium heat and simmer, stirring often, until the mixture is thick, about 10 minutes. Season with 1 teaspoon of the salt and pepper to taste. Keep warm.
- Preheat a grill or broiler. Remove the chicken from the lime juice and grill or broil until just cooked through, about 4 minutes per side. While the chicken is cooking, stir together the remaining lime juice and salt, the cilantro, jalapeno, lime zest and olive oil.
- Divide the corn mixture among 4 plates, placing it in the center. Lay a piece of chicken over the corn and spoon the cilantro mixture on top. Serve immediately.

Nutrition Information

- 165: calories;
- 4 grams: carbohydrates;
- 1 gram: polyunsaturated fat;
- 0 grams: dietary fiber;
- 2 grams: sugars;
- 27 grams: protein;
- 387 milligrams: sodium;

166. Linguine With Lentils And Prosciutto

Serving: 6 servings | Prep: | Cook: | Ready in: 35mins

Ingredients

- 1 stalk celery, chopped
- 1 carrot, chopped
- 4 or 5 ounces onion, diced
- 1 tablespoon minced garlic
- 1 jalapeno, chopped
- ¼ teaspoon hot red pepper flakes
- 3 ounces prosciutto, diced
- 2 tablespoons olive oil
- 1 heaping cup red lentils
- Salt to taste
- 1 ½ pounds linguine
- 1 red onion, chopped

Direction

- Saute celery, carrot, onion, garlic, jalapeno, pepper flakes and prosciutto in the oil in a large, deep skillet for about 10 minutes, until very soft and fragrant.
- Add lentils and 5 cups water, and bring to a boil. Reduce heat, and boil gently until lentils are soft but not mushy, about 10 minutes. Season with salt.
- Cook the pasta according to the package directions. Drain, and add to the lentil mixture; toss well. Serve topped with chopped red onion.

Nutrition Information

- 626: calories;
- 527 milligrams: sodium;
- 8 grams: dietary fiber;
- 1 gram: polyunsaturated fat;
- 4 grams: monounsaturated fat;
- 111 grams: carbohydrates;

- 6 grams: sugars;
- 27 grams: protein;

167. Lucky's Clams Provencal

Serving: Serves six as an appetizer or three as a main course | Prep: | Cook: | Ready in: 40mins

Ingredients

- 1 pound red potatoes, cleaned, with skins on
- 2 medium onions
- 1 bulb fennel
- 1 jalapeno pepper
- 1 sweet red pepper
- 36 littleneck clams, cleaned and scrubbed
- ¾ cup dry white wine
- ½ cup water
- 2 tablespoons minced fresh garlic
- 1 ½ cups (28-ounce can) tinned Italian plum tomatoes, drained and chopped
- 1 tablespoon fresh tarragon leaves (optional)
- 1 tablespoon cilantro leaves
- 4 ounces unsalted butter, cut up
- 2 teaspoons Pernod
- 3 scallions, cut into a fine julienne
- 1 lemon, cut into 6 wedges

Direction

- Slice the potatoes about one-quarter inch thick and place in a pot filled with cold water. Bring to a boil and boil for seven minutes. Drain and set aside.
- Peel the onions, halve them and slice them about one-quarter-inch thick. Trim the fennel bulb and slice about one-quarter-inch thick. Seed the peppers, remove the membranes and dice.
- Preheat the oven to 500 degrees.
- Lay out the clams in a single layer in a baking dish. In a bowl, combine the onions, fennel, peppers, wine, water, garlic, plum tomatoes, tarragon, cilantro, butter and Pernod. Top the clams with this mixture. Roast the clams for eight minutes. Turn them and roast for about eight minutes more, until the clams open (discard any unopened clams).
- To serve, place six clams into each of six heated bowls. With tongs, distribute the tomatoes, onions, fennel and potatoes around the clams. Pour equal amounts of the broth and remaining solids over the clams. Garnish with the scallions and lemon wedges. Serve immediately with garlic mayonnaise on the side. (See recipe.)

Nutrition Information

- 357: calories;
- 31 grams: carbohydrates;
- 6 grams: dietary fiber;
- 9 grams: sugars;
- 572 milligrams: sodium;
- 17 grams: protein;
- 10 grams: saturated fat;
- 1 gram: polyunsaturated fat;
- 4 grams: monounsaturated fat;

168. Mark Strausman's Grilled Mushrooms

Serving: 4 servings | Prep: | Cook: | Ready in: 20mins

Ingredients

- 1 anchovy mashed, or 1 1/2 teaspoons anchovy paste
- 2 cloves garlic, minced
- ¼ cup lemon juice
- ⅓ cup extra-virgin olive oil
- Salt and freshly ground black pepper to taste
- 1 pound mushrooms with large caps (portobello, cremini, oyster, shiitake or a mixture)
- ¼ cup vegetable oil
- 1 tablespoon chopped Italian parsley

Direction

- Preheat the grill.
- Mash the anchovy or anchovy paste with the garlic in a mortar. Blend in the lemon juice and olive oil. Season to taste with salt and pepper, and set aside.
- Wipe any soil from the mushrooms with a damp paper towel. Remove stems from the mushrooms, and discard or set aside for another use, like making stock. (It is not necessary to do this with oyster mushrooms.) Brush the caps with the vegetable oil, and sprinkle with salt and pepper.
- Place the caps on the grill, top side down, and grill for a minute or two. Give each cap a quarter turn to set crisscross grill marks, and continue grilling another minute. Turn the caps over, and grill another minute or two, until a knife can easily pierce the cap.
- Remove the mushrooms from the grill, and arrange them on a plate. Beat the dressing to reblend it, and sprinkle it over the warm mushrooms. Scatter the parsley on top, and serve.

Nutrition Information

- 317: calories;
- 33 grams: fat;
- 5 grams: polyunsaturated fat;
- 383 milligrams: sodium;
- 3 grams: sugars;
- 0 grams: trans fat;
- 23 grams: monounsaturated fat;
- 6 grams: carbohydrates;
- 1 gram: dietary fiber;
- 4 grams: protein;

169. Mashed Potatoes

Serving: 4 servings | Prep: | Cook: | Ready in: 45mins

Ingredients

- 1 ½ pounds baking potatoes
- 1 ½ teaspoons salt
- 7 tablespoons butter, chilled
- 1 cup milk, heated
- Salt to taste
- Dash nutmeg (optional)

Direction

- Peel potatoes, cut into quarters and wash thoroughly. Put in a saucepan and cover with cold water. Add 1 1/2 teaspoons salt. Bring to boil and boil until cooked, about 15 to 18 minutes, or until you can slip the tip of a knife into a potato. Don't overcook.
- Drain water and rapidly push potatoes through a food mill; they must stay hot. Return potatoes to saucepan and put on a very low flame to dry the potatoes for about eight minutes, moving with spatula. Add butter in pieces. Be sure butter is cold and hard. Beat vigorously with a wooden spoon to make the puree light and white. Then add very hot milk in small quantities, working with spoon and wooden spatula until totally absorbed and smooth. Do not boil after this step. Add a dash of nutmeg. Add salt if necessary. Serve as soon as possible. Once prepared, the puree should not be reheated

Nutrition Information

- 350: calories;
- 34 grams: carbohydrates;
- 2 grams: dietary fiber;
- 22 grams: fat;
- 14 grams: saturated fat;
- 1 gram: polyunsaturated fat;
- 6 grams: protein;
- 4 grams: sugars;
- 595 milligrams: sodium;

170. Mashed Potatoes With Chives

Serving: 4 servings | Prep: | Cook: | Ready in: 30mins

Ingredients

- 1 ½ pounds russet potatoes
- Salt to taste
- 1 cup milk
- 4 tablespoons butter
- 4 tablespoons chopped chives

Direction

- Peel the potatoes and cut them into 2-inch cubes.
- Put the potatoes in a saucepan and cover with water. Add salt and bring to a boil. Simmer 20 minutes or until the potatoes are tender. Do not overcook them.
- Meanwhile, heat the milk until it is hot.
- Drain the potatoes and put them through a food mill or ricer or mash them well with a potato masher. Return them to the saucepan. Using a wooden spatula, add the butter and chives and blend well. Mix in the milk and keep warm until ready to serve.

Nutrition Information

- 274: calories;
- 14 grams: fat;
- 8 grams: saturated fat;
- 3 grams: monounsaturated fat;
- 2 grams: dietary fiber;
- 6 grams: protein;
- 0 grams: trans fat;
- 1 gram: polyunsaturated fat;
- 34 grams: carbohydrates;
- 4 grams: sugars;
- 577 milligrams: sodium;

171. Matchstick Potatoes

Serving: 6 servings | Prep: | Cook: | Ready in: 1hours30mins

Ingredients

- 3 medium baking potatoes (russets)
- 1 quart vegetable (not olive) oil
- Medium-grain sea salt

Direction

- Peel potatoes and cut sides and ends flat so that potato is a solid rectangle four inches long. Adjusting your mandolin accordingly, cut potatoes into matchstick shapes or, using a sharp knife, cut them by hand, rinsing blade frequently to remove starch. Place matchsticks in a bowl of ice cold water. After five minutes pour off starchy water and refill. Put bowl in the refrigerator and let potatoes soak for an hour, then drain in a colander and pat them dry with a paper towel. You might hasten the drying by spinning them in a salad spinner.
- In a deep, heavy kettle with a frying basket, heat oil, which should be about two inches deep, to 350 degrees. Add potatoes a handful at a time. (Do not add too many potatoes at once or you will reduce temperature. Potatoes will be soggy and won't brown.) As they begin to cook, shake basket to separate them. If they clump, poke them with a wooden spoon or tongs. When they are crisp and golden, remove them from oil with tongs. Drain on paper towels. Add salt. Repeat in batches. Keep them warm and crisp in a low oven.

172. Matelote Of Monkfish (Monkfish Stew)

Serving: 4 servings | Prep: | Cook: | Ready in: 20mins

Ingredients

- 2 tablespoons olive oil

- 12 pearl onions, peeled
- 16 small mushrooms
- 4 tablespoons finely chopped shallots
- 1 bay leaf
- 4 sprigs fresh thyme or 1/2 teaspoon dried
- 1 tablespoon finely chopped garlic
- 2 tablespoons flour
- 2 cups red wine like Cotes du Rhone or cabernet sauvignon
- 1 cup fresh fish broth or bottled clam juice
- 2 cloves
- Salt and freshly ground pepper to taste
- 1 ¾ pounds monkfish fillets, cut into 1/2-inch cubes
- 2 tablespoons butter
- 4 tablespoons finely chopped parsley

Direction

- Heat oil in a nonstick saucepan over medium-high heat. Add onions, mushrooms, shallots, bay leaf, thyme sprigs and garlic. Cook, stirring, until wilted, about 3 minutes.
- Add flour and blend well. Add wine, fish broth, cloves, salt and pepper. Blend well with a wire whisk. Bring to a boil and simmer 10 minutes.
- Add fish cubes, bring to a simmer and cook about 4 minutes or until done. Add butter and blend well. Remove thyme sprigs and bay leaf. Sprinkle with parsley and serve hot with croutons (see recipe) on the side.

Nutrition Information

- 433: calories;
- 16 grams: carbohydrates;
- 7 grams: monounsaturated fat;
- 4 grams: sugars;
- 1150 milligrams: sodium;
- 5 grams: saturated fat;
- 0 grams: trans fat;
- 2 grams: polyunsaturated fat;
- 3 grams: dietary fiber;
- 36 grams: protein;

173. Mediterranean Lentil Salad With Lemon Thyme Vinaigrette

Serving: Four servings | Prep: | Cook: |Ready in: 30mins

Ingredients

- The salad:
- 1 cup lentils
- 5 cups water
- 1 tomato, cored and chopped
- ½ cup oil-cured black olives, pitted and coarsely chopped
- ½ cup crumbled feta cheese
- 2 stalks celery, trimmed, peeled and thinly sliced
- Salt and freshly ground pepper to taste
- 1 tablespoon chopped fresh parsley, for garnish
- The vinaigrette:
- ¼ cup fresh lemon juice
- 2 large cloves garlic, peeled and minced
- 2 teaspoons minced fresh thyme leaves
- 2 tablespoons plus 2 teaspoons olive oil
- ½ teaspoon salt
- Freshly ground pepper to taste

Direction

- To make the salad, combine the lentils and water in a large saucepan and bring to a boil. Reduce heat and simmer until tender but not mushy, about 20 minutes. Drain, place in a large bowl and let cool. Toss the tomato, olives, feta and celery with the lentils.
- To make the vinaigrette, whisk together the lemon juice, garlic and thyme in a medium bowl. Slowly whisk in the olive oil. Whisk in the salt and pepper. Toss the vinaigrette with the salad and season to taste. Divide among 4 plates, garnish with chopped parsley and serve.

Nutrition Information

- 338: calories;
- 4 grams: saturated fat;
- 9 grams: monounsaturated fat;
- 2 grams: polyunsaturated fat;
- 38 grams: carbohydrates;
- 7 grams: dietary fiber;
- 3 grams: sugars;
- 15 grams: fat;
- 16 grams: protein;
- 1067 milligrams: sodium;

174. Melon Sorbet

Serving: 4 to 6 servings | Prep: | Cook: | Ready in: 4hours45mins

Ingredients

- ¼ cup water
- 65 grams (about 1/4 cup plus 1 teaspoon) sugar
- 33 grams (about 1 tablespoon plus 2 teaspoons) corn syrup
- 680 grams (1 1/2 pounds) peeled diced ripe cantaloupe, honeydew or similar yellow or green-fleshed melons (about 1 medium melon)
- 1 tablespoon lime juice (optional)
- Pinch of salt (optional)

Direction

- Combine the water and sugar in a saucepan and bring to a boil. Reduce the heat and simmer until the sugar has dissolved. Remove from the heat and allow to cool.
- In a blender, purée the melon with the sugar solution and remaining ingredients until smooth. Chill in the refrigerator for 2 hours or overnight.
- Chill a container in the freezer. Blend the mixture for 30 seconds with an immersion blender, then freeze in an ice cream maker following the manufacturer's instructions.

Transfer to the chilled container and place in the freezer for 2 hours to pack. Allow to soften in the refrigerator for 15 to 30 minutes before serving.

Nutrition Information

- 96: calories;
- 0 grams: polyunsaturated fat;
- 24 grams: sugars;
- 1 gram: protein;
- 22 milligrams: sodium;

175. Melon And Lime Parfait

Serving: Serves 6 | Prep: | Cook: | Ready in: 1hours20mins

Ingredients

- 1 small Cavaillon melon or cantaloupe, seeded and flesh cut into chunks
- ½ cup plain full-fat yogurt
- Grated zest of 1 lime
- ½ cup 2-percent milk
- ½ teaspoon Banyuls or other flavorful white-wine vinegar

Direction

- Purée the melon in a food processor, then refrigerate for at least 1 hour. Combine the yogurt and lime zest. Divide the yogurt mixture among six glasses. Chill.
- Just before serving, carefully pour the melon purée atop the yogurt in each glass.
- In a food processor, combine the milk and vinegar and pulse until solidly foamy on top. Place a spoonful of the foam in each glass and serve immediately.

Nutrition Information

- 60: calories;

- 0 grams: polyunsaturated fat;
- 11 grams: carbohydrates;
- 10 grams: sugars;
- 2 grams: protein;
- 35 milligrams: sodium;
- 1 gram: dietary fiber;

176. Mexican Chicken Soup With Chick Peas, Avocado And Chipotles

Serving: Serves six | Prep: | Cook: | Ready in: 40mins

Ingredients

- 2 quarts defatted chicken broth
- 1 medium onion, preferably a white onion, finely chopped
- 2 garlic cloves, minced
- ¾ cup diced carrot
- 1 ½ cups (1 15-ounce can) cooked chick peas, rinsed
- Salt, preferably kosher salt, to taste
- 1 cup diced zucchini
- 1 large whole chicken breast or 2 boneless, skinless breasts, poached and shredded (about 4 cups shredded chicken)
- 2 chipotle chiles, rinsed, seeded and cut into thin strips
- 3 to 4 tablespoons chopped cilantro
- 1 medium avocado, sliced
- Lime wedges for serving

Direction

- Combine the chicken stock, onion, garlic, carrot, chick peas and salt to taste in a large soup pot, and bring to a simmer. Cover and simmer over low heat for 15 minutes. Add the zucchini, and simmer for another 10 to 15 minutes, until the vegetables are tender and the broth fragrant but the zucchini has not lost all of its brightness. Taste and adjust salt.
- Just before serving, stir in the chicken, chipotles and cilantro, and heat through. Ladle the soup into bowls. Place a few avocado slices in each bowl, squeeze in a little lime juice and serve, passing additional lime wedges at the table.

Nutrition Information

- 372: calories;
- 39 grams: carbohydrates;
- 24 grams: protein;
- 1266 milligrams: sodium;
- 3 grams: polyunsaturated fat;
- 0 grams: trans fat;
- 7 grams: monounsaturated fat;
- 12 grams: sugars;
- 14 grams: fat;
- 9 grams: dietary fiber;

177. Middle Eastern Meat Loaf

Serving: 6 to 8 servings | Prep: | Cook: | Ready in: 1hours15mins

Ingredients

- For the meatloaf
- 1 pound lean ground beef
- 1 pound ground lamb
- 2 eggs
- 1 cup milk
- ½ cup rolled oats
- ½ cup chopped parsley
- 1 cup onion, minced
- ½ cup green pepper, minced
- Juice of 1/2 lemon
- Grated zest of 1/2 orange
- 1 cup pine nuts
- 1 cup raisins
- 1 teaspoon ground allspice
- 1 teaspoon dried thyme

- 1 ½ teaspoons salt
- 1 teaspoon black pepper
- 2 cloves garlic, minced
- 3 tablespoons Worcestershire sauce
- 2 tablespoons melted butter
- FOR THE SAUCE
- 2 tablespoons butter
- 1 cup finely chopped onions
- ½ cup finely chopped green pepper
- 1 bay leaf
- 1 clove garlic, minced
- Juice of 1 lemon
- ½ cup raisins
- 1 teaspoon dried thyme
- 1 teaspoon ground allspice
- 4 cups canned tomatoes, with their juice
- 2 tablespoons tomato paste
- 3 tablespoons chopped parsley

Direction

-
-

178. Millet And Greens Gratin

Serving: 4 to 6 servings | Prep: | Cook: |Ready in: 1hours10mins

Ingredients

- 1 generous bunch beet greens
- Salt to taste
- 2 tablespoons extra virgin olive oil
- ½ medium onion, finely chopped
- 2 large garlic cloves, minced
- 1 teaspoon chopped fresh thyme
- 1 teaspoon chopped fresh rosemary
- 2 eggs plus 1 egg yolk
- ½ cup low-fat milk
- 1 to 1 ¼ cups cooked millet
- 3 ounces Gruyère cheese, grated (3/4 cup)

Direction

- Stem the greens and wash the leaves in 2 changes of water. To blanch the greens, bring a large pot of water to a rolling boil, salt generously and add the greens. Blanch for 1 minute or until tender. Alternatively, steam the greens over 1 inch of boiling water for about 2 minutes, until tender. Transfer to a bowl of cold water and drain. Taking the greens up by the handful, squeeze hard to expel excess water. Chop medium-fine. You should have about 11/4 cups.
- Preheat the oven to 375 degrees. Oil a 2-quart gratin or baking dish. Heat 1 tablespoon of the oil in a heavy skillet over medium heat and add the onion. Cook, stirring often, until tender, about 5 minutes. Add a generous pinch of salt and the garlic and cook, stirring, until the garlic is fragrant, 30 seconds to a minute. Add the herbs, beet greens, and salt and pepper to taste, and stir and toss in the pan for about a minute, until the mixture is nicely infused with the oil, garlic and herbs. Remove from the heat.
- In a large bowl, beat together the eggs, egg yolk and milk. Add salt to taste (about 1/2 teaspoon), pepper, the millet, the greens and the cheese and stir together until the mixture is well blended. Scrape into the oiled baking dish. Drizzle the remaining tablespoon of olive oil on top.
- Bake in the preheated oven for 35 minutes, or until it is sizzling and set, and the top is just beginning to color. Remove from the oven and allow to sit for 10 minutes or longer before serving.

Nutrition Information

- 194: calories;
- 1 gram: dietary fiber;
- 2 grams: sugars;
- 10 grams: protein;
- 280 milligrams: sodium;
- 12 grams: fat;
- 5 grams: saturated fat;
- 0 grams: trans fat;

- 6 grams: monounsaturated fat;
- 11 grams: carbohydrates;

179. Minestrone With Giant White Beans And Winter Squash

Serving: 6 generous servings | Prep: | Cook: | Ready in: 2hours

Ingredients

- For the beans
- 6 ounces (1 cup) giant white beans such as Royal Coronas, gigandes (giant white beans), or large dried limas, washed, picked over and soaked for 4 hours or longer (no need to soak limas or large white beans)
- ½ medium onion
- 1 bay leaf
- 2 quarts water
- Salt to taste
- 2 garlic cloves, peeled and crushed
- For the soup:
- 2 tablespoons extra virgin olive oil
- 1 medium onion, chopped
- 1 large or 2 medium carrots, peeled and diced (1/2 inch dice or smaller if desired)
- 1 celery stalk, diced
- 2 tablespoons chopped fresh parsley
- 1 or 2 leeks, white and light green parts only, halved, cleaned well and sliced thin
- 3 or 4 garlic cloves (to taste), minced
- 1 14-ounce can chopped tomatoes, with juice
- A bouquet garni made with a Parmesan rind, a bay leaf and a couple of sprigs each parsley and thyme, tied into one of the leek leaves if desired
- Salt and freshly ground pepper
- 1 pound winter squash, diced
- Lots of chopped flat leaf parsley or basil (or both)
- Freshly grated Parmesan for serving

Direction

- First simmer beans. Drain soaked beans and place in a large saucepan with 2 quarts water, halved onion, crushed garlic and bay leaf. Bring to a gentle boil, reduce heat and simmer 45 minutes. Add salt to taste (I usually use 1 teaspoon salt per quart of water) and continue to simmer another 30 minutes. Beans should be almost tender. Remove from heat and use tongs to remove and discard onion half, garlic cloves and bay leaf.
- While beans are simmering you can make tomato base. Heat olive oil over medium heat in a heavy soup pot or Dutch oven, and add onion, carrot and celery. Add a pinch of salt and cook, stirring, until vegetables are just about tender, about 5 minutes, and add parsley and leeks. Cook, stirring, until leeks are slightly wilted, about 3 minutes, and stir in garlic along with another generous pinch of salt. Cook, stirring, just until the garlic smells fragrant, 30 seconds to a minute, and stir in tomatoes with their juice and salt to taste. Bring to a simmer and cook, stirring often, for about 10 minutes, until tomatoes have cooked down somewhat and smell fragrant. Remove from heat until beans are ready.
- Add beans and their broth to tomato base, stir together, add bouquet garni and bring to a simmer. Cover and simmer over low heat for 30 minutes. Add winter squash and continue to simmer for another 30 to 45 minutes, until squash and beans are very tender. Taste, adjust salt, and add freshly ground pepper to taste.
- Just before serving heat through and stir in a generous handful of chopped fresh parsley or basil, or a mix of the two. Serve, topping each bowl with freshly grated Parmesan.

Nutrition Information

- 211: calories;
- 3 grams: monounsaturated fat;
- 35 grams: carbohydrates;
- 9 grams: protein;
- 7 grams: sugars;

- 1321 milligrams: sodium;
- 5 grams: fat;
- 1 gram: polyunsaturated fat;

180. Mini Bell Peppers Stuffed With Goat Cheese

Serving: Serves 6 | Prep: | Cook: | Ready in: 40mins

Ingredients

- ¾ pound mini sweet peppers (1 package, usually 12) or small lipstick peppers
- 6 ounces goat cheese (1/2 of a 12-ounce log)
- ⅓ cup low-fat (not nonfat) cottage cheese
- 3 tablespoons plain low-fat (not nonfat) Greek yogurt

Direction

- Preheat oven to 425 degrees. Line a sheet pan with foil. Place peppers on the baking sheet and roast 8 to10 minutes (small peppers – less than 2 inches long – will cook faster), turning them over halfway through. The peppers should be soft but not charred, except perhaps in a few spots. Remove from heat and allow to cool. If there are some larger peppers in the bag and they haven't softened in 10 minutes, return to oven for another 5.
- While peppers are cooling, make filling. Combine goat cheese, cottage cheese and yogurt in a food processor fitted with a steel blade and process until mix is very smooth, at least one minute. Scrape down sides of bowl and process for another minute. Transfer to a pastry bag fitted with a 3/8-inch star tip.
- When peppers have cooled, slice off ends just below the shoulders. Carefully remove any seeds and membranes. The peppers should be intact, but sometimes, they split down one side. Place any that have not split upright in a small glass or cup to facilitate filling, and pipe in goat cheese mix. Lay those that have split on a plate, pipe on the filling and close the pepper around the filling. Arrange stuffed peppers on a plate or platter. Serve at once, or chill until 30 minutes before serving. Bring to room temperature so cheese is soft and creamy.

Nutrition Information

- 97: calories;
- 165 milligrams: sodium;
- 6 grams: fat;
- 4 grams: carbohydrates;
- 0 grams: polyunsaturated fat;
- 1 gram: dietary fiber;
- 2 grams: sugars;
- 8 grams: protein;

181. Mini Peppers Stuffed With Tuna And Olive Rillettes

Serving: Serves 6 | Prep: | Cook: | Ready in: 30mins

Ingredients

- 1 pound mini bell peppers (usually 2 bags)
- 2 ounces / about 1/3 cup imported black olives, pitted
- 1 plump garlic clove, peeled, green shoot removed
- 1 tablespoon capers, rinsed
- 1 can olive oil-packed tuna, drained
- 1 teaspoon Dijon mustard
- 2 tablespoons extra virgin olive oil
- 2 tablespoons Greek yogurt
- 2 to 3 teaspoons fresh lemon juice (more to taste)
- 1 teaspoon finely chopped fresh rosemary
- 1 teaspoon thyme leaves, chopped

Direction

- Heat oven to 425 degrees. Line a sheet pan with foil. Place peppers on baking sheet and roast very small peppers (less than 2 inches

long) for 8 to 10 minutes, larger peppers for 15 minutes, turning them over halfway through. They should be soft but only charred in a few spots. Remove from oven and allow to cool.
- Meanwhile, in a mini-chop or in a mortar and pestle, pulse or grind olives, garlic and capers to a paste.
- In a bowl, mash tuna with a fork and work in olive mixture, mustard, olive oil, yogurt, lemon juice, rosemary and thyme.
- When peppers have cooled, slice off ends just below shoulders. Carefully remove any seeds and membranes. The peppers should be intact, but sometimes they split down one side. Cut large peppers in half lengthwise. Spoon tuna rillettes into peppers and arrange on a plate or platter. Serve at once, or chill until 30 minutes before serving. Bring to room temperature before serving so that the rillettes are soft.

Nutrition Information

- 188: calories;
- 2 grams: dietary fiber;
- 0 grams: trans fat;
- 6 grams: carbohydrates;
- 3 grams: sugars;
- 17 grams: protein;
- 341 milligrams: sodium;
- 11 grams: fat;

182. Mint Syrup

Serving: Two and two-thirds cups | Prep: | Cook: | Ready in: 2hours15mins

Ingredients

- 2 cups water
- 2 cups sugar
- 1 bunch fresh mint, with stems

Direction

- Stir water and sugar together in a saucepan until sugar dissolves. Add the mint. Place over medium heat and bring to a boil. Reduce to a simmer and cook for 5 minutes. Remove from heat and let stand for 2 hours. Strain and refrigerate until cold. Either use to sweeten a pitcher of iced tea or place in a pitcher and let guests sweeten their tea to taste.

Nutrition Information

- 781: calories;
- 16 milligrams: sodium;
- 0 grams: protein;
- 201 grams: carbohydrates;
- 1 gram: dietary fiber;
- 200 grams: sugars;

183. Mole Coloradito

Serving: 6 servings | Prep: | Cook: | Ready in: 1hours45mins

Ingredients

- 6 pieces chicken: 3 half breasts, 3 thigh-legs
- 1 small onion, halved
- 9 cloves garlic, unpeeled
- 10 dried ancho chilies (see note)
- 1 dried pasilla chilies (see note)
- 4 large plum tomatoes, stem end removed
- 6 tablespoons vegetable oil
- 2 slices stale country bread
- ½ cup sesame seeds
- 15 blanched almonds
- 10 black peppercorns
- 1 tablespoon dried Mexican oregano
- 3 whole cloves
- 1 2-inch stick cinnamon, preferably Mexican canela or Sri Lankan, in pieces
- 1 tablespoon sugar
- Salt and freshly ground black pepper

Direction

- In a large pot, boil 12 cups salted water. Add chicken, onion and 3 garlic cloves. Reduce to simmer. Cook 25 minutes or until chicken is just cooked through. Remove chicken to a plate, and keep warm. Pour broth through a sieve into a bowl; reserve.
- Stem and seed chilies. In a large skillet over medium-high heat, roast chilies 3 to 5 minutes until they smoke and blister. Transfer to a medium bowl, and cover with boiling water. Soak for 20 minutes.
- In same skillet, roast remaining garlic cloves and tomatoes over medium-high heat 12 to 15 minutes. Turn to blister all surfaces. Garlic should be soft and tomatoes evenly covered with brown/black spots. When garlic cools, remove skin.
- In same skillet, heat 3 tablespoons oil over medium-high heat until it shimmers. Add bread, and fry until pale gold, about 2 minutes, turning once. Remove bread from skillet. Add sesame seeds, almonds, peppercorns, oregano and cloves. Cook, stirring frequently, about 4 minutes, until fragrant and seeds are lightly colored. Reserve.
- Drain chilies, discarding soaking liquid. Transfer to a blender with 1/2 cup reserved chicken broth. Puree, pushing down and scraping sides, as needed. In same skillet, heat remaining oil over medium-high heat. Add paste made from chilies and cook, stirring occasionally, 8 to 10 minutes, until paste darkens and oil is absorbed. Transfer to pot chicken was cooked in.
- In blender, puree fried bread, roasted garlic, tomatoes, seeds, almonds and spices with 2 cups broth. Scrape down sides as needed. Transfer to pot with chili paste.
- Place cinnamon in blender with 1/4 cup broth. Puree. Press through sieve over chili paste mixture. Add 1 quart broth to pot, stirring to combine. Increase to high heat. Bring to a boil. Add sugar, salt and pepper. Reduce heat and cook 40 to 50 minutes, until thick enough to coat the back of a spoon.
- Add reserved chicken. Simmer over medium-low heat for 10 minutes. Serve with rice and corn tortillas.

184. Momma Iquana's Fresh Vegetabel Chili

Serving: 6 to 8 servings | Prep: | Cook: | Ready in: 1hours

Ingredients

- 2 cups diced onions
- 2 cups diced celery
- 2 tablespoons olive oil
- 3 cups potatoes cut in 1/2-inch cubes
- 1 ½ cups carrots cut in 1/4-inch cubes
- 2 cups zucchini cut in 1-inch cubes
- 1 cup red pepper cored, seeded and cut in 1-inch cubes
- 2 cups cooked pinto or kidney beans
- 1 cup corn kernels
- 1 tablespoon minced garlic
- 4 cups crushed fresh or canned, drained tomatoes
- 1 cup tomato sauce
- 2 tablespoons ground cumin
- ½ cup very mild pure chili powder (see note)
- ½ cup water

Direction

- Saute onions and celery in hot oil until soft.
- Add remaining ingredients; cover and simmer until vegetables are tender, about 30 minutes.

Nutrition Information

- 346: calories;
- 6 grams: fat;
- 1 gram: saturated fat;
- 62 grams: carbohydrates;
- 21 grams: dietary fiber;
- 12 grams: sugars;
- 3 grams: monounsaturated fat;

- 2 grams: polyunsaturated fat;
- 17 grams: protein;
- 572 milligrams: sodium;

185. Moroccan Cooked Carrot Salad

Serving: Serves 4 | Prep: | Cook: | Ready in: 15mins

Ingredients

- 1 pound carrots, peeled and thinly sliced
- 3 to 4 tablespoons extra virgin olive oil (to taste)
- 2 large garlic cloves, minced or pureed in a mortar and pestle with 1/4 teaspoon salt
- Salt to taste
- ½ teaspoon freshly ground pepper
- 1 teaspoon cumin seeds, lightly toasted and ground
- 2 to 3 tablespoons fresh lemon juice (to taste)
- ¼ cup chopped flat-leaf parsley
- For the garnish
- Imported black olives
- 2 hard boiled eggs, cut in wedges (optional)

Direction

- Place the carrots in a steamer above 1 inch of boiling water, cover and steam 5 to 8 minutes, until tender. Remove from the heat, rinse with cold water, and drain on paper towels.
- Heat 2 tablespoons of the olive oil in a large, heavy skillet and add the garlic and cumin. Cook, stirring, for about 30 seconds, until the garlic smells fragrant, and stir in the carrots, pepper, and salt to taste. Stir together for a few minutes, until the carrots are nicely seasoned. Remove from the heat and stir in the lemon juice, remaining olive oil, and the parsley. Taste and adjust salt and lemon juice as desired. Transfer to a platter, and decorate with olives and hard-boiled eggs if desired. Serve at room temperature.

186. Moroccan Marinated Fish

Serving: 4 servings | Prep: | Cook: | Ready in: 1hours30mins

Ingredients

- 1 ¾ pound whole red snapper or striped bass, head on
- 1 small bunch fresh coriander, leaves only
- 2 cloves garlic, peeled
- 2 tablespoons vinegar
- Juice of 1 lemon or lime
- 1 tablespoon paprika
- 1 tablespoon cumin
- ½ teaspoon crushed chili
- Cayenne pepper to taste
- 2 tablespoons olive oil

Direction

- Wipe the fish dry with paper towels.
- Combine all the ingredients in a blender and mix until smooth. Coat the fish, inside and out, with the marinade and leave for an hour at room temperature.
- Preheat oven to 375 degrees.
- Bake the fish for 20 to 30 minutes or until cooked.

Nutrition Information

- 278: calories;
- 4 grams: carbohydrates;
- 1 gram: sugars;
- 42 grams: protein;
- 135 milligrams: sodium;
- 10 grams: fat;
- 2 grams: polyunsaturated fat;
- 6 grams: monounsaturated fat;

187. Mousse Au Chocolat

Serving: | Prep: | Cook: | Ready in: 15mins

Ingredients

- ½ pound sweet chocolate
- 3 tablespoons water
- ¼ cup sugar
- 4 eggs, separated
- 1 inch scraped vanilla bean
- 1 cup heavy cream, whipped

Direction

- In top of double boiler over hot water, melt the chocolate with the water and the sugar. Remove and cool.
- Add the yolks, one at a time, mixing well after each addition. Add the vanilla bean.
- Beat the whites until stiff. Fold into chocolate mixture. Spoon into six or eight individual pots, souffle dishes or ramekins. Refrigerate.
- To serve, top with whipped cream.

Nutrition Information

- 252: calories;
- 0 grams: trans fat;
- 24 grams: carbohydrates;
- 21 grams: sugars;
- 4 grams: protein;
- 41 milligrams: sodium;
- 17 grams: fat;
- 10 grams: saturated fat;
- 6 grams: monounsaturated fat;
- 1 gram: polyunsaturated fat;
- 2 grams: dietary fiber;

188. Mushroom Stuffed Tomatoes

Serving: | Prep: | Cook: | Ready in: 41mins

Ingredients

- 2 tablespoons unsalted butter
- 2 tablespoons fruity olive oil
- ⅓ cup shallots, peeled and thinly sliced (4 to 6 shallots)
- 4 medium cloves garlic, peeled, minced and mashed
- 2 teaspoons kosher salt
- Freshly ground black pepper
- 6 large ripe tomatoes or 10 small ones (about 3 pounds)
- ¾ pound chanterelles, cleaned, trimmed and sliced 1/2-inch thick
- 1 teaspoon fresh marjoram leaves
- 2 teaspoons fresh thyme
- ⅓ cup orzo pasta
- ¼ cup fresh Italian parsley, minced
- 4 ounces mozzarella, cut into 1/4-inch cubes

Direction

- In a 10-inch quiche dish, combine butter, olive oil, shallots, garlic and salt. Cook, covered tightly with microwave plastic wrap, at 100 percent for 4 minutes.
- Core tomatoes. Cut a "lid" from the top of each, and, if necessary, a small slice from the bottom so that it will stand upright. Scoop flesh and seeds from each tomato to leave a shell for stuffing. Coarsely chop flesh and tops and set aside.
- Prick each tomato shell through the skin 5 to 6 times. Sprinkle the inside with salt and pepper. Arrange tomatoes in a ring in a dish just large enough to hold them and at least 2 inches deep.
- Stir chopped tomatoes, chanterelles, herbs and orzo into shallot mixture. Cover tightly with microwave plastic wrap and cook at 100 percent for 7 minutes. Uncover and stir in parsley, mozzarella and pepper. Divide mixture among tomato shells. Cover tightly with microwave plastic wrap and cook 100 percent for 5 minutes. Serve immediately, or let cool to room temperature and refrigerate;

reheat, covered, for 1 minute 30 seconds before serving.

Nutrition Information

- 224: calories;
- 1 gram: polyunsaturated fat;
- 7 grams: sugars;
- 8 grams: protein;
- 6 grams: dietary fiber;
- 13 grams: fat;
- 0 grams: trans fat;
- 20 grams: carbohydrates;
- 765 milligrams: sodium;

189. My Pain Catalan With Extra Tomatoes And Goat Cheese

Serving: 1 serving, or 2 servings as an appetizer | Prep: | Cook: | Ready in: 10mins

Ingredients

- 2 slices whole-wheat country bread
- 1 garlic clove, cut in half, or Dijon mustard to taste
- 1 large or 2 smaller ripe tomatoes in season
- Salt to taste
- ½ ounce goat cheese, crumbled or thinly sliced

Direction

- If desired, toast the bread. Rub with the cut side of the garlic clove or spread with mustard. Cut one of the tomatoes in half and rub the cut side against the bread until the bread is nicely saturated with the juice and pulp of the tomato. Slice the remaining tomato and layer over the bread. Season to taste with salt, crumble the goat cheese on top, add a few torn basil leaves if desired and enjoy.

Nutrition Information

- 218: calories;
- 461 milligrams: sodium;
- 5 grams: fat;
- 1 gram: polyunsaturated fat;
- 7 grams: sugars;
- 34 grams: carbohydrates;
- 4 grams: dietary fiber;
- 10 grams: protein;
- 3 grams: saturated fat;
- 0 grams: trans fat;

190. Noodles With Egg And Parsley Topping

Serving: 4 servings | Prep: | Cook: | Ready in: 10mins

Ingredients

- ½ pound fine noodles
- Salt to taste
- 3 tablespoons butter
- Freshly ground pepper to taste
- 1 hard-cooked egg, peeled and coarsely chopped
- ⅛ teaspoon freshly grated nutmeg
- ¼ cup finely chopped parsley

Direction

- Cook the noodles in salted water until tender. Drain and add 1 tablespoon of the butter, salt and pepper. Toss well.
- Heat the remaining 2 tablespoons of butter in a skillet over medium-high heat, and add the chopped egg and nutmeg. Cook briefly, shaking the skillet. Add the parsley, and cook for 30 seconds. Pour over the noodles and toss. Serve immediately.

Nutrition Information

- 312: calories;

- 3 grams: monounsaturated fat;
- 1 gram: sugars;
- 189 milligrams: sodium;
- 0 grams: trans fat;
- 12 grams: fat;
- 6 grams: saturated fat;
- 41 grams: carbohydrates;
- 2 grams: dietary fiber;
- 10 grams: protein;

191. Not Too Sweet Wok Popped Coconut Kettle Corn

Serving: About 12 cups popcorn | Prep: | Cook: | Ready in: 5mins

Ingredients

- 2 tablespoons coconut oil
- 6 tablespoons popcorn
- 2 tablespoons raw brown sugar
- Kosher salt to taste

Direction

- Place the coconut oil in a 14-inch lidded wok over medium heat. When the coconut oil melts add a few kernels of popcorn and cover. When you hear a kernel pop, quickly lift the lid and pour in all of the popcorn. Cover, turn the heat to medium-low, and cook, shaking the wok constantly, until you no longer hear the kernels popping against the lid. Turn off the heat, uncover and add the sugar and salt. Cover again and shake the wok vigorously for 30 seconds to a minute. Transfer the popcorn to a bowl, and if there is any caramelized sugar on the bottom of the wok scrape it out. Stir or toss the popcorn to distribute the caramelized bits throughout, and serve.

Nutrition Information

- 159: calories;

- 1 gram: monounsaturated fat;
- 0 grams: protein;
- 10 grams: carbohydrates;
- 9 grams: sugars;
- 56 milligrams: sodium;
- 14 grams: fat;
- 12 grams: saturated fat;

192. Oats With Amaranth, Chia Seeds And Blueberries

Serving: Serves 1 | Prep: | Cook: | Ready in: 15mins

Ingredients

- For each bowl
- ¼ cup regular or quick cooking steel-cut oats
- 1 tablespoon amaranth seeds
- 1 teaspoon chia seeds
- Salt to taste (I use a generous pinch)
- 1 heaped tablespoon fresh or frozen blueberries, or more to taste
- ¾ cup water
- 1 teaspoon honey or maple syrup, plus more as desired for drizzling
- Optional toppings: milk, chopped toasted skinned hazelnuts, chopped toasted almonds, grated apple or pear, freeze-dried blueberries

Direction

- The night before, stir together steel-cut oats, amaranth seeds, chia seeds, salt and blueberries in a medium microwave-proof bowl. Bring water to a boil and pour over mixture. Add honey or maple syrup and stir, then cover bowl with a plate.
- In the morning, microwave mixture for 2 minutes on 100 percent power. Remove bowl from microwave and carefully remove plate (bowl will be hot and steam will rise from cereal). Stir mixture, cover again and return to microwave. Heat for 2 minutes more, or until mixture is no longer watery.

- Transfer to a serving dish and sprinkle on toppings of your choice.

193. Octopus, Galician Style

Serving: 4 to 8 servings | Prep: | Cook: | Ready in: 2hours

Ingredients

- 1 octopus, about 3 pounds
- Coarse salt
- 4 medium to large potatoes
- Smoked pimentón
- Olive oil

Direction

- Thaw octopus if necessary, either for 24 hours in refrigerator, or for a few hours in a couple of changes of cold water. With a scissors, remove skinny tips of tentacles and, cutting through webbing that connects them, separate the 8 tentacles and discard head. (Alternatively, you can cook the octopus whole and cut it up after cooking.)
- Bring a large pot of water to a boil and salt it well. Put octopus in water and, when it returns to boil, cover and adjust heat so water simmers gently. Cook an hour or so, until octopus is tender. Meanwhile peel potatoes and cut into 2-inch slices. Lower them into water and cook until tender, about a half hour. Remove if they're done before octopus, and keep warm.
- When octopus is tender, remove it and drain. Put potatoes on a platter and cut octopus into pieces (again, a scissors is easiest); top potatoes with it. Drizzle all liberally with pimentón, olive oil and coarse salt, and serve hot or warm.

194. Olive Oil Poached Bay Scallops With Chickpeas

Serving: Four servings | Prep: | Cook: | Ready in: 1hours

Ingredients

- The cream:
- 1 sprig fresh rosemary
- ½ cup heavy cream
- The chickpeas:
- 1 tablespoon peanut oil
- 1 small carrot, scraped and cut into 2-inch pieces
- 1 small rib of celery, trimmed and cut into 2-inch pieces
- 1 small onion, cut in half
- ½ cup chick peas, soaked overnight
- 1 ½ cups chicken stock
- 1 bay leaf
- The scallops:
- 1 cup extra-virgin olive oil
- 1 pound bay scallops
- ⅓ cup diced tomato, skin and seeds removed
- ¼ teaspoon rosemary leaves
- Salt and freshly ground black pepper to taste

Direction

- In a small saucepan, heat the cream until just warm, being careful not to let it bubble. Add the rosemary, turn off the heat and let it steep for a half hour. Refrigerate the cream until cold and then whip it into soft peaks. Set aside.
- In a medium-sized saucepan, heat the peanut oil over medium-high heat. Add the carrot, celery and onion, adjust the heat to low, cover and sweat the vegetables for about three to four minutes. Add the chickpeas, stock and bay leaf, then cook gently over medium heat, uncovered, until the peas are soft and cooked through, 30 to 45 minutes. Let them cool, then peel. Discard the vegetables.
- In a medium-sized saucepan, heat the oil over medium heat, until fairly warm, but not hot. Add the scallops and cook them gently until barely cooked through, about one-and-a-half

minutes. Drain off most of the oil, then add the chickpeas, tomato and rosemary leaves. Season with salt and pepper. Ladle the scallops and chickpea mixture into soup bowls, top with a dollop of rosemary cream and serve.

Nutrition Information

- 757: calories;
- 0 grams: trans fat;
- 5 grams: sugars;
- 18 grams: protein;
- 857 milligrams: sodium;
- 70 grams: fat;
- 15 grams: carbohydrates;
- 45 grams: monounsaturated fat;
- 8 grams: polyunsaturated fat;
- 3 grams: dietary fiber;

195. Orange Cheese Poundcake

Serving: Twenty servings | Prep: | Cook: |Ready in: 1hours30mins

Ingredients

- 1 ½ cups unsalted butter, at room temperature, plus some for greasing the pan
- 3 cups flour, plus some for dusting the pan
- 8 ounces cream cheese, at room temperature
- 3 cups sugar
- 6 eggs
- 1 teaspoon vanilla extract
- 1 teaspoon orange extract
- 1 ½ teaspoons grated orange zest
- Powdered sugar and mint sprigs for garnish
- Whipped cream

Direction

- Preheat the oven to 325 degrees. Grease a cake pan, 12 inches in diameter and 2 inches deep; dust it with flour.
- In a large mixing bowl, cream the butter, the cream cheese and sugar until smooth and well blended. Beat in the eggs, one at a time, until well incorporated. Add the flour, a little at a time, until smooth. Stir in the vanilla extract, orange extract and zest.
- Pour the mixture into the prepared pan and bake for one hour to one hour and 15 minutes, or until a toothpick inserted in the center comes out almost clean. Remove and cool. Unmold, sprinkle with powdered sugar and garnish with sprigs of mint. Serve with whipped cream on the side.

196. Orange Glaze

Serving: Glaze for 1 cake | Prep: | Cook: |Ready in: 2mins

Ingredients

- 2 cups confectioners' sugar
- 4 tablespoons orange juice
- 1 tablespoon lemon juice
- 1 teaspoon grated orange rind

Direction

- Combine the ingredients and stir thoroughly to blend.

Nutrition Information

- 483: calories;
- 0 grams: protein;
- 124 grams: carbohydrates;
- 120 grams: sugars;
- 3 milligrams: sodium;

197. Orzo With Fresh Tomato

Serving: Four servings | Prep: | Cook: | Ready in: 30mins

Ingredients

- 4 cups water
- Salt to taste
- 3 cups fresh orzo
- 2 tablespoons olive oil
- 4 tablespoons finely chopped onions
- ¾ pound ripe fresh tomatoes, peeled and cut into 1/2-inch cubes
- Freshly ground pepper to taste
- ¼ teaspoon hot red-pepper flakes

Direction

- Bring the water to a boil in a saucepan. Add salt. Cook the orzo according to package directions. Drain.
- Meanwhile, heat the oil in a saucepan. Cook the onions until they are wilted. Add the tomatoes, sprinkle with salt and pepper and the pepper flakes. Stir gently and bring the pan juices to a boil.
- Add the orzo and stir gently to blend.

Nutrition Information

- 385: calories;
- 5 grams: monounsaturated fat;
- 2 grams: dietary fiber;
- 3 grams: sugars;
- 1035 milligrams: sodium;
- 13 grams: protein;
- 9 grams: fat;
- 1 gram: saturated fat;
- 63 grams: carbohydrates;

198. Osso Buco Alla Milanese

Serving: 6 servings | Prep: | Cook: | Ready in: 1hours25mins

Ingredients

- 4 to 6 tablespoons olive oil
- 6 portions of veal shank (about 6 pounds total), see note
- ¼ cup flour
- 1 cup finely chopped onions
- ½ cup finely chopped carrots
- ½ cup finely chopped celery
- 1 large clove garlic, minced
- 1 ½ cups dry white wine
- 1 ½ cups peeled, seeded, chopped fresh tomatoes (canned Italian tomatoes, drained and chopped, may be substituted)
- 1 ¼ cups well-flavored veal, beef or chicken stock
- ½ teaspoon dried thyme
- Salt and freshly ground black pepper
- Gremolata (see recipe)

Direction

- Melt the oil in a heavy casserole large enough to hold the veal in a single layer. Dust shank pieces with flour and lightly brown on all sides over medium heat. You may find the browning easier if you do not put all the shanks in the pan at once. Do not allow them to become dark or blackened. Remove the shanks from the casserole and lower heat.
- Preheat oven to 350 degrees.
- To the casserole, add onions, carrots and celery and saute, stirring until they begin to soften. Add garlic and saute a minute longer. Add wine and cook over medium-high heat, scraping the pan until all the brown bits clinging to it have dissolved. Stir in the tomatoes, stock and thyme.
- Return the shanks to the casserole, basting with the sauce. Season with salt and pepper, cover and bake in the preheated oven about one and one-half hours until the meat is tender when pierced with a fork. Baste the shanks several times during baking.
- Remove shanks to a serving dish and keep warm. Taste sauce and season with salt and pepper if necessary. If the sauce is too thin (it

should be about the consistency of cream), place the pan on top of the stove and boil down the sauce for several minutes.
- Pour sauce over the shanks and top with a little of the gremolata. Pass the rest on the side.

Nutrition Information

- 777: calories;
- 3 grams: polyunsaturated fat;
- 2 grams: dietary fiber;
- 4 grams: sugars;
- 30 grams: fat;
- 14 grams: carbohydrates;
- 99 grams: protein;
- 1648 milligrams: sodium;
- 7 grams: saturated fat;
- 15 grams: monounsaturated fat;

199. Oven Poached Pacific Sole With Lemon Caper Sauce

Serving: Serves 4 | Prep: | Cook: | Ready in: 40mins

Ingredients

- 1 ½ pounds Pacific sole or flounder fillets
- Salt and freshly ground pepper
- 1 tablespoon extra-virgin olive oil
- 3 tablespoons finely chopped shallot
- 1 cup dry white wine (you can also use rosé; the sauce will have a pink hue)
- For the sauce
- 1 plump garlic clove, minced or puréed (more to taste)
- 2 tablespoons capers, rinsed and coarsely chopped
- ¼ cup fresh lemon juice
- 3 tablespoons extra-virgin olive oil
- 2 to 4 tablespoons finely chopped parsley

Direction

- Preheat the oven to 400 degrees. Oil or butter one or two baking dishes large enough to accommodate the fish fillets in one layer. Lay the fish in the dish(es) and season with salt and pepper.
- Heat the olive oil over medium heat in a small or medium skillet and add the shallot. Cook, stirring, until tender and translucent, about 3 minutes. Add the wine to the pan, bring to a boil, and pour the wine and shallots over the fish. Return the skillet to the stove (make sure the heat is off) for later use. Cover the baking dish with foil and place in the oven. Bake 8 to 10 minutes, or 5 minutes for each 1/2 inch of thickness, until the fish is opaque and pulls apart easily with a fork.
- While the fish is in the oven, whisk together the garlic, capers, lemon juice and olive oil. You can also mash the garlic in a mortar and pestle and work in the capers, lemon juice and olive oil, though I prefer the capers chopped, even some intact, and not puréed.
- When the fish is done remove it from the oven and carefully transfer to a platter or plates. Cover and keep warm. Pour the liquid in the baking dish into the skillet and turn the heat on high. Reduce, stirring often, to about 1/4 cup – it should be thick – and stir in the garlic and caper mixture and the parsley. Whisk together, taste and adjust seasoning, pour over the fish and serve.

Nutrition Information

- 299: calories;
- 17 grams: fat;
- 3 grams: saturated fat;
- 0 grams: trans fat;
- 11 grams: monounsaturated fat;
- 2 grams: sugars;
- 5 grams: carbohydrates;
- 1 gram: dietary fiber;
- 22 grams: protein;
- 632 milligrams: sodium;

200. Oysters With Linguine

Serving: 4 servings | Prep: | Cook: | Ready in: 17mins

Ingredients

- 6 scallions, chopped
- 2 tablespoons chopped parsley
- 2 tablespoons minced garlic in oil
- 2 or 3 tablespoons olive oil
- Freshly ground black pepper to taste
- Crushed red-hot pepper to taste
- 2 teaspoons Dijon-style mustard
- ⅔ cup dry white wine
- 3 tablespoons flour
- 2 pints shucked oysters, liquor reserved
- 2 12-ounce cans corn niblets
- 12 to 16 ounces fresh or dried linguine
- ¾ cup grated cheddar cheese

Direction

- Bring 3 or 4 quarts of water to boil in a covered pot for linguine.
- Saute scallions, parsley and garlic in hot oil over medium heat until softened.
- Season with peppers, and add mustard and wine; reduce heat and cook slowly for a minute or two.
- Mix flour with enough of the reserved oyster liquor to make a paste. Add the paste and remaining liquor to pan and cook, stirring, until the mixture thickens a little.
- Add oysters and corn with liquid from can; cook 3 or 4 minutes over moderate heat, just until oysters begin to curl.
- Cook linguine in boiling water according to package directions for dried, or about one minute for fresh.
- Serve oyster sauce over linguine, sprinkled with cheese.

Nutrition Information

- 898: calories;
- 26 grams: fat;
- 7 grams: saturated fat;
- 121 grams: carbohydrates;
- 772 milligrams: sodium;
- 0 grams: trans fat;
- 9 grams: sugars;
- 4 grams: polyunsaturated fat;
- 41 grams: protein;

201. Paglia E Fieno With Corn

Serving: 2 servings | Prep: | Cook: | Ready in: 30mins

Ingredients

- 2 tablespoons butter
- ¼ cup finely chopped onion
- 1 clove of garlic, minced
- Kernels from 1 ear of yellow corn
- 2 ounces prosciutto, minced
- 1 cup heavy cream
- Freshly ground black pepper
- ¼ pound each fresh green and white tagliolini or linguine noodles
- Freshly grated Parmesan cheese

Direction

- Bring a large pot of water to a boil.
- Heat butter in a heavy skillet, add the onion and saute over medium heat until tender but not brown. Stir in the garlic, corn and prosciutto and cook a few minutes longer. Add the cream and allow to simmer several minutes to thicken slightly. Season to taste with pepper.
- Boil the noodles for about three minutes, until just done. Transfer to a warm serving dish. Pour the sauce over the noodles, toss and serve. Pass the cheese alongside.

202.   Papaya Sorbet

Serving: about 2 cups | Prep: | Cook: | Ready in: 10mins

Ingredients

- 2 medium papayas, seeded, peeled and cut into chunks
- 1 cup simple syrup (see note)
- Juice of 3 limes

Direction

- Puree papaya until smooth. There should be about 1 1/2 cups puree. Add the simple syrup and lime juice.
- Freeze in an ice cream machine according to the manufacturer's directions.

Nutrition Information

- 212: calories;
- 1 gram: protein;
- 42 milligrams: sodium;
- 0 grams: polyunsaturated fat;
- 57 grams: carbohydrates;
- 3 grams: dietary fiber;
- 50 grams: sugars;

203.   Papaya Tart

Serving: 4 to 6 servings | Prep: | Cook: | Ready in: 1hours

Ingredients

- 1 sheet frozen puff pastry (8 1/2 ounces)
- 2 teaspoons milk
- 3 tablespoons dark brown sugar
- 2 medium papayas, peeled and cut lengthwise into 1/4-inch-thick slices (any left over can be used for the sorbet)
- Juice of 2 or 3 limes (to taste)

Direction

- Allow 1 piece of puff pastry dough to defrost at room temperature (about 30 minutes).
- Place a rack in the middle of oven, and heat to 400 degrees.
- Open out the sheet of puff pastry. On a lightly floured surface, roll it out until it is about 1/8 inch thick. Cut out a 9-inch circle. Place on a parchment-covered baking sheet (or a baking sheet covered with greased aluminum foil). Leaving a 1/4-inch rim, prick the center of the dough all over with the tines of a fork. With a pastry brush, lightly coat the center of the dough with the milk. Push 1 tablespoon of the sugar through a coarse sieve to distribute evenly over the center of the dough. Bake for 5 minutes.
- Gently toss the papaya with the lime juice. Remove the tart shell from the oven, and lay the papaya slices in a spoke pattern on the shell. Push the remaining 2 tablespoons of sugar through a coarse sieve evenly over the top of the fruit.
- Return to the oven for 15 minutes, until the crust is golden and the sugar is caramelized. Remove from the oven, and slide off the baking pan onto a rack. Cool slightly and serve, or cool completely and reheat slightly just before serving. Cut into wedges with large kitchen scissors.

Nutrition Information

- 308: calories;
- 4 grams: protein;
- 9 grams: monounsaturated fat;
- 2 grams: polyunsaturated fat;
- 41 grams: carbohydrates;
- 114 milligrams: sodium;
- 16 grams: sugars;

204. Parsley Salad With Country Ham, Tomatoes And Asiago

Serving: 4 servings | Prep: | Cook: |Ready in: 20mins

Ingredients

- 4 plum tomatoes
- ¼ cup plus 2 tablespoons olive oil
- ½ teaspoon sugar
- Kosher salt and freshly ground black pepper
- 2 cloves garlic, minced
- 2 tablespoons lemon juice
- 4 cups loosely packed flat-leaf parsley leaves
- ¾ cup croutons, made with country bread
- 3 tablespoons grated Wisconsin asiago or Parmesan
- 4 paper-thin slices Smithfield country ham or prosciutto

Direction

- The night before serving, prepare the tomatoes: preheat the oven to its lowest setting, about 160 degrees. In a medium bowl, combine the tomatoes with 2 tablespoons olive oil and the sugar. Season to taste with salt and pepper. Arrange tomatoes on a baking rack fitted on top of a baking sheet. Bake overnight, 6 to 8 hours, until the tomatoes are shriveled and partially dried. Remove from oven, and let cool. Thinly slice, drain juices and reserve.
- In a small bowl, whisk remaining olive oil, garlic and lemon juice. Season to taste with salt and pepper. In a large bowl, combine parsley, croutons, cheese and tomatoes. Slowly add dressing; toss until coated. Place a slice of ham on each of 4 plates; mound salad on top of each slice. Serve.

Nutrition Information

- 313: calories;
- 13 grams: carbohydrates;
- 11 grams: protein;
- 627 milligrams: sodium;
- 25 grams: fat;
- 5 grams: saturated fat;
- 17 grams: monounsaturated fat;
- 3 grams: sugars;

205. Passion Fruit Salad With White Pepper Ice Cream

Serving: 6 servings | Prep: | Cook: |Ready in: 30mins

Ingredients

- For the ice cream:
- 6 large egg yolks
- 1 ½ cups milk
- 1 ⅓ cups heavy cream
- 1 ½ cups plus 1 tablespoon sugar
- 4 teaspoons freshly ground white pepper
- For the fruit salad:
- 1 ½ cups passion-fruit puree (see note)
- 1 cup water
- 7 tablespoons sugar
- ½ pineapple, peeled, cored and cut into bite-size wedges
- 3 kiwis, peeled and cut into 8 wedges each
- 2 bananas, peeled and thinly sliced
- 3 passion fruits, halved, flesh scooped out (if unavailable, substitute 1 mango, peeled and pitted)
- 3 plums, diced

Direction

- To make the ice cream, place the yolks in a large bowl and whisk until smooth. Place the milk, cream, sugar and pepper in a saucepan and bring just to a boil. Remove from heat and slowly whisk 1/3 of the hot liquid into the yolks. Whisk in the remainder. Strain mixture through a fine-mesh sieve and refrigerate until chilled. Freeze according to the ice-cream maker's instructions.
- To make the fruit salad, combine the puree, water and sugar in a small saucepan and bring just to a boil without stirring. Remove from

the heat and cool. Combine the fruits in a large bowl and toss with the cooled fruit syrup. Divide the salad among 6 deep plates, and then top each serving with a scoop of ice cream.

Nutrition Information

- 788: calories;
- 27 grams: fat;
- 9 grams: protein;
- 15 grams: saturated fat;
- 8 grams: monounsaturated fat;
- 2 grams: polyunsaturated fat;
- 135 grams: carbohydrates;
- 7 grams: dietary fiber;
- 113 grams: sugars;
- 61 milligrams: sodium;

206. Pasta With Fresh Tomato Sauce

Serving: 4 to 6 servings | Prep: | Cook: | Ready in: 20mins

Ingredients

- Salt
- 3 tablespoons butter or olive oil
- 1 ½ to 2 pounds tomatoes, cored and roughly chopped
- 1 pound linguine, spaghetti or other long pasta
- ½ cup freshly grated Parmigiano-Reggiano
- Salt and freshly ground black pepper to taste

Direction

- Bring a large pot of water to a boil, and salt it. Place the butter or oil in an 8- or 10-inch skillet, and turn heat to medium. When butter melts or oil is hot, add tomatoes and turn heat to high.
- Cook, stirring occasionally, until tomatoes begin to juice up, then turn the heat to low and keep warm, stirring occasionally, while you cook pasta.
- Cook pasta until it is tender but firm. Drain, and toss with tomatoes and cheese. Season with salt and pepper, toss again and serve immediately.

Nutrition Information

- 403: calories;
- 523 milligrams: sodium;
- 11 grams: fat;
- 3 grams: saturated fat;
- 1 gram: polyunsaturated fat;
- 4 grams: dietary fiber;
- 14 grams: protein;
- 6 grams: sugars;
- 62 grams: carbohydrates;

207. Pasta With Portobello Mushrooms

Serving: 4 servings | Prep: | Cook: | Ready in: 20mins

Ingredients

- 1 pound pappardelle or fettuccine, fresh or dried
- 2 tablespoons olive oil
- 6 large shallots, finely minced
- ¼ cup coarsely grated ginger
- 1 pound portobello mushrooms or any assortment of wild and common white mushrooms (champignons de Paris), cleaned, trimmed and sliced
- 1 ¼ cups reduced-fat ricotta cheese
- 1 ¼ cups nonfat plain yogurt
- 1 tablespoon cornstarch
- ¼ teaspoon salt
- Freshly ground black pepper to taste
- ¼ cup chopped parsley
- ½ cup coarsely grated Parmigiano Reggiano

Direction

- Cook the pasta in boiling water.
- Heat the oil in a large skillet, and saute the shallots, ginger and mushrooms until the mushrooms soften and release their liquid.
- Blend the ricotta and yogurt thoroughly. Then, thoroughly blend a little of the yogurt mixture with the cornstarch to form a smooth paste. Spoon the cornstarch mixture into the remaining yogurt-ricotta mixture, and blend thoroughly.
- Reduce the heat under the mushrooms to very low. Stir in the yogurt mixture, and cook until the sauce is warmed, but not hot. If it gets hot, it will separate.
- Season with salt and pepper, and spoon over the pasta. Sprinkle with parsley. Serve with cheese.

Nutrition Information

- 843: calories;
- 121 grams: carbohydrates;
- 21 grams: sugars;
- 40 grams: protein;
- 10 grams: saturated fat;
- 2 grams: polyunsaturated fat;
- 494 milligrams: sodium;
- 23 grams: fat;
- 9 grams: dietary fiber;

208. Pasta With Smoked Mussels And Tomatoes

Serving: Four servings | Prep: | Cook: | Ready in: 20mins

Ingredients

- 1 pound linguine
- ¼ cup plus 2 teaspoons olive oil
- 3 cloves garlic, peeled and minced
- 8 plum tomatoes, cut into 1/2-inch dice
- 2-3 2/3-ounce cans smoked mussels, drained
- 5 tablespoons chopped Italian parsley
- ½ cup fresh basil leaves, cut across into thin strips
- 3 teaspoons salt
- Freshly ground pepper to taste

Direction

- Bring a large pot of salted water to a boil. Add the linguine and cook until al dente, about 10 minutes. Drain.
- Meanwhile, heat 1/4 cup of olive oil in a medium skillet over medium heat. Add the garlic and saute for 2 minutes; do not let it brown. Add the tomatoes and cook just until heated through, about 4 minutes. Remove from heat and stir in the mussels, parsley, basil, salt and pepper.
- Place the linguine in a large bowl and toss with the mussel mixture and the remaining 2 teaspoons of olive oil. Divide among 4 plates and serve immediately.

Nutrition Information

- 625: calories;
- 661 milligrams: sodium;
- 19 grams: fat;
- 3 grams: polyunsaturated fat;
- 12 grams: monounsaturated fat;
- 93 grams: carbohydrates;
- 6 grams: sugars;
- 21 grams: protein;

209. Paul Buxman's Biscuits

Serving: 12-14 biscuits | Prep: | Cook: | Ready in: 35mins

Ingredients

- ⅓ cup stone-ground whole-wheatpastry flour
- 1 ⅔ cups all-purpose flour
- 1 tablespoon baking powder
- ½ teaspoon baking soda
- Generous 1/2 teaspoon kosher salt

- ⅓ cup frozen unsalted butter
- 1 ¼ cups buttermilk

Direction

- Preheat oven to 500 degree. In a large bowl, mix dry ingredients, cut butter into small chips adding into the mix. Use a pastry cutter to incorporate butter into flour until mixture becomes mealy. Create a small indentation in center of mix and add buttermilk. Fold dry mix into wet center with wooden spoon until dough ball is formed.
- Transfer dough to work surface that has been floured with mix of wholewheat flour and all-purpose flour. Press dough into a flattened round and fold over; flatten again and fold, then flatten and fold the dough once more. With palm of hand, press dough to 1/2-inch thickness. (Do not use a rolling pin — biscuits will not rise properly.)
- Cut out biscuits with sharp biscuit cutter into 2 1/4-inch rounds, if possible. (Make sure the cutter is sharp. A dull one seals the dough around the edges, and the biscuit will not rise properly). Place biscuits on baking tray 2 inches apart and place in upper third of the oven.
- Bake for 3 minutes, then reduce the heat to 450 degrees and bake for 7 minutes or until golden brown. Place the biscuits in a basket with a paper towel on the bottom, and cover with a kitchen towel (don't wrap them in the towel).
- Preslice chilled butter to serve with biscuits. It saves time as biscuits are passed around table.

Nutrition Information

- 120: calories;
- 5 grams: fat;
- 3 grams: protein;
- 0 grams: polyunsaturated fat;
- 1 gram: sugars;
- 16 grams: carbohydrates;
- 178 milligrams: sodium;

210. Pea Dip With Parmesan

Serving: At least 8 servings | Prep: | Cook: |Ready in: 10mins

Ingredients

- 3 cups peas (frozen are fine; no need to defrost)
- About 1 cup stock or water, as needed
- 3 tablespoons toasted pine nuts, roughly chopped
- 1 cup freshly grated Parmesan
- ½ teaspoon minced garlic
- ¼ cup chopped fresh mint or more to taste
- 2 tablespoons extra virgin olive oil
- Salt
- freshly ground black pepper

Direction

- Put peas in a pan with just enough stock or water to come half way up their height. Cook for about 3 minutes, or until peas are bright green and tender. Put all but 1 cup of peas in a food processor or blender, and add just enough cooking liquid to start purée. When purée is relatively smooth, transfer it to a bowl and stir in remaining cup of peas.
- Add pine nuts, cheese, garlic, mint and olive oil. Sprinkle with salt and pepper; taste and adjust seasoning, then thin with more liquid if necessary. Serve or refrigerate.

Nutrition Information

- 164: calories;
- 10 grams: carbohydrates;
- 3 grams: dietary fiber;
- 4 grams: sugars;
- 2 grams: polyunsaturated fat;
- 9 grams: protein;
- 252 milligrams: sodium;

211. Penne With Corn And Hot Sausage

Serving: 4 to 6 servings | Prep: | Cook: | Ready in: 1hours

Ingredients

- 2 tablespoons olive oil
- ¾ cup chopped onions
- 1 green pepper, seeded and chopped
- 1 sweet red pepper, seeded and chopped
- 2 large cloves garlic, finely chopped
- 1 pound penne
- 3 cups finely chopped fresh tomato pulp (about six medium ripe tomatoes)
- Kernels stripped from 4 ears of corn
- Salt and freshly ground black pepper
- ¼ teaspoon hot red pepper flakes, or to taste
- ½ pound Italian hot sausage removed from its casing
- 4 tablespoons butter
- 1 tablespoon chopped fresh coriander leaves
- Freshly grated Parmesan or aged Monterey Jack cheese

Direction

- Heat the oil in a heavy saucepan, add the onion, green and red pepper and cook slowly until the vegetables are tender but not brown. At the same time bring a large pot of water to a boil for the pasta.
- Stir the garlic into the sauce, cook a moment longer then add the tomatoes. Simmer 10 to 15 minutes.
- Add the corn, salt and pepper and hot red pepper flakes. Continue to simmer the sauce for another five minutes or so.
- Meanwhiie, crumble the sausage in a skillet and saute it, stirring to break up the pieces, until they are lightly browned.
- Cook the penne until it is al dente, six to eight minutes. When the pasta is cooked, drain it well and transfer it to a warm serving dish. Toss with the sausage.
- Reheat the sauce, adding the butter. Pour over the pasta and toss. Sprinkle coriander on top and serve. Pass the grated cheese alongside.

212. Penne With Peas, Pea Greens And Parmesan

Serving: 4 servings | Prep: | Cook: | Ready in: 20mins

Ingredients

- 1 pound fresh peas, shelled (about 3/4 cup)
- 6 ounces pea shoots (tendrils, shoots, leaves) (1/2 big bunch), curly tendrils removed and discarded
- 1 tablespoon extra virgin olive oil
- 1 bunch young spring onions or scallions, cleaned and finely chopped (about 1/2 cup)
- Salt and freshly ground pepper
- 1 tablespoon chopped fresh tarragon
- 1 tablespoon chopped fresh parsley
- ¾ pound penne
- 1 to 2 ounces Parmesan, grated (1/4 to 1/2 cup, to taste)

Direction

- Begin heating a large pot of water for the pasta. Meanwhile, steam the peas over an inch of boiling water for 4 minutes, until just tender. Transfer to a bowl. Add the pea shoots to the steamer and steam 2 minutes, until just wilted. Remove from the heat and allow to cool until you can handle them. Do not discard the steaming water; pour it into a measuring cup. Squeeze out excess water from the pea greens and chop medium-fine. You should have about 1 cup chopped leaves and tender stems.
- Heat the olive oil over medium heat in a large skillet and add the chopped spring onion or scallions. Cook, stirring, until wilted, about 3 minutes. Add the pea shoots and stir together for about a minute. Season to taste with salt and pepper. Add the peas, tarragon and

parsley and about 1/4 cup of the steaming water and heat through.

- When the water in the pot comes to a boil, salt generously and add the pasta. Cook al dente, using the timing instructions on the package as a guide but checking the pasta a minute before the time indicated is up. When the pasta is ready, using a ladle transfer 1/2 cup of the pasta cooking water to the pan with the peas and pea shoots. Drain the pasta and toss at once with the vegetables and Parmesan. Serve hot.

Nutrition Information

- 426: calories;
- 6 grams: dietary fiber;
- 18 grams: protein;
- 426 milligrams: sodium;
- 8 grams: fat;
- 1 gram: polyunsaturated fat;
- 71 grams: carbohydrates;
- 3 grams: monounsaturated fat;
- 4 grams: sugars;

213. Perfect White Rice, Spanish Caribbean Style

Serving: Four to six servings | Prep: | Cook: | Ready in: 35mins

Ingredients

- 2 cups white rice
- About 2 1/2 tablespoons freshly squeezed lime juice
- 3 cups water
- 2 tablespoons olive oil
- Salt to taste

Direction

- Place the rice in a colander and rinse it thoroughly, adding a few drops of fresh lime juice to the rinsing water (the lime juice helps take away the musty smell that rice gets from sitting in the package).
- In a saucepan, bring the water, 1 tablespoon of the lime juice, 1 tablespoon of the olive oil and salt to a boil. (To make the con conor delicately flavored crusts of rice, use a very light pan; do not use a pot with an enamel or Teflon surface.)
- Stir in the rice. Return to a boil, cover tightly and simmer over low heat for 15 to 20 minutes, or until the rice is tender and dry.
- Turn off the heat and let stand for a few minutes. Gently stir in 1 tablespoon olive oil. The sides and bottom of the pan will be covered with a crust of browned rice, the con con Scrape off the browned bits and serve separately.

Nutrition Information

- 275: calories;
- 52 grams: carbohydrates;
- 0 grams: sugars;
- 4 grams: protein;
- 452 milligrams: sodium;
- 5 grams: fat;
- 1 gram: polyunsaturated fat;
- 3 grams: monounsaturated fat;

214. Persian Spinach, Potatoes And Peas

Serving: 2 servings | Prep: | Cook: | Ready in: 20mins

Ingredients

- 1 pound tiny new potatoes
- 12 ounces whole onion or 11 ounces ready-cut (2 1/4 to 2 1/2 cups)
- 2 teaspoons olive oil
- 2 cloves garlic
- 1 10-ounce package fresh spinach or 1 pound loose spinach

- 1 cup frozen peas
- ⅛ teaspoon nutmeg
- 1 cup nonfat plain yogurt
- ⅛ teaspoon salt
- Freshly ground black pepper to taste

Direction

- Scrub potatoes, and put in a pot with water to cover. Cover pot, and cook until fork-tender, about 20 minutes, depending on size.
- Chop whole onion. Saute onion in a nonstick pan in very hot oil over medium-high heat, until it begins to soften and brown.
- Mince garlic, and add to onion as it cooks.
- Wash spinach; remove tough stems, and cook spinach in covered pot in the water clinging to it, until it wilts, 4 or 5 minutes, stirring once or twice.
- Stir peas into onion mixture and cook 2 or 3 minutes.
- When spinach is cooked, drain it, thoroughly pressing the water out. Cut up and add to cooked onion, along with nutmeg and yogurt.
- When potatoes are cooked, drain and cut into bite-size pieces and stir into spinach mixture. Season with salt and pepper, and serve.

Nutrition Information

- 454: calories;
- 84 grams: carbohydrates;
- 23 grams: sugars;
- 22 grams: protein;
- 446 milligrams: sodium;
- 6 grams: fat;
- 3 grams: monounsaturated fat;
- 1 gram: polyunsaturated fat;
- 15 grams: dietary fiber;

215. Pheasant With Cabernet Sauce

Serving: Eight servings | Prep: | Cook: | Ready in: 40mins

Ingredients

- 2 tablespoons vegetable oil
- 2 pheasants (about 2 1/2 pounds each), each cut into 8 serving pieces
- Salt and freshly ground pepper to taste
- 4 tablespoons finely chopped shallots
- ½ cup finely diced carrots
- ½ cup finely diced celery
- 16 small white mushrooms
- 16 small white pearl onions
- 1 teaspoon finely chopped garlic
- 6 juniper berries
- 2 whole cloves
- 1 tablespoon butter
- 2 tablespoons flour
- 2 tablespoons Cognac
- 4 cups cabernet wine
- 1 cup fresh or canned chicken broth
- 1 bouquet garni consisting of 4 parsley sprigs, 1 bay leaf and 4 sprigs of fresh thyme or 1 teaspoon dried

Direction

- Heat the oil in large casserole or heavy cast-iron skillet over medium-high heat. Add the pheasant pieces skin side down. Sprinkle with salt and pepper to taste. Cook, stirring occasionally, until the meat is golden brown. Add the shallots, carrots, celery, mushrooms, pearl onions, garlic, juniper berries and cloves. Cook, stirring, until the vegetables are wilted, about 2 to 3 minutes.
- Drain the fat and add the butter and flour; stir and blend well. Pour the Cognac over the pheasant pieces and let it ignite.
- Add the wine, chicken broth and bouquet garni. Stir and blend well. Bring to a boil, cover and simmer about 30 minutes, or until

tender. Remove the bouquet garni and serve hot.

Nutrition Information

- 629: calories;
- 28 grams: fat;
- 8 grams: saturated fat;
- 0 grams: trans fat;
- 2 grams: dietary fiber;
- 3 grams: sugars;
- 57 grams: protein;
- 13 grams: monounsaturated fat;
- 4 grams: polyunsaturated fat;
- 11 grams: carbohydrates;
- 1186 milligrams: sodium;

216. Pho With Carrots, Turnips, Broccoli And Tofu

Serving: 6 servings | Prep: | Cook: | Ready in: 20mins

Ingredients

- 1 recipe vegetarian pho broth (see recipe)
- ½ pound firm tofu, cut in dominoes (optional)
- Soy sauce to taste (optional)
- 12 ounces soba or wide rice noodles
- 1 broccoli stem, peeled and cut in 1 1/2-inch julienne, steamed for 1 minute
- 1 broccoli crown, sliced thin and steamed for 1 minute
- 1 large carrot (about 5 ounces) peeled and cut in 1 1/2-inch julienne
- 1 medium turnip, peeled and cut in 1 1/2-inch julienne
- ½ cup Asian or purple basil leaves, slivered
- 4 scallions, chopped
- 1 cup chopped cilantro
- 2 to 4 bird or serrano chilies, sliced thin or finely chopped (to taste)
- 6 mint sprigs
- 3 to 4 limes, cut in wedges

Direction

- Have the broth at a simmer in a soup pot. Place the tofu in a bowl and season with soy sauce if desired.
- For soba: Bring 3 or 4 quarts of water to a boil in a large pot. Add the noodles gradually, so that the water remains at a boil, and stir once with a long-handled spoon or pasta fork so that they don't stick together. Wait for the water to come back up to a rolling boil; it will bubble up, so don't fill the pot all the way; and add 1 cup of cold water. Allow the water to come back to a rolling boil and add another cup of cold water. Allow the water to come to a boil one more time and add a third cup of water. When the water comes to a boil again, the noodles should be cooked through. Drain and divide among 6 large soup bowls. For rice noodles: Bring a large pot of water to a boil and add the noodles. Cook until just al dente, firm to the bite, following the timing instructions on the package (my wide noodles take about 5 minutes). Drain and divide among 6 large soup bowls.
- Add the turnips and carrots to the simmering broth and simmer until just tender, about 2 minutes. Divide the tofu and the steamed broccoli crowns and stems among the bowls. Ladle in the hot broth with carrots and turnips. Sprinkle on half the cilantro, half the basil leaves and the green onions. Pass the chopped chilies, the mint sprigs and the remaining basil and cilantro for guests to add as desired, and the lime wedges for guests to squeeze on. Serve with chopsticks for the noodles and soup spoons for the soup.

Nutrition Information

- 250: calories;
- 1 gram: fat;
- 0 grams: polyunsaturated fat;
- 56 grams: carbohydrates;
- 4 grams: dietary fiber;
- 3 grams: sugars;
- 5 grams: protein;

- 147 milligrams: sodium;

217. Pierogi Ruskie (Potato And Cheese Pierogi)

Serving: 24 to 30 pierogi | Prep: | Cook: | Ready in: 1hours30mins

Ingredients

- For the Dough:
- 2 cups/255 grams all-purpose flour (preferably unbleached), plus more as needed
- 1 teaspoon kosher salt
- 3 tablespoons unsalted butter
- 1 large egg, beaten
- For the Filling:
- ½ pound waxy or all-purpose potatoes
- Salt and pepper
- 3 tablespoons unsalted butter
- 3 medium yellow onions (about 8 ounces each), finely chopped
- ½ cup quark cheese, cottage cheese or sour cream (about 4 ounces)
- For Serving:
- Butter, for pan-frying (optional)
- Sour cream, for garnish
- Chopped fresh parsley or dill, for garnish

Direction

- Prepare the dough: Add the flour and salt to a large bowl; whisk to combine. In a small saucepan, heat 1/2 cup water and the butter over medium-high until butter is melted, about 3 minutes. Pour the buttery liquid into the flour gradually, stirring it in as you add it. (The dough will be quite crumbly and flaky at this point, like a biscuit dough.) Stir in the egg until combined then move the dough to a lightly floured surface and knead until smooth, 5 to 7 minutes. Cover the dough with a dampened towel or plastic wrap and let rest at room temperature for 30 minutes.
- Prepare the filling: Peel the potatoes and cut into 1-inch cubes. Add them to a large pot, sprinkle with 1 tablespoon salt and cover with cold water by about 2 inches. Bring to a boil over high and continue to cook at a simmer until potatoes are tender, about 25 minutes.
- While the potatoes cook, prepare the onions: In a large skillet, melt the butter over medium-high. Add the onions, season generously with salt and pepper, and cook, stirring occasionally, until golden-brown and softened, about 12 minutes. Set aside about 1 cup of onions for garnish and add the rest to a medium bowl.
- Transfer the cooked potatoes to a colander to drain, then transfer to the medium bowl with the onions. Add the cheese, stir to combine, season generously with salt and pepper, then let cool.
- Bring a large pot of heavily salted water to a boil over high.
- Prepare the wrappers: Cut the dough into two even pieces. (You'll want to leave one piece under the towel to stay moist while you work with the other piece.) You'll also want a small bowl of flour, a small bowl of water and a towel handy for keeping your hands clean. Dust some flour onto a baking sheet (for holding the pierogi) and your work surface, then roll out one portion of dough until 1/8-inch thick. Using a 3-inch cookie cutter or inverted glass, punch 12 to 15 disks of dough. (Save and refrigerate the scraps to boil as a rustic pasta, in soup or another use.)
- Assemble the pierogi: Working with one disk at time, spoon a scant tablespoon of filling onto the middle of it. Fold the dough in half to enclose the filling, bringing the edges together to form a crescent shape. Pinch the two sides together at the top, then work your way down on both sides, pinching the dough over the filling and pushing in the filling as needed, making sure the potato mixture does not break the seal. If needed, you can dip your fingertip into water and moisten the dough in spots as needed to help the two sides adhere together.

- To form a rustic pattern on the curved seal, pinch the rounded rim underneath using your pointer finger and middle finger and press an indentation on top with your thumb, working your way along the rounded rim. Transfer to the prepared baking sheet. (If you've gotten some filling on your fingers, dip your fingertips into the bowl of water then dry them off on the towel.)
- Repeat with remaining disks, then repeat the entire process with the remaining portion of dough. You'll want to work fairly quickly, as the pierogi can be harder to seal if they start to dry out. (If cooking the pierogi at a later point, transfer them on the baking sheet to the freezer until frozen solid, then transfer the pierogi to a resealable bag and freeze.)
- To cook the pierogi, add a single layer of pierogi to the pot of boiling water. Let them cook until they rise to the surface, about 2 minutes, then cook another 2 to 3 minutes until puffy. (With frozen dumplings, you will need to increase the cooking time by a couple of minutes.) Use a slotted spoon to transfer cooked dumplings to a colander to drain, then boil remaining dumplings.
- If you want to pan-fry your pierogi, working in batches, melt 1 to 2 tablespoons of butter in a large skillet over medium-high until crackling. Add a few boiled pierogi in a single layer to avoid overcrowding, and cook until crisp and golden, 1 to 2 minutes per side. Repeat with remaining pierogi, adding butter as needed.
- Serve hot. Top with any browned butter from the pan, warmed reserved onions, sour cream and herbs.

218. Pimms Gelée With Raspberries And Fromage Blanc

Serving: Serves 4 | Prep: | Cook: | Ready in: 15mins

Ingredients

- 16 ounces raspberries
- ¼ cup, plus 2 tablespoons, sugar
- 2 teaspoons unflavored gelatin
- ½ cup Pimms or a sweet rosé
- 1 tablespoon orange juice
- 1 cup fromage blanc

Direction

- In a small saucepan, mix 10 ounces of the raspberries and 1/4 cup sugar. Cook over medium heat until the sugar is dissolved and the raspberries are soft and breaking apart. Let cool.
- Soften the gelatin in 3 tablespoons of the Pimms. In another small saucepan, combine the orange juice and the remaining Pimms. Place over medium heat until very warm, then remove from heat and stir in the gelatin. Place a fine-meshed sieve over the pan and pour in the raspberries and their juice. Mash and press the raspberries to extract as much juice as possible. Pour into a shallow dish and chill until firm.
- Mix the fromage blanc with the remaining sugar. Using a whisk or fork, stir the Pimms gelée until broken into small beads. In each of 4 small tumblers, spoon a layer of Pimms gelée, using it all up. Top with a layer of fromage blanc, followed by a layer of fresh raspberries.

Nutrition Information

- 247: calories;
- 40 milligrams: sodium;
- 5 grams: fat;
- 2 grams: saturated fat;
- 7 grams: dietary fiber;
- 22 grams: sugars;
- 8 grams: protein;
- 0 grams: polyunsaturated fat;
- 33 grams: carbohydrates;

219. Pissaladieres

Serving: Two servings | Prep: | Cook: | Ready in: 15mins

Ingredients

- 1 loaf French or Italian bread (stale or fresh)
- 4 garlic cloves, halved
- About 1/4 cup extra-virgin olive oil
- 2 Italian plum tomatoes, sliced
- 8 anchovy fillets (preferably from whole Italian anchovies packed in salt)
- 8 calamata olives
- About 1/4 pound mozzarella cheese (plain or smoked), sliced

Direction

- Slice off 8 1/2-inch rounds of the bread and toast lightly.
- Rub each bread slice with a garlic clove half. With a pastry brush, apply a layer of olive oil to each slice.
- On each piece of bread, place a slice of plum tomato, an anchovy fillet, 2 olive halves; top with a slice of mozzarella. Place on a baking sheet and broil 2 to 3 minutes, or until the cheese bubbles and the toast threatens to ignite and burst into flames.

Nutrition Information

- 921: calories;
- 14 grams: saturated fat;
- 6 grams: dietary fiber;
- 32 grams: protein;
- 50 grams: fat;
- 27 grams: monounsaturated fat;
- 87 grams: carbohydrates;
- 4 grams: sugars;
- 2069 milligrams: sodium;

220. Pizza Fantasy

Serving: 2 servings | Prep: | Cook: | Ready in: 45mins

Ingredients

- 1 pound new potatoes
- Nonstick pan spray
- 12 ounces whole red or yellow peppers, or 11 ounces ready-cut (about 3 cups)
- 1 tablespoon olive oil
- 8 ounces whole zucchini, or 7 ounces ready-cut (about 1 1/3 cups)
- 6 ounces whole mushrooms, or 5 ounces ready-cut (2 cups)
- 4 7-to-8-inch flour tortillas (the no-oil variety, if possible)
- 10 medium imported olives
- 6 ounces cooked peeled shrimp
- ⅛ teaspoon salt
- 1 ounce Parmigiano Reggiano (1/3 cup grated)

Direction

- Prepare stove-top grill; turn oven to 450 degrees.
- Scrub and slice potatoes thin (less than 1/4-inch). Spray on both sides with nonstick pan spray, and grill until brown on both sides.
- Wash, trim, seed and slice whole peppers.
- Heat a large nonstick pan until very hot. Reduce heat to medium-high; add oil and saute peppers until soft.
- Meanwhile wash, trim and slice whole zucchini, and add.
- Wash, trim and slice whole mushrooms, and add. Cook until vegetables have softened.
- Wrap two tortillas in aluminum foil, and heat in oven or toaster oven for 3 to 5 minutes.
- Pit olives and stir into vegetables along with the shrimp and the grilled potatoes. Add salt.
- Grate cheese.
- Arrange half of the topping on two hot tortillas. Sprinkle with half the cheese.
- Heat remaining two tortillas while eating the first two, and add the rest of the topping.

Nutrition Information

- 814: calories;
- 6 grams: polyunsaturated fat;
- 0 grams: trans fat;
- 16 grams: monounsaturated fat;
- 107 grams: carbohydrates;
- 1701 milligrams: sodium;
- 30 grams: fat;
- 11 grams: dietary fiber;
- 8 grams: sugars;
- 35 grams: protein;

221. Platanos Maduros (Fried Yellow Plantains)

Serving: Six to eight servings | Prep: | Cook: | Ready in: 5mins

Ingredients

- 3 ripe yellow plantains
- Oil for frying

Direction

- Peel and slice the plantains in half crosswise, then again lengthwise. Cut each piece into 2 or 3 1/4-inch slices.
- Heat the oil (a depth of about 1/2 inch) in an cast-iron skillet until very hot. Add the plantain slices and fry until soft and golden brown, about 45 seconds to 1 minute.

Nutrition Information

- 171: calories;
- 1 gram: protein;
- 0 grams: trans fat;
- 6 grams: monounsaturated fat;
- 21 grams: carbohydrates;
- 2 grams: dietary fiber;
- 3 milligrams: sodium;
- 3 grams: polyunsaturated fat;
- 10 grams: sugars;

222. Poached Chicken Breasts With Tomatillos And Jalapeños

Serving: 4 servings | Prep: | Cook: | Ready in: 2hours

Ingredients

- 1 quart chicken stock, plus more as needed (or use salted water)
- 1 ¼ pounds boneless, skinless chicken breasts (3 medium breasts)
- 1 ½ pounds tomatillos, cut into 1/2-inch chunks
- 2 to 3 jalapeños, thinly sliced
- 6 tablespoons extra-virgin olive oil, plus more as needed
- ¾ teaspoon kosher salt, plus more as needed
- 1 teaspoon cumin seeds
- 4 garlic cloves, thinly sliced
- ¾ cup cilantro leaves, roughly chopped
- 3 scallions, thinly sliced
- Finely grated zest of 1/2 lime
- 1 avocado, sliced
- Fresh lime juice, to taste

Direction

- Place racks in the top and bottom third of the oven and heat to 275 degrees. In the microwave or in a small pot on the stove, heat chicken stock until it comes to a simmer.
- Place chicken in a small baking dish and cover with hot chicken stock.
- On a rimmed baking sheet, toss together tomatillos, jalapeños, 2 tablespoons oil, 3/4 teaspoon salt, and cumin seeds. Spread into a single layer on the sheet, then nudge the tomatillos aside to make room in 1 corner for a small ramekin. Fill ramekin with garlic and remaining 4 tablespoons oil or more as needed to cover the garlic.
- Place chicken on top oven rack until chicken is cooked through (a thermometer inserted in the

center should read 155 degrees), 55 minutes to 1 hour and 10 minutes. At the same time, bake tomatillos on bottom rack, tossing occasionally, until they are tender, and garlic is light golden, 1 to 1 1/2 hours. If chicken is ready before the tomatillos, remove it from the oven and leave it in the pan covered in stock to keep it warm until everything is done.
- Use a slotted spoon to remove garlic from oil and coarsely chop. Remove chicken from stock (save stock for another use; it can be frozen for up to 3 months), and slice the meat.
- To assemble, toss together tomatillos, chopped garlic, cilantro, scallions, lime zest and salt to taste. Drizzle fresh lime juice and garlic oil all over the chicken and avocado if you like, and season with salt. Serve with the tomatillo salsa.

Nutrition Information

- 573: calories;
- 26 grams: carbohydrates;
- 8 grams: dietary fiber;
- 12 grams: sugars;
- 765 milligrams: sodium;
- 36 grams: fat;
- 6 grams: saturated fat;
- 22 grams: monounsaturated fat;
- 39 grams: protein;
- 0 grams: trans fat;
- 5 grams: polyunsaturated fat;

223. Pork Burgers With Caraway

Serving: 4 servings | Prep: | Cook: | Ready in: 20mins

Ingredients

- 1 ½ pounds lean ground pork
- 1 teaspoon caraway seeds
- ½ teaspoon ground cumin
- Salt and freshly ground pepper to taste
- 1 tablespoon vegetable oil
- 1 tablespoon olive oil
- ½ cup finely chopped onion
- 1 teaspoon finely chopped garlic
- 1 tablespoon red-wine vinegar
- 4 ripe plum tomatoes, cut into 1/4-inch cubes
- 1 tablespoon chopped fresh sage or 2 teaspoons dried

Direction

- Place the pork in a mixing bowl. Add the caraway seeds, cumin, salt and pepper. Blend with the fingers. Do not overmix.
- Divide the mixture into 8 portions of equal size. Using the fingers, shape the portions into neat round flat patties about 1/2-inch thick.
- Heat the vegetable oil in a nonstick skillet over medium heat and add the patties. Cook on one side about 5 minutes. Turn and cook for 5 minutes more or until well done. Remove to a warm serving platter. Cover with foil and keep warm.
- Pour off the fat from the skillet and add the olive oil, onion and garlic. Cook until wilted. Do not brown the garlic. Add the vinegar, tomatoes, sage, salt and pepper. Cook, stirring, about 3 minutes. Pour over the patties and serve.

Nutrition Information

- 299: calories;
- 37 grams: protein;
- 14 grams: fat;
- 3 grams: sugars;
- 2 grams: dietary fiber;
- 7 grams: carbohydrates;
- 621 milligrams: sodium;
- 0 grams: trans fat;
- 8 grams: monounsaturated fat;

224. Pork Chops Baked With Apples And Onions

Serving: Four servings | Prep: | Cook: | Ready in: 30mins

Ingredients

- 1 teaspoon vegetable oil
- 4 1/2-inch-thick pork chops
- 1 medium onion, peeled and thinly sliced
- ¼ cup sherry
- ¼ cup apple cider
- 3 large Macintosh apples, peeled, cored and cut into 1/4-inch-thick slices
- ½ teaspoon salt, plus more to taste
- Freshly ground pepper to taste

Direction

- Preheat oven to 350 degrees. Heat the vegetable oil in a large, ovenproof skillet over medium-high heat. Add the pork chops and sear until golden brown, about 1 1/2 minutes per side. Place the pork chops on a plate and set aside.
- Add the onion to the skillet and cook, stirring often, for 2 minutes. Add the sherry and the cider and cook, stirring contantly, scraping up any browned bits stuck to the bottom of the pan. Add the apples, 1/2 teaspoon salt and pepper to taste. Lower the heat and cook for 5 minutes.
- Push the pork chops down into the apple mixture and pour any juices accumulated on the plate over them. Cover with foil and bake until the pork chops are tender and cooked through, about 15 minutes. Uncover and season with additional salt and pepper to taste. Divide among 4 plates and serve.

Nutrition Information

- 467: calories;
- 6 grams: saturated fat;
- 3 grams: polyunsaturated fat;
- 42 grams: protein;
- 29 grams: carbohydrates;
- 5 grams: dietary fiber;
- 404 milligrams: sodium;
- 20 grams: sugars;
- 0 grams: trans fat;
- 8 grams: monounsaturated fat;

225. Pork Chops Smothered With Fennel And Garlic

Serving: Four servings | Prep: | Cook: | Ready in: 45mins

Ingredients

- 2 teaspoons vegetable oil
- 4 center-cut loin pork chops, 1 inch thick
- 4 to 8 cloves garlic, peeled and slivered
- 1 ¼ cups chicken broth
- ⅔ cup dry white wine
- 2 fennel bulbs, trimmed, quartered, and cut into very thin slices
- 2 teaspoons cornstarch
- Salt, freshly ground pepper

Direction

- Preheat oven to 225 degrees.
- Heat oil in a large skillet over medium-high heat. Pat chops dry and add to skillet. Cook 5 to 6 minutes on each side or until deep golden brown. Pour off fat.
- Remove skillet from heat (leave pork chops in skillet) and add garlic. Cook 1 minute in the hot skillet.
- Return skillet to heat and add 1 cup broth, the wine and fennel, and bring to a boil. Lower heat and simmer covered 5 minutes.
- Remove chops to a pie plate or other ovenproof dish and cover lightly with foil (set skillet aside). Place chops in the oven and cook 10 to 15 minutes, or until a meat thermometer registers 160 degrees when placed near the bone.
- Meanwhile, simmer the sauce in the skillet 5 minutes or until reduced slightly.

- In a small cup or bowl mix remaining 1/4 cup broth (it should be cold or room temperature) with the cornstarch. Add this mixture to the sauce and boil 1 minute, or until lightly thickened. Taste, adding salt and pepper, if desired. Serve chops "smothered" with sauce.

Nutrition Information

- 465: calories;
- 6 grams: sugars;
- 9 grams: monounsaturated fat;
- 15 grams: carbohydrates;
- 1016 milligrams: sodium;
- 21 grams: fat;
- 0 grams: trans fat;
- 3 grams: polyunsaturated fat;
- 4 grams: dietary fiber;
- 45 grams: protein;

226. Potato Gratin

Serving: 6 servings | Prep: | Cook: | Ready in: 1hours40mins

Ingredients

- Light vegetable-oil cooking spray
- 3 medium baking potatoes, thinly sliced
- 2 tablespoons flour
- ¼ teaspoon salt, optional
- 1 medium onion, trimmed, thinly sliced and separated into rings
- ⅛ teaspoon cayenne pepper
- 1 teaspoon paprika
- ½ teaspoon freshly ground black pepper
- 2 tablespoons freshly grated Parmesan cheese
- 1 small zucchini, trimmed and thinly sliced
- ¼ teaspoon ground nutmeg
- ½ teaspoon Spike seasoning (an herb mixture available in supermarkets)
- 12 ounces evaporated skim milk
- 2 tablespoons chopped fresh parsley

Direction

- Preheat the oven to 400 degrees.
- Coat an 11-inch gratin dish or glass pie plate with 3 sprays of the vegetable oil.
- Layer a third of the potatoes over the bottom of the prepared gratin dish or pie plate, overlapping the slices in a spiral pattern. Sprinkle 1 tablespoon of the flour and some of the optional salt over the potatoes; arrange the onion rings on top. Dust with the cayenne pepper and 1/2-teaspoon of the paprika.
- Layer another third of the potatoes, adding the remaining tablespoon of flour, the black pepper and 1 tablespoon of the Parmesan cheese.
- For the next layer, scatter the zucchini, and dust with the nutmeg, Spike seasoning and remaining optional salt. Top with a spiral layer of the remaining potatoes.
- Pour the evaporated milk over the gratin, and add the remaining paprika and Parmesan cheese.
- Cover with aluminum foil, and bake for 45 minutes. Remove the foil, lower the oven to 350 degrees and bake for about 15 minutes more, until the top is golden brown. Remove from the oven, and allow to cool for 10 minutes.
- Garnish with chopped parsley.

Nutrition Information

- 171: calories;
- 4 grams: fat;
- 27 grams: carbohydrates;
- 5 grams: sugars;
- 7 grams: protein;
- 1 gram: polyunsaturated fat;
- 0 grams: trans fat;
- 2 grams: dietary fiber;
- 103 milligrams: sodium;

227. Potato Lasagnas With Monkfish And Shallot Vinaigrette

Serving: Serves 4 | Prep: | Cook: | Ready in: 45mins

Ingredients

- 2 large Idaho potatoes (about 1 pound each, skins removed)
- 4 6-ounce pieces of center-cut monkfish
- 1 ½ tablespoons olive oil
- Salt and freshly ground pepper
- 5 tablespoons clarified butter
- 1 tablespoon balsamic vinegar
- 3 tablespoons olive oil mixed with 1 tablespoon water
- 2 tablespoons chopped chives
- 3 teaspoons shallots
- 1 cup mixed salad greens

Direction

- Preheat oven to 350 degrees.
- Cut each potato into a brick, 3 by 1 3/4 inches. Place in cold water.
- Brush the monkfish fillets with the undiluted olive oil and season with salt and pepper. Lay a fillet on the edge of a sheet of aluminum foil. Roll the fillet tightly in the foil to form a cylinder and twist the ends tightly to secure. Repeat with the other fillets.
- Cut each potato brick into 20 thin slices (roughly 1/8-inch thick). Brush the slices with clarified butter and place on a cookie sheet that has been lined with wax paper and greased with clarified butter. Season well with salt and pepper. Cover tightly with aluminum foil. Place the potatoes on the bottom shelf of the preheated oven. Bake for 12 to 15 minutes (they should still be slightly undercooked). Brush again with clarified butter. Set aside, covered.
- Boil water in the bottom of a steamer. Place the monkfish rolls on the top rack of the steamer. Cover and cook for about 15 minutes, turning the rolls 3 times. Remove from the steamer rack and let sit for 5 minutes.
- In a mixing bowl, whisk together the vinaigrette ingredients: balsamic vinegar, olive oil with water, chives, shallots and salt and pepper to taste. Toss well with greens, and taste for seasoning.
- To assemble the dish, unwrap the monkfish fillets. Slice each fillet widthwise into four equal pieces. Lay 1 rectangle of potato on a warm serving plate. Place a slice of fish over it. Lay another potato slice on top, followed by another slice of fish. Repeat until you have 5 potato slices holding 4 layers of fish. Repeat with rest of the potatoes and fish. Garnish with mixed greens tossed in vinaigrette.

Nutrition Information

- 556: calories;
- 34 grams: carbohydrates;
- 13 grams: saturated fat;
- 16 grams: monounsaturated fat;
- 5 grams: dietary fiber;
- 2 grams: sugars;
- 29 grams: protein;
- 939 milligrams: sodium;
- 3 grams: polyunsaturated fat;

228. Potato And Goat Cheese Pizza With Rosemary

Serving: 4 main-course servings | Prep: | Cook: | Ready in: 2hours25mins

Ingredients

- Basic dough (see recipe)
- 2 large baking potatoes, preferably long and thin
- 2 tablespoons plus 1/2 teaspoon olive oil
- 1 teaspoon salt
- Freshly ground pepper to taste
- 4 ounces goat cheese, crumbled

- 2 teaspoons minced fresh rosemary

Direction

- Prepare the dough and roll it out according to directions in basic dough recipe. While dough is rising, preheat oven to 375 degrees. Peel the potatoes, and cut them crosswise into slices 1/8-inch thick. Toss the slices with 1/2 teaspoon of the olive oil and place them in a single layer on a large baking sheet. Bake until the slices are tender, about 15 minutes.
- Increase oven temperature to 425 degrees. When the dough is rolled out, arrange the potato slices over the dough in concentric circles. Season with the salt and pepper. Sprinkle with the crumbled goat cheese and rosemary. Drizzle the remaining 2 tablespoons olive oil over the top, and bake until the crust is golden brown, about 20 minutes. Cut into wedges, and serve immediately.

229. Potato And Pea Patties With Indian Spices

Serving: 8 patties | Prep: | Cook: | Ready in: 45mins

Ingredients

- ¾ pound sweet potatoes, preferably light-fleshed, baked and cooled
- ½ pound red boiling potatoes, scrubbed and quartered
- ½ cup finely chopped fresh cilantro leaves
- 6 tablespoons grape seed oil
- 2 dried red chiles, coarsely ground in a mortar and pestle or spice mill, or 1/2 to 3/4 teaspoon red pepper flakes (to taste)
- 1 tablespoon coriander seeds
- 2 teaspoons cumin seeds
- ¼ teaspoon cayenne pepper
- 2 teaspoons fresh lemon juice
- Salt to taste (Suvir Saran uses about 1 1/2 teaspoons kosher salt)
- 1 cup frozen peas, thawed, or 1 cup fresh peas, steamed or boiled for 5 minutes
- 1 cup panko or chickpea flour (you will not use all of it)

Direction

- Peel cooled baked sweet potatoes and place in a large bowl.
- Place quartered red potatoes in a steamer over 1 inch of boiling water and steam for 15 to 20 minutes, until tender. Remove from heat and add to bowl with sweet potatoes. Mash potatoes together. The red skins will fall apart. Stir in cilantro.
- Combine 2 tablespoons of the oil with ground red chiles or red pepper flakes, coriander seeds and cumin seeds in a large, heavy skillet and heat over medium-high heat until cumin is fragrant and golden-brown, 1 to 2 minutes. Stir in cayenne and then scrape in potato mixture and salt to taste. Stir in peas and cook just until potatoes and peas are warmed through, about 2 minutes, stirring and scraping the bottom of the skillet often to work in any browned bits. Transfer mixture to a large bowl. Stir in lemon juice, taste and adjust salt, and set aside to cool completely.
- Take up about 1/3 cup of the mixture and form into a ball (you can wet your hands to reduce sticking). Roll ball in the panko or chickpea flour, then gently flatten into a patty. Set on a plate and continue with the rest of the mixture. Refrigerate uncovered for 1 hour or longer (the longer the better).
- When you're ready to cook, place a rack over a sheet pan. Heat 2 tablespoons of oil in a 12-inch, heavy nonstick frying pan over high heat. Swirl pan to coat with the hot oil. Lower heat to medium. Place 4 to 5 patties in the pan (do not crowd), and cook until well browned on one side, about 4 minutes. Turn and brown for about 4 more minutes. Remove to rack. Heat remaining oil in the pan and cook remaining patties. Keep patties warm in a low oven until ready to serve. Serve with a salad and your choice of toppings, such as the usual

(ketchup, mustard, relish), or yogurt raita, garlic yogurt, or chutney.

Nutrition Information

- 211: calories;
- 11 grams: fat;
- 1 gram: saturated fat;
- 2 grams: monounsaturated fat;
- 5 grams: protein;
- 263 milligrams: sodium;
- 8 grams: polyunsaturated fat;
- 23 grams: carbohydrates;
- 4 grams: sugars;

230. Potato, Grilled Pancetta And Chive Salad

Serving: 4 servings | Prep: | Cook: | Ready in: 25mins

Ingredients

- 2 pounds Yukon Gold potatoes
- 4 slices pancetta, grilled until crisp
- 1 tablespoon Dijon mustard
- 1 clove garlic
- 2 to 3 tablespoons balsamic vinegar (or to taste)
- Coarse salt and freshly ground pepper to taste
- ¾ cup extra-virgin olive oil
- 1 bunch fresh chives, minced

Direction

- Steam the potatoes until tender (about 20 minutes). Crumble the pancetta.
- Make the dressing. Place the mustard in a bowl large enough to hold the potatoes. Peel the garlic and crush it into the mustard with a fork. Add the vinegar, salt and pepper. Gradually beat in the olive oil, a little at a time, creating an emulsion.
- When the potatoes are cooked, remove the garlic from the dressing. Add the potatoes and

chives and toss thoroughly. Serve at room temperature and correct seasoning just before serving.

Nutrition Information

- 669: calories;
- 52 grams: fat;
- 0 grams: trans fat;
- 6 grams: polyunsaturated fat;
- 43 grams: carbohydrates;
- 4 grams: sugars;
- 10 grams: saturated fat;
- 35 grams: monounsaturated fat;
- 5 grams: dietary fiber;
- 9 grams: protein;
- 732 milligrams: sodium;

231. Provençal Artichoke Ragout

Serving: Serves 6 to 8 | Prep: | Cook: | Ready in: 1hours15mins

Ingredients

- 2 pounds baby artichokes or globe artichokes if baby artichokes aren't available, trimmed (see below)
- 1 lemon, cut in half
- 2 tablespoons olive oil
- 1 large sweet onion, such as Vidalia or Maui, chopped, or 1 bunch of spring onions, chopped
- 2 celery stalks, from the inner hart, sliced
- 1 large or 2 small red bell peppers, diced
- 4 large garlic cloves, minced or pressed
- Salt
- 1 28-ounce can chopped tomatoes with juice, peeled, seeded and chopped
- ¾ to 1 cup water, as needed
- Freshly ground pepper
- 1 teaspoon fresh thyme leaves, or 1/2 teaspoon dried thyme

- 1 bay leaf
- 2 to 4 tablespoons chopped fresh basil or parsley
- 2 to 3 teaspoons fresh lemon juice

Direction

- How to trim artichokes: Fill a bowl with water, and add the juice of 1/2 lemon. Cut the stems off the artichokes, and with a sharp knife, cut away the tops — about 1/2 inch from the top for baby artichokes, 1 inch for larger artichokes. Rub the cut parts with the other half of the lemon. Break off the tough outer leaves until you reach the lighter green leaves near the middle. With a paring knife, trim the bottom of the bulb right above the stem by holding the knife at an angle and cutting around the artichoke, until you reach the light flesh beneath the tough bottoms of the leaves. Cut small baby artichokes in half, or large artichokes into quarters, and cut away the chokes if the artichokes are mature. Immediately place in the bowl of acidulated water.
- Heat the oil in a large, heavy nonstick skillet or casserole over medium heat, and add the onion and celery. Cook, stirring, until tender, about three to five minutes. Add the red pepper and about 1/4 teaspoon salt, and stir together for three to five minutes until the pepper begins to soften. Add the garlic, and stir together for another minute, until the garlic is fragrant. Add the tomatoes and a little more salt, and cook, stirring from time to time, for 10 minutes, until the tomatoes have cooked down and smell fragrant. Add the artichokes, thyme, bay leaf and enough water to cover the artichokes halfway, and bring to a simmer. Add salt and pepper, then cover and simmer 30 to 40 minutes, until the artichokes are tender and the sauce fragrant. Check from time to time and add water if necessary. Add the lemon juice, taste and adjust salt and pepper.

Nutrition Information

- 113: calories;
- 4 grams: sugars;
- 1 gram: polyunsaturated fat;
- 3 grams: monounsaturated fat;
- 19 grams: carbohydrates;
- 9 grams: dietary fiber;
- 5 grams: protein;
- 643 milligrams: sodium;

232. Prune Plum And Peach Compote

Serving: Forty servings | Prep: | Cook: | Ready in: 20mins

Ingredients

- 4 pounds prune plums
- 12 to 15 sprigs fresh mint, washed and tied with kitchen string
- 3 cups fruit preserves (a mixture of plum, raspberry and blueberry jam and currant jelly)
- 3 cups (1 bottle) dry red wine (a cabernet or merlot)
- 3 pounds ripe but firm peaches

Direction

- Halve the prune plums and discard the pits. Place the plums in a large stainless-steel saucepan with the mint, jam and wine.
- Peel the peaches with a sharp paring knife or vegetable peeler and cut each of them into six wedges, discarding the pits.
- Bring the plum mixture to a boil, stirring occasionally, and boil gently, covered, for 2 minutes. Add the peach wedges and bring the mixture back to a boil. Immediately remove the saucepan from the heat and let the mixture cool in the pan. When at room temperature, transfer to a bowl, cover with plastic wrap and refrigerate for at least 4 to 5 hours but for up to 5 to 6 days.
- At serving time, remove and discard the mint.

Nutrition Information

- 204: calories;
- 4 grams: dietary fiber;
- 32 grams: sugars;
- 1 gram: protein;
- 9 milligrams: sodium;
- 0 grams: polyunsaturated fat;
- 49 grams: carbohydrates;

233. Pumpkin Ginger Pie

Serving: 6 to 8 servings. | Prep: | Cook: | Ready in: 1hours10mins

Ingredients

- 2 cups cooked, strained pumpkin
- 1 ¼ cups lightly packed light brown sugar
- ½ teaspoon salt
- 1 ½ teaspoons cinnamon
- ¼ teaspoon freshly grated nutmeg
- 2 tablespoons finely chopped crystalized ginger, plus extra for garnish
- Grated zest of 1 lemon, orange or tangerine
- 2 eggs, well beaten
- 2 tablespoons brandy
- 1 tablespoon bourbon
- 1 partly baked 9-inch pie shell

Direction

- Preheat oven to 325 degrees.
- Combine all the ingredients for the filling and beat well. Pour into the partly baked pie shell.
- Bake for about 50 minutes or until the center of the pie is set. Garnish with a little crystalized ginger.

Nutrition Information

- 300: calories;
- 1 gram: dietary fiber;
- 52 grams: carbohydrates;
- 35 grams: sugars;
- 279 milligrams: sodium;
- 8 grams: fat;
- 3 grams: protein;
- 0 grams: trans fat;

234. Pumpkin Seed Battered 'Chicken' With Cranberry Cabernet Sauce

Serving: 6 servings. | Prep: | Cook: | Ready in: 20mins

Ingredients

- Cranberry Cabernet Sauce
- 3 tablespoons olive oil
- 1 large shallot, diced
- 4 sprigs thyme
- ¼ cup dried cranberries
- Salt to taste
- Pepper to taste
- 1 cup Cabernet wine
- 1 cup vegetable stock
- 1 tablespoon arrowroot powder
- 2 tablespoons water
- 3 tablespoons non-hydrogenated margarine, divided
- Pumpkin Seed Battered Cutlets
- 1 tablespoon minced fresh sage
- 1 cup toasted, shelled pumpkin seeds
- 1 teaspoon paprika
- 1 cup panko breadcrumbs
- 2 tablespoons nutritional yeast
- Salt to taste
- Pepper to taste
- 12 vegan "chicken" cutlets, thawed
- 1 cup unbleached white flour
- 2 cups unsweetened soy milk
- Olive oil

Direction

- Make the sauce. In a sauté pan over medium heat, heat olive oil. Add shallot and sauté for 3 minutes. Add thyme and cranberries and

sauté for another 2 minutes. Season with salt and pepper. Add wine and scrape the bottom of the pan, then cook until the liquid is reduced by half.
- Add vegetable stock and reduce by half again. In a small bowl, combine arrowroot and water. Add the arrowroot mixture to the pan, stir well, and continue to cook for 2 minutes. Turn off heat and whisk in margarine, 1 tablespoon at a time. Remove thyme stems before serving.
- To make the cutlets, use a food processor to combine sage, pumpkin seeds, paprika, breadcrumbs, nutritional yeast, salt and pepper until well incorporated.
- Dredge each cutlet in flour, dip into soy milk, and then into seasoned breadcrumbs.
- Heat olive oil in a large sauté pan. Using medium-high heat, sauté cutlets on each side until browned and crisp. Serve with the cranberry Cabernet sauce.

235. Pumpkin Soup

Serving: Serves 4 to 6 | Prep: | Cook: | Ready in: 1hours30mins

Ingredients

- 1 3- to 3 1/2-pound pumpkin, halved, scraped and seeded
- 2 tablespoons sweet butter
- 1 large white potato, peeled and cut into 1/2-inch cubes
- 2 leeks, cleaned and trimmed, leaving about 1/2 inch of the green, chopped
- 3 cups chicken stock
- 3 cups water
- Salt and white pepper to taste
- ⅓ cup cream
- Freshly grated nutmeg to taste

Direction

- Cut the pumpkin halves into 4 to 6 wedges each and remove the rind. Chop pumpkin flesh into chunks about 3/4 inch thick.
- In a deep soup pot, melt the butter over medium-low heat and cook the potatoes, leeks and pumpkin for about 20 minutes, stirring occasionally.
- Add chicken stock and water to the pot, cover, bring to a boil, reduce heat and simmer for 1 hour or until pumpkin chunks are soft.
- Add the soup to the bowl of an electric blender or food mill, a little at a time, and puree well. When all the soup is pureed, return it to the soup pot over medium heat. Salt and pepper to taste. Add cream and stir. Add grated nutmeg to taste, stir and serve. (For a dramatic note, the soup can be served in a well-cleaned pumpkin that has been warmed in the oven.)

236. Pureed Potatoes With Carrots And Onions

Serving: Four servings | Prep: | Cook: | Ready in: 35mins

Ingredients

- 3 potatoes, about 1 1/4 pounds
- 4 carrots, trimmed, scraped and cut into 1-inch lengths (about 2 cups)
- ½ cup sliced onions
- Salt to taste
- 2 tablespoons butter
- Freshly ground pepper to taste
- ⅛ teaspoon freshly grated nutmeg
- ½ cup hot milk
- 2 tablespoons chopped parsley (optional)

Direction

- Peel the potatoes and cut them into eighths. Place the carrots, sliced onions and potatoes in a saucepan. Add cold water to cover and salt to taste. Bring to a boil and simmer about 20 minutes or until the vegetables are tender. Do not overcook or they will become mushy.

- Put the vegetables through a food mill or potato ricer. Blend until smooth, but no more. Return to a clean saucepan.
- Add more salt (if necessary), the butter, pepper and nutmeg and blend well. Place over low heat and stir in the milk, then the parsley. Serve.

Nutrition Information

- 184: calories;
- 594 milligrams: sodium;
- 7 grams: fat;
- 4 grams: protein;
- 0 grams: polyunsaturated fat;
- 2 grams: monounsaturated fat;
- 28 grams: carbohydrates;
- 6 grams: sugars;

237. Puréed Beets With Yogurt And Caraway

Serving: 2 2/3 cups, serving 6 to 8 | Prep: | Cook: | Ready in:

Ingredients

- 1 ½ pounds beets (4 medium), roasted beets
- 2 garlic cloves, crushed
- 1 cup plain Greek yogurt
- 1 tablespoon agave syrup or date syrup
- 3 tablespoons olive oil, plus additional for drizzling
- 1 teaspoon ground caraway seeds
- ⅛ to ¼ teaspoon cayenne, to taste
- Salt to taste
- For garnish: a handful of chopped, toasted almonds (2 to 4 tablespoons)
- Pita bread for serving

Direction

- Peel beets and cut into wedges. Allow to cool completely.
- Turn on a food processor fitted with a steel blade and drop in garlic. When it is chopped and adhering to the sides of the bowl, stop machine and scrape down bowl with a spatula. Add beets and pulse to finely chop. Add yogurt and process to a smooth purée. Add agave nectar or date syrup, olive oil, caraway, cayenne and salt to taste and process until well blended.
- Mound into a wide bowl and run a fork over the surface. Drizzle on a little bit of olive oil, sprinkle with almonds and serve with pita bread.

Nutrition Information

- 77: calories;
- 0 grams: polyunsaturated fat;
- 8 grams: sugars;
- 290 milligrams: sodium;
- 2 grams: fat;
- 1 gram: saturated fat;
- 11 grams: carbohydrates;
- 3 grams: dietary fiber;
- 4 grams: protein;

238. Puréed Broccoli And Celery Soup

Serving: Serves 6 | Prep: | Cook: | Ready in: 45mins

Ingredients

- 1 tablespoon extra virgin olive oil
- 1 medium onion, chopped
- 4 stalks celery, diced
- 2 to 4 garlic cloves, to taste, minced
- 2 pounds broccoli, mostly crowns, chopped; stems, if using, peeled and diced
- 6 ounces potatoes, peeled and diced, or 1/2 cup medium grain rice
- 2 quarts water or vegetable stock

- A bouquet garni made with a bay leaf, a Parmesan rind, and a couple of sprigs each thyme and parsley
- Salt and freshly ground pepper to taste
- 1 ½ ounces spinach leaves or baby spinach (1 cup, tightly packed)
- 2 tablespoons chopped fresh herbs, such as parsley, tarragon, chives, for garnish
- optional garnishes
- A drizzle of olive oil
- a swirl of crème fraiche or plain yogurt
- a sprinkle of freshly grated Parmesan

Direction

- Heat the olive oil over medium heat in a large, heavy soup pot or Dutch oven and add the onion and celery. Cook, stirring, until tender, about 5 to 8 minutes. Do not allow these ingredients to brown. Add a generous pinch of salt to prevent this from happening (the salt draws out liquid from the vegetables). Add the garlic and cook, stirring, until the garlic smells fragrant, 30 seconds to 1 minute.
- Add the broccoli, potatoes or rice, water or stock, bouquet garni, and salt, and bring to a boil. Reduce the heat, cover and simmer 30 minutes. Remove the bouquet garni. Stir in the spinach and let sit for a minute off the heat. Add freshly ground pepper, taste and adjust salt.
- Using a hand blender, or in batches in a regular blender, purée the soup. If using a regular blender fill only half way and cover the top with a towel pulled down tight, rather than airtight with the lid, because hot soup will jump and push the top off if the blender is closed airtight. Return to the pot and heat through, stirring. Adjust seasoning to taste with salt and pepper. Serve, topping each bowl with a sprinkle of chopped herbs and with other garnishes of your choice.

Nutrition Information

- 158: calories;
- 0 grams: polyunsaturated fat;
- 22 grams: carbohydrates;
- 9 grams: protein;
- 1355 milligrams: sodium;
- 6 grams: sugars;
- 2 grams: monounsaturated fat;

239. Puréed Trahana And Vegetable Soup

Serving: Serves 6 to 8 | Prep: | Cook: | Ready in: 1hours

Ingredients

- 3 tablespoons extra virgin olive oil
- 1 large red or yellow onion, chopped
- Salt to taste
- 2 garlic cloves, minced
- ¾ pound carrots, diced
- 2 large leeks, white and light green parts only, rinsed of all sand and chopped
- 1 1/2 cups sour bulgur trahana
- 2 quarts vegetable stock, chicken stock or water
- A bouquet garni made with a bay leaf and a couple of sprigs each parsley and thyme or oregano
- Freshly ground pepper
- Additional olive oil and chopped fresh herbs such as dill, parsley or mint, for garnish
- Red pepper flakes or cayenne for garnish (optional)

Direction

- Heat 2 tablespoons of olive oil over medium heat in a heavy soup pot and add onion. Cook, stirring often, until onion is soft, 5 to 8 minutes, and add a generous pinch of salt, garlic, carrots and leeks. Continue to cook, stirring often, until carrots and leeks are beginning to soften, 3 to 5 minutes.
- Add remaining olive oil and stir in trahana. Stir until trahana is coated with oil, about 1 minute, and add stock or water and bouquet garni. Bring to a boil, add salt to taste, reduce

heat and simmer 30 minutes, until vegetables are tender and trahana has fallen apart in the soup and is tender. Taste and adjust salt. Remove and discard bouquet garni.

- For a coarse purée, use an immersion blender to purée the soup. For a finer purée, transfer, in batches, to a blender or a food processor. If using a blender do not put the top on tight; leave out the center of the lid and cover tightly with a towel. Purée until smooth and if desired, strain. Return to the pot, taste and adjust salt. Add freshly ground pepper to taste.
- Reheat gently and serve, garnishing each serving with a drizzle of olive oil and a sprinkling of herbs. If you want spice, sprinkle with red pepper flakes or a little bit of cayenne.

Nutrition Information

- 181: calories;
- 4 grams: protein;
- 31 grams: carbohydrates;
- 805 milligrams: sodium;
- 6 grams: dietary fiber;
- 1 gram: polyunsaturated fat;

240. Puréed Winter Squash Soup With Ginger

Serving: 4 to 6 servings | Prep: | Cook: | Ready in: 1hours30mins

Ingredients

- 1 tablespoon canola or rice bran oil
- 1 medium onion, chopped
- 1 carrot, diced
- 2 pounds peeled winter squash, like butternut or kabocha
- 2 garlic cloves, minced
- 1 tablespoon minced ginger
- 6 ½ cups water, chicken stock or vegetable stock
- ⅓ cup rice
- Salt and freshly ground pepper
- ½ teaspoon ginger juice (made by grating a teaspoon of fresh ginger, wrapping in cheesecloth and squeezing the cheesecloth)
- Pinch of freshly grated nutmeg
- ½ lime
- 4 to 6 tablespoons plain yogurt

Direction

- Heat the oil over medium heat in a large, heavy soup pot or Dutch oven and add the onion and carrot. Cook, stirring, until the vegetables are tender, about 5 minutes. Add the winter squash, garlic and minced ginger and cook, stirring, until the mixture smells fragrant, about 1 minute
- Add the water or stock, the rice and salt to taste and bring to a boil. Reduce the heat, cover and simmer 45 minutes to 1 hour, until the squash is very tender
- Using a hand blender, or in batches in a regular blender, purée the soup. If using a regular blender, cover the top with a towel pulled down tight, rather than airtight with the lid. Return to the pot and heat through. Stir in the ginger juice, taste and season with salt and pepper. If desired, thin out with a little more water or stock
- Ladle the soup into bowls and add a tablespoon of yogurt (more to taste), then slowly swirl the yogurt into the soup with a spoon. Squeeze a few drops of lime juice onto each serving and sprinkle with whisper of nutmeg

Nutrition Information

- 154: calories;
- 5 grams: sugars;
- 1094 milligrams: sodium;
- 3 grams: protein;
- 1 gram: polyunsaturated fat;
- 32 grams: carbohydrates;

- 4 grams: dietary fiber;

241. Quick Chile Sauce

Serving: 1 1/2 cups | Prep: | Cook: | Ready in: 5mins

Ingredients

- 9 Fresno chiles (about 5 ounces/140 grams) or other medium-heat chiles, preferably red, such as jalapeño or serrano, destemmed and roughly chopped
- 1 ¼ teaspoons kosher salt
- 3 ounces/85 grams cherry tomatoes (about 12) or 1 small vine tomato, roughly chopped
- 3 tablespoons white wine vinegar, apple cider vinegar or other light vinegar
- ¼ cup/60 milliliters extra-virgin olive oil

Direction

- Place the chiles and salt in the bowl of a food processor, and pulse a few times until chiles are chopped. (You don't want to go too far and turn them into paste.)
- Add the tomatoes and vinegar, and pulse again in two or three short bursts, just enough to break down the tomatoes.
- Transfer to a lidded container and top with the oil. Cover and keep in the fridge up to 1 week.

242. Quick Quesadilla With Dukkah

Serving: 1 serving | Prep: | Cook: | Ready in: 10mins

Ingredients

- 2 corn tortillas
- 1 ounce melting cheese, like Monterey Jack, mozzarella or Mexican string cheese, shredded
- ½ to 1 teaspoon pumpkin seed dukkah (to taste) (see recipe)

Direction

- Top one of the tortillas with the cheese and the dukkah. Place the other tortilla on top. Zap for 1 minute in the microwave, or heat in a dry skillet, flipping the quesadilla from time to time, until the cheese melts. The tortilla will be crispier using the pan method. Cut into quarters and serve.

Nutrition Information

- 225: calories;
- 1 gram: sugars;
- 23 grams: carbohydrates;
- 10 grams: fat;
- 5 grams: saturated fat;
- 3 grams: dietary fiber;
- 11 grams: protein;
- 41 milligrams: sodium;
- 0 grams: trans fat;

243. Quinoa And Carrot Kugel

Serving: 6 servings | Prep: | Cook: | Ready in: 2hours

Ingredients

- 2 tablespoons extra virgin olive oil
- ½ medium onion, finely chopped
- ½ cup quinoa
- 1 ¼ cups water
- Salt to taste
- 1 pound carrots, peeled and cut into 3-inch-long sticks
- ½ cup low-fat cottage cheese
- 3 eggs
- 1 scant teaspoon caraway seeds, lightly crushed
- Freshly ground pepper

Direction

- Heat 1 tablespoon of the olive oil in a medium saucepan and add the onion. Cook, stirring, until the onion is just about tender, 3 to 5 minutes, and add the quinoa. Cook, stirring, for another 2 to 3 minutes, until the quinoa begins to smell toasty and the onion is tender. Add the water and salt to taste and bring to a boil. Add the carrots, cover, reduce the heat and simmer 15 to 20 minutes, until the quinoa and carrots are tender and the grains display a threadlike spiral. Uncover and use tongs to transfer the carrot sticks to a bowl. If any water remains in the pot, drain the quinoa through a strainer, then return to the pot. Place a dish towel over the pot, then return the lid and let sit undisturbed for 10 to 15 minutes

- Meanwhile, preheat the oven to 375 degrees and oil a 2-quart baking dish or gratin
- In a food processor fitted with the steel blade, purée the cooked carrots. Scrape down the sides of the bowl, add the cottage cheese and purée until the mixture is smooth. Add the eggs, salt (I suggest about 1/2 teaspoon), pepper and caraway, and purée until smooth. Scrape into a large mixing bowl. Add the quinoa and mix together thoroughly. Scrape into the oiled baking dish. Drizzle the remaining oil over the top and place in the oven
- Bake 40 to 45 minutes, until the top is lightly browned. Remove from the oven and allow to cool for at least 15 minutes before serving. Serve warm or at room temperature, cut into squares or wedges

Nutrition Information

- 175: calories;
- 0 grams: trans fat;
- 451 milligrams: sodium;
- 4 grams: dietary fiber;
- 1 gram: polyunsaturated fat;
- 19 grams: carbohydrates;
- 5 grams: sugars;
- 8 grams: protein;
- 2 grams: saturated fat;

244. Rabbit Fricassee With Tomatoes And White Wine

Serving: 4 servings | Prep: | Cook: | Ready in: 45mins

Ingredients

- 1 rabbit, cut into eight pieces
- Coarse salt and freshly ground pepper to taste
- 3 tablespoons olive oil
- 1 cup dry white wine
- 1 tablespoon fresh thyme leaves
- 3 cloves garlic, boiled in their skins
- 2 tomatoes, peeled and chopped
- 1 tablespoon unsalted butter

Direction

- Season the rabbit with salt and pepper. Heat the olive oil in a large skillet and brown the rabbit pieces a few at a time. Add the wine, scraping up the cooking juices, sprinkle with thyme, cover and cook over low heat for 20 minutes, turning occasionally. If the sauce gets too dry, add a little water. Simmer the garlic cloves in their skins in water for 20 minutes.
- Add the tomatoes to the rabbit, and cook for another 15 minutes. Test the rabbit for doneness. When it is ready, mash the garlic into the sauce, discarding the skins. Swirl in the butter and serve.

Nutrition Information

- 721: calories;
- 6 grams: carbohydrates;
- 80 grams: protein;
- 1241 milligrams: sodium;
- 10 grams: saturated fat;
- 14 grams: monounsaturated fat;
- 1 gram: dietary fiber;
- 2 grams: sugars;
- 35 grams: fat;
- 0 grams: trans fat;

245. Radicchio Or Red Endive Risotto

Serving: Serves four to six | Prep: | Cook: |Ready in: 40mins

Ingredients

- 2 quarts well seasoned chicken or vegetable stock, as needed
- 2 tablespoons extra virgin olive oil
- ½ cup minced onion
- 1 ½ cups arborio or carnaroli rice
- 1 to 2 garlic cloves (to taste), green shoots removed, minced
- Freshly ground pepper to taste
- ½ cup red wine or dry white wine, such as pinot grigio or sauvignon blanc
- 2 medium heads radicchio or 4 or 5 purple Belgian endives, quartered, cored and cut crosswise in thin slivers
- ½ cup freshly grated Parmesan cheese (2 ounces)
- 2 tablespoons minced flat-leaf parsley

Direction

- Put your stock or broth into a saucepan, and bring it to a simmer over low heat with a ladle nearby or in the pot. Make sure that it is well seasoned.
- Heat the olive oil over medium heat in a wide, heavy skillet or in a large, wide saucepan. Add the onion and a generous pinch of salt, and cook gently until it is just tender, about three minutes. Do not brown.
- Add the rice and the garlic, and stir until the grains separate and begin to crackle. Add the wine, and stir until it has been absorbed. Begin adding the simmering stock, a couple of ladlefuls (about 1/2 cup) at a time. The stock should just cover the rice and should be bubbling, not too slowly but not too quickly. Cook, stirring often, until it is just about absorbed. Add another ladleful or two of the stock, and continue to cook in this fashion, stirring in more stock when the rice is almost dry. You do not have to stir constantly, but stir often. After 10 minutes, stir in the radicchio or endive, and continue to cook in the same fashion until the rice is tender all the way through but still chewy, about 15 minutes. Taste now and adjust seasoning, adding salt and pepper to taste. Add another ladleful of stock to the rice, along with the Parmesan and the parsley, and remove from the heat. The mixture should be creamy (add more stock if it isn't). Stir for about half a minute, then serve in wide soup bowls or on plates, spreading the risotto in a thin layer rather than a mound.

Nutrition Information

- 400: calories;
- 6 grams: sugars;
- 1 gram: polyunsaturated fat;
- 55 grams: carbohydrates;
- 15 grams: protein;
- 590 milligrams: sodium;
- 11 grams: fat;
- 3 grams: dietary fiber;

246. Ramps Braised In Olive Oil

Serving: 6 servings as a side dish | Prep: | Cook: |Ready in: 50mins

Ingredients

- 2 cups olive oil, plus more if necessary
- 2 pounds ramps (approximately 6 bunches), cleaned
- Salt and freshly ground pepper to taste

Direction

- Place olive oil in a large, shallow pan with a tight-fitting lid over high heat. When oil is warm, roll a bunch of ramps in paper towels to remove excess moisture, and unwrap. Reduce heat to medium, and add ramps to pan. Toss to coat each leaf with oil. Working quickly, dry second bunch and add to oil, tossing until ramps wilt. Continue with remaining ramps, adding more oil if necessary.

- When all ramps are wilted, season to taste and reduce heat to low, then stir and cover pot. Cook 5 to 10 minutes, depending on the size of the ramps, stirring frequently to avoid burning. When ramps are very, very tender, remove pan from heat and let sit, covered, for 10 minutes. Season again if desired, and serve.

Nutrition Information

- 687: calories;
- 4 grams: sugars;
- 3 grams: protein;
- 10 grams: saturated fat;
- 8 grams: polyunsaturated fat;
- 12 grams: carbohydrates;
- 521 milligrams: sodium;
- 72 grams: fat;
- 53 grams: monounsaturated fat;

247. Raspberry Mousse

Serving: 12 servings | Prep: | Cook: | Ready in: 3hours40mins

Ingredients

- For the filling:
- ½ cup sugar
- 1 ⅓ cup fresh raspberries
- 2 tablespoons raspberry-flavored vodka, or kirsch
- For the mousse:
- 2 cups fresh raspberries
- 1 envelope (2 1/4 teaspoons) unflavored gelatin
- ½ cup sugar
- 2 tablespoons light corn syrup
- 3 large egg whites
- 1 cup heavy cream
- Prepared raspberry syrup, for serving
- Mascarpone cheese, for serving

Direction

- To make the filling, combine sugar and 1/2 cup water in a small nonreactive, heavy saucepan, and bring to a boil over medium heat. Add 1 1/3 cups of the raspberries and return to a boil without stirring. Transfer to a small bowl and allow to cool completely. Add the vodka. Cover and refrigerate.
- To make the mousse, puree the 2 cups of raspberries in a blender and set aside. Sprinkle the gelatin into 1/4 cup of cool water and set aside for 3 minutes. Pour 1/4 cup water, 1/2 cup sugar and the corn syrup into a small, heavy saucepan and place over medium-high heat. Insert a candy thermometer.
- Meanwhile, place the egg whites into the bowl of a mixer and whip until they form soft peaks. When the sugar water has reached 250 degrees, pour it down the sides of the bowl (not directly onto the beaters) into the egg whites while continuing to whip. Add the gelatin mixture and continue to whip until the outside of the bowl is warm, but not hot, about 5 minutes, and the meringue is stiff and glossy.
- Pour the heavy cream into a large mixing bowl and whisk until it forms soft peaks. Fold half of the raspberry puree into the whipped cream and the other half into the meringue, being careful not to deflate either mixture. Fold the meringue and whipped cream together until combined.
- Place the mousse in a pastry bag with a large opening, and pipe the mousse into twelve nonreactive cup molds, filling them halfway. Spread the mousse up the sides of the mold. Place a spoonful of the filling into the center of each mold and top with more mousse. Place the molds in the refrigerator to set for at least 3 hours. To serve, drizzle each plate with

raspberry syrup, and unmold the mousses in the center of each plate and serve with a dollop of mascarpone on the side.

Nutrition Information

- 172: calories;
- 0 grams: polyunsaturated fat;
- 24 grams: carbohydrates;
- 22 grams: sugars;
- 25 milligrams: sodium;
- 8 grams: fat;
- 5 grams: saturated fat;
- 2 grams: protein;

248. Ratatouille

Serving: 9 to 10 cups | Prep: | Cook: | Ready in: 50mins

Ingredients

- 2 ½ pounds eggplant, scrubbed, unpeeled and cut into 1-inch cubes
- 7 sprigs of fresh dill, tough stems removed
- 2 ½ pounds zucchini, washed, trimmed and cut into slices 1/4-inch thick
- 1 ¼ pounds onions, peeled and sliced 1/4-inch thick
- 3 green peppers, seeded, cored and cut into 1-inch pieces
- 2 large or 3 medium-sized cloves garlic, put through garlic press
- 6 sprigs fresh parsley
- 1 teaspoon dried oregano
- 1 pound fresh, ripe plum tomatoes
- 3 tablespoons drained capers
- 6 to 8 tablespoons distilled white vinegar
- Freshly ground black pepper to taste

Direction

- Place all of the ingredients in one large pot or two small ones. Mix contents to distribute seasonings.
- Cover and cook over low heat, just below simmer, for 45 minutes. Ratatouille is cooked when vegetables are soft. Drain well and divide in half.

Nutrition Information

- 231: calories;
- 2 grams: fat;
- 1 gram: polyunsaturated fat;
- 18 grams: dietary fiber;
- 28 grams: sugars;
- 196 milligrams: sodium;
- 0 grams: monounsaturated fat;
- 50 grams: carbohydrates;
- 10 grams: protein;

249. Red Cabbage Glazed With Maple Syrup

Serving: Four to six servings | Prep: | Cook: | Ready in: 45mins

Ingredients

- 5 strips bacon, minced
- 1 onion, minced
- 1 medium firm, tart apple, peeled, cored and sliced
- 1 pound red cabbage (about 1/2 head), cored, outer leaves removed and remainder shredded
- 1 bay leaf
- ½ cup maple syrup
- Salt and freshly ground pepper to taste

Direction

- Preheat the oven to 350 degrees.
- In an oven-proof saucepan or a flame-proof casserole large enough to hold all the ingredients, saute the bacon until crisp. Add the onion and saute until translucent. Add the remaining ingredients, cover and bake in the oven for 1/2 hour.

Nutrition Information

- 217: calories;
- 22 grams: sugars;
- 10 grams: fat;
- 2 grams: polyunsaturated fat;
- 29 grams: carbohydrates;
- 4 grams: protein;
- 396 milligrams: sodium;
- 3 grams: dietary fiber;
- 0 grams: trans fat;

250. Rhubarb Ice Cream With A Caramel Swirl

Serving: One scant quart | Prep: | Cook: | Ready in: 1hours15mins

Ingredients

- 1 and 1/2 cups whole milk
- 1 and 3/4 cup plus 6 tablespoons granulated sugar
- Pinch fine sea salt
- 1 vanilla bean, split and scraped
- 4 large egg yolks, lightly beaten
- 1 and 1/2 cups sour cream
- ¾ pound rhubarb, cut into 1/2-inch dice
- ½ cup heavy cream

Direction

- In a heavy-bottomed pot over medium heat, whisk together the milk, 3/4 cup sugar, the salt, the vanilla bean seeds and its pod. Simmer gently until sugar dissolves, about 5 minutes. Remove from heat, cover, and steep 30 minutes. Discard the vanilla pod and return mixture to a bare simmer.
- Place the yolks in a large bowl. Slowly whisk in hot milk mixture. Scrape the custard back into the pot and cook over medium-low heat, stirring constantly, until mixture is thick enough to coat the back of a spoon, about 5 minutes. Strain through a fine-mesh sieve into a bowl. Whisk in sour cream. Chill at least 3 hours or overnight.
- In a saucepan, combine the rhubarb with 1 cup sugar. Simmer until rhubarb is just tender and has begun releasing its juices, but has not started to fall apart, 4 to 5 minutes. Using a slotted spoon, transfer rhubarb to a bowl. Continue to simmer the juices until syrupy, 5 to 10 minutes more. Pour the syrup over the rhubarb. Cool completely.
- In a clean, dry and preferably nonstick skillet, sprinkle 2 tablespoons sugar over medium heat. When it begins to melt and lightly color, sprinkle in 2 more tablespoons and start swirling pan to help evenly distribute sugar. Add the final 2 tablespoons and cook, swirling pan until all the sugar has melted. Let cook, swirling occasionally, until the sugar syrup caramelizes and turns dark brown. Pour in the heavy cream and 2 tablespoons water (stand back; it may splatter). Simmer, stirring with a heatproof rubber spatula until smooth. Cool completely.
- Pour the custard base into an ice cream machine and churn. Add rhubarb compote for the last minute of churning.
- Scrape a quarter of the caramel into the bottom of a freezer-proof quart container. Top with a quarter of the ice cream. Repeat layering until all of the caramel and ice cream has been used, ending with the ice cream. Freeze until firm for at least 2 hours and up to 1 week.

251. Risotto With Asparagus And Morels

Serving: 4 servings | Prep: | Cook: | Ready in: 30mins

Ingredients

- 2 ounces dried morels, soaked for 30 minutes in warm water
- 6 ounces fresh morels

- 2 shallots, minced
- 3 tablespoons unsalted butter
- About 5 cups hot chicken stock
- 1 tablespoon olive oil
- 1 ½ cups Arborio rice
- Coarse salt and freshly ground pepper to taste
- ½ cup dry white wine
- 8 asparagus spears, sliced on the bias into one-inch pieces
- ½ cup freshly grated Parmesan cheese
- 1 tablespoon parsley, chopped

Direction

- Scoop the dried morels up from their soaking liquid and squeeze them, letting them drain back into the bowl. Follow by straining the soaking liquid through several layers of cheesecloth and then rinse the morels under running water before slicing them.
- Prepare the fresh morels. Rinse the morels quickly under cold running water and dry them with paper towels. Slice the tops and stems. In a small skillet, soften the shallots in one tablespoon of the butter over moderate heat. Add all the mushrooms and the strained soaking liquid, cover and cook gently for five minutes. Meanwhile, bring the chicken stock to a slow simmer.
- Heat one tablespoon butter and the olive oil in a large, heavy skillet and add the rice. Cook, stirring, until the grains are coated with the butter. Add a cup of the hot stock and cook, stirring frequently, until the rice has absorbed the liquid. Add the mushrooms and season them with salt and pepper to taste, and add the white wine.
- When the liquid has evaporated, add the asparagus, reserving the tips in another one-half cup of the stock. Continue adding the stock, one-half cup at a time as the rice absorbs the liquid, stirring continuously. Add the asparagus tips after the rice has cooked for about 12 minutes, and continue adding the broth, one-half cup at a time, stirring frequently. Continue adding liquid and stirring until the rice is creamy and tender, but just slightly al dente. Correct seasoning, stir in the Parmesan cheese and the remaining butter and sprinkle with parsley.

Nutrition Information

- 606: calories;
- 9 grams: saturated fat;
- 8 grams: sugars;
- 80 grams: carbohydrates;
- 5 grams: dietary fiber;
- 1226 milligrams: sodium;
- 20 grams: protein;
- 0 grams: trans fat;
- 2 grams: polyunsaturated fat;

252. Risotto With Broccoli

Serving: Serves 4 to 6 | Prep: | Cook: | Ready in: 45mins

Ingredients

- 2 quarts well-seasoned chicken or vegetable stock, as needed
- 2 tablespoons extra virgin olive oil
- ½ cup minced onion
- 1 ½ cups arborio or carnaroli rice
- 1 to 2 garlic cloves (to taste), green shoots removed, minced
- Freshly ground pepper to taste
- ½ cup dry white wine, such as pinot grigio or sauvignon blanc
- 1 pound broccoli (2 good-size stalks), stems peeled and cut in small dice, flowers thinly sliced
- ½ cup freshly grated Parmesan cheese
- 2 tablespoons minced flat-leaf parsley

Direction

- Put your stock or broth into a saucepan, and bring it to a simmer over low heat with a ladle nearby or in the pot. Make sure that the stock is well seasoned.

- Heat the olive oil over medium heat in a wide, heavy skillet or in a large, wide saucepan. Add the onion and a generous pinch of salt, and cook gently until it is just tender, about three minutes. Do not brown.
- Add the rice and the garlic, and stir until the grains separate and begin to crackle. Add the wine, and stir until it has been absorbed. Begin adding the simmering stock, a couple of ladlefuls (about 1/2 cup) at a time. The stock should just cover the rice and should be bubbling, not too slowly but not too quickly. Cook, stirring often, until it is just about absorbed. Add another ladleful or two of the stock, and continue to cook in this fashion, stirring in more stock when the rice is almost dry. You do not have to stir constantly, but stir often. After 10 minutes, stir in the diced broccoli stems. Continue to add broth and stir the rice for another five minutes. Stir in the thinly sliced flowers. Continue to add broth and stir the rice for another 10 minutes or so. When the rice is tender all the way through but still chewy, it is done. Taste now and adjust seasoning, adding salt and pepper to taste. Add another ladleful of stock to the rice, along with the Parmesan and the parsley, and remove from the heat. The mixture should be creamy (add more stock if it isn't). Stir for about half a minute, then serve in wide soup bowls or on plates, spreading the risotto in a thin layer rather than a mound.

Nutrition Information

- 423: calories;
- 3 grams: saturated fat;
- 7 grams: sugars;
- 17 grams: protein;
- 614 milligrams: sodium;
- 11 grams: fat;
- 6 grams: monounsaturated fat;
- 1 gram: polyunsaturated fat;
- 59 grams: carbohydrates;
- 4 grams: dietary fiber;

253. Risotto With Pumpkin

Serving: 4 servings | Prep: | Cook: | Ready in: 35mins

Ingredients

- Generous pinch of saffron
- 5 cups boiling chicken stock
- 3 tablespoons olive oil
- 2 cloves garlic, minced
- 2 cups pumpkin, in 1/2-inch dice
- 1 ½ cups arborio rice
- 1 tablespoon butter
- Salt and freshly ground black pepper
- Freshly grated Parmesan cheese

Direction

- Place the saffron in a small dish, add a little of the chicken stock and allow to steep for a few minutes.
- Heat the oil in a heavy saucepan. Add the garlic, saute briefly then stir in the pumpkin. When the pumpkin is coated with oil, stir in the rice. Add the saffron. Stir.
- Stirring constantly, begin adding the remaining stock, about one-half cup at a time, adding additional stock as each portion is absorbed by the rice.
- After about 20 minutes, when all the stock has been added, the rice should be just tender and the pumpkin should be quite soft. Don't worry if some of the pumpkin has disintegrated.
- Stir in the butter, season to taste with salt and pepper and stir in a couple of tablespoons of Parmesan cheese. Serve at once with remaining Parmesan cheese on the side.

254. Risotto With Tomato Consomme And Fresh Cheese

Serving: Four servings | Prep: | Cook: | Ready in: 40mins

Ingredients

- 6 tomatoes, chopped
- 1 medium carrot, peeled and diced
- 1 red bell pepper, seeded and diced
- 7 cups basic vegetable broth (see recipe)
- 1 teaspoon olive oil
- 1 leek, white part only, rinsed well and minced
- 1 clove garlic, peeled and finely minced
- 1 ½ cups Arborio rice
- ½ teaspoon salt, plus more to taste
- 1 ½ teaspoons freshly ground pepper, plus more to taste
- 1 pound fresh mozzarella, diced
- 1 cup roughly chopped basil leaves
- 1 tablespoon cracked black peppercorns

Direction

- Put the chopped tomatoes, carrot and bell pepper into a blender, add the vegetable broth and puree until smooth. Strain the broth into a large, heavy-bottomed skillet or pot and simmer.
- Heat the olive oil in a large saucepan at medium heat. Add the leek and the garlic and saute until soft, about 5 minutes. Add the rice and stir. Ladle in 1/2 cup of the vegetable broth and stir. Increase the heat to medium-high and, for the next 25 minutes, continue adding the broth, 1/2 cup at a time, stirring constantly. Season to taste with salt and pepper. The rice should be tender but firm. If not, add more vegetable broth until the rice is tender. Remove the rice from the heat immediately. Quickly stir in the mozzarella and the basil leaves. Divide among 4 bowls and garnish with the cracked black pepper.

Nutrition Information

- 694: calories;
- 33 grams: protein;
- 1092 milligrams: sodium;
- 78 grams: carbohydrates;
- 7 grams: dietary fiber;
- 28 grams: fat;
- 15 grams: saturated fat;
- 9 grams: sugars;
- 1 gram: polyunsaturated fat;

255. Roast Chicken With Tarragon

Serving: 4 servings | Prep: | Cook: |Ready in: 1hours10mins

Ingredients

- 1 5-pound chicken
- 1 lemon, halved
- Kosher salt to taste
- Freshly ground black pepper to taste
- 4 cloves garlic, smashed and peeled
- 2 bunches fresh tarragon (3/4 ounce each); stem one of the bunches and leave the other intact
- ½ cup dry white wine

Direction

- Preheat oven to 500 degrees. Remove fat from the crop and cavity of the chicken. Remove the neck, gizzards and liver and freeze for another use.
- Squeeze half the lemon all over the skin of the chicken. Season the skin with salt and pepper. Stuff the cavity with the remaining half lemon, garlic and 1 bunch whole tarragon.
- Put the chicken in a roasting pan, breast side up, and roast 45 minutes to 1 hour, or until the juices run clear. During the first few minutes, either shake the chicken or move it frequently with a wooden spoon to keep it from sticking.
- When chicken is done, tilt it over the roasting pan to let the cavity juices run into the pan. Remove the chicken to a platter. Pour off the fat from the roasting pan.
- Put the pan on top of the stove. Add the wine and bring the contents of the pan to a boil, while scraping the bottom vigorously with a wooden spoon. Stir in tarragon leaves. Let

simmer 5 minutes once the pan is thoroughly deglazed. Serve the pan juices over the chicken or pass it separately in a sauce boat.

Nutrition Information

- 897: calories;
- 17 grams: saturated fat;
- 10 grams: carbohydrates;
- 75 grams: protein;
- 2 grams: dietary fiber;
- 1 gram: sugars;
- 1454 milligrams: sodium;
- 59 grams: fat;
- 0 grams: trans fat;
- 24 grams: monounsaturated fat;
- 13 grams: polyunsaturated fat;

256. Roast Cornish Hens With Herbs And Pancetta

Serving: 4 servings | Prep: | Cook: | Ready in: 45mins

Ingredients

- 4 fresh sage leaves
- 2 teaspoons fresh rosemary leaves
- 2 teaspoons fresh thyme
- 2 tablespoons unsalted butter, softened
- 4 poussins or Cornish hens, air-dried overnight in the refrigerator
- Coarse salt and freshly ground pepper to taste
- 8 slices smoked pancetta
- 2 tablespoons olive oil

Direction

- Preheat the oven to 375 degrees. Chop the sage, rosemary and thyme and mix with the butter. Push the herb butter under the loosened skin of the breasts of the poussins or hens. Truss the poussins, season with salt and pepper and cover the breasts with pancetta. Sprinkle with olive oil.

- Place the poussins in a roasting pan and roast for 45 minutes to 1 hour. Degrease the pan juices and season to taste. Place each poussin on a heated plate and pour a serving of sauce around each one.

Nutrition Information

- 1032: calories;
- 25 grams: saturated fat;
- 14 grams: polyunsaturated fat;
- 83 grams: fat;
- 0 grams: trans fat;
- 37 grams: monounsaturated fat;
- 2 grams: carbohydrates;
- 1 gram: sugars;
- 65 grams: protein;
- 955 milligrams: sodium;

257. Roasted Apple And Pear Compote With Candied Ginger

Serving: Serves six | Prep: | Cook: | Ready in: 2hours

Ingredients

- 4 apples, preferably on the tart side, peeled, cored and cut into sixths
- 3 ripe but firm pears, peeled, cored and cut into sixths
- 2 tablespoons freshly squeezed lemon juice (more to taste)
- 1 cup apple juice
- A handful of golden raisins
- 2 tablespoons chopped candied ginger
- 2 tablespoons agave syrup
- ¼ to ½ teaspoon ground cinnamon (to taste)
- ½ teaspoon freshly grated nutmeg
- 1 tablespoon whisky

Direction

- Preheat the oven to 375 degrees. Butter a baking dish large enough to accommodate all

of the fruit. Fill a bowl with water, and add 1 tablespoon of the lemon juice. As you prepare the fruit, put it into the water. When all of the fruit is peeled and sliced, drain and toss with the remaining lemon juice in the baking dish.
- Combine the apple juice, raisins, ginger, agave syrup, cinnamon, nutmeg and whisky in a small saucepan, and bring to a simmer. Remove from the heat, and pour over the fruit.
- Place in the oven, and bake 1 to 1 1/2 hours until the fruit is very soft. Stir gently every 10 to 15 minutes to keep all the fruit moist. Serve warm.

Nutrition Information

- 183: calories;
- 6 grams: dietary fiber;
- 35 grams: sugars;
- 9 milligrams: sodium;
- 1 gram: protein;
- 0 grams: polyunsaturated fat;
- 46 grams: carbohydrates;

258. Roasted Brussels Sprouts With A Pomegranate Reduction

Serving: 4 servings | Prep: | Cook: | Ready in: 1hours15mins

Ingredients

- 1 pound brussels sprouts, washed, trimmed and halved
- 2 tablespoons olive oil
- Fine sea salt, to taste
- 1 cup pomegranate juice
- ⅓ cup sugar (can be maple, brown, date, coconut, granulated)
- 3 tablespoons pomegranate seeds

Direction

- Position the baking rack in the middle of the oven and heat the oven to 425[dg]F. In a large bowl, toss the brussels sprouts with oil and a few pinches of salt. Spread the brussels sprouts over a shallow baking pan and roast for about 30 to 35 minutes, or until the sprouts are lightly browned and crispy.
- While the brussels sprouts are roasting, in a small saucepan combine the pomegranate juice with the sugar and set over medium heat, stirring until the sugar is completely dissolved. When the liquid comes to a simmer, reduce the heat to medium-low and gently simmer until the liquid is reduced to one quarter of the original amount and is thick and syrupy, about 25 minutes. Toward the end, watch the reduction carefully — it can go from thick to burned in a matter of seconds. Transfer the reduction to a cooling rack and let it come to room temperature. Do not refrigerate.
- Drizzle the reduction over the brussels sprouts and sprinkle with the pomegranate seeds.

Nutrition Information

- 184: calories;
- 4 grams: protein;
- 5 grams: monounsaturated fat;
- 22 grams: carbohydrates;
- 12 grams: sugars;
- 11 grams: fat;
- 1 gram: polyunsaturated fat;
- 6 grams: dietary fiber;
- 472 milligrams: sodium;

259. Roasted Carrot, Parsnip And Potato Soup

Serving: 6 servings | Prep: | Cook: | Ready in: 1hours

Ingredients

- 1 ½ pounds carrots, peeled and cut in 3/4 inch pieces
- ½ pound (2 large) parsnips, peeled, quartered, cored and cut in 3/4 inch pieces
- 1 medium or large red onion, cut in large dice
- 1 medium (about 6 ounces) Yukon gold potato, quartered
- 2 garlic cloves, in the skin
- 2 tablespoons extra virgin olive oil
- Salt and freshly ground pepper
- 6 cups chicken or vegetable stock or broth
- Chopped fresh herbs, such as parsley, thyme, tarragon or chives, for garnish
- Crème fraîche or yogurt for garnish (optional)

Direction

- Preheat oven to 425 degrees. Line a sheet pan or a baking dish with parchment or foil. Toss vegetables, including garlic cloves, with olive oil and salt and pepper to taste. Spread in baking dish or on sheet pan in an even layer and place in oven. Set timer for 20 minutes.
- After 20 minutes, stir vegetables and turn heat down to 400 degrees. Roast for another 20 to 30 minutes (or longer; I have found every oven I've used to be different, thus the range), or until very tender and caramelized on the edges, stirring every 10 minutes. Remove from the heat. You should have about 4 cups roasted vegetables.
- Hold garlic cloves with a towel so that you don't burn your fingers. Squeeze out the pulp into a blender. Add half the vegetables and 2 cups of the stock. Cover the top of the blender with a towel pulled down tight, rather than airtight with the lid, because hot mixture will jump and push the top off if the blender is closed airtight. Blend until smooth and transfer to a soup pot. Repeat with the second half of the roasted vegetables. Transfer to the pot and whisk in remaining broth. Season to taste with salt and pepper and heat through. Serve each bowl with a sprinkle of chopped fresh herbs and if you wish, a swirl of crème fraîche or yogurt.

Nutrition Information

- 243: calories;
- 1 gram: polyunsaturated fat;
- 5 grams: monounsaturated fat;
- 12 grams: sugars;
- 9 grams: protein;
- 1066 milligrams: sodium;
- 8 grams: fat;
- 36 grams: carbohydrates;
- 7 grams: dietary fiber;

260. Roasted Cauliflower With Tahini Parsley Sauce

Serving: Serves four to six, with some sauce left over | Prep: | Cook: | Ready in: 1hours

Ingredients

- 1 large cauliflower, broken into florets
- Salt to taste
- Freshly ground pepper to taste
- 2 tablespoons extra virgin olive oil
- 2 to 3 garlic cloves, to taste, cut in half, green shoots removed
- 1 cup sesame tahini
- ¼ to ¾ cup fresh lemon juice, to taste
- 1 cup finely chopped flat-leaf parsley (2 bunches)

Direction

- Preheat the oven to 400 degrees. Meanwhile, bring a large pot of water to a boil, and fill a bowl with ice water. When the water comes to a boil, salt generously and add the cauliflower. Blanch for two minutes, and transfer to the ice water. Drain and blot dry. Transfer to a baking dish.
- Season the cauliflower with salt and pepper, and toss with the olive oil. Place in the oven, and roast for 30 to 40 minutes, stirring from time to time, until tender and lightly browned.

- Puree the garlic cloves with 1/4 teaspoon salt in a mortar and pestle. Transfer to a bowl, and whisk in the sesame tahini. Whisk in the lemon juice, beginning with the smaller amount. The mixture will stiffen up. Gradually whisk in up to 1/2 cup water, until the sauce has the consistency of thick cream (or runny yogurt). Stir in the parsley. Taste, and adjust salt and lemon juice. Serve with the cauliflower. You will have some sauce left over.

Nutrition Information

- 328: calories;
- 27 grams: fat;
- 4 grams: sugars;
- 12 grams: monounsaturated fat;
- 10 grams: protein;
- 19 grams: carbohydrates;
- 7 grams: dietary fiber;
- 527 milligrams: sodium;

261. Roasted Garlic And Shallot Soup

Serving: 6 to 8 servings | Prep: | Cook: | Ready in: 2hours30mins

Ingredients

- 5 whole heads garlic, cloves from 2 1/2 heads peeled
- ¾ pound shallots, half of them peeled and coarsely chopped
- 4 tablespoons olive oil
- Kosher salt and freshly ground pepper
- 4 tablespoons unsalted butter
- 2 large yellow onions, peeled and coarsely chopped
- ¾ pound russet potatoes, peeled and quartered
- 4 cups well-seasoned chicken stock, approximately
- 1 cup heavy cream, half-and-half or milk, approximately
- 1 tablespoon fresh thyme leaves

Direction

- Preheat oven to 350 degrees.
- Combine unpeeled garlic heads and unpeeled shallots in large bowl, pour the olive oil over them and toss to coat. Season generously with salt and pepper and place them in a single layer in a baking dish along with any oil remaining in bowl. Cover with foil and bake 35 minutes. If shallots are soft by then, remove them. Bake them a little longer if necessary. Continue baking the garlic another 30 minutes or so until it is soft. Allow garlic and shallots to cool.
- Meanwhile, melt the butter in a heavy three- to four-quart saucepan. Add onions and cook gently for 15 minutes. Do not allow to brown. Add peeled, unroasted shallots and peeled garlic cloves. Cook over low heat 10 minutes longer. Add potatoes, about 1/2 teaspoon salt or to taste, the chicken stock, cream and thyme. Cover and cook about 40 minutes, until potatoes are very soft.
- Peel roasted shallots. Cut roasted garlic heads in half horizontally and squeeze in a potato ricer or by hand to extract the soft pulp. Add garlic pulp and shallots to saucepan and cook 10 minutes longer.
- Puree the soup in a blender or food processor. Season to taste with salt and pepper and, if desired, adjust the consistency of the soup with some additional stock, cream or milk or water. Reheat before serving.

Nutrition Information

- 386: calories;
- 0 grams: trans fat;
- 2 grams: polyunsaturated fat;
- 35 grams: carbohydrates;
- 4 grams: dietary fiber;
- 12 grams: saturated fat;
- 8 grams: protein;

- 743 milligrams: sodium;
- 25 grams: fat;
- 10 grams: monounsaturated fat;

262. Roasted Root Vegetables With Polenta

Serving: Serves 4 to 6 | Prep: | Cook: | Ready in: 1hours30mins

Ingredients

- 2 large carrots (3/4 to 1 pound), peeled and cut into 3/4-inch pieces (quarter at the fat ends, cut in half at the thin ends, then cut in thick slices)
- 1 large parsnip (about 1/2 pound), quartered, cored and cut in 3/4-inch pieces
- 1 medium-size fennel bulb, quartered, cored and cut in 3/4 inch pieces
- 1 medium or large red onion, cut in large dice
- 2 tablespoons extra virgin olive oil
- Salt and freshly ground pepper to taste
- Chopped fresh rosemary, thyme or sage, about 2 teaspoons (optional)
- 1 cup polenta
- 1 quart water
- 1 teaspoon salt
- 1 tablespoon unsalted butter
- ½ cup freshly grated Parmesan (optional but recommended)
- 1 batch marinara sauce (optional)

Direction

- Preheat oven to 375 degrees. Line a sheet pan or a baking dish with parchment or foil. Toss vegetables with the olive oil and salt and pepper to taste. Add fresh herbs if using. Spread vegetables in an even layer.
- Combine polenta, water, and salt in a 2-quart baking dish and stir together. Place polenta and vegetables in the oven. If you can't fit both pans on the same (middle) rack, place vegetables on a lower rack. Roast vegetables for 30 to 40 minutes, stirring every 10 minutes or until soft and beginning to caramelize. Remove from the oven.
- If serving this with marinara sauce, make the sauce while the vegetables and polenta are in the oven.
- Continue to bake the polenta until it has been in the oven for 40 to 45 minutes and has absorbed the water. Remove from oven and stir in butter. Use a fork or a spatula to stir the polenta well, and return to oven for 5 to 10 more minutes. Remove from oven and stir again. Carefully taste a little bit of the polenta; if it is not completely soft, return to the oven for 5 to 10 more minutes.
- Remove polenta from oven and stir in 1/3 cup grated Parmesan, if using. Immediately spoon polenta onto plates and make a depression in the middle. Ladle on some marinara sauce and top with a generous spoonful of roasted vegetables. Sprinkle on remaining Parmesan and serve.

Nutrition Information

- 264: calories;
- 5 grams: monounsaturated fat;
- 38 grams: carbohydrates;
- 859 milligrams: sodium;
- 0 grams: trans fat;
- 1 gram: polyunsaturated fat;
- 6 grams: dietary fiber;
- 7 grams: protein;
- 10 grams: fat;
- 4 grams: saturated fat;

263. Roasted Sweet Potatoes And Fresh Figs

Serving: 4 servings | Prep: | Cook: | Ready in: 45mins

Ingredients

- 4 small sweet potatoes (2 1/4 pounds total)

- 5 tablespoons olive oil
- Scant 3 tablespoons balsamic vinegar (you can use a commercial rather than a premium aged grade)
- 1 ½ tablespoons superfine sugar
- 12 green onions, halved lengthwise and cut into 1 1/2-inch segments
- 1 red chili, thinly sliced
- 6 ripe figs (8 1/2 ounces total), quartered
- 5 ounces soft goat's milk cheese (optional)
- Maldon sea salt and freshly ground black pepper

Direction

- Preheat oven to 475 degrees. Wash the sweet potatoes, halve them lengthwise, and then cut each half into 3 long wedges. Mix with 3 tablespoons of the olive oil, 2 teaspoons salt and some black pepper.
- Spread the wedges out, skin side down, on a baking sheet and cook for about 25 minutes, until they are soft but not mushy. Remove from the oven and leave to cool.
- To make the balsamic reduction, place the balsamic vinegar and sugar in a small saucepan. Bring to a boil, then decrease the heat and simmer for 2 to 4 minutes, until it thickens. Be sure to remove the pan from the heat when the vinegar is still runnier than honey; it will continue to thicken as it cools. Stir in a drop of water before serving if it does become too thick to drizzle
- Arrange the sweet potatoes on a serving platter. Heat the remaining oil in a medium saucepan over medium heat and add the green onions and chili. Fry for 4 to 5 minutes, stirring often to make sure not to burn the chili. Spoon the oil, onions and chili over the sweet potatoes. Dot the figs among the wedges, and then drizzle over the balsamic reduction. Serve at room temperature. Crumble the cheese over the top, if using.

Nutrition Information

- 343: calories;
- 47 grams: carbohydrates;
- 7 grams: dietary fiber;
- 619 milligrams: sodium;
- 17 grams: fat;
- 2 grams: polyunsaturated fat;
- 12 grams: monounsaturated fat;
- 26 grams: sugars;
- 3 grams: protein;

264. Roasted Vegetable Galette With Olives

Serving: 8 servings | Prep: | Cook: | Ready in: 1hours40mins

Ingredients

- Crust
- 1 ¼ cups all-purpose flour
- 1 cup whole-wheat pastry flour
- 2 teaspoons baking powder
- 1 teaspoon sugar
- ½ teaspoon salt
- ⅓ cup water
- ¼ cup extra-virgin olive oil
- ½ cup finely chopped pitted Kalamata olives
- Filling
- 1 ½ cups diced peeled carrots (3 medium)
- 1 ½ cups diced peeled parsnips (3 medium)
- 1 ½ cups diced peeled butternut squash (1/2 medium)
- 1 cup diced peeled beet (1 medium)
- 2 tablespoons extra-virgin olive oil, divided
- 2 teaspoons chopped fresh rosemary or 1/2 teaspoon dried
- ½ teaspoon salt, or to taste
- Freshly ground pepper to taste
- 1 head garlic
- 1 cup crumbled creamy goat cheese (4 ounces), divided
- 1 egg mixed with 1 tablespoon water for glazing

Direction

- To prepare crust: Combine all-purpose flour, whole-wheat flour, baking powder, sugar and salt in a food processor; pulse several times. Mix water and oil; sprinkle over the dry ingredients and pulse just until blended. Add olives and pulse to mix. (Alternatively, combine dry ingredients in a large bowl. Make a well in the center and add the water-oil mixture, stirring until well blended. Stir in olives.)
- Press the dough into a disk; if it seems dry, add a little more water. Wrap in plastic wrap and refrigerate for 30 minutes or longer. The unbaked crust will keep, well wrapped, in the refrigerator for up to 2 days.
- Meanwhile, preheat oven to 400 degrees Fahrenheit. Coat a large baking sheet with cooking spray.
- To prepare filling: Combine carrots, parsnips, squash, beet, 1 tablespoon oil, rosemary, salt and pepper in a large bowl; toss to coat. Spread the vegetables on the prepared baking sheet. Cut the tip off the head of garlic. Set on a square of foil, sprinkle with a tablespoon of water and pinch the edges of the foil together. Place the packet on the baking sheet with the vegetables. Roast, stirring the vegetables every 10 minutes, until they are tender and beginning to brown and the garlic is soft, about 35 minutes. (The garlic may take a little longer.)
- Transfer the vegetables to a bowl. Unwrap the garlic and let cool slightly. Squeeze the garlic cloves into a small bowl; add the remaining 1 tablespoon oil and mash with a fork. Add the mashed garlic to the roasted vegetables and toss to mix. Add 3/4 cup goat cheese and toss to coat.
- To assemble galette: Roll the dough into a rough 14-inch circle about 1/4 inch thick. Coat a baking sheet with cooking spray and place the dough on it. Arrange the roasted vegetables on the dough, leaving a 2-inch border all around. Fold the border up and over the filling to form a rim, pleating as you go. Scatter the remaining 1/4 cup goat cheese over the vegetables. Stir egg and water briskly; brush lightly over the crust.
- Bake the galette at 400 degrees until the crust is golden, 30 to 35 minutes. Let cool for 10 minutes. Serve warm.

Nutrition Information

- 317: calories;
- 15 grams: fat;
- 2 grams: polyunsaturated fat;
- 5 grams: sugars;
- 8 grams: protein;
- 413 milligrams: sodium;
- 4 grams: saturated fat;
- 9 grams: monounsaturated fat;
- 41 grams: carbohydrates;
- 6 grams: dietary fiber;

265. Roasted Winter Vegetable Medley

Serving: Serves 6 | Prep: | Cook: | Ready in: 30mins

Ingredients

- 1 medium butternut squash (about 1 1/2 pounds), peeled, seeds and membranes scraped away, and cut into 3/4 to 1-inch dice
- 2 large carrots, peeled and cut into 3/4-inch pieces (quarter at the fat ends, cut in half at the thin ends, then cut in thick slices)
- 1 large parsnip, quartered, cored, and cut in 3/4-inch pieces
- 1 medium-size fennel bulb, quartered, cored and cut in 3/4 inch pieces
- 1 medium or large red onion, cut in large dice
- 3 tablespoons extra virgin olive oil
- Salt and freshly ground pepper to taste
- Optional: Chopped fresh rosemary, thyme or sage, about 2 teaspoons

Direction

- Preheat oven to 425 degrees. Line 2 baking sheets or roasting pans with parchment or foil. Place squash on one and remaining vegetables on the other, and toss each batch with 1 tablespoon olive oil and salt and pepper to taste. If desired, add fresh herbs such as rosemary, thyme or sage, and toss together. Spread vegetables in an even layer.
- Place in the oven, on the same shelf if both pans will fit, or on the middle and lower shelves, and roast for 20 minutes, stirring halfway through. Switch pans top to bottom halfway through if on separate shelves Turn heat down to 400 degrees and continue to roast for another 10 to 20 minutes (the squash may be ready sooner than the root vegetables), stirring halfway through, until tender and caramelized.
- Remove from oven, combine squash and other vegetables and stir together.

Nutrition Information

- 155: calories;
- 6 grams: dietary fiber;
- 2 grams: protein;
- 545 milligrams: sodium;
- 7 grams: sugars;
- 1 gram: polyunsaturated fat;
- 5 grams: monounsaturated fat;
- 24 grams: carbohydrates;

266. Saag Tofu (Tofu With Spinach, Ginger, Coriander And Turmeric)

Serving: 4 servings | Prep: | Cook: | Ready in: 30mins

Ingredients

- ¾ pound firm tofu, cut into 1-inch cubes
- 2 tablespoons canola oil
- ½ cup coarsely chopped shallot or red onion
- 4 lengthwise slices peeled fresh ginger (2 inches long, 1 inch wide, 1/8 inch thick), coarsely chopped
- 1 teaspoon cumin seeds
- ½ teaspoon fennel seeds
- 2 whole dried red chilies, like Thai, cayenne or arbol
- 1 tablespoon coriander seeds, ground
- Salt to taste
- ¼ teaspoon cayenne
- ¼ teaspoon ground turmeric
- 1 ½ pounds fresh spinach, stems trimmed at the end and washed in 2 changes of water, or 12 ounces baby spinach, rinsed
- ½ cup drained yogurt
- ¼ teaspoon cornstarch

Direction

- Drain the tofu on paper towels. Heat 1 tablespoon of the oil over medium-high heat in a wok or a large, heavy lidded skillet and add the tofu. Stir-fry until golden brown and remove from the heat.
- Combine the shallot or onion and the ginger in a food processor or mini-chop and blend until finely minced, almost a paste.
- Heat the remaining oil over medium-high heat in a wok or skillet and add the cumin seeds, fennel seeds and whole chiles. Cook, stirring, for about 15 seconds, or until the spices are fragrant and reddish-brown. Add the onion and ginger and stir-fry until it is lightly browned, about 3 minutes. Add the coriander, salt, cayenne and turmeric, stir for about 10 seconds and add the spinach in batches, adding the next batch after the first batch wilts and stirring and scraping the bottom of the pan to deglaze.
- Stir in the tofu, cover, reduce the heat to medium-low and simmer, stirring occasionally, for 2 to 3 minutes, until the spinach is uniformly wilted and the tofu is warmed through.
- Whisk the cornstarch into the yogurt. Remove the pan from the heat, remove the chilies, and

stir in the yogurt. Taste, adjust salt and serve with rice or other grains.

Nutrition Information

- 274: calories;
- 17 grams: fat;
- 0 grams: trans fat;
- 6 grams: monounsaturated fat;
- 22 grams: protein;
- 751 milligrams: sodium;
- 3 grams: sugars;
- 7 grams: dietary fiber;
- 15 grams: carbohydrates;

267. Salade Niçoise With Yogurt Vinaigrette

Serving: 6 servings | Prep: | Cook: | Ready in: 45mins

Ingredients

- For the vinaigrette:
- 2 tablespoons good-quality red or white wine vinegar or sherry vinegar
- 1 tablespoon fresh lemon juice
- 1 garlic clove, small or large to taste, green shoot removed, puréed with a garlic press or in a mortar and pestle
- Salt and freshly ground pepper to taste
- 1 teaspoon Dijon mustard
- ¼ cup extra virgin olive oil
- 5 tablespoons plain low-fat yogurt (you can omit this and use a total of 1/2 cup extra virgin olive oil)
- For the salad:
- ¾ pound medium Yukon gold or fingerling potatoes, cut in 3/4-inch dice
- 1 5 1/2-ounce can light (not albacore) tuna packed in water, drained
- 6 ounces green beans, trimmed, and cut in half if long
- 1 small red or green pepper, thinly sliced or diced
- 1 small cucumber (preferably Persian), cut in half lengthwise and then sliced in half-moons
- 2 hard-cooked eggs, preferably free range, peeled and cut in wedges
- 1 small head of Boston lettuce, 1 romaine heart, or 4 to 5 cups mixed baby salad greens, washed and dried
- 2 to 4 tablespoons chopped fresh herbs, like parsley, basil, tarragon, chives and marjoram
- 3 or 4 tomatoes, cut in wedges, or 1/2 pint cherry tomatoes, cut in half
- Optional:
- 6 to 12 anchovy fillets, rinsed and drained on paper towels
- 12 imported black olives

Direction

- Using a fork or a small whisk, mix together the vinegar and lemon juice with the garlic, salt, pepper and Dijon mustard. Whisk in the olive oil and yogurt.
- Steam the potatoes above 1 inch simmering water for 10 to 15 minutes, until tender. Transfer to a large salad bowl and season with salt and pepper. Add the tuna and toss with 1/4 cup of the dressing while the potatoes are hot.
- Bring a pot of water to a boil, and fill a bowl with ice water. When the water comes to a boil, add a generous amount of salt and add the green beans. Cook 4 to 5 minutes, until just tender. Transfer to the ice water, then drain. Dry on paper towels. Add to the salad bowl, along with the red or green pepper, cucumber, hard-boiled eggs, lettuce and herbs. Garnish with the tomatoes, anchovies and olives, and serve.

Nutrition Information

- 218: calories;
- 2 grams: polyunsaturated fat;
- 0 grams: trans fat;
- 3 grams: dietary fiber;
- 12 grams: protein;
- 8 grams: monounsaturated fat;

- 17 grams: carbohydrates;
- 4 grams: sugars;
- 536 milligrams: sodium;

268. Salmon Fillet With Ginger And Capers

Serving: 2 servings | Prep: | Cook: | Ready in: 1hours10mins

Ingredients

- 1 salmon fillet (about 1 pound)
- Juice 1/2 lemon
- 2 teaspoons fresh thyme leaves
- 3 tablespoons salt-packed capers, soaked for one hour and rinsed thoroughly
- 3 tablespoons fresh ginger, minced
- 2 tablespoons grape-seed or vegetable oil
- Freshly ground pepper to taste
- 2 tablespoons chopped chives

Direction

- Pat the salmon dry with paper towels and rub with the lemon juice. Sprinkle with thyme leaves and set aside.
- Dry the capers with a salad spinner. Heat the oil in a frying pan large enough to hold the salmon comfortably. Add the capers and ginger and saute for two minutes.
- Add the salmon skin side down and cook for two minutes, using a spatula to prevent the skin from sticking to the bottom. Turn and brown on the other side. Stir the ginger and capers from time to time to prevent them from burning. Cook the fish to the desired degree and remove it to a heated serving dish. Spoon the capers and ginger on top. Season with pepper, sprinkle with chives and serve.

Nutrition Information

- 614: calories;
- 4 grams: carbohydrates;
- 11 grams: polyunsaturated fat;
- 0 grams: trans fat;
- 19 grams: monounsaturated fat;
- 1 gram: sugars;
- 47 grams: protein;
- 438 milligrams: sodium;
- 45 grams: fat;
- 8 grams: saturated fat;

269. Salmon Tacos With Greens And Tomatillo Salsa

Serving: 8 to 10 tacos | Prep: | Cook: | Ready in: 50mins

Ingredients

- 1 pound salmon or arctic char fillets
- Salt and freshly ground pepper
- 1 bunch spinach or chard (about ¾ pound), stemmed and washed well in 2 changes of water
- 1 tablespoon extra virgin olive oil
- 1 to 2 garlic cloves (to taste), minced
- 1 to 3 serrano or jalapeño chiles (to taste), minced
- 1 cup cooked tomatillo salsa (see recipe)
- 2 to 3 ounces crumbled queso fresco or feta (optional)
- Shredded cabbage (optional)
- 8 to 10 corn tortillas
- Chopped cilantro

Direction

- Preheat the oven to 300 degrees. Cover a baking sheet with foil and lightly oil the foil. Place the salmon or arctic char on top. Season with salt and gently rub the salt into the surface of the salmon. Add pepper to taste. Fill a roasting pan or cake pan halfway with boiling water and place it on the oven floor. Place the fish in the oven and bake 10 to 20 minutes (depending on the thickness), until white beads of protein appear on the surface and the fish can be pulled apart with a fork. Remove from the heat and allow to cool until you can handle it. If desired, scrape away the white protein beads, then flake the fish and place in a bowl. Discard the skin. Season the fish well with salt and pepper.

- Steam the spinach or chard just until wilted, about 1 minute for spinach, 2 minutes for chard, or blanch in boiling salted water (20 seconds for spinach, about 1 minute for chard). Transfer to a bowl of cold water, then drain and, taking the greens up by the handful, squeeze out excess water. Chop medium-fine.
- Heat the olive oil over medium heat in a heavy, medium size skillet and add the garlic and chile. Stir until fragrant, 30 seconds to a minute, and add the greens and salt and pepper to taste. Stir and toss in the pan for about a minute, until nicely infused with the oil, garlic and chile. Remove from the heat and add to the fish. Stir in 1/2 cup of the salsa. Taste and adjust seasonings.
- Heat the tortillas: wrap in a kitchen towel and place in a steamer basket over 1 inch of boiling water. Bring to a boil, cover the pot and steam 1 minute. Turn off the heat and allow to sit for 10 to 15 minutes without uncovering. Top the hot tortillas with the fish. Spoon on a little more salsa and if desired, garnish with crumbled cheese and shredded cabbage. Fold the tortillas over and serve.

Nutrition Information

- 191: calories;
- 344 milligrams: sodium;
- 9 grams: fat;
- 2 grams: sugars;
- 3 grams: dietary fiber;
- 15 grams: carbohydrates;
- 13 grams: protein;

270.   Sauce

Serving: Six cups | Prep: | Cook: | Ready in: 40mins

Ingredients

- 2 tablespoons olive oil
- ½ cup finely diced celery
- ½ cup finely diced green pepper
- 1 bay leaf
- 1 large clove garlic, minced
- 1 ½ teaspoons dried basil
- 1 teaspoon dried thyme
- ½ teaspoon dried oregano
- 1 teaspoon salt
- 1 teaspoon black pepper
- 2 tablespoons Worcestershire sauce
- 2 dashes Tabasco sauce
- 4 cups canned tomatoes, with their juice
- 1 tablespoon tomato paste
- 3 tablespoons chopped parsley

Direction

- Heat the olive oil in a large skillet and saute the vegetables for 5 minutes or until soft. Add the bay leaf, garlic, herbs, salt and pepper, Worcestershire and Tabasco. Cook over low heat for 3 minutes, or until all ingredients are combined.
- Chop the tomatoes and add to the skillet with their juice. Cook gently until the sauce begins to thicken, about 20 minutes.
- Stir in the tomato paste. Cook 5 minutes. Add the parsley and stir well. Serve over Basic Texas Meat Loaf.

Nutrition Information

- 40: calories;
- 1 gram: protein;
- 230 milligrams: sodium;
- 3 grams: sugars;
- 0 grams: polyunsaturated fat;
- 2 grams: dietary fiber;
- 5 grams: carbohydrates;

271. Sausage Stuffing

Serving: 6 to 8 servings | Prep: | Cook: | Ready in: 20mins

Ingredients

- ½ pound ground sausage meat
- 2 cups finely chopped onions
- 1 teaspoon finely minced garlic
- 2 apples, preferably Granny Smiths, about 1 pound
- 2 cups bread slices cut into 1/2-inch cubes, toasted
- Salt to taste if desired
- Freshly ground pepper to taste
- 2 teaspoons finely chopped leaf sage
- 1 cup fresh or canned chicken broth
- ½ cup finely chopped parsley
- 2 tablespoons butter
- 1 egg, well beaten

Direction

- Put sausage in skillet and cook, breaking up any lumps, until the meat has lost its raw look.
- Add onions and garlic and cook, stirring, until wilted.
- Meanwhile, peel apples; remove and discard stems and cores. Cut apples into quarters. Cut apple quarters crosswise into very thin slices. There should be about 3 cups.
- Add apples and stir. Add toasted bread cubes, salt and pepper. Add sage, broth and parsley. Cover and cook over low heat about 10 minutes. Add butter and egg and blend well. Remove from heat and keep warm.

Nutrition Information

- 190: calories;
- 16 grams: carbohydrates;
- 7 grams: protein;
- 389 milligrams: sodium;
- 4 grams: monounsaturated fat;
- 0 grams: trans fat;
- 11 grams: fat;
- 2 grams: polyunsaturated fat;
- 3 grams: dietary fiber;

272. Sauteed Wild Mushrooms With Shallots And Garlic

Serving: 4 servings | Prep: | Cook: | Ready in: 15mins

Ingredients

- 1 pound fresh wild mushrooms, like chanterelles, morels, porcini or any cultivated mushrooms of your choice
- 2 tablespoons olive oil
- Salt and freshly ground pepper to taste
- 1 tablespoon butter
- 2 tablespoons fine bread crumbs
- 1 tablespoon finely chopped shallots
- 1 teaspoon finely chopped garlic
- 2 tablespoons finely chopped parsley

Direction

- Trim the mushrooms, wash them in cold water and drain well.
- If the mushrooms are large, slice them or cut them in halves or quarters.
- Heat a large, heavy skillet and add the olive oil. When it is very hot and almost smoking, add the mushrooms, salt and pepper. Cook over high heat, shaking and tossing the skillet so that the mushrooms cook evenly until they are browned and crisp. They should be almost mahogany in color.
- Add the butter, and quickly sprinkle in the bread crumbs, shallots and garlic, and toss well for 10 seconds. Add the parsley and serve immediately.

Nutrition Information

- 128: calories;

- 4 grams: protein;
- 308 milligrams: sodium;
- 3 grams: sugars;
- 0 grams: trans fat;
- 6 grams: monounsaturated fat;
- 2 grams: dietary fiber;
- 10 grams: fat;
- 1 gram: polyunsaturated fat;
- 7 grams: carbohydrates;

- 136: calories;
- 10 grams: carbohydrates;
- 425 milligrams: sodium;
- 0 grams: polyunsaturated fat;
- 2 grams: sugars;
- 4 grams: dietary fiber;
- 3 grams: protein;
- 8 grams: fat;
- 5 grams: saturated fat;

273. Sautéed Chanterelles

Serving: 4 servings | Prep: | Cook: | Ready in: 20mins

Ingredients

- 1 pound chanterelles
- 2 to 3 tablespoons unsalted butter
- ¼ cup dry white wine
- About 3/4 cup chicken stock, preferably homemade
- Coarse salt and freshly ground pepper to taste
- 1 tablespoon chopped parsley, fresh thyme leaves or chives

Direction

- Cut the base of the stems of the chanterelles. If the mushrooms are very gritty, rinse them quickly under cold running water and pat them dry. Otherwise, clean them carefully with a soft paint or pastry brush. Cut the large mushrooms into bite-size pieces; leave the smaller ones whole.
- Heat the butter in a frying pan. Add the chanterelles and saute for two to three minutes or until they start to become soft. Add the wine and when it has evaporated, add the chicken stock. Cook over high heat until it has almost evaporated. Season to taste with salt and pepper and sprinkle with parsley, thyme or chives.

Nutrition Information

274. Sautéed Shredded Cabbage And Squash

Serving: The sautéed vegetables alone serve 4; the gratin serves 6. | Prep: | Cook: | Ready in: 1hours30mins

Ingredients

- For the shredded vegetable sauté:
- 2 tablespoons extra virgin olive oil
- 1 pound winter squash, peeled and shredded
- ½ cup chopped onion
- ¾ pound green cabbage, shredded
- 2 garlic cloves, minced
- 2 teaspoons finely chopped fresh sage
- 2 teaspoons chopped fresh thyme leaves
- For the gratin:
- 3 eggs
- ½ cup low-fat milk
- Salt and freshly ground pepper
- 1 cup cooked barley, rice (preferably brown) or quinoa
- 2 ounces Gruyère, grated (1/2 cup)
- 1 ounce Parmesan, grated (1/4 cup)

Direction

- If serving the vegetables with grains, begin cooking the grains of your choice first.
- Heat 1 tablespoon of the olive oil over medium heat in a large, heavy skillet or a wok and add the onion. Cook, stirring, until it begins to soften, about 3 minutes. Add the shredded winter squash and the garlic and a generous pinch of salt. Cook, stirring often, until not

quite tender, about 10 minutes, and add the remaining oil, the cabbage, sage, thyme, and salt and pepper to taste. Continue to cook, stirring often, until the vegetables are tender and fragrant, 8 to 10 minutes. Serve with grains or use the vegetables for the gratin below.

- If making a gratin, preheat the oven to 375 degrees and oil a 2-quart baking dish or gratin dish. In a large bowl, whisk together the eggs and milk. Add salt to taste (about 1/2 teaspoon) and freshly ground pepper, and stir in the cooked grains (I used cooked purple barley, and it was a beautiful and tasty combination with lots of texture) and the cooked vegetables. Add the cheeses and stir everything together, then scrape into the prepared baking dish.
- Bake 40 to 45 minutes, or until the top is lightly browned and the gratin is set. Allow to cool for 15 minutes or longer before cutting into wedges and serving. The gratin is good hot, warm or at room temperature, and you can cut it into smaller pieces to serve as an hors d'oeuvre.

Nutrition Information

- 448: calories;
- 21 grams: protein;
- 833 milligrams: sodium;
- 7 grams: saturated fat;
- 0 grams: trans fat;
- 9 grams: monounsaturated fat;
- 48 grams: carbohydrates;
- 8 grams: sugars;
- 20 grams: fat;
- 3 grams: polyunsaturated fat;

275. Sautéed Spinach

Serving: 4 servings. | Prep: | Cook: | Ready in: 10mins

Ingredients

- 1 ½ pounds fresh spinach
- 2 tablespoons olive oil
- 1 clove garlic, peeled
- Salt and freshly ground pepper to taste

Direction

- Discard blemished spinach leaves and tough stems. Rinse the spinach and drain well.
- Heat the oil in a skillet large enough to hold all the spinach. Add the spinach, garlic, salt and pepper. Cook over high heat, stirring rapidly, until the spinach is wilted and most of the moisture has evaporated. Remove the garlic and serve immediately.

Nutrition Information

- 101: calories;
- 7 grams: carbohydrates;
- 1 gram: sugars;
- 5 grams: protein;
- 4 grams: dietary fiber;
- 414 milligrams: sodium;

276. Savory Bread Pudding With Kale And Mushrooms

Serving: 6 servings. | Prep: | Cook: | Ready in: 1hours20mins

Ingredients

- 1 bunch kale, any type, stemmed and washed thoroughly in 2 changes of water (more if necessary)
- 1 tablespoon extra virgin olive oil
- ½ pound mushrooms, sliced
- 1 teaspoon fresh thyme leaves, coarsely chopped
- 1 to 2 garlic cloves (optional)
- Salt and freshly ground pepper
- ½ pound stale bread, preferably whole-grain, sliced about 1 inch thick

- 2 ounces Gruyère cheese, grated (1/2 cup)
- 1 ounce Parmesan cheese, grated (1/4 cup)
- Salt and freshly ground pepper
- 4 eggs
- 2 cups low-fat milk

Direction

- Bring a medium or large pot of water to a boil, salt generously and add the kale. Cook 2 to 3 minutes, until tender but still colorful. Transfer to a bowl of cold water, then drain and squeeze out excess water. Chop coarsely and set aside.
- If using garlic, cut one of the garlic cloves in half and rub the slices of bread with the cut side. Then mince all of the garlic. Cut the bread into 1-inch squares.
- Heat the oil over medium-high heat in a heavy, wide skillet and add the mushrooms. Cook, stirring often, until they begin to soften, and add the thyme, garlic and salt and pepper to taste. Continue to cook for another minute or two, until the mushrooms are tender and fragrant. Stir in the kale, toss together and remove from the heat.
- Preheat the oven to 350 degrees. Oil or butter a 2-quart baking dish, soufflé dish or gratin. In a large bowl, combine the bread cubes, the mushrooms and kale, and the two cheeses and toss together. Transfer to the prepared baking dish.
- Beat together the eggs and milk. Add salt to taste and a few twists of the pepper mill, and pour over the bread mixture. Let sit for 5 to 10 minutes before baking so that the bread can absorb some of the liquid.
- Place in the oven and bake 40 to 50 minutes, until puffed and browned. Remove from the oven and serve hot or warm.

Nutrition Information

- 288: calories;
- 5 grams: monounsaturated fat;
- 0 grams: trans fat;
- 28 grams: carbohydrates;
- 3 grams: dietary fiber;
- 8 grams: sugars;
- 555 milligrams: sodium;
- 12 grams: fat;
- 2 grams: polyunsaturated fat;
- 17 grams: protein;

277. Savory Oatmeal Pan Bread

Serving: Serves 8 to 10 | Prep: | Cook: |Ready in: 1hours

Ingredients

- 110 grams (1 1/8 cups) rolled oats
- 70 grams (1/2 cup plus 1 tablespoon) whole wheat pastry flour
- 10 grams (2 1/4 teaspoons) baking powder
- 4 ½ grams (scant 3/4 teaspoon) salt
- 1 gram (1/4 teaspoon) freshly ground pepper
- 150 grams (1/2 cup plus 1 tablespoon) milk
- 110 grams (2 extra large) egg
- ½ cup fresh herbs, such as parsley leaves, sage, marjoram, thyme, dill, chopped (1/3 cup chopped)
- 50 grams (3 tablespoons) grated onion
- 4 tablespoons extra virgin olive oil

Direction

- Preheat the oven to 400 degrees.
- Place the oats in the bowl of a stand mixer or into the bowl of a food processor fitted with the steel blade. Sift together the flour, baking powder, salt, and ground pepper and add to the oats. Add the remaining ingredients except 2 tablespoons of the olive oil and mix at medium speed or pulse together until well blended. Scrape down the sides of the bowl and the beater and mix again for about 30 seconds.
- Add 2 tablespoons of the oil to a 9-inch cast iron skillet and place in the oven for 5 minutes. Remove from the oven and spread the batter in the pan.

- Place in the oven and bake 30 minutes, until the top is nicely browned and a tester comes out clean when inserted in the middle. Remove from the heat and serve hot, or allow to cool on a rack.

Nutrition Information

- 140: calories;
- 0 grams: trans fat;
- 5 grams: monounsaturated fat;
- 1 gram: sugars;
- 14 grams: carbohydrates;
- 4 grams: protein;
- 130 milligrams: sodium;
- 8 grams: fat;
- 2 grams: dietary fiber;

278. Scallop Cakes With Artichoke Hearts

Serving: Four servings | Prep: | Cook: | Ready in: 20mins

Ingredients

- ½ pound sea scallops, coarsely chopped
- 3 artichoke hearts, cooked until tender, cooled and coarsely chopped
- 1 tablespoon minced fresh parsley
- 1 teaspoon minced fresh mint
- 1 egg, beaten
- ½ teaspoon salt
- Freshly ground black pepper to taste
- ¼ cup cracker crumbs

Direction

- Combine all ingredients in a medium bowl. With slightly moistened hands, form the mixture into 8 cakes, each about 1/2 inch thick.
- Coat a large nonstick skillet lightly with oil. Heat over medium-low heat until hot. Add as many fish cakes as will comfortably fit in pan.

Cook until nicely browned on both sides and scallops are cooked through, about 4 minutes per side.

Nutrition Information

- 88: calories;
- 292 milligrams: sodium;
- 2 grams: dietary fiber;
- 1 gram: sugars;
- 0 grams: trans fat;
- 8 grams: carbohydrates;
- 10 grams: protein;

279. Scallop Napoleon With Crisp Potatoes

Serving: Six servings | Prep: | Cook: | Ready in: 25mins

Ingredients

- Juice of 1 lemon
- Juice of 1 lime
- Juice of 1/2 orange
- ½ teaspoon each minced fresh rosemary, tarragon and thyme
- ½ teaspoon fresh minced tarragon
- ½ teaspoon fresh minced thyme
- 2 tablespoons Champagne vinegar
- ½ cup chicken broth
- ½ cup, plus 2 tablespoons, extra-virgin olive oil
- Salt and freshly ground black pepper to taste
- 2 pounds Idaho potatoes, peeled
- 3 tablespoons minced fresh chives
- ½ tablespoon unsalted butter
- 1 ½ pounds sea scallops (about 18 large scallops)

Direction

- Combine the juices, minced herbs, vinegar and chicken broth in a small, nonreactive saucepan and cook over high heat until the mixture is

reduced to about 1/3 cup. Beat in the half cup of olive oil and season to taste with salt and pepper. Set aside in the saucepan.
- Using a grater or food processor, shred the potatoes. Mix with 2 tablespoons of the chives and season to taste with salt and pepper. Heat 1 tablespoon of olive oil with the butter in a heavy, nonstick skillet. Spoon the potato mixture into the skillet in 3-inch disks, patting them down to flatten. Fry over medium-high heat until golden brown and crusty, about 3 to 4 minutes per side; drain on paper towels. Repeat until you have 12 disks. Set aside in a 150-degree oven to keep warm.
- Preheat a grill until very hot. Brush the scallops with the remaining olive oil and grill until just seared, about 2 to 3 minutes per side. Slice each in half horizontally.
- To assemble, place a potato disk on each of 6 plates, top with three slices of scallop, another disk and another trio of scallops, seared side up. Sprinkle with the remaining chives. Gently reheat the dressing until warm, beat it and pour a few tablespoons of it around each napoleon. Serve at once.

Nutrition Information

- 222: calories;
- 4 grams: dietary fiber;
- 15 grams: protein;
- 713 milligrams: sodium;
- 3 grams: sugars;
- 1 gram: monounsaturated fat;
- 0 grams: polyunsaturated fat;
- 34 grams: carbohydrates;

280. Scallops And Nectarines

Serving: 8 servings | Prep: | Cook: | Ready in: 10mins

Ingredients

- 3 pounds scallops
- ½ cup butter
- 4 cloves garlic, peeled and minced
- Salt and freshly ground black pepper to taste
- 8 medium-size nectarines, sliced
- ½ cup fresh lemon juice
- 4 tablespoons chopped fresh parsley

Direction

- Wash and dry scallops; cut large scallops in half.
- In large skillet heat butter; add garlic and scallops, salt and pepper. Cook quickly over high heat, stirring occasionally until scallops begin to brown, about 5 minutes.
- Add nectarines for last 2 or 3 minutes of cooking time. Add lemon juice. Remove from heat and sprinkle dish with parsley.

Nutrition Information

- 290: calories;
- 13 grams: fat;
- 1 gram: polyunsaturated fat;
- 12 grams: sugars;
- 805 milligrams: sodium;
- 23 grams: carbohydrates;
- 22 grams: protein;
- 8 grams: saturated fat;
- 0 grams: trans fat;
- 3 grams: dietary fiber;

281. Seared Red Rice With Spinach, Mushrooms, Carrot And Egg

Serving: 4 to 6 servings | Prep: | Cook: | Ready in: 15mins

Ingredients

- 2 tablespoons rice bran oil
- 1 small or medium onion, sliced

- 1 large carrot, peeled and cut in 2-inch-long julienne
- 4 ounces tofu, patted dry and cut in 1/2-inch dice
- 6 white or cremini mushrooms, cut in thick slices
- 4 large garlic cloves, minced
- 2 serrano chilies, minced
- 1 generous bunch spinach (3/4 to 1 pound), ends trimmed, rinsed thoroughly in 2 changes of water
- Salt and freshly ground pepper to taste
- 2 eggs, beaten and seasoned with salt and pepper
- 5 cups cooked red rice
- 1 tablespoon fish sauce or soy sauce (more to taste, optional)
- 1 bunch scallions, both white and green parts, chopped (optional)
- Optional garnishes
- Chopped cilantro
- Thinly sliced cucumber
- Lime wedges
- Scallions
- Fish sauce with hot chilies (nam pla prik)

Direction

- Heat a 14-inch wok or large, heavy skillet over high heat until a drop of water evaporates upon contact. Swirl in the oil and add the onion, carrot, tofu and mushrooms. Stir-fry until the vegetables are crisp-tender and the tofu is lightly colored, about 2 minutes. Add the garlic and chili, stir-fry for no more than 10 seconds, and add the spinach. Stir-fry until the spinach wilts, season to taste with salt and pepper, and pour in the beaten egg. Stir-fry until the egg is scrambled, and add the rice. Cook, scooping up the rice with your paddle, then pressing it into the pan and scooping it up again, for about 2 minutes, until the mixture has a nice seared aroma. Add the fish sauce or soy sauce and chopped scallions, stir together for about half a minute, and serve, passing the optional garnishes.

282. Seared Sea Scallops With Lime Ginger Sauce And Caramelized Endive

Serving: Six first-course servings | Prep: | Cook: | Ready in: 45mins

Ingredients

- The endive:
- 2 tablespoons unsalted butter
- 3 heads Belgian endive, halved lengthwise
- ¼ teaspoon kosher salt
- Freshly ground pepper to taste
- 1 tablespoon sugar
- 1 tablespoon fresh lime juice
- The scallops:
- 1 tablespoon canola oil
- 1 pound sea scallops
- ¼ teaspoon kosher salt
- Freshly ground pepper to taste
- The sauce and garnish:
- 1 shallot, peeled and minced
- ½ clove garlic, peeled and thinly sliced
- 1 tablespoon grated fresh ginger
- 1 ½ tablespoons fresh lime juice
- 6 tablespoons imported white port or dry white wine
- ¼ cup heavy cream
- 4 tablespoons cold unsalted butter, cut into small pieces
- ½ teaspoon kosher salt
- Freshly ground pepper to taste
- Cayenne pepper to taste
- 2 scallions, trimmed and thinly sliced on the diagonal
- 1 large ripe tomato, peeled, seeded and diced small

Direction

- To make the endive, melt the butter in a large nonstick skillet over medium-low heat. Season the endive with salt and pepper and place cut

side down in the skillet. Cook until lightly browned on the bottom, about 8 minutes.
- Sprinkle the sugar and lime juice over the top and cook, turning occasionally, until the endive are caramelized and tender when pierced with a knife, about 15 minutes longer. Cover and keep warm (can be prepared ahead and reheated in the oven).
- To make the scallops, heat the oil in a large skillet over medium-high heat. Season the scallops with salt and pepper, place them in the skillet and sear until lightly browned and warm in the center, about 1 minute per side.
- To make the sauce, combine the shallot, garlic, ginger, lime juice and port in a nonreactive saucepan over medium-high heat. Simmer until nearly all of the liquid has evaporated, about 3 minutes. Add the cream, bring to a boil and remove from the heat. Whisk in the butter a few pieces at a time until all is incorporated. Strain the sauce and season with salt, pepper and a touch of cayenne. Keep warm.
- To serve, place 1 endive half on each of 6 plates. Divide the scallops among the plates and spoon the sauce over and around them. Sprinkle with the scallions and tomato. Serve immediately.

Nutrition Information

- 253: calories;
- 1 gram: polyunsaturated fat;
- 11 grams: carbohydrates;
- 2 grams: dietary fiber;
- 18 grams: fat;
- 10 grams: protein;
- 0 grams: trans fat;
- 6 grams: monounsaturated fat;
- 439 milligrams: sodium;
- 4 grams: sugars;

283. Seitan Roulade With Oyster Mushroom Stuffing

Serving: 8 servings. | Prep: | Cook: | Ready in: 2hours

Ingredients

- Seitan
- 1 cup vital wheat gluten flour
- ¾ cup vegetable stock
- Roulade
- 1 pound uncooked seitan (see recipe)
- ½ cup soy sauce
- 3 tablespoons olive oil
- 1 small yellow onion, minced
- 1 cup oyster mushrooms, coarsely chopped
- 1 cup vegan sausage, cooked and crumbled
- 1 tablespoon minced fresh parsley
- 1 teaspoon minced fresh thyme
- Salt to taste
- Freshly ground black pepper to taste
- 4 cups finely diced bread

Direction

- Make the seitan. In a large bowl, combine flour and vegetable stock. Stir to make a soft dough. Knead for 3 minutes and let rest for 5 minutes.
- Place seitan in a shallow baking dish. Cover with soy sauce and marinate for 30 minutes at room temperature.
- Preheat oven to 375 degrees Fahrenheit. In a large skillet over medium heat, heat olive oil. Add onion, cover, and cook, stirring a few times until softened, about 5 minutes.
- Add mushrooms, vegan sausage, parsley, thyme, salt and pepper. Stir for 5 minutes longer, then transfer to a large bowl. Stir in the bread and mix well. Add a small amount of water if the stuffing mixture is too dry. Set aside.
- Place the uncooked seitan (reserve the marinade) between two sheets of plastic wrap and roll out with a rolling pin until it is approximately 1/4-inch thick. Using your hands, spread the stuffing over seitan to within 1/2-inch of the edges, then roll it up. In

a lightly oiled shallow baking pan, place rolled seitan seam-side down. Pierce in several places with a fork.
- Pour the reserved marinade over the roast and bake uncovered for 40 to 45 minutes, basting once after 20 minutes. When the surface of the roast is firm and golden brown, remove from oven and let rest for 10 minutes.
- Using a serrated knife, cut the roast into 1/2-inch-thick slices. Arrange on serving platter and serve with remaining marinade and your favorite vegan gravy.

284. Shell Bean Succotash

Serving: Serves 6 | Prep: | Cook: | Ready in: 1hours15mins

Ingredients

- 1 pound shell beans (about 1 3/4 cups)
- 1 onion, halved
- 7 cups water
- 3 large garlic cloves, crushed
- A bouquet garni made with a few sprigs each of parsley and thyme, a sprig of sage and a bay leaf
- Salt to taste
- 2 tablespoons extra virgin olive oil
- 1 small red onion, finely chopped
- ½ pound summer squash, cut in small dice
- 2 garlic cloves, minced (optional)
- Kernels from 4 ears of corn
- 2 or 3 sage leaves, minced
- Freshly ground pepper

Direction

- Combine the beans, onion, water, garlic, bouquet garni and salt in a heavy saucepan or soup pot, and bring to a simmer. Cover and simmer 45 minutes, or until the beans are tender. Taste and adjust salt. Remove and discard the onion, the bouquet garni and the garlic cloves. Drain though a strainer or colander set over a bowl.
- Heat the olive oil in a large, heavy skillet over medium heat, and add the red onion. Cook, stirring, until it begins to soften, for about three minutes. Add the squash, and salt to taste. Cook, stirring, until the squash begins to soften and look translucent, three to four minutes. Add the garlic and corn. Cook for about four minutes, stirring often. Season with salt and pepper. Add the beans and sage, and continue to cook, stirring, for another minute or two. Taste and adjust seasonings. If you want this to be more moist, stir in some of the bean broth.

Nutrition Information

- 90: calories;
- 2 grams: sugars;
- 900 milligrams: sodium;
- 5 grams: fat;
- 1 gram: polyunsaturated fat;
- 3 grams: protein;
- 10 grams: carbohydrates;

285. Show Me Bar B Q Meat Loaf

Serving: 4 servings | Prep: | Cook: | Ready in: 1hours

Ingredients

- ⅔ cup Show-Me Bar-B-Q Sauce
- 1 egg
- 1 cup bread crumbs
- 1 teaspoon salt
- 1 ½ pounds ground beef

Direction

- Mix 2/3 cup of the barbecue sauce with remaining ingredients.
- Form a loaf, and put into a pan.

- Bake for 45 minutes at 350 degrees.
- Pour another 2/3 cup of the sauce over the loaf, and bake 15 minutes more.

286. Shrimp Broth

Serving: About four cups | Prep: | Cook: |Ready in: 30mins

Ingredients

- Shells from raw shrimp
- 5 cups water
- 6 black peppercorns
- ¼ cup coarsely chopped onions
- 2 ribs celery coarsely chopped
- 1 bay leaf

Direction

- Put all the ingredients in a saucepan and bring to a boil. Simmer for 20 minutes and strain.

287. Shrimp Stuffed With Spicy Dal

Serving: 4 servings | Prep: | Cook: |Ready in: 1hours20mins

Ingredients

- ½ cup yellow split peas, picked over and rinsed well
- 2 cups water
- ⅛ teaspoon ground turmeric
- ½ teaspoon ground cumin
- 2 small jalapenos, halved lengthwise, not seeded
- 1 teaspoon vegetable oil
- 2 cloves garlic, peeled and minced
- 2 tablespoons chopped shallots
- ¼ teaspoon dried red pepper flakes
- ½ teaspoon kosher salt, plus more to taste
- 32 large shrimp, in the shell
- Curry-mustard steaming liquid (see recipe)

Direction

- Place the split peas, water, turmeric, cumin and jalapenos in a small saucepan and bring to a boil over medium-high heat. Reduce heat to a simmer, cover partly and cook for 45 minutes.
- Meanwhile, heat the oil in a small saucepan over medium heat. Add the garlic, shallots and pepper flakes and cook until softened, about 2 minutes.
- Remove the jalapenos from the split pea mixture and discard. Stir in the shallot mixture. Continue cooking, uncovered, until mixture forms a thick paste, about 20 minutes more, stirring often. Season with salt.
- With a small, sharp knife, make a slit down the back of each shrimp and use your finger to make a pocket on each side of the shrimp between the shell and the meat.
- Place about 1/2 teaspoon of the dal into each side of each shrimp. Press the shell firmly back against the shrimp.
- Place the shrimp in a steamer, cover and steam over the liquid until shrimp are just cooked through, about 3 1/2 minutes. Divide among 4 plates and serve immediately.

Nutrition Information

- 146: calories;
- 18 grams: carbohydrates;
- 7 grams: dietary fiber;
- 3 grams: sugars;
- 14 grams: protein;
- 0 grams: trans fat;
- 1 gram: polyunsaturated fat;
- 2 grams: fat;
- 494 milligrams: sodium;

288. Sicilian Cauliflower And Black Olive Gratin

Serving: Serves 6 | Prep: | Cook: | Ready in: 45mins

Ingredients

- 1 generous head green or white cauliflower (2 to 2 1/2 pounds)
- Salt
- 1 small onion, finely chopped
- 3 tablespoons extra virgin olive oil
- 2 garlic cloves, minced
- 16 imported oil-cured black olives, pitted and cut in half
- 2 tablespoons minced fresh parsley
- Freshly ground pepper
- ½ cup freshly grated Pecorino or Parmesan, or a combination

Direction

- Break up the cauliflower into small florets while you bring a large pot of water to a boil. Salt the water generously and drop in the cauliflower. Boil 5 minutes while you fill a bowl with ice and water. Transfer the cauliflower to the ice water, let sit for a couple of minutes, then drain and place on paper towels.
- Preheat the oven to 375 degrees. Oil a 2-quart baking dish or gratin dish. Heat 1 tablespoon of the olive oil over medium heat in a large, heavy skillet and add the onion. Cook, stirring, until tender, about 3 minutes, and add a pinch of salt and the garlic. Cook, stirring, for about 30 seconds, until fragrant and translucent. Remove from the heat and stir in the olives.
- Place the cauliflower in the baking dish and add the onion and olive mixture, the remaining olive oil, the parsley and half the cheese. Season to taste with salt and pepper and stir together well. Spread out in the dish and sprinkle the remaining cheese on top.
- Bake in the preheated oven for 25 to 30 minutes, until the cheese is nicely browned. Serve hot or warm.

Nutrition Information

- 163: calories;
- 491 milligrams: sodium;
- 11 grams: carbohydrates;
- 3 grams: saturated fat;
- 7 grams: protein;
- 1 gram: polyunsaturated fat;
- 4 grams: sugars;

289. Skillet Collards And Winter Squash

Serving: 4 to 6 servings | Prep: | Cook: | Ready in: 1hours30mins

Ingredients

- 1 cup barley (regular or purple)
- 1 quart water
- Salt to taste
- 2 tablespoons extra virgin olive oil
- 2 pounds butternut squash, peeled and diced
- 1 generous bunch collard greens (about 1 pound), stemmed, washed thoroughly in 2 changes of water and sliced crosswise in ribbons
- 2 garlic cloves, minced
- Freshly ground pepper
- 2 teaspoons slivered fresh sage
- Lemon juice to taste

Direction

- Combine the barley and water in a medium saucepan, add salt to taste and bring to a boil. Reduce the heat and simmer 50 minutes to an hour (longer for purple barley), until the barley is tender. There should still be plenty of water in the pot. Place a strainer over a bowl and drain the barley. Measure out 1 cup of the cooking water. Transfer the barley to a serving bowl and keep warm.

- Heat 1 tablespoon of the oil over medium-high heat and sear the squash for 5 to 10 minutes, until it is lightly colored. Add the greens and cook, stirring, until they are wilted, about 5 minutes. Add the garlic, salt, pepper and sage and cook, stirring, for a couple of minutes, until the mixture is fragrant, then add the stock or barley water and bring to a simmer. Reduce the heat to low, cover and simmer 10 minutes, until the squash and greens are tender. Add lemon juice to taste, drizzle on the remaining olive oil, adjust seasoning and serve with the barley.

Nutrition Information

- 248: calories;
- 1 gram: polyunsaturated fat;
- 4 grams: sugars;
- 8 grams: protein;
- 983 milligrams: sodium;
- 6 grams: fat;
- 3 grams: monounsaturated fat;
- 46 grams: carbohydrates;
- 12 grams: dietary fiber;

290. Skillet Soba, Baked Tofu And Green Bean Salad With Spicy Dressing

Serving: Serves 6 | Prep: | Cook: |Ready in: 45mins

Ingredients

- For the tofu
- ½ pound tofu
- 1 tablespoon low-sodium soy sauce
- 1 teaspoon minced ginger
- 1 garlic clove, minced
- 1 teaspoon agave nectar
- 1 tablespoon canola, rice bran oil or grape seed oil
- 1 teaspoon dark sesame oil
- For the salad
- ½ pound green beans, trimmed and cut into 1-inch lengths (about 2 cups)
- Salt to taste
- ¾ pound soba noodles
- ¼ cup dark sesame oil
- 1 tablespoon of the tofu marinade
- 2 tablespoons rice vinegar
- 1 garlic clove, minced or pureed
- 2 teaspoons minced ginger
- ½ teaspoon hot chile oil or 1/8 to 1/4 teaspoon cayenne pepper (to taste)
- 1 tablespoon soy sauce
- ⅓ cup buttermilk
- ¼ to ½ cup chopped cilantro (to taste)
- 1 tablespoon lightly toasted sesame seeds or black sesame seeds

Direction

- Make the baked tofu: Preheat the oven to 375 degrees. Line a sheet pan with parchment. Pat the tofu dry with paper towels and cut into dominoes, about 1/3 inch thick. In a large, wide bowl whisk together all of the marinade ingredients for the tofu. Pat each piece of tofu with paper towels, then dip into the marinade, making sure to coat both sides. Transfer to the baking sheet. Bake for 7 to 10 minutes, until the edges are just beginning to color and the marinade sets on the surface of the tofu. Remove from the heat and keep warm.
- Bring 3 or 4 quarts of water to a boil in a large pot. Add salt to taste and the green beans. Boil 5 minutes and using a slotted spoon or skimmer, transfer to a bowl of cold water and drain. Set aside.
- Bring the water back to a boil. Add the soba gradually, so that the water remains at a boil, and stir once with a long-handled spoon or pasta fork so that the noodles don't stick together. Wait for the water to come back up to a rolling boil – it will bubble up, so don't fill the pot all the way – and add 1 cup of cold

water. Allow the water to come back to a rolling boil and add another cup of cold water. Allow the water to come to a boil one more time and add a third cup of water. When the water comes to a boil again, the noodles should be cooked through. Drain and toss with 2 tablespoons of the sesame oil. (If using rice noodles, boil 5 to 6 minutes without adding the water, until cooked al dente).
- Whisk together 1 tablespoon of the tofu marinade, the rice vinegar, garlic, ginger, hot chile oil or cayenne, soy sauce, remaining sesame oil and buttermilk. Pour over the noodles, add the beans, tofu and cilantro, and gently toss together.
- Heat a wide skillet over medium-high heat and add the noodle salad. Toss in the pan until heated through and serve.

Nutrition Information

- 362: calories;
- 15 grams: fat;
- 2 grams: dietary fiber;
- 0 grams: trans fat;
- 3 grams: sugars;
- 13 grams: protein;
- 6 grams: polyunsaturated fat;
- 48 grams: carbohydrates;
- 715 milligrams: sodium;

291.   Sloppy Joes

Serving: 6 servings | Prep: | Cook: |Ready in: 22mins

Ingredients

- For the sauce:
- 1 8-ounce can tomato sauce
- ½ cup ketchup
- 1 ½ tablespoons Worcestershire sauce
- 1 teaspoon prepared yellow mustard
- ½ teaspoon dry mustard
- 1 teaspoon molasses
- 1 garlic clove, finely minced
- ¼ teaspoon orange zest
- Pinch of ground cloves
- Hot sauce to taste
- For the meat:
- 1 pound ground beef
- ½ small onion, finely chopped
- 6 whole-wheat hamburger buns, toasted if desired

Direction

- In a saucepan over low heat combine the sauce ingredients. Season to taste with salt and pepper. Mix well, and simmer while preparing the meat.
- Heat a heavy nonstick or cast-iron skillet, at least 10 inches in diameter, over medium-high heat. Add the ground sirloin, and saute, stirring occasionally, for 4 to 5 minutes, or until the meat is no longer pink. Turn the meat into a strainer or colander lined with paper towels, allowing the fat to drain off.
- Add the onion to the pan, and sauté, stirring frequently, for about 5 minutes, or until the onion is translucent. Return the meat to the pan, and add the sauce. Heat for 3 minutes, stirring occasionally. Taste and season with salt, pepper or more hot sauce, if desired. Spoon 1/2 cup of the mixture over each bun. Serve immediately.

Nutrition Information

- 299: calories;
- 1 gram: polyunsaturated fat;
- 10 grams: sugars;
- 21 grams: protein;
- 4 grams: saturated fat;
- 0 grams: trans fat;
- 5 grams: monounsaturated fat;
- 3 grams: dietary fiber;
- 650 milligrams: sodium;
- 11 grams: fat;
- 30 grams: carbohydrates;

292. Smashed Turnips With Fresh Horseradish

Serving: 4 to 6 servings | Prep: | Cook: | Ready in: 45mins

Ingredients

- 8 large turnips (about 2 pounds), peeled and quartered
- ½ cup sour cream
- 6 scallions, thinly sliced
- 2 tablespoons freshly grated horseradish, or more to taste
- 2 teaspoons salt

Direction

- Place the turnips in a large pot with enough water to cover by 2 inches. Bring to a boil over high heat, then reduce the heat to low and simmer until fork-tender, about 25 minutes. Drain thoroughly, until completely dry.
- Place the turnips in a bowl and, while they are still hot, add the sour cream, scallions, horseradish and salt. Mash with a wire whisk or potato masher until well combined but still chunky. Serve immediately.

Nutrition Information

- 78: calories;
- 1 gram: monounsaturated fat;
- 0 grams: polyunsaturated fat;
- 10 grams: carbohydrates;
- 4 grams: fat;
- 2 grams: protein;
- 3 grams: dietary fiber;
- 6 grams: sugars;
- 443 milligrams: sodium;

293. Smoked Lobster Chowder

Serving: Four servings | Prep: | Cook: | Ready in: 45mins

Ingredients

- 3 1 1/2-pound lobsters
- 1 teaspoon olive oil
- 1 1/4-inch-thick slice pancetta, diced small
- 2 large cloves garlic, peeled and minced
- 1 medium onion, peeled and diced
- 2 ½ cups milk
- ¼ cup heavy cream
- 8 medium-small red potatoes, each cut into 8 wedges
- 2 carrots, peeled and julienned
- 1 teaspoon salt, plus more to taste
- Freshly ground pepper to taste
- 1 tablespoon chopped Italian parsley
- 8 basil leaves, cut across into thin strips

Direction

- Steam the lobsters in 2 cups of boiling water for 10 minutes. Reserve 1 cup of the steaming liquid. Follow the directions for smoking lobster as above. Cut the lobster meat into large chunks and set aside.
- Combine the olive oil and pancetta in a large saucepan over medium-high heat. Cook for 2 minutes. Lower the heat, add the garlic and onion and saute for 5 minutes. Add the steaming liquid and cook, stirring constantly, for 1 minute. Add the milk, cream and potatoes and bring to a simmer; do not boil. Cook until potatoes are tender, about 12 minutes.
- Stir in the carrots, lobster meat, salt and pepper. Cook for 2 minutes. Taste and adjust seasoning with additional salt and pepper if needed. Stir in the parsley. Divide among 4 bowls, garnish with basil and serve immediately.

294. Soba And Herb Salad With Roasted Eggplant And Pluots

Serving: Serves 6 | Prep: | Cook: | Ready in: 45mins

Ingredients

- 2 long eggplants, about 1 pound, cut in 3/4-inch dice
- Salt to taste
- ⅓ cup sunflower oil
- 9 ounces (1 package) soba noodles
- 1 tablespoon dark sesame oil
- 6 ounces firm tofu, cut in 1/2-inch dice and blotted dry
- 1 tablespoon soy sauce
- 1 to 2 serrano or Thai chiles, minced (to taste)
- 2 firm but ripe plums or pluots, cut in thin slices
- 1 cup basil leaves (preferably Thai basil), chopped, torn or cut in slivers
- 1 cup chopped cilantro
- 2 to 4 tablespoons chopped chives
- ⅓ cup seasoned rice vinegar
- Juice and grated zest of 1 lime
- 1 large garlic clove, minced or pureed

Direction

- Preheat the oven to 450 degrees. Cover a sheet pan with foil. Place the eggplant in a large bowl and season with salt to taste. Add 2 tablespoons of the oil and toss well. Spread on the baking sheet in an even layer. Place in the oven and roast for 20 minutes, or until the eggplant is soft when you pierce it with a fork and beginning to brown on the edges. It will look dry on the outside surfaces. Remove from the oven and very carefully fold over the foil and crimp the edges so that the eggplant is now contained within a foil envelope, where it will steam and become softer. Set aside until the eggplant cools.
- Meanwhile, cook the soba noodles. When they're done, drain, rinse with cold water, shake well in the colander and transfer to a bowl. Add the sesame oil and stir together.
- Heat a wok or a large heavy frying pan over high heat until a drop of water evaporates within a few seconds when added to the pan. Add 1 tablespoon of the sunflower oil and the tofu. Let sit in the pan to sear for 30 seconds, then stir-fry until lightly browned. Add 1 teaspoon of the soy sauce, toss together, then remove from the heat and add to the noodles. Add the roasted eggplant and the minced chiles, the plums or pluots and all of the chopped herbs if serving right away, half of them if serving later.
- In a small bowl or measuring cup mix together the seasoned wine vinegar, the remaining soy sauce, salt to taste, the lime juice and zest, and the garlic. Whisk in the remaining oil. Taste and adjust seasoning. Toss with the noodle salad and serve.

Nutrition Information

- 382: calories;
- 2 grams: saturated fat;
- 7 grams: dietary fiber;
- 49 grams: carbohydrates;
- 10 grams: sugars;
- 13 grams: protein;
- 784 milligrams: sodium;
- 18 grams: fat;

295. Soft Shell Crabs With Tomato Buttermilk Sauce

Serving: 2 servings | Prep: | Cook: | Ready in: 20mins

Ingredients

- 2 medium cloves garlic
- Pan spray
- ½ teaspoon ground cumin
- ⅛ teaspoon crushed red pepper flakes
- ¼ teaspoon sugar

- ½ of a 28-ounce can of no-salt-added tomatoes
- 2 tablespoons plus 1 teaspoon flour
- ½ cup nonfat buttermilk
- 4 cleaned soft-shell crabs
- 1 teaspoon toasted sesame oil

Direction

- Mince garlic.
- Over high heat, heat nonstick saute pan large enough to hold the crabs. Spray lightly with pan spray. Stir in the garlic and cook for 30 seconds over medium heat.
- Remove from heat, and stir in cumin, red pepper and sugar. Add the tomatoes, crushing them between your fingers before adding to the pan. Simmer for a few minutes.
- Mix 1 teaspoon of flour with a little of the buttermilk to make a paste; then, add the paste to the remaining buttermilk, and stir it into the tomato mixture. Cook over low heat until mixture thickens. Remove from saute pan, and set aside.
- Wash crabs and dip into remaining flour, coating both sides.
- Return pan to medium-high heat, and add oil. When pan is hot, add the crabs, and brown on both sides, allowing 2 to 3 minutes a side, depending on the size of the crabs.
- Spoon the reserved tomato sauce over the crabs, and cook just to heat sauce through.

Nutrition Information

- 148: calories;
- 5 grams: sugars;
- 1 gram: dietary fiber;
- 2 grams: polyunsaturated fat;
- 14 grams: carbohydrates;
- 11 grams: protein;
- 297 milligrams: sodium;

296. Sole With Julienne Of Pumpkin

Serving: Serves 2 | Prep: | Cook: | Ready in: 20mins

Ingredients

- 1 pound gray sole (about 3 fillets)
- 2 teaspoons lemon juice
- ½ cup water
- ¼ cup white wine
- Salt and white pepper to taste
- 5 tablespoons sweet butter
- 1 ½ cups loosely packed julienne of pumpkin flesh (strips about 2 inches long)

Direction

- Place the sole fillets in a pan just large enough to hold them. Add the lemon juice, water, white wine, sacreamlt and pepper. Bring to a boil, reduce to simmer and cook for 4 to 5 minutes. Carefully remove sole from the pan and place on a dish in a warm oven. Reserve cooking liquid.
- Meanwhile, melt 2 tablespoons of the butter in a skillet and saute the julienne strips of pumpkin over medium heat, stirring occasionally, for 3 to 5 minutes, or until they are soft. Remove pumpkin and keep warm.
- Add any juice that has accumulated in the dish holding the sole to the cooking liquid and reduce the liquid over high heat by half. Pour the reduced liquid into an electric blender. Add about 1/2 cup of the pumpkin strips and 3 tablespoons of cold butter. Blend well.
- Put fillets on warm plates, garnish with sauce and arrange remaining pumpkin strips on top.

Nutrition Information

- 473: calories;
- 19 grams: saturated fat;
- 1 gram: trans fat;
- 7 grams: carbohydrates;
- 0 grams: dietary fiber;
- 32 grams: protein;

- 34 grams: fat;
- 9 grams: monounsaturated fat;
- 2 grams: polyunsaturated fat;
- 3 grams: sugars;
- 1069 milligrams: sodium;

297. Sour Orange Mignonette

Serving: 2 cups, enough for 120 oysters | Prep: | Cook: | Ready in: 30mins

Ingredients

- 1 ¾ cups Seville orange juice (about 8 oranges)
- ¼ cup Champagne vinegar
- 2 large shallots, finely chopped
- ½ teaspoon granulated sugar

Direction

- Whisk ingredients together in a small bowl until sugar dissolves. Cover with plastic wrap and chill in refrigerator for half an hour.

Nutrition Information

- 165: calories;
- 0 grams: polyunsaturated fat;
- 37 grams: carbohydrates;
- 3 grams: dietary fiber;
- 26 grams: sugars;
- 4 grams: protein;
- 12 milligrams: sodium;
- 1 gram: fat;

298. Southeast Asian Shrimp And Grapefruit Salad

Serving: 4 servings | Prep: | Cook: | Ready in: 30mins

Ingredients

- 1 to 1 ½ pounds shrimp
- Salt
- 3 tablespoons nam pla (fish sauce) or soy sauce
- 1 tablespoon sugar
- Juice of 2 limes
- 6 cups lettuce or mesclun, washed and dried
- 2 grapefruit, peeled and sectioned, tough white pith removed, each section cut in half
- ¼ cup chopped mint
- ¼ cup chopped cilantro
- Minced chilies or dried red pepper flakes, optional
- ½ cup chopped dry-roasted peanuts, optional

Direction

- Put shrimp in a saucepan with salted water to cover; bring to a boil, then turn off heat and let sit for 5 minutes, or until shrimp are opaque in center. (Alternatively, grill or saute, sprinkling shrimp with salt as they cook.) Cool in refrigerator or under cold running water, then peel (and devein if you like). Cut shrimp in half if they're large.
- Combine nam pla or soy sauce with 2 tablespoons water, sugar and lime juice, and blend or whisk until smooth.
- Arrange the lettuce on 4 plates; top each portion with a few grapefruit pieces, some shrimp, and the mint and cilantro; drizzle with the dressing, then sprinkle with a little of the minced chilies and chopped peanuts if you like, or pass them at the table.

Nutrition Information

- 182: calories;
- 2 grams: fat;
- 13 grams: sugars;
- 1468 milligrams: sodium;
- 0 grams: monounsaturated fat;
- 1 gram: polyunsaturated fat;
- 21 grams: carbohydrates;
- 4 grams: dietary fiber;
- 23 grams: protein;

299. Spaghetti With Tomatoes And Garlic

Serving: 4 servings | Prep: | Cook: | Ready in: 15mins

Ingredients

- ¾ pound spaghetti
- ¾ pound ripe plum tomatoes with skin removed or 1 cup canned crushed tomatoes
- 2 tablespoons olive oil
- 1 tablespoon finely chopped garlic
- 1 teaspoon finely chopped jalapeno pepper (optional)
- Salt and pepper to taste
- 2 tablespoons fresh chopped basil or Italian parsley
- 4 tablespoons grated Parmesan or pecorino cheese

Direction

- Bring two quarts of salted water to boil in a kettle. Add the spaghetti, stir well and bring back to a boil, stirring while cooking. Cook to the desired degree of doneness. Reserve a quarter-cup of the cooking liquid.
- Meanwhile, cut the tomatoes into 1/4 inch cubes.
- In a skillet or kettle, add olive oil and the garlic. Cook briefly, stirring. Do not brown. Add the tomatoes, jalapeno pepper, salt and pepper to taste. Cook for 2 minutes, stirring. Add the spaghetti, basil or parsley, reserved cooking liquid and cheese, toss well and serve.

Nutrition Information

- 440: calories;
- 441 milligrams: sodium;
- 11 grams: fat;
- 3 grams: saturated fat;
- 1 gram: polyunsaturated fat;
- 71 grams: carbohydrates;
- 5 grams: dietary fiber;
- 6 grams: sugars;
- 15 grams: protein;

300. Sparkling Pineapple Soup

Serving: | Prep: | Cook: | Ready in: 10mins

Ingredients

- 2 cups sparkling wine
- 3 cupsgrated pineapple flesh
- 2 tablespoons lemon juice
- Toasted coconut

Direction

- In a bowl, whisk together 2 cups sparkling wine
- In another bowl, combine 3 cups grated pineapple flesh, 2 tablespoons lemon juice
- Combine everything in one bowl, stir gently and serve immediately; do not refrigerate.
- Garnish: Toasted coconut.

301. Spartina's Roasted Cod With Nicoise Vinaigrette

Serving: 4 servings | Prep: | Cook: | Ready in: 30mins

Ingredients

- 8 marinated anchovy fillets, minced
- 1 tablespoon capers, minced
- 1 tablespoon nicoise olives, minced
- 1 tablespoon minced shallot
- 1 teaspoon finely slivered garlic
- ½ cup extra-virgin olive oil
- 3 tablespoons sherry wine vinegar
- Salt and freshly ground black pepper
- 4 cod fillets, each about 6 ounces

Direction

- Preheat oven to 500 degrees. Mix anchovies, capers, olives, shallot and garlic with 1/3 cup olive oil and the vinegar. Season with salt and pepper.
- Heat remaining oil in an oven-proof skillet. Season cod with salt and pepper, place in skillet and sear on one side until golden, about 2 minutes. Turn and place in oven until done, about 5 minutes.
- Place a cod fillet on each of 4 plates. Spoon about 2 tablespoons of anchovy sauce on top.

Nutrition Information

- 404: calories;
- 4 grams: saturated fat;
- 20 grams: monounsaturated fat;
- 3 grams: polyunsaturated fat;
- 1 gram: carbohydrates;
- 33 grams: protein;
- 29 grams: fat;
- 0 grams: sugars;
- 522 milligrams: sodium;

302. Spiced Lamb Loaf

Serving: 6 or more servings | Prep: | Cook: | Ready in: 1hours15mins

Ingredients

- 2 pounds ground lean meat, preferably lamb
- 1 tablespoon corn, peanut or vegetable oil
- 1 cup finely chopped onion
- 1 cup finely diced celery
- 1 cup finely chopped green pepper
- 1 teaspoon finely minced garlic
- Salt to taste if desired
- Freshly ground pepper to taste
- ⅛ teaspoon freshly grated nutmeg
- 1 teaspoon ground cumin
- 2 teaspoons Worcestershire sauce
- ⅛ teaspoon Tabasco sauce
- 1 tablespoon Dijon-style mustard
- ½ cup fine, fresh bread crumbs
- 1 egg, lightly beaten

Direction

- Preheat oven to 400 degrees.
- Put meat in mixing bowl and set aside.
- Heat oil in saucepan and add onion, celery, green pepper and garlic. Cook, stirring, until vegetables are wilted. Set aside to cool briefly.
- Add cooked vegetables to meat. Add salt, pepper, nutmeg, cumin, Worcestershire sauce, Tabasco sauce, mustard, bread crumbs and egg. Blend well with the fingers.
- Pack mixture into 6-cup loaf pan. Smooth over the top.
- Place pan in oven and bake 50 minutes. Remove from oven and let stand 10 minutes. Slice and serve.

Nutrition Information

- 1072: calories;
- 0 grams: trans fat;
- 12 grams: protein;
- 2 grams: dietary fiber;
- 3 grams: sugars;
- 568 milligrams: sodium;
- 108 grams: fat;
- 54 grams: saturated fat;
- 5 grams: polyunsaturated fat;
- 44 grams: monounsaturated fat;

303. Spiced Manhattan Clam Chowder

Serving: Four servings | Prep: | Cook: | Ready in: 1hours10mins

Ingredients

- 4 ripe tomatoes, peeled, cored, seeded and diced
- ¼ cup grated lemon rind

- ¼ cup minced mint leaves
- 32 littleneck clams, scrubbed
- 2 cloves garlic, peeled and minced
- 1 cup dry white wine
- 2 cups water
- 2 slices smoked bacon, chopped
- 1 white onion, minced
- 1 teaspoon orange zest
- 3 cups fresh or canned plum tomatoes, with juice
- 1 1/8-inch cinnamon stick
- 3 boiling potatoes, peeled and cut into 1/2-inch cubes
- ¼ teaspoon saffron threads
- Salt and freshly ground pepper to taste

Direction

- Combine the tomatoes, lemon rind and mint. Set aside. Combine the clams, garlic, wine and water in a pot and bring to a boil. Cover, lower the heat and simmer until the clams open, about 5 minutes. Remove from the heat. Strain, reserve the broth and set the clams aside.
- Fry the bacon in a large saucepan until golden, about 5 minutes. Add the onion and half the orange zest. Continue cooking until the onion is translucent, about 5 minutes. Add the tomatoes, their juice and the cinnamon stick. Simmer for 30 minutes. Remove the cinnamon and discard. Pour the tomato broth into a blender or food processor. Puree until smooth. Transfer to a clean saucepan. Add the clam broth and potatoes. Simmer until the potatoes are tender, about 5 to 8 minutes.
- Take the clams out of their shells. Add the saffron and the remaining orange zest to the chowder and simmer for one minute. Add the clam meat. Continue cooking for about 2 minutes. Season to taste with salt and pepper. Ladle into 4 bowls. Garnish with the tomato-lemon-mint mixture.

Nutrition Information

- 400: calories;
- 1 gram: polyunsaturated fat;
- 50 grams: carbohydrates;
- 1739 milligrams: sodium;
- 0 grams: trans fat;
- 8 grams: fat;
- 2 grams: saturated fat;
- 3 grams: monounsaturated fat;
- 9 grams: dietary fiber;
- 10 grams: sugars;
- 25 grams: protein;

304. Spicy Carrot And Spinach Latkes

Serving: Makes 15 to 16, serving 4 | Prep: | Cook: | Ready in: 40mins

Ingredients

- 1 pound carrots, peeled and grated (3 cups, tightly packed, grated carrots)
- 6 ounces baby spinach or stemmed washed spinach, chopped (3 cups tightly packed chopped spinach)
- 1 teaspoon baking powder
- Salt to taste
- 1 tablespoon nigella seeds (more to taste)
- 2 to 3 teaspoons mild chili powder, to taste
- 3 tablespoons oat bran
- 3 tablespoon matzo meal or all-purpose flour
- 2 eggs, beaten
- About 1/4 cup canola, grape seed or rice bran oil

Direction

- Begin heating a large heavy skillet over medium-high heat. Heat the oven to 300 degrees and line a sheet pan with parchment. Place a rack over another sheet pan.
- In a large bowl mix together the carrots, spinach, baking powder, salt, nigella seeds, chili powder, oat bran and matzo meal or flour. Taste and adjust salt. Add the eggs and stir together. If the mixture seems dry add a little more egg.

- Pack about 3 tablespoons of the mixture into a 1/4 cup measuring cup. Reverse onto the parchment-lined baking sheet. Repeat with the remaining latke mix. You should have enough to make 15 or 16 latkes.
- Add the oil to the pan and when it is hot (hold your hand a few inches above – you should feel the heat), use a spatula to transfer one portion of the latke mixture to the pan. Press down with the spatula to flatten. Repeat with more mounds. In my 10-inch pan I can cook three or four at a time without crowding; my 12-inch pan will accommodate four or five. Cook on one side until golden brown, about three minutes. Slide the spatula underneath and flip the latkes over. Cook on the other side until golden brown, another two to three minutes. Transfer to the rack set over a baking sheet and place in the oven to keep warm.
- Serve hot topped with low-fat sour cream, Greek yogurt or crème fraîche, or with other toppings of your choice such as chutney or raita.

Nutrition Information

- 64: calories;
- 4 grams: fat;
- 1 gram: sugars;
- 0 grams: trans fat;
- 2 grams: protein;
- 5 grams: carbohydrates;
- 120 milligrams: sodium;

305. Spicy Celery With Garlic

Serving: 6 servings | Prep: | Cook: | Ready in: 35mins

Ingredients

- 1 bunch celery (2 pounds)
- 4 cloves garlic, peeled and thinly sliced (2 tablespoons)
- ½ cup chicken stock, preferably unsalted homemade stock, or canned light chicken broth
- ¼ cup hot red salsa
- ¼ cup olive oil
- Salt to taste

Direction

- Using a vegetable peeler, remove the tough, fibrous strings from the celery ribs. Cut the celery into 2-inch pieces. You should have about 8 cups.
- Place the celery pieces in a large bowl, cover with cold water and wash them thoroughly.
- Place the celery, still wet, in a large saucepan with the remainder of the ingredients. Bring the mixture to a boil, uncovered; then, reduce the heat, cover and cook gently for about 25 minutes until most of the liquid has evaporated and the celery is tender.
- Serve immediately, or if you want to serve the dish later, cool, cover, refrigerate and reheat briefly in a microwave oven or in a saucepan on top of the stove.

Nutrition Information

- 118: calories;
- 10 grams: fat;
- 1 gram: polyunsaturated fat;
- 7 grams: carbohydrates;
- 3 grams: sugars;
- 2 grams: protein;
- 451 milligrams: sodium;

306. Spicy Coleslaw

Serving: Serves 6 | Prep: | Cook: | Ready in: 10mins

Ingredients

- 1 medium head green cabbage
- 2 carrots, peeled and grated

- ½ cup mayonnaise
- 2 tablespoons pickle relish
- 1 tablespoon Dijon mustard
- 1 tablespoon cider vinegar
- 2 teaspoons pepper sauce, like Frank's, or to taste
- Kosher salt
- Freshly ground black pepper

Direction

- Cut the cabbage in half and remove the core. Cut each half in half and slice each resulting quarter into thin ribbons. Mix with carrots in a large, nonreactive bowl.
- In a separate bowl, whisk together the remaining ingredients.
- Pour the dressing over the cabbage and toss. Season to taste.
- The coleslaw may be covered with plastic wrap and refrigerated for a few hours. Toss again before serving.

Nutrition Information

- 190: calories;
- 2 grams: protein;
- 4 grams: monounsaturated fat;
- 13 grams: carbohydrates;
- 7 grams: sugars;
- 472 milligrams: sodium;
- 15 grams: fat;
- 0 grams: trans fat;
- 9 grams: polyunsaturated fat;
- 5 grams: dietary fiber;

307. Spicy Pork

Serving: 2 servings | Prep: | Cook: | Ready in: 15mins

Ingredients

- 1 tablespoon coarsely grated fresh or frozen ginger
- 1 large garlic clove
- 8 ounces pork tenderloin
- 1 teaspoon olive oil
- 1 teaspoon ground cumin
- ¼ teaspoon turmeric
- ⅛ teaspoon hot pepper flakes
- ½ teaspoon ground coriander
- ½ cup no-salt-added beef stock or broth
- Freshly ground black pepper to taste
- 1 teaspoon lime juice

Direction

- Grate ginger; mince garlic.
- Trim fat from pork and cut remainder into bite-size chunks.
- Heat oil until it is very hot in nonstick pot. Saute ginger and garlic for 30 seconds. Add the pork and brown on both sides.
- Stir in cumin, turmeric, hot pepper flakes and coriander and cook about 30 seconds.
- Stir in beef stock and cook over medium-high heat until stock is reduced a little. Season with pepper and lime juice. Serve.

Nutrition Information

- 178: calories;
- 2 grams: saturated fat;
- 1 gram: dietary fiber;
- 25 grams: protein;
- 7 grams: fat;
- 0 grams: sugars;
- 3 grams: monounsaturated fat;
- 4 grams: carbohydrates;
- 181 milligrams: sodium;

308. Spicy Rum Punch

Serving: Two gallons, or about 90 servings | Prep: | Cook: | Ready in: 40mins

Ingredients

- The syrup:
- 2 oranges
- 2 lemons
- 4 cups granulated sugar
- 1 teaspoon ground nutmeg
- 2 teaspoons ground cinnamon
- 2 teaspoons anise seeds
- 1 teaspoon red pepper flakes
- 1 teaspoon black peppercorns
- 2 tablespoons coriander seeds
- 20 bay leaves
- ½ cup vanilla extract
- 8 cups water
- The punch:
- 2 quarts syrup (above)
- 2 liters white rum
- 2 12-ounce cans frozen orange concentrate
- 2 12-ounce cans frozen grapefruit concentrate
- 2 quarts cranberry juice

Direction

- For the syrup, remove the skin from the oranges and lemons with a vegetable peeler and place the peelings in a large saucepan. Extract the juice from the oranges and lemons and add it to the saucepan with the remaining ingredients. Bring to a boil, reduce the heat and boil gently, uncovered, for 30 minutes. Strain through a fine strainer and cool. You should have 2 quarts.
- For the punch, combine the punch ingredients in a large container and mix well. Transfer to gallon jugs, cover and refrigerate until serving time.
- For each serving, place 1/2 cup ice cubes in an old-fashioned glass and pour 1/3 cup of the punch over the ice. Stir well and serve.

309. Spinach Bites

Serving: Thirty-six spinach balls | Prep: | Cook: |Ready in: 30mins

Ingredients

- 2 packages of frozen chopped spinach, thawed and drained
- 2 cups Pepperidge Farm stuffing
- 1 onion, chopped
- 4 eggs, beaten
- ½ cup melted butter plus butter for the pan
- ½ cup grated parmesan

Direction

- Preheat the oven to 375 degrees.
- Combine all ingredients in a large bowl. Form into bite-size balls and place on a lightly buttered cookie sheet. Bake for 20 minutes and serve.

Nutrition Information

- 77: calories;
- 0 grams: trans fat;
- 2 grams: protein;
- 1 gram: sugars;
- 4 grams: carbohydrates;
- 114 milligrams: sodium;
- 6 grams: fat;
- 3 grams: saturated fat;

310. Spinach And Onion Tart

Serving: 6 servings | Prep: | Cook: |Ready in: 1hours30mins

Ingredients

- 1 yeasted olive oil pastry (1/2 recipe)
- 1 ½ pounds fresh spinach, stemmed and washed in 2 changes of water, or 3/4 pound baby spinach, rinsed
- 1 tablespoon extra virgin olive oil
- 1 medium onion, finely chopped
- Salt and freshly ground pepper to taste
- 1 teaspoon fresh thyme leaves, coarsely chopped, or 1/2 teaspoon dried thyme

- 4 eggs
- ¾ cup low-fat milk
- 2 ounces Gruyere cheese, grated (1/2 cup)
- 1 ounce freshly grated Parmesan (1/4 cup)

Direction

- Preheat the oven to 350 degrees. Oil a 10-inch tart pan and line it with the pastry. Keep it in the refrigerator while you prepare the filling.
- Steam the spinach above an inch of boiling water for 2 to 3 minutes, until wilted. You will probably have to do this in batches. I like to use a pasta pot with an insert for steaming spinach, as I can get a lot of it into the insert. Rinse briefly with cold water, squeeze out excess water and chop medium-fine.
- Heat the olive oil over medium heat in a large, heavy skillet and add the onion. Cook, stirring often, until it is tender and beginning to color, about 8 minutes. Add the spinach, thyme and salt and pepper to taste, and stir together. Remove from the heat.
- Whisk the eggs in a large bowl. Add salt to taste (I use about 1/2 teaspoon) and whisk in the milk. Stir in the onion and spinach mixture and the cheeses. Scrape into the pastry-lined tart pan. Place in the oven and bake 40 to 45 minutes, until tart is set and beginning to color on the top. Remove from the heat and allow to cool for at least 15 minutes before cutting. Serve warm or room temperature.

Nutrition Information

- 216: calories;
- 5 grams: saturated fat;
- 0 grams: trans fat;
- 6 grams: monounsaturated fat;
- 2 grams: polyunsaturated fat;
- 14 grams: protein;
- 12 grams: carbohydrates;
- 3 grams: sugars;
- 506 milligrams: sodium;

311. Spinach And Yogurt Dip

Serving: 2 cups | Prep: | Cook: | Ready in: 20mins

Ingredients

- 1 ½ pounds spinach, stemmed and washed thoroughly in 2 changes of water (or 12 ounces baby spinach)
- 1 to 2 large garlic cloves (to taste)
- Salt to taste
- 1 cup thick plain yogurt
- 2 tablespoons extra virgin olive oil
- 2 allspice berries, ground, or 1/8 teaspoon ground allspice (more to taste)
- 1 clove, ground, or 1/8 teaspoon ground clove
- ⅛ teaspoon freshly grated nutmeg
- ⅛ teaspoon ground cinnamon
- 1 scant teaspoon coriander seeds, or 1 teaspoon freshly ground coriander
- Chopped walnuts for garnish (optional)

Direction

- Blanch the spinach for 20 to 30 seconds or steam for 2 to 3 minutes. Rinse and squeeze out excess water and chop coarsely.
- Pound the garlic to a paste with salt in a mortar and pestle. Stir into the yogurt and set aside.
- Heat the olive oil over medium heat in a wide, heavy skillet and add the spices. Cook, stirring, until they begin to sizzle, and add the spinach. Cook, stirring, until heated through and coated with the oil and spices, 2 to 3 minutes. Transfer to a food processor and pulse to a puree. Add the yogurt and blend together. Transfer to a bowl or platter. Serve on croutons or with crudités such as red pepper squares, or with pita triangles. Garnish with chopped walnuts if desired. Serve with pita bread.

Nutrition Information

- 143: calories;
- 10 grams: fat;

- 562 milligrams: sodium;
- 11 grams: carbohydrates;
- 4 grams: sugars;
- 7 grams: protein;
- 2 grams: saturated fat;
- 0 grams: trans fat;
- 6 grams: monounsaturated fat;
- 1 gram: polyunsaturated fat;

312. Spring Rolls With Beets, Brown Rice, Eggs And Herbs

Serving: 8 spring rolls | Prep: | Cook: | Ready in: 30mins

Ingredients

- 3 eggs
- Salt to taste
- 1 ½ teaspoons rice bran oil or canola oil
- 1 ¾ cups cooked brown rice
- ¼ cup rice vinegar
- 3 to 4 medium-size beets (about 1 pound), peeled and grated
- ⅓ cup mint leaves, coarsely chopped, plus additional leaves
- ¼ cup Thai basil leaves, coarsely chopped, plus additional leaves (may substitute regular basil if you can't get the Thai variety)
- 2 cups shredded cabbage
- 8 8 1/2-inch rice flour spring roll wrappers

Direction

- Make three egg "pancakes": heat an 8-inch omelet pan over medium-high heat and beat 1 egg in a bowl. Season to taste with salt. When the pan is hot add 1/2 teaspoon oil and pour in the egg, scraping all of it out of the pan with a heat-proof rubber spatula. Swirl the pan so that the egg covers the bottom in an even layer, and lift the edges of the thin omelet with your spatula to let the egg run underneath. Push the pan away from you and quickly jerk it toward you to flip or fold the omelet over (if it just folds, that's fine). Turn out of the pan onto a plate. Repeat with the other two eggs and remaining oil. Slice the omelets into 1/2-inch-wide pieces and set aside
- Toss the rice with 1 tablespoon of the rice vinegar
- Combine the shredded beets and chopped herbs in a bowl and toss with 2 tablespoons of the rice vinegar and salt to taste. Place the shredded cabbage in another bowl and toss with the remaining vinegar and salt to taste
- Fill a bowl with warm water and place a spring roll wrapper in it just until it is pliable, about 30 seconds. Remove from the water and drain briefly on a kitchen towel. Place the wrapper on your work surface in front of you and arrange several whole mint and basil leaves, vein side up, on the wrapper. Place a large spoonful or handful of beets (wear plastic gloves if you don't want the beets to color your hands) down the middle of the wrapper but slightly closer to the bottom, leaving a 2-inch margin on the sides. Place a handful of cabbage over the beets, then a handful of rice. Arrange 3 slices of omelet over the rice. Fold the sides in, then roll up the spring rolls tightly, squeezing the filling to get a tight roll. Refrigerate until ready to serve. Serve with a dipping sauce of your choice if desired

Nutrition Information

- 183: calories;
- 1 gram: polyunsaturated fat;
- 0 grams: trans fat;
- 32 grams: carbohydrates;
- 5 grams: protein;
- 481 milligrams: sodium;
- 4 grams: sugars;

313. Spring Rolls With Shredded Broccoli Stems, Vermicelli And Red Pepper

Serving: Makes 8 spring rolls | Prep: | Cook: | Ready in: 1hours

Ingredients

- 2 ounces rice vermicelli (thin rice sticks)
- ¼ cup rice vinegar
- 2 teaspoons soy sauce
- 3 cups grated broccoli stems (it's fine to use a packaged mix of grated broccoli stems and carrots)
- Salt to taste
- 4 ounces firm tofu, cut in 1x1/2-inch dominoes
- 1 tablespoon light miso
- 1 tablespoon chopped chives
- 2 tablespoons chopped Thai basil or tarragon
- 2 tablespoons mint leaves, coarsely chopped, plus additional leaves
- ½ cup cilantro, chopped, plus additional sprigs
- 8 inner romaine lettuce leaves, chopped
- 16 to 24 pieces pickled ginger (to taste)
- 8 8-1/2-inch rice flour spring roll wrappers

Direction

- Place the rice noodles in a large bowl and cover with hot water. Soak for 20 minutes, or until pliable. Meanwhile, bring a large pot of water to a boil. Drain the noodles and add to the boiling water. Boil 1 minute and drain. Rinse with cold water and transfer to a bowl. Cut the noodles into 2-inch lengths with kitchen scissors. Toss with 2 teaspoons of the rice vinegar and the soy sauce.
- Place the shredded broccoli stems in a colander and toss with salt to taste. Let drain for 15 minutes and squeeze out excess water. (This step can be omitted if serving the spring rolls right away).
- Combine shredded broccoli stems with chopped herbs and 2 tablespoons of the rice vinegar in a large bowl. Place lettuce in another bowl and toss with remaining vinegar and salt to taste.
- Pat tofu pieces dry with paper towels and spread a little miso on each piece.
- Fill a bowl with warm water and place a spring roll wrapper in it just until it is pliable, about 30 seconds. Remove from water and drain briefly on a kitchen towel. Place wrapper on your work surface and arrange several cilantro sprigs and whole mint leaves, vein side up, on wrapper. Leaving a 2-inch margin on the sides, place a handful of the broccoli stem mixture on the wrapper, slightly nearer to the edge closest to you. Top with a handful of lettuce, then a handful of noodles. Arrange 2 pieces of tofu and 2 or 3 slices of pickled ginger on top of the noodles. Fold in sides of wrapper, then roll up tightly. To really firm up the rolls, wrap tightly in plastic wrap. Refrigerate until ready to serve.

Nutrition Information

- 175: calories;
- 2 grams: sugars;
- 0 grams: saturated fat;
- 1 gram: polyunsaturated fat;
- 33 grams: carbohydrates;
- 3 grams: dietary fiber;
- 6 grams: protein;
- 382 milligrams: sodium;

314. Spring Rolls With Spinach, Mushrooms, Sesame, Rice And Herbs

Serving: 8 spring rolls | Prep: | Cook: | Ready in: 30mins

Ingredients

- For the filling
- 1 ¾ cups cooked rice (brown, basmati or jasmine)
- 3 tablespoons rice vinegar

- 2 teaspoons soy sauce
- 1 pound baby spinach or 2 pounds bunch spinach, stemmed and washed
- 2 teaspoons black sesame seeds or lightly toasted regular hulled sesame seeds
- ¼ pound firm tofu, cut into dominoes 1/4 inch thick by 1/2 inch wide and drained on paper towels
- 2 tablespoons peanut sauce
- 2 large carrots (about 1 pound), peeled and grated
- 6 shiitake mushrooms, stems removed, thinly sliced
- ½ cup cilantro, coarsely chopped, plus additional sprigs
- ⅓ cup mint leaves, coarsely chopped, plus additional leaves
- ¼ cup Thai basil leaves, coarsely chopped, plus additional leaves (may substitute regular basil if you can't get the Thai variety)
- Salt to taste
- 8 8 1/2-inch rice flour spring roll wrappers

Direction

- Toss the rice with 1 tablespoon of the rice vinegar and the soy sauce
- Wash the spinach and steam 1 to 2 minutes, tossing halfway through. It should wilt but still have some texture. Rinse with cold water, squeeze dry and coarsely chop. Season with salt to taste
- Spread each tofu domino with about 1/4 teaspoon peanut sauce
- Place the shredded carrots, slivered mushrooms and chopped herbs in a large bowl and toss with the remaining rice vinegar and salt to taste
- Fill a bowl with warm water and place a spring roll in it just until it is pliable, about 30 seconds. Remove from the water and drain briefly on a kitchen towel. Place the wrapper on your work surface in front of you and arrange several cilantro sprigs, whole mint leaves and basil leaves, vein side up, on the wrapper. Leaving a 2-inch margin on the sides, place a handful of the carrot mixture on the wrapper, slightly nearer to the edge closest to you. Top with a handful of rice, then a handful of spinach. Place 3 tofu dominoes down the length of the spinach. Fold the sides in, then roll up the spring rolls tightly, squeezing the filling to get a tight roll. Refrigerate until ready to serve. Serve with a dipping sauce of your choice

Nutrition Information

- 214: calories;
- 2 grams: polyunsaturated fat;
- 39 grams: carbohydrates;
- 6 grams: dietary fiber;
- 5 grams: sugars;
- 9 grams: protein;
- 1 gram: monounsaturated fat;
- 0 grams: trans fat;
- 651 milligrams: sodium;
- 4 grams: fat;

315. Steamed Fava Beans With Thyme

Serving: 4 servings | Prep: | Cook: | Ready in: 30mins

Ingredients

- 3 pounds fava beans (in their pods)
- 1 teaspoon fresh thyme leaves
- 1 tablespoon unsalted butter
- Coarse salt and freshly ground pepper to taste

Direction

- Remove the pods from the fava beans. If you like, peel their skins.
- Put beans in top of a steamer and sprinkle them with thyme. Cook them until they are tender (this depends on their size and whether they are peeled, but it shouldn't take longer than 15 minutes).

- Put the beans in a warm serving bowl, add the butter, salt and pepper and toss them. Serve immediately.

Nutrition Information

- 328: calories;
- 61 grams: carbohydrates;
- 0 grams: trans fat;
- 1 gram: polyunsaturated fat;
- 2 grams: saturated fat;
- 26 grams: dietary fiber;
- 31 grams: sugars;
- 27 grams: protein;
- 802 milligrams: sodium;
- 5 grams: fat;

316. Stir Fried Sesame Shrimp And Spinach

Serving: 3 to 4 servings | Prep: | Cook: | Ready in: 15mins

Ingredients

- 1 pound large shrimp, peeled and deveined
- Salt to taste
- ⅛ teaspoon sugar
- 2 tablespoons canola oil or light sesame oil
- 1 tablespoon minced ginger
- 1 tablespoon minced garlic
- ¼ to ½ teaspoon crumbled dried red chili
- 2 tablespoons sesame seeds
- 1 generous bunch spinach (about 1 pound), stems trimmed at the end, rinsed in 2 changes water
- 2 teaspoons dark sesame oil

Direction

- Place the shrimp in a large colander and rinse with water. Sprinkle generously with salt and toss together for about a minute. Rinse with water and repeat. After rinsing one more time, drain on paper towels. Pat dry with more paper towels.
- Combine 1/4 to 1/2 teaspoon salt (to taste) and the sugar in a small bowl and place close to your wok.
- Heat a 14-inch flat-bottomed wok over high heat until a drop of water evaporates within a second or two when added to the pan. Swirl in 1 tablespoon of the oil by adding it to the sides of the pan and swirling the pan, then add the garlic, ginger and chili flakes and stir-fry for no more than 10 seconds. Push to the sides of the pan and add the shrimp in one layer. Let cook undisturbed for 1 minute, then add the remaining oil and stir-fry for 1 minute.
- Add the sesame seeds and spinach and stir-fry for 1 minute, until it has begun to wilt but the wilting is still uneven. Add the salt and sugar, sprinkling it evenly over the spinach, and continue to stir-fry until the spinach has wilted but is still bright and the shrimp are cooked through and bright pink, about 2 more minutes. Remove from the heat, drizzle on the sesame oil, toss together and serve, with rice, noodles or other grains.

Nutrition Information

- 219: calories;
- 1 gram: sugars;
- 13 grams: fat;
- 2 grams: saturated fat;
- 0 grams: trans fat;
- 6 grams: monounsaturated fat;
- 4 grams: polyunsaturated fat;
- 7 grams: carbohydrates;
- 3 grams: dietary fiber;
- 20 grams: protein;
- 733 milligrams: sodium;

317. Strata With Mushrooms And Chard

Serving: Serves four to six | Prep: | Cook: | Ready in: 2hours

Ingredients

- ½ pound stale bread, sliced about 3/4 to 1 inch thick
- ¾ ounce dried mushrooms
- 8 ounces Swiss chard, stemmed and cleaned
- 2 garlic cloves, 1 cut in half, green shoots removed, the other minced
- 1 ½ cups low-fat milk
- 2 ounces Gruyère cheese, grated (1/2 cup, tightly packed)
- 1 ounce Parmesan cheese, grated (1/4 cup, tightly packed)
- 2 tablespoons extra virgin olive oil
- 1 teaspoon chopped fresh rosemary
- Salt
- freshly ground pepper
- 4 large eggs
- ½ teaspoon salt

Direction

- If the bread is soft, toast it lightly and rub each slice front and back with the cut clove of garlic. Cut in 1-inch dice. If the bread is stale, just rub the slices with garlic and cut them into 1-inch dice. Place in a very large bowl, and toss with 2/3 cup of the milk. Set aside.
- Place the dried mushrooms in a bowl or a Pyrex measuring cup, and cover with 1 1/2 cups boiling water. Allow to sit for 30 minutes. Set a strainer over a bowl, line with cheesecloth, a coffee filter or paper towels, and drain the mushrooms. Squeeze the mushrooms over the strainer to extract all of the broth. Rinse, away from the strainer, in several changes of water to wash off sand. Squeeze out excess water. Chop coarsely. Measure out 1 cup of the mushroom broth, and combine with the remaining milk.
- Preheat the oven to 350 degrees. Oil or butter a 2-quart baking dish or gratin. Heat a large skillet over medium-high heat, and add the chard. Stir until the leaves begin to wilt in the liquid left on them after washing. Cover the pan, and let the chard steam until it has completely collapsed, about two minutes. Uncover and stir. When all of the chard has wilted, remove from the pan and rinse briefly with cold water. Press or squeeze out excess liquid. Chop coarsely and set aside.
- Add 1 tablespoon of the olive oil to the pan, turn the heat down to medium and add the minced garlic. Cook, stirring, until fragrant, about 30 seconds, and stir in the reconstituted mushrooms, the rosemary and the chard. Stir together for a couple of minutes, and season to taste with salt and pepper. Remove from the heat, and transfer to the bowl with the bread cubes. Add the cheeses, and toss together. Arrange in the baking dish.
- Beat together the eggs in a medium bowl. Add salt to taste (I use 1/2 to 3/4 teaspoon), the remaining milk and the mushroom broth. Add a few twists of the peppermill and pour over the bread. Press the bread down into the custard mixture. Sprinkle a little Parmesan over the top, and drizzle on the remaining olive oil. Place in the oven, and bake 40 to 50 minutes, until puffed and browned. Remove from the oven, and serve hot or warm.

Nutrition Information

- 292: calories;
- 27 grams: carbohydrates;
- 14 grams: fat;
- 5 grams: saturated fat;
- 0 grams: trans fat;
- 6 grams: sugars;
- 2 grams: dietary fiber;
- 15 grams: protein;
- 473 milligrams: sodium;

318. Strawberry Orange Soup

Serving: | Prep: | Cook: |Ready in: 15mins

Ingredients

- 2 cups yogurt
- ¼ cup orange juice
- 1 tablespoon sugar
- 1 cupchopped mint leaves
- 2 cups sliced strawberries
- 2 tablespoons limejuice
- 2 tablespoons sugar
- 1 teaspoon chili powder

Direction

- In a bowl, whisk together 2 cups yogurt, 1/4 cup orange juice, 1 tablespoon sugar and 1 cup chopped mint leaves until mint is fragrant; strain and discard solids.
- In another bowl, combine two cups sliced strawberries, 2 tablespoons lime juice, add 2 tablespoons sugar and 1 teaspoon chili powder; refrigerate bowls for 2 hours, stirring once
- To serve, spoon yogurt onto strawberries and stir.
- Garnish with whipped cream and mint.

Nutrition Information

- 159: calories;
- 21 grams: sugars;
- 6 grams: protein;
- 84 milligrams: sodium;
- 5 grams: fat;
- 3 grams: saturated fat;
- 1 gram: monounsaturated fat;
- 0 grams: polyunsaturated fat;
- 26 grams: carbohydrates;
- 4 grams: dietary fiber;

319. Stuffed Squid, Lisbon Style

Serving: Six servings | Prep: | Cook: |Ready in: 1hours45mins

Ingredients

- ¼ pound slab bacon, cut into small dice
- 3 tablespoons olive oil
- 2 medium yellow onions, peeled and sliced thin
- 2 medium carrots, peeled and sliced thin
- 1 large garlic clove, peeled and minced
- ½ cup fish stock or bottled clam juice
- ½ cup dry white wine
- 3 tablespoons tomato paste
- Juice of 1 large lemon
- 1 whole bay leaf (do not crumble)
- 1 ½ pounds squid, cleaned, tentacles separated from body and reserved
- The stuffing:
- 2 tablespoons olive oil
- 1 tablespoon bacon drippings
- 1 medium yellow onion, peeled and chopped
- 1 small garlic clove, peeled and minced
- 1 small carrot, peeled and chopped
- Reserved squid tentacles, washed well and coarsely chopped
- ¼ pound prosciutto, finely minced
- 2 tablespoons tomato paste
- 2 cups fine, soft bread crumbs
- ¼ cup dry white wine
- ⅓ cup water
- ¼ teaspoon freshly ground pepper
- 1 tablespoon minced parsley
- 2 egg yolks, lightly beaten

Direction

- In a small, heavy skillet, saute the bacon in 1 tablespoon of the olive oil over moderate heat 5 to 6 minutes, or until the bacon bits are crisp; remove with a slotted spoon and drain on a paper towel.
- Spoon 2 tablespoons of the bacon drippings into a large, heavy kettle, add the remaining

olive oil and turn heat to high; reserve remaining 1 tablespoon dripping for the stuffing. When oil is very hot, add the onions, carrots and garlic. Saute over moderate heat, stirring often, about 5 minutes or until onions turn glassy. Mix in fish stock, wine, tomato paste and lemon juice; add the bay leaf. Bring to a low boil, then lower heat and simmer gently while you make the stuffing.
- Make the stuffing: In a large, heavy skillet, heat the 2 tablespoons olive oil and the reserved 1 tablespoon of the bacon drippings. Add the onion, garlic and carrot and saute over moderate heat 5 minutes, or until the onions begin to turn glassy.
- Add the chopped squid tentacles; turn heat to low, cover and steam 20 minutes.
- Mix in the prosciutto, tomato paste, bread crumbs, wine, water, pepper and parsley and cook, stirring, 2 to 3 minutes, or until the mixture is very thick and pastelike.
- Remove from heat, let cool slightly, then blend in the egg yolks.
- Push the stuffing into each squid until about 3/4 inch from the top; close top with a toothpick. Do not stuff too near the top or too compactly, since the stuffing will expand when cooked.
- Lay the squid in the kettle of simmering sauce; cover and simmer 1 hour. Remove the squid, spoon the sauce over it and serve with bacon bits sprinkled on top.

320. Summer Aioli Feast

Serving: 10 servings | Prep: | Cook: | Ready in: 1hours30mins

Ingredients

- 3 large artichokes
- 1 lemon, cut in half
- 5 medium carrots, peeled, trimmed and cut in half lengthwise
- 5 medium or 10 small potatoes, cut in half
- 4 beets, scrubbed and roasted, cut in wedges
- ¾ pound green beans, trimmed
- 1 pound asparagus, trimmed
- 1 to 1 ½ pounds mixed summer squash, cut in half lengthwise and into 3-inch pieces or, if using pattypans, cut into wedges
- 5 hard-boiled eggs, peeled and halved or quartered
- ¾ pound chickpeas, cooked, or 2 cans, drained and rinsed
- 2 pounds cod fillets, seasoned with salt and pepper and steamed until tender and flaky, 5 to 10 minutes depending on the thickness (optional)
- 2 cups aioli

Direction

- Fill a bowl with water and add the juice of half a lemon. Cut the tops off the artichokes, about 1 inch from the end, and snip the spiny tops off the remaining leaves. Break off the leaves around the base, and cut away the stem. Rub the cut edges with the other lemon half as you work. Cut the artichokes into quarters, and cut away the chokes. Place the pieces in the bowl of acidulated water as you work. When all of the artichokes are ready, steam them above an inch of simmering water for 30 to 40 minutes, until the leaves pull away easily and the heart can be easily pierced with the tip of a knife. Remove from the heat and set aside.
- Steam the carrots above an inch of boiling water for about 10 minutes, or until tender. A pasta pot with an insert is a good pot to do this in. Remove from the steamer and set aside. Steam the potatoes until tender, about 20 minutes. Arrange on the platter or in a separate bowl.
- Steam the squash for 5 minutes, or until just tender. Steam the green beans and asparagus or cook in boiling salted water for about 4 minutes, until just tender. Transfer to a bowl of ice cold water. Let sit for a minute, then drain.
- Arrange all the vegetables, fish and the eggs on platters, the chickpeas in a bowl and the

aioli in bowls. Serve the vegetables hot or at room temperature. To serve them hot, bring a large pot of water to a boil. In batches, tip the vegetables into the water for 30 seconds, transfer to platters with a slotted spoon or skimmer, and serve, with generous helpings of aioli and lots of chilled dry rosé.

Nutrition Information

- 625: calories;
- 6 grams: saturated fat;
- 23 grams: polyunsaturated fat;
- 54 grams: carbohydrates;
- 12 grams: sugars;
- 401 milligrams: sodium;
- 40 grams: fat;
- 10 grams: monounsaturated fat;
- 13 grams: dietary fiber;
- 16 grams: protein;

321. Summer Tomato Gratin

Serving: Serves four | Prep: | Cook: | Ready in: 1hours30mins

Ingredients

- 2 pounds ripe, firm tomatoes, sliced
- Salt
- freshly ground pepper to taste
- ½ teaspoon sugar
- ½ cup fresh or dry bread crumbs, preferably whole wheat
- 2 tablespoons chopped flat-leaf parsley
- 2 tablespoons extra virgin olive oil

Direction

- Preheat the oven to 400 degrees. Oil a 2-quart gratin or baking dish. Layer the tomatoes in the dish, seasoning each layer with salt, pepper and a small sprinkle of sugar.
- Toss together the bread crumbs, parsley and olive oil. Spread over the tomatoes in an even layer. Place in the oven, and bake for 1 to 1 1/2 hours, until the juices are thick and syrupy and the top is golden. Remove from the oven, and allow to cool for at least 15 minutes before serving.

Nutrition Information

- 175: calories;
- 599 milligrams: sodium;
- 8 grams: fat;
- 1 gram: polyunsaturated fat;
- 6 grams: dietary fiber;
- 5 grams: monounsaturated fat;
- 26 grams: carbohydrates;
- 7 grams: sugars;
- 4 grams: protein;

322. Sunchoke And Apple Salad

Serving: 8 servings | Prep: | Cook: | Ready in: 50mins

Ingredients

- 12 sunchokes
- Olive oil to coat the sunchokes
- 4 apples, sliced
- 2 tablespoons toasted pumpkin seeds
- Mixed greens: radicchio, bok choy, mizuna, celery leaves
- ½ cup celery, minced
- 1 tablespoon shallot, minced
- Apple cider vinaigrette
- 1 cup apple cider
- 2 Tablespoons apple cider vinegar
- 1 teaspoon Dijon mustard
- 1 tablespoon maple syrup
- ½ cup olive oil
- ¼ cup lemon juice
- Salt to taste

- Pepper to taste

Direction

- Prepare the sunchokes. Wash sunchokes with the skin on. Slice 2 sunchokes, raw, into thin strips using a mandoline; set aside. Roast the remaining sunchokes. Preheat oven to 375 degrees. Place them in a pan with olive oil, and roast for about 40 minutes.
- Toss the hot sunchokes with the remaining salad ingredients.
- Prepare the cider vinaigrette by combining all the vinaigrette ingredients; dress the salad and season with salt and pepper to taste. Garnish with raw sunchoke slices.

Nutrition Information

- 230: calories;
- 20 grams: fat;
- 3 grams: protein;
- 13 grams: monounsaturated fat;
- 2 grams: sugars;
- 16 grams: carbohydrates;
- 10 grams: dietary fiber;
- 169 milligrams: sodium;

323. Suvir Saran's Guacamole With Toasted Cumin

Serving: | Prep: | Cook: | Ready in: 10mins

Ingredients

- 4 ripe Hass avocados, halved and pitted
- 1 small tomato, chopped
- 1 small red onion, finely diced
- ½ cup chopped cilantro
- 1 jalapeño, minced (seeded for a milder flavor)
- ¼ to ½ teaspoon toasted cumin seeds, ground if desired
- ½ teaspoon kosher salt, or to taste
- ½ teaspoon freshly ground peppercorns
- Juice of 2 limes

Direction

- Cut avocados into small dice. The easiest way to do this is to cross-hatch the flesh with a paring knife while still in the skin, then scoop out into a bowl.
- Add remaining ingredients and combine. Taste, adjust salt, and serve.

324. Sweet Potato And Apple Latkes With Ginger And Sweet Spices

Serving: About 40 small latkes, serving 6 to 8 | Prep: | Cook: | Ready in: 45mins

Ingredients

- 1 ½ pound red-fleshed sweet potatoes (yams), peeled and grated – about 5 cups grated
- 1 cup grated apple, preferably a slightly tart variety such as Braeburn
- 2 teaspoons fresh lime juice
- 1 to 2 teaspoons grated fresh ginger (to taste)
- 2 teaspoons ground cinnamon
- ½ teaspoon freshly grated nutmeg
- 1 teaspoon baking powder
- Salt to taste
- 3 tablespoons oat bran
- 3 tablespoon matzo meal or all-purpose flour
- 2 eggs, beaten
- About 1/4 cup canola, grape seed or rice bran oil

Direction

- Begin heating a large heavy skillet over medium heat. Heat the oven to 350 degrees. Line a sheet pan with parchment and place a rack over another sheet pan.
- Place the grated sweet potatoes in a large bowl. Toss the grated apple with the lime juice and add to the sweet potatoes, along with the

ginger, spices, baking powder, salt, oat bran and matzo meal or flour. Taste and adjust salt. Add the beaten eggs and stir together.

- Take a 1/4 cup measuring cup and fill with 2 tablespoons of the mixture. Reverse onto the parchment-lined baking sheet. Repeat with the remaining latke mix. You should have enough to make about 40 latkes.
- Add the oil to the pan and when it is hot (hold your hand a few inches above – you should feel the heat), slide a spatula under one portion of the latke mixture and press down with the spatula to flatten. Repeat with more mounds. In my 10-inch pan I can cook four at a time without crowding; my 12-inch pan will accommodate five or six. Cook on one side until golden brown, about three minutes. Slide the spatula underneath and flip the latkes over. Cook on the other side until golden brown, another two to three minutes. Transfer to the rack set over a baking sheet. Try one latke and if it is still a bit chewy in the middle transfer them to the baking sheet and place in the oven for 10 minutes, until golden brown and soft in the center.
- Serve hot topped with applesauce and low-fat sour cream, thick Greek yogurt or crème fraîche if desired.

Nutrition Information

- 175: calories;
- 5 grams: sugars;
- 8 grams: fat;
- 2 grams: saturated fat;
- 3 grams: protein;
- 0 grams: trans fat;
- 24 grams: carbohydrates;
- 4 grams: dietary fiber;
- 289 milligrams: sodium;

325. Sweet Potatoes Anna With Prunes

Serving: 6 to 10 servings | Prep: | Cook: | Ready in: 1hours30mins

Ingredients

- 1 cup (2 sticks) unsalted butter
- 1 cup port
- 10 pitted prunes
- 5 to 6 small sweet potatoes, peeled and very thinly sliced
- Salt and freshly ground black pepper

Direction

- Clarify the butter: In a small saucepan set over low heat, melt the butter. Skim off any foam, then pour the clear liquid into a bowl, leaving behind the solids.
- Heat the port to a simmer in a small saucepan over medium heat. Add the prunes, turn off the heat and let them soak until plumped, about 20 minutes. Drain and chop the prunes coarsely.
- Heat oven to 450 degrees.
- Brush a layer of clarified butter onto your favorite 8- or 9-inch round baking dish or ovenproof frying pan.
- Arrange a layer of potatoes, overlapping in circles, in the dish. Brush with the clarified butter and season with salt and pepper. Arrange another layer of potatoes and sprinkle with about half the prune pieces. Season with salt and pepper. Brush with clarified butter. Repeat with one more layer of potatoes and prunes, then end with a layer of potatoes. Remember to brush each layer with clarified butter and salt and pepper. You can do four layers of potatoes or six; it's up to you. Pack the potatoes tightly by pressing down on them with your palms. If there's a little butter left at the end, it's no big deal.
- Bake until crisp and tender, 35 to 45 minutes.
- Remove from the oven and let cool in the pan for a few minutes. Then flip the cake onto a

serving plate and cut into wedges. If desired, finish with a dusting of sugar and a couple of minutes of broiling, for a brûlée top. It can also be made using apples and prunes, or just apples.

Nutrition Information

- 311: calories;
- 3 grams: dietary fiber;
- 2 grams: protein;
- 1 gram: polyunsaturated fat;
- 23 grams: carbohydrates;
- 15 grams: saturated fat;
- 6 grams: monounsaturated fat;
- 8 grams: sugars;
- 280 milligrams: sodium;

326. Sweet And Sour Butternut Squash Or Pumpkin

Serving: 4 to 5 servings | Prep: | Cook: | Ready in: 20mins

Ingredients

- 3 tablespoons mustard oil or olive oil
- A generous pinch of ground asafetida
- ½ teaspoon whole brown or yellow mustard seeds
- 4 cups (1 1/4 pounds) peeled and seeded butternut squash or pumpkin, cut into segments 3/4- to 1-inch in size
- ¾ to 1 teaspoon salt
- 1 ½ teaspoons sugar
- ⅛ to ¼ teaspoon cayenne pepper
- 1 tablespoon plain yogurt
- 2 tablespoons chopped cilantro

Direction

- Pour the oil into a frying pan and set over medium heat. When hot, add the asafetida and mustard seeds. As soon as the mustard seeds start to pop, a matter of seconds, add the squash. Continue to cook, stirring, for about 3 minutes, or until the squash pieces just start to brown.
- Add 1/4 cup of water, cover, turn heat to low, and cook for about 10 minutes, or until the squash is tender.
- Add the salt, sugar, cayenne and yogurt. Stir and cook, uncovered, over medium heat until the yogurt is absorbed and no longer visible. Sprinkle in the cilantro and stir a few times.

Nutrition Information

- 133: calories;
- 9 grams: fat;
- 1 gram: protein;
- 5 grams: monounsaturated fat;
- 2 grams: dietary fiber;
- 15 grams: carbohydrates;
- 4 grams: sugars;
- 296 milligrams: sodium;

327. Swiss Chard Souffle With Fresh Tomato Sauce

Serving: Six to eight servings | Prep: | Cook: | Ready in: 1hours15mins

Ingredients

- 1 tablespoon unsalted butter
- 3 tablespoons dry bread crumbs
- 4 tablespoons olive oil
- 1 medium onion, finely chopped
- 1 large garlic clove, minced
- 1 bunch, about 3/4 pound, Swiss chard, chopped
- 2 cups part-skim ricotta
- 2 tablespoons flour
- 1 large egg yolk
- 1 teaspoon dried thyme
- Salt and freshly ground pepper to taste

- 1 ½ pounds fresh plum tomatoes, finely chopped
- 6 large egg whites

Direction

- Butter an eight-cup souffle dish and dust it with the bread crumbs. Set aside.
- Heat two tablespoons of the oil in a large, heavy skillet. Add half the chopped onion and saute over medium heat until it is soft but not brown. Add the garlic and stir, then add the Swiss chard. Stir-fry the mixture over high heat until the Swiss chard has wilted, about five minutes.
- Chop the mixture in a food processor until very fine. Add the ricotta, flour and egg yolk, and process until smooth. Stir in one-half teaspoon of the thyme. Season with salt and pepper and set aside. (The souffle can be prepared ahead up to this point.)
- For the sauce, heat the remaining olive oil in the same skillet and saute the remaining onion until it is soft but not brown. Stir in the tomatoes and cook over medium-high heat for 10 to 15 minutes, until the mixture is thick. Add the remaining thyme, season with salt and pepper and set aside.
- Preheat the oven to 425 degrees.
- Beat the egg whites until they hold firm peaks. Stir one-third of the egg whites into the ricotta mixture, then fold the ricotta mixture into the remaining egg whites.
- Spoon the mixture into the dish. Bake 20 minutes. Reduce the temperature to 375 degrees and bake about 25 minutes longer, until the souffle is puffed, lightly browned and firm.
- While the souffle is baking, reheat the tomato sauce. Serve at once, with the tomato sauce on the side.

Nutrition Information

- 227: calories;
- 1 gram: polyunsaturated fat;
- 2 grams: dietary fiber;
- 4 grams: sugars;
- 569 milligrams: sodium;
- 14 grams: carbohydrates;
- 5 grams: saturated fat;
- 7 grams: monounsaturated fat;
- 0 grams: trans fat;
- 12 grams: protein;

328. Swordfish Hash

Serving: 4 servings | Prep: | Cook: |Ready in: 40mins

Ingredients

- 2 medium to large boiling potatoes, peeled and diced
- Salt
- 2 tablespoons cooking oil
- 1 large onion, chopped
- 1 ½ cups cooked swordfish, diced
- Juice of 1 lemon
- Salt and freshly ground black pepper
- 1 tablespoon minced fresh parsley
- 1 tablespoon minced scallion
- Poached eggs (optional)

Direction

- Place potatoes in boiling salted water and cook about 10 minutes, until barely tender. Drain.
- Heat oil in large, heavy skillet. Add the potatoes and saute over medium-high heat until they begin to color. Add onion and continue to saute until onion and potato are golden. Fold in swordfish and cook for several minutes. Add lemon juice and cook a minute or so longer.
- Season to taste with salt and pepper and fold in the parsley and scallion. Serve at once, topped, if desired, with poached eggs.

Nutrition Information

- 239: calories;

- 4 grams: dietary fiber;
- 511 milligrams: sodium;
- 11 grams: fat;
- 1 gram: saturated fat;
- 0 grams: trans fat;
- 6 grams: monounsaturated fat;
- 3 grams: sugars;
- 24 grams: carbohydrates;
- 13 grams: protein;

329. Taking Stock After Thanksgiving

Serving: Makes about 5 quarts | Prep: | Cook: | Ready in: 7hours45mins

Ingredients

- For the turkey stock
- 1 turkey carcass, plus the neck if you kept it
- 6 quarts water (more if needed)
- 3 or 4 carrots, peeled and sliced
- 3 or 4 stalks celery, sliced
- 2 leeks, trimmed, cleaned, and sliced optional
- ½ head garlic, cut in half across the middle
- 2 bay leaves
- 6 sprigs parsley
- 4 sprigs thyme
- 12 peppercorns
- 1 teaspoon salt
- For the day-after-thanksgiving turkey soup
- 2 quarts turkey stock
- Salt
- freshly ground pepper to taste
- 2 carrots, diced
- 2 stalks celery, diced
- Leftover vegetables from dinner
- Leftover turkey from dinner, diced
- ½ cup soup pasta, such as shells or macaroni
- Chopped fresh parsley or cilantro

Direction

- Rinse the turkey, making sure to wash away any stuffing that may be sticking to the walls of the cavity. Break apart if necessary, so the wing bones and thigh bones are detached. Place in a large stockpot, and add the water. It should cover the carcass.
- Place over medium heat, and bring to a simmer. The bubbles should just break gently on the surface. Skim off any foam that rises to the surface. Cover partially, turn the heat to very low and simmer two hours, skimming as necessary. Add the remaining ingredients, and simmer for another four hours, partially covered. Keep your eye on the pot, and skim as necessary.
- Before draining such a big pot of stock, I find it easiest to remove the carcass and bones using tongs. Gently strain the soup through a strainer, colander or conical chinois into a very large bowl. Line a strainer with cheesecloth, and strain once again. Place in the refrigerator, uncovered, and chill. Lift off any fat that has congealed on the top, and discard. Keep in the refrigerator, or freeze in small containers.
- Combine the stock, salt, pepper, carrots and celery, and bring to a simmer. Cover and simmer over low heat for 30 minutes. Add the leftover vegetables and turkey, and simmer for another 10 to 15 minutes. Add the soup pasta, and simmer until tender, five to 10 minutes. Taste, adjust seasonings and stir in the parsley or cilantro. Serve.

330. Tangerine Sorbet

Serving: About 5 cups, serving 6 | Prep: | Cook: | Ready in: 5hours

Ingredients

- 125 grams (1/2 cup) water
- 150 grams sugar (approximately 3/4 cup)
- 50 grams corn syrup or mild honey (approximately 2 tablespoons)

- 1000 grams freshly squeezed tangerine, Clementine or mandarin juice (1 quart)

Direction

- Combine the water and sugar in a saucepan and bring to boil. Reduce the heat and simmer until the sugar has dissolved. Stir in the corn syrup or honey, remove from the heat and allow to cool. Stir in the tangerine juice. Transfer to a container and chill in the refrigerator for two hours or overnight.
- Chill a container in the freezer. Freeze the juice mixture in an ice cream maker following the manufacturer's instructions. Transfer to the chilled container and place in the freezer for two hours to pack. Allow to soften in the refrigerator for 15 to 30 minutes before serving.

Nutrition Information

- 193: calories;
- 3 milligrams: sodium;
- 0 grams: dietary fiber;
- 49 grams: carbohydrates;
- 48 grams: sugars;
- 1 gram: protein;

331. Teff And Oatmeal Pancakes

Serving: 20 pancakes | Prep: | Cook: |Ready in: 40mins

Ingredients

- 1 cup (200 grams) ground teff or teff flour
- 1 cup (140 grams) whole-wheat flour
- 2 teaspoons baking powder
- 1 teaspoon baking soda
- ¼ teaspoon salt
- 2 eggs
- 2 tablespoons agave nectar or 1 tablespoon blackstrap molasses and 1 tablespoon agave nectar
- 1 ¾ cups buttermilk
- 2 tablespoons canola oil
- 1 teaspoon vanilla extract
- 1 cup (270 grams) cooked oatmeal (rolled oats, not steel-cut; 1/2 cup uncooked)
- Butter or oil as needed for cooking
- 1 cup blueberries, preferably organic
- 1 teaspoon unbleached all-purpose flour

Direction

- Sift together the flours, baking powder, baking soda and salt
- In a medium bowl, whisk the eggs. Whisk in the agave syrup and molasses (if using), buttermilk, canola oil and vanilla. Quickly whisk in the flour mix. Do not overwork the batter. Stir in the cooked oatmeal
- Heat a griddle or a large skillet, either nonstick or seasoned cast iron, over medium-high heat. Brush with butter or oil. Use a 1/4-cup ladle or cup measure to drop 3 to 4 tablespoons of batter per pancake onto your heated pan or griddle
- Toss the berries with 1 teaspoon flour in a bowl. Place 6 to 7 berries on each pancake (more if using small wild blueberries), gently pressing them down into the batter. When bubbles break through the pancakes, flip the pancakes over and cook for another minute, or until they are brown on the other side. Serve right away, or allow to cool and wrap individual servings in plastic, then place in a freezer bag and freeze

Nutrition Information

- 118: calories;
- 4 grams: protein;
- 163 milligrams: sodium;
- 3 grams: fat;
- 1 gram: polyunsaturated fat;
- 0 grams: trans fat;
- 19 grams: carbohydrates;

- 2 grams: dietary fiber;

332. Three Greens Gratin

Serving: Serves 6 generously | Prep: | Cook: | Ready in: 1hours15mins

Ingredients

- 2 generous bunches Swiss chard (about 2 to 2 1/4 pounds), stemmed and washed in 2 changes of water
- Salt
- 1 pound beet greens or spinach, stemmed and washed in 2 changes of water
- 3 tablespoons extra virgin olive oil, plus additional for oiling baking dish
- 1 onion, chopped
- ½ pound leeks (1 large or 2 smaller), white and light green parts only, cleaned and chopped
- 3 garlic cloves, minced
- 1 teaspoon chopped fresh thyme leaves
- 1 pound cabbage (1/2 medium), cored and chopped
- 4 eggs
- 1 cup cooked rice or farro
- Nutmeg
- Freshly ground pepper
- 2 ounces Gruyère, grated (1/2 cup)
- 1 ounce Parmesan, grated (1/4 cup)
- ¼ cup breadcrumbs (optional)

Direction

- Bring a large pot of water to a boil while you stem and wash the greens. When the water comes to a boil salt generously and add chard. Blanch for 1 minute, until just wilted, and using a skimmer or a slotted spoon, transfer to a bowl of cold water. Drain and squeeze out excess water, taking the chard up by the handful. Chop medium-fine and set aside. You should have about 2 cups.
- Bring the water back to a boil and blanch beet greens for 1 minute; if using spinach, blanch for 20 seconds only. Transfer to a bowl of cold water, drain and squeeze out excess water. Chop medium-fine. You should have about 1 cup (less for spinach).
- Preheat oven to 375 degrees. Oil a 2-quart baking dish with olive oil.
- Heat 2 tablespoons olive oil over medium heat in a large, heavy skillet and add onion. Cook, stirring often, until tender, about 5 minutes, and add leeks. Cook, stirring, until leeks begin to soften, 2 to 3 minutes, and add garlic and a generous pinch of salt. Cook, stirring, until garlic is fragrant, 30 seconds to a minute, and add cabbage and thyme. Cook, stirring often, until cabbage collapses in pan, about 5 minutes, and add another generous pinch of salt. Continue to cook the mixture until the cabbage is tender, sweet, and beginning to color, about 10 minutes. Stir in chopped blanched greens and season to taste with salt and pepper. Stir together for about a minute and remove from the heat.
- Beat eggs in a large bowl and add a pinch of nutmeg and salt and pepper to taste. Stir in rice or farro, vegetable mixture and cheeses. Scrape into prepared baking dish. If using breadcrumbs, toss with remaining tablespoon olive oil and sprinkle over the top. If not using breadcrumbs drizzle remaining oil over the top.
- Bake 40 to 45 minutes, until top is lightly browned. Remove from heat and allow to sit for at least 10 minutes before serving. Serve hot, warm or room temperature.

Nutrition Information

- 302: calories;
- 0 grams: trans fat;
- 8 grams: monounsaturated fat;
- 30 grams: carbohydrates;
- 16 grams: protein;
- 15 grams: fat;
- 5 grams: saturated fat;
- 2 grams: polyunsaturated fat;
- 9 grams: dietary fiber;

- 7 grams: sugars;
- 1049 milligrams: sodium;

333. Tomato Bluefish Pasta

Serving: | Prep: | Cook: |Ready in: 24mins

Ingredients

- ¾ pound spaghetti
- ½ pound fresh fennel
- ¼ cup olive oil
- ½ yellow onion, peeled and cut into 1 inch wedges
- 6 cloves garlic, peeled and mashed
- 2 cups lightly cooked crushed tomatoes (see recipe) or 2 cups canned crushed tomatoes in juice, drained
- 2 tablespoons capers, drained
- Freshly ground black pepper
- 4 bluefish fillets, 4 ounces each
- 1 ½ tablespoons fresh lemon juice
- Kosher salt

Direction

- On the stove, bring a large pot of salted water to boil.
- Trim fennel by removing the feathery tops. Chop tops finely and reserve. Cut fennel bulb in half through the core. Slice each half through the core into 4 wedges.
- In a glass or ceramic oval dish (11 by 9 by 2 inches), stir fennel, olive oil, onion and garlic until vegetables are coated with oil. Push vegetables to the sides of the dish, leaving the center empty. Cook, uncovered, at 100 percent for 4 minutes.
- Add the spaghetti to the boiling water.
- Pour tomatoes into the center of the dish of vegetables. Sprinkle reserved fennel tops and capers over tomatoes. Sprinkle a small amount of black pepper on top. Cover tightly with microwave plastic wrap. Cook at 100 percent for 5 minutes.
- Carefully uncover the dish. Arrange fish fillets spoke-fashion over tomatoes and vegetables. Cover tightly with microwave plastic wrap. Cook at 100 percent for 5 minutes.
- When pasta is cooked, remove 1/2 cup of the cooking water and pour it into a large bowl. Drain the pasta and add it to the bowl. Gently set the fish fillets on top of the pasta, arranging them around the sides of the bowl. Place vegetables in the center.
- Taste the tomato sauce and season with lemon juice and salt, if desired. Pour sauce over all. Work a small wooden spoon down into the spaghetti in several places so some of the tomato sauce trickles down. Serve immediately.

Nutrition Information

- 260: calories;
- 3 grams: dietary fiber;
- 15 grams: protein;
- 4 grams: sugars;
- 391 milligrams: sodium;
- 8 grams: fat;
- 1 gram: polyunsaturated fat;
- 5 grams: monounsaturated fat;
- 32 grams: carbohydrates;

334. Tournedos De La Foret (Filet Mignons With Morels)

Serving: 4 servings | Prep: | Cook: |Ready in: 45mins

Ingredients

- 4 filet mignons, each about 1 1/2 inches thick, about 1 1/4 pounds
- Salt to taste if desired
- Freshly ground pepper to taste
- ¾ cup dried morels, about 1 ounce
- 1 tablespoon corn, peanut or vegetable oil
- 4 tablespoons butter
- 2 tablespoons finely chopped shallots

- ¼ cup dry red wine
- ¼ cup rich beef broth
- 2 tablespoons Cognac, optional
- 2 tablespoons finely chopped parsley

Direction

- Sprinkle fillets with salt and pepper and set aside.
- Put dried morels in mixing bowl and add warm water to cover. Let stand 30 minutes or longer. Drain.
- Heat heavy skillet and add oil. When quite hot add fillets. Cook about 3 minutes on one side until browned. Turn and continue cooking about 7 minutes on second side.
- Transfer fillets to a warm serving dish.
- Pour off all fat from skillet. Add 2 tablespoons of butter, shallots and drained morels. Cook briefly, stirring, and add wine. Cook down about 1 minute over high heat and add beef broth. Cook down briefly and add Cognac. Heat sauce and swirl in remaining butter. Pour sauce over beef and garnish with chopped parsley.

Nutrition Information

- 592: calories;
- 19 grams: monounsaturated fat;
- 1 gram: sugars;
- 567 milligrams: sodium;
- 47 grams: fat;
- 20 grams: saturated fat;
- 0 grams: trans fat;
- 2 grams: polyunsaturated fat;
- 3 grams: carbohydrates;
- 36 grams: protein;

335. Tuna Mushroom Burgers

Serving: Serves 4 | Prep: | Cook: | Ready in: 1hours

Ingredients

- 10 ounces sushi grade or ahi tuna, trimmed of blood lines
- 10 ounces roasted mushroom mix
- 1 to 2 teaspoons wasabi paste (more to taste)
- 2 tablespoons capers, coarsely chopped if desired
- Salt to taste
- black pepper to taste
- 1 small shallot, finely minced
- Oil for the pan (no more than 1 tablespoon)

Direction

- Chop tuna very fine. I find a cleaver works well for this. It should be like ground beef and it is best to do this by hand because a food processor will make the fish pasty.
- In a large bowl mix together all of the ingredients except the oil, and season to taste. Combine well. Shape 4 patties with moistened hands, or shape by setting a 2-1/2- or 3-inch ring on a plate and filling the ring with the mixture. Carefully remove the ring.
- Heat a large, heavy nonstick skillet over medium-high heat and brush lightly with olive oil or add a small amount to the pan and swirl the pan. Carefully add burgers to pan, taking care not to crowd them. Turn heat to medium and either sear for only 30 seconds to a minute on each side, or cook 2 minutes on each side if desired. Remove to a plate and serve, on buns if desired. Chef Pleau serves these with "avocado crema," a blend of avocado, yogurt, lime juice, cilantro and wasabi powder.

Nutrition Information

- 122: calories;
- 3 grams: fat;
- 0 grams: trans fat;
- 1 gram: dietary fiber;
- 5 grams: carbohydrates;
- 2 grams: sugars;
- 20 grams: protein;
- 371 milligrams: sodium;

336. Turkey Normande

Serving: 2 servings | Prep: | Cook: | Ready in: 35mins

Ingredients

- 10 ounces turkey breast, preferably in one piece
- 1 teaspoon canola oil
- 2 tart medium apples
- 3 tablespoons apple brandy
- ¼ cup low-fat sour cream
- Freshly ground black pepper
- 5 sprigs parsley to yield 1 tablespoon chopped

Direction

- Wash and dry turkey breast, and slice on the diagonal into 1/4-inch-thick slices.
- Heat oil in nonstick skillet until it is medium hot.
- Saute turkey breast slices until they are brown on both sides.
- Meanwhile, wash, quarter and core the apples and cut each quarter into thin slices.
- Add the apples and the brandy to the turkey; cover, and cook about 3 minutes, until the apples are tender.
- Stir in the sour cream and pepper, and cook just until the sour cream is heated.
- Wash, dry and chop parsley, and sprinkle it over turkey to serve.

Nutrition Information

- 434: calories;
- 17 grams: fat;
- 5 grams: dietary fiber;
- 0 grams: trans fat;
- 3 grams: polyunsaturated fat;
- 28 grams: carbohydrates;
- 6 grams: monounsaturated fat;
- 19 grams: sugars;
- 34 grams: protein;
- 107 milligrams: sodium;

337. Turkish Pumpkin Soup

Serving: Serves 4 to 6 | Prep: | Cook: | Ready in: 1hours

Ingredients

- 2 tablespoons extra virgin olive oil
- 1 large onion, chopped
- 1 large leek, white and light green part only, thinly sliced
- 2 to 4 garlic cloves (to taste), minced
- Salt to taste
- 1 teaspoon ground allspice
- 1 teaspoon ground cinnamon
- 2 pounds peeled, seeded butternut or kabocha squash, diced (about 6 cups)
- 6 cups chicken stock, vegetable stock or water
- 3 tablespoons rice
- 1 teaspoon honey or sugar
- Freshly ground pepper to taste
- ½ cup Greek style yogurt
- Aleppo pepper, Turkish red pepper or mild chili powder for garnish

Direction

- Heat the olive oil over medium heat in a large, heavy soup pot or Dutch oven and add the onion and the sliced leek. Cook, stirring, until tender, about 5 minutes. Do not brown. Add a generous pinch of salt and the garlic and cook, stirring, until the garlic smells fragrant, 30 seconds to 1 minute.
- Add the squash, allspice, cinnamon, stock or water, rice, honey or sugar, and salt, and bring to a boil. Reduce the heat, cover and simmer 45 minutes.
- Using a hand blender, or in batches in a regular blender, purée the soup. If using a regular blender fill only half way and cover the top with a towel pulled down tight, rather than airtight with the lid, because hot soup will jump and push the top off if the blender is closed airtight. Return to the pot and heat

through, stirring. Season to taste with salt and pepper.
- Ladle the soup into serving bowls. Swirl a tablespoon or two of yogurt into each bowl and sprinkle with Aleppo pepper, Turkish red pepper or chili powder.

Nutrition Information

- 241: calories;
- 10 grams: protein;
- 9 grams: fat;
- 2 grams: saturated fat;
- 5 grams: monounsaturated fat;
- 1 gram: polyunsaturated fat;
- 32 grams: carbohydrates;
- 3 grams: dietary fiber;
- 1021 milligrams: sodium;

338. Turmeric Raisin Rice

Serving: 4 servings | Prep: | Cook: | Ready in: 25mins

Ingredients

- 2 tablespoons butter
- ¼ cup finely chopped onion
- 1 teaspoon finely chopped garlic
- 1 cup converted rice
- ⅓ cup raisins
- 1 teaspoon turmeric
- 2 sprigs fresh thyme or 1/2 teaspoon dried
- 4 drop Tabasco sauce
- 1 bay leaf
- 1 ½ cups water
- Salt and ground pepper to taste

Direction

- Melt 1 tablespoon of the butter in a saucepan and add the onion and garlic. Cook, stirring, until wilted. Add the rice, raisins, turmeric, thyme, Tabasco, bay leaf, water, salt and

pepper. Bring to a boil, stirring. Cover the pot tightly and simmer for 17 minutes.
- Discard the thyme sprigs and bay leaf. Distribute the remaining butter through the rice. Keep the rice covered in a warm place until it is served.

Nutrition Information

- 273: calories;
- 8 grams: sugars;
- 6 grams: fat;
- 4 grams: protein;
- 2 grams: monounsaturated fat;
- 51 grams: carbohydrates;
- 1 gram: dietary fiber;
- 0 grams: polyunsaturated fat;
- 396 milligrams: sodium;

339. Turmeric Rice

Serving: 4 servings | Prep: | Cook: | Ready in: 25mins

Ingredients

- 1 tablespoon butter
- 1 tablespoon olive oil
- ¼ cup finely chopped onions
- 1 teaspoon finely chopped garlic
- 1 cup converted rice
- 2 teaspoons turmeric
- 1 ½ cups fresh or canned chicken broth
- 1 bay leaf
- 2 sprigs fresh thyme or 1 teaspoon dried
- Tabasco to taste
- Salt and pepper to taste

Direction

- In a heavy saucepan with a tight-fitting lid, melt the butter and add the olive oil. Add onions and garlic and cook until wilted. Add rice and turmeric. Stir to coat.

- Add broth, bay leaf, thyme, Tabasco, salt and pepper. Blend well, bring to a boil and simmer for 17 minutes. Uncover and stir with a fork. Remove bay leaf.

Nutrition Information

- 249: calories;
- 4 grams: protein;
- 42 grams: carbohydrates;
- 7 grams: fat;
- 2 grams: saturated fat;
- 0 grams: trans fat;
- 3 grams: monounsaturated fat;
- 1 gram: sugars;
- 380 milligrams: sodium;

---

340. Two Bean And Tuna Salad

Serving: 6 Servings | Prep: | Cook: | Ready in: 15mins

Ingredients

- ¾ pound green beans, trimmed
- 1 small red onion, cut in half and sliced in half-moons (optional)
- 2 5-ounce cans tuna (packed in water or olive oil), drained
- 1 ½ cups cooked Good Mother Stallard, borlotti, pinto or white beans (if using canned beans, rinse)
- 2 tablespoons chopped fresh parsley
- 2 tablespoons chopped chives
- 2 teaspoons chopped fresh marjoram or sage
- 2 tablespoons sherry vinegar or red wine vinegar
- Salt to taste
- 1 garlic clove, minced or puréed
- 1 teaspoon Dijon mustard
- 2 tablespoons bean broth
- 6 tablespoons extra-virgin olive oil

Direction

- Bring a medium-size pot of water to a boil and add salt to taste. Blanch green beans for 4 minutes (5 minutes if beans are thick), until just tender. Transfer to a bowl of cold water and drain. (Alternatively, steam beans for 4 to 5 minutes). Cut or break beans in half if very long.
- Meanwhile, place sliced onion, if using, in a bowl and cover with cold water. Soak 5 minutes. Drain, rinse and drain again on paper towels.
- Drain tuna and place in a salad bowl. Break up with a fork. Add cooked dried beans, green beans, onion and herbs. Toss together.
- In a small bowl or measuring cup, whisk together vinegar, salt, garlic, mustard and bean broth. Whisk in olive oil. Toss with tuna and bean mixture, and serve.

Nutrition Information

- 256: calories;
- 2 grams: sugars;
- 10 grams: monounsaturated fat;
- 18 grams: carbohydrates;
- 5 grams: dietary fiber;
- 15 grams: protein;
- 0 grams: trans fat;
- 457 milligrams: sodium;
- 14 grams: fat;

---

341. Veal In Red Wine Sauce (Meurettes De Veau)

Serving: 6 to 8 servings | Prep: | Cook: | Ready in: 2hours

Ingredients

- 4 pounds boneless shoulder of veal, cut into 1 1/2-inch cubes
- Salt to taste, if desired
- Freshly ground pepper to taste
- ¼ cup corn, peanut or vegetable oil

- 3 carrots, trimmed and scraped, cut into 1/2-inch cubes, about 1 1/4 cups
- 1 onion, about 1/2 pound, peeled and cut into 1/2-inch dice, about 1 1/2 cups
- 1 tablespoon garlic, peeled and finely minced
- ¼ cup flour
- 4 sprigs fresh thyme
- 10 sprigs parsley
- 1 bay leaf
- 3 ½ cups (1 bottle) dry red wine
- 1 teaspoon sugar
- 1 tablespoon marc de bourgogne, Italian grappa or Calvados
- Croutons, optional (see recipe)

Direction

- Sprinkle the veal with salt and pepper.
- Heat the oil in a large, heavy skillet over high heat, add the veal pieces a few at a time and cook, stirring, until lightly browned on all sides, about 8 to 10 minutes. Transfer the pieces as they are browned to a large, heavy casserole and continue cooking in the casserole over high heat. Add more pieces to the skillet and continue cooking and browning and transferring the pieces to the casserole until all are browned and added.
- Add the carrots, onion and garlic to the meat and stir. Cook 10 minutes and sprinkle with flour, salt and pepper, stirring. Tie the thyme, parsley and bay leaf into a bundle and add it. Add the wine and sugar and bring to the boil. Cover and let simmer over low heat about one and one-half hours. Remove and discard the herb bundle. Add the marc de bourgogne and cook about three minutes longer. Serve with croutons, if desired, on the side.

Nutrition Information

- 487: calories;
- 9 grams: monounsaturated fat;
- 12 grams: carbohydrates;
- 3 grams: sugars;
- 918 milligrams: sodium;
- 19 grams: fat;
- 0 grams: trans fat;
- 2 grams: dietary fiber;
- 45 grams: protein;
- 5 grams: saturated fat;

342. Veal Shanks With Oriental Vegetables

Serving: Six servings | Prep: | Cook: | Ready in: 1hours45mins

Ingredients

- 1 veal shank, about 3 pounds
- 4 cloves garlic, cut lengthwise into 3 strips
- Freshly ground pepper to taste
- 4 cups fresh or canned chicken broth
- 2 cups water
- ¼ cup dark soy sauce
- 2 whole cloves
- 1 teaspoon anise seed
- 1 cup dry white wine
- 1 ½ cups scallions cut into 1-inch lengths
- 5 cups coarsely chopped kale
- ½ head Chinese cabbage, coarsely chopped (about 5 cups)
- 12 baby carrots, peeled
- ½ cup chopped fresh coriander
- ½ pound snow peas
- 1 ½ cups bean sprouts

Direction

- Make small incisions around the veal shank and insert the strips of garlic. Rub the shank with pepper.
- In a large kettle, combine the veal shank, broth, water, soy sauce, cloves, anise seed and wine. Bring to a boil, cover and simmer for one hour and 15 minutes, or until tender. Add the scallions, kale, Chinese cabbage and carrots. Cook for 15 minutes. Add the coriander, snow peas and bean sprouts. Cook for five minutes. Taste for seasonings and serve.

Nutrition Information

- 312: calories;
- 7 grams: sugars;
- 0 grams: trans fat;
- 19 grams: carbohydrates;
- 2 grams: monounsaturated fat;
- 1 gram: polyunsaturated fat;
- 6 grams: dietary fiber;
- 39 grams: protein;
- 1423 milligrams: sodium;

343. Vegan Chocolate Chip Banana Cake

Serving: 1 bundt or 5- by 10-inch loaf | Prep: | Cook: | Ready in: 1hours15mins

Ingredients

- 2 cups all-purpose flour (or gluten-free all-purpose flour plus 1 teaspoon xanthan gum)
- 1 cup sugar
- 1 teaspoon baking powder
- ½ teaspoon baking soda
- 1 teaspoon salt
- ½ teaspoon ground cinnamon
- ½ teaspoon ground nutmeg
- ½ teaspoon ground cloves
- ½ teaspoon ground ginger
- 1 cup mashed bananas (approximately 2 very ripe bananas, mashed on a plate using the back of a fork)
- 1 cup canned coconut milk, mixed well before measuring
- ½ cup canola oil
- 2 teaspoons white or apple cider vinegar
- 1 tablespoon pure vanilla extract
- 1 ½ cups semisweet chocolate chips (dairy free)
- Powdered sugar for garnish

Direction

- Heat oven to 350 degrees. Lightly grease a Bundt pan or a 5- by 10-inch loaf pan.
- In a large bowl, whisk together flour, sugar, baking powder, baking soda, salt, cinnamon, nutmeg, cloves and ginger. In a separate bowl, whisk together bananas, coconut milk, oil, vinegar and vanilla. Pour the wet mixture into the dry mixture and whisk until just combined. Fold in the chocolate chips; do not over-mix.
- Spread the batter evenly into the prepared pan. Bake for about 40 to 45 minutes in a Bundt pan or 50 to 60 minutes in a loaf pan until a toothpick inserted in the center of the cake comes out with a few crumbs clinging to it. Check the cake often and if it gets too brown on top, cover with foil and continue to bake. Rotate the pan halfway through baking time. Let cool, then sift powdered sugar over top.

344. Vegan Pumpkin Tiramisu

Serving: 1 (8-inch) trifle or 6 to 8 mini-trifles | Prep: | Cook: | Ready in: 1hours15mins

Ingredients

- For the Pumpkin Crème
- ⅓ cup cornstarch or arrowroot
- ¼ cup water
- ¾ cup canned coconut milk, mixed well before measuring
- 1 (15-ounce) can pumpkin purée
- ¾ cup maple syrup
- 2 teaspoons pumpkin pie spice
- ½ teaspoon salt
- For the Vanilla Cake
- 3 cups all-purpose flour (or gluten-free all-purpose flour plus 1 1/2 teaspoons xanthan gum)
- 2 cups sugar
- 2 teaspoons baking soda
- 1 teaspoon salt
- 1 ¾ cups soy, almond or rice milk

- 1 cup canola oil
- ¼ cup white or apple cider vinegar
- 1 tablespoon pure vanilla or almond extract
- For the espresso soak
- ½ cup amaretto
- ¼ cup water
- 3 tablespoons instant espresso
- For assembly
- 12 ounces semisweet chocolate chips (dairy-free), ground in a food processor or finely chopped

Direction

- To make the Pumpkin Crème: In a small bowl, thoroughly mix cornstarch and water with a whisk or fork and set aside.
- In a medium saucepan, whisk together coconut milk, pumpkin purée, maple syrup, pumpkin pie spice and salt, and heat over medium heat until it just begins to boil, about 5 minutes. Slowly drizzle cornstarch mixture into the saucepan, whisking continuously. Cook until the mixture becomes very thick, about 5 minutes, whisking frequently. Pour the crème into a bowl and let cool about 15 minutes. Cover the bowl with plastic wrap so that the plastic wrap is touching the top of the crème. Refrigerate for a few hours or overnight.
- To make the Vanilla Cake: Preheat oven to 350 degrees. Lightly grease three 8- or 9-inch round cake pans or one 9-by-13-inch pan and line the bottoms with parchment paper.
- In a large bowl, whisk together flour, sugar, baking soda and salt. In a separate bowl, whisk together nondairy milk, oil, vinegar and vanilla. Pour the wet mixture into the dry mixture and whisk until just combined. Do not overmix.
- Fill each prepared cake pan evenly with batter. Bake for 18 to 20 minutes, or until a toothpick inserted in the center of the cake comes out mostly clean, with a few crumbs clinging to it. Rotate the cakes halfway through the baking time. Cool the cakes completely before assembly.
- To make the Espresso Soak: In a small bowl, whisk amaretto, water and espresso until espresso dissolves.
- To assemble: In a large bowl or trifle dish, place one layer of cake (trim to fit) at the bottom and drizzle it with the Espresso Soak. Spread a layer of Pumpkin Crème on top and generously sprinkle with ground chocolate. Repeat this process for 2 more layers until all components are used up. You could also cut the cake into mini rounds for individual servings in mini trifle dishes or ramekins.

Nutrition Information

- 1184: calories;
- 113 grams: sugars;
- 52 grams: fat;
- 27 grams: monounsaturated fat;
- 10 grams: polyunsaturated fat;
- 7 grams: dietary fiber;
- 9 grams: protein;
- 922 milligrams: sodium;
- 16 grams: saturated fat;
- 0 grams: trans fat;
- 171 grams: carbohydrates;

345. Venison And Trotter Pie

Serving: 1 9-inch deep dish pie, 4 servings | Prep: | Cook: | Ready in: 9hours

Ingredients

- For the filling:
- 5 cups/1.2 liters chicken stock
- 1 pig trotter, split lengthways
- 2 tablespoons olive oil
- 1 ½ pounds/700 grams venison shoulder or leg meat, cut into about 2-inch pieces
- Kosher salt
- 4 tablespoons/40 grams all-purpose flour
- ¾ cup/188 milliliters white wine
- ½ onion

- 6 cloves garlic, peeled and halved
- 6 sprigs thyme
- 1 bay leaf
- 1 cup fingerling potatoes or new potatoes, boiled until tender
- 1 5- to 6-inch marrow bone, outside scraped clean
- For the crust:
- 2 ½ cups/300 grams all-purpose flour
- 2 tablespoons/30 grams sugar
- ½ teaspoon baking powder
- 1 teaspoon kosher salt
- 5 ½ tablespoons/75 grams cold unsalted butter, coarsely grated
- 5 ½ tablespoons/75 grams cold beef suet, coarsely grated (or use additional butter)
- ¾ cup/200 milliliters ice water
- To assemble:
- 1 egg, beaten

Direction

- Make the filling: In a heavy-bottomed pot that fits the trotter pieces in a single layer, bring the stock and trotter to a boil. Reduce the heat to medium, cover and simmer gently for about 3 hours or until the trotter skin and meat is very tender. Remove trotter pieces and strain the liquid, reserving both the trotters and liquid, separately.
- Heat oven to 325 degrees. In a large Dutch oven, heat the oil over high heat. Generously season the venison all over with kosher salt and, working in batches, sear the meat on all sides until deep golden brown. Return all meat to the pot, reduce heat to medium and sprinkle the flour over the meat, stirring gently. When flour is slightly brown, add the wine, scraping all the browned bits from the bottom of the pan. Cook until the liquid thickens, about 1 minute, then add about 4 cups of the braising liquid from the trotters, so the meat is covered, along with the onion, garlic and herbs. Bring up to a boil, then cover tightly and place in the oven to cook until tender, about 3 hours. Fish out and discard the onion, garlic, thyme and bay leaf.
- Once the trotter pieces are cool enough, pick off all of the meat, silken tendons and skin from the bones, and discard the bones and any tough bits. Chop trotter meat, tendon and skin roughly and add to the braised venison, along with the potatoes. Taste for seasoning and adjust if necessary with more salt.
- Make the crust: Combine the flour, sugar, baking powder and salt in a food processor and pulse to mix. Add the butter and suet and pulse until mixture has a cornmeal-like texture. Slowly stream in a little cold water and continue pulsing, adding water a little at a time until dough comes together; you may not need all the water. Turn dough out onto a lightly floured surface and knead until smooth, dusting with flour as needed to avoid sticking. Wrap in plastic wrap and chill in the refrigerator for at least 30 minutes or up to 1 day.
- When ready to bake the pie, heat oven to 375 degrees. Put a 9- or 10-inch deep-dish pie plate on a foil-lined baking tray and stand the marrow bone up in the center of the pan. Spoon all the meat, potato filling and gravy around it. On a lightly floured surface, roll dough into a 12-inch round and cut a small cross at the center. Drape dough over the pie plate, pushing the marrow bone right through the center, so it's sticking out. Use scissors to cut excess dough away, leaving at least an inch hanging off the edge all around. Use a fork to press down and crimp the dough where it's touching the edge of the pan, leaving the overhang attached. (It will make a kind of curtain around the the dish.) Generously brush the dough all over with the beaten egg, and bake until the crust is deep golden brown, about 1 hour and 15 minutes. Let cool for 10 minutes, then season the open top of the marrow bone with a little salt and serve.

346. Veracruzana Vinegar Bathed Shrimp

Serving: Serves 8 | Prep: | Cook: | Ready in: 45mins

Ingredients

- 2 pounds medium shrimp
- 3 cups water
- 3 tablespoons extra-virgin olive oil
- 1 large white or red onion, thinly sliced
- 2 large carrots, thinly sliced
- Salt to taste
- 4 to 6 garlic cloves, minced or puréed
- 2 fresh or pickled serrano or jalapeño chiles, or chipotle chiles in adobo sauce, minced
- 2 large or 4 small bay leaves
- ⅓ cup seasoned rice vinegar
- ¼ teaspoon freshly ground pepper
- ½ teaspoon ground cloves (more to taste)
- 1 teaspoon dried Mexican oregano or 1 tablespoon chopped fresh mint
- ⅓ cup chopped cilantro
- Lettuce leaves for serving (optional)

Direction

- Peel and devein shrimp, saving the shells.
- Bring water to a boil in a medium saucepan and add shrimp shells. Simmer 30 minutes. Line a strainer with cheesecloth and set over a bowl. Strain broth into bowl and discard shells. You will need only 1/2 cup of the broth; the rest can be frozen, or used to cook rice if you choose it to accompany the shrimp.
- Heat 2 tablespoons olive oil over medium heat in a large, heavy skillet and add onion, carrots and a generous pinch of salt. Cook, stirring often, until tender, 5 to 8 minutes. Add garlic and shrimp and cook, stirring, until shrimp begins to turn pink, about 3 minutes.
- Add chiles, bay leaves, vinegar, pepper, ground cloves, salt to taste and 1/2 cup shrimp stock and bring to a simmer. Reduce heat to low and simmer for 5 minutes or until the shrimp is cooked through, stirring occasionally. Remove from heat and transfer mix to a bowl. Refrigerate for 30 minutes or longer.
- Stir in remaining tablespoon of olive oil, the oregano or mint and cilantro. Taste and adjust seasonings. If desired, line a platter or plates with lettuce leaves and spoon shrimp mix over the lettuce.

Nutrition Information

- 146: calories;
- 6 grams: fat;
- 2 grams: sugars;
- 16 grams: protein;
- 660 milligrams: sodium;
- 1 gram: dietary fiber;
- 0 grams: trans fat;
- 4 grams: monounsaturated fat;
- 5 grams: carbohydrates;

347. Warm Millet, Carrot And Kale Salad With Curry Scented Dressing

Serving: Serves 4 to 5 | Prep: | Cook: | Ready in: 2hours

Ingredients

- 1 bunch of black kale (cavolo nero), 10 to 12 ounces, stemmed and washed thoroughly
- Salt to taste
- 2 teaspoons canola oil, rice bran oil or extra virgin olive oil
- ⅔ cup millet
- 2 cups water or blanching water from the kale
- 2 teaspoons extra virgin olive oil
- ½ pound carrots, peeled and thinly sliced on the diagonal
- ½ cup chopped cilantro
- 1 tablespoon nigella seeds
- For the Dressing
- 2 tablespoons fresh lemon juice
- 2 teaspoons seasoned rice vinegar

- 1 teaspoon sweet curry powder
- Salt and freshly ground pepper
- 4 tablespoons grape seed oil, rice bran oil, canola oil or extra virgin olive oil
- ¼ cup buttermilk

Direction

- Separate the kale into two unequal bunches, with about two thirds in one bunch. Wash and dry the smaller bunch, roll the leaves in paper towels and set aside. Blanch the rest in a pot of boiling salted water for 1 to 2 minutes. Remove from the pot with a slotted spoon or skimmer, transfer to a bowl of cold water, drain and squeeze out excess water. Cut the squeezed bunch of kale crosswise into thin slices and set aside. Measure out 2 cups of the blanching water.
- Heat 2 teaspoons of oil over medium-high heat in a heavy 2- or 3-quart saucepan. Add the millet and toast, stirring, until it begins to smell fragrant and toasty, 3 to 5 minutes. Add the 2 cups of kale water. If not using the kale water add 2 cups water and salt to taste, and bring back to a boil. Reduce the heat to low, cover and simmer 25 to 30 minutes, until the liquid in the saucepan has evaporated and the grains are fluffy. Turn off the heat, place a clean dish towel over the pot and return the lid. Let sit for 10 to 15 minutes, then transfer the cooked millet to a baking sheet or a shallow pan and spread out in an even layer to cool. This helps prevent clumping.
- Meanwhile, make crispy kale with the remaining kale. Heat the oven to 300 degrees. Line 2 baking sheets with parchment. Make sure that your kale leaves are dry. Tear them into medium-size pieces and toss with the olive oil. Gently knead the leaves between your thumbs and fingers to make sure they are coated with oil. Place in an even layer on the baking sheets. Do this in batches if necessary. Place in the oven and roast for 22 to 25 minutes, until the leaves are crisp but not browned. If some of the leaves crisp before others, remove them to a bowl or sheet pan and return the remaining kale to the oven. Watch closely as once the kale browns it will taste bitter. Once the kale is crisp, season to taste with salt. Allow to cool.
- Whisk the dressing ingredients together in a small bowl or measuring cup, then transfer to a wide skillet. Add the millet, blanched kale, carrots, and nigella seeds and heat everything together over medium heat, stirring to combine well, until sizzling. Stir in the cilantro just before serving. Serve with the crispy kale crumbled over the top.

Nutrition Information

- 287: calories;
- 29 grams: carbohydrates;
- 2 grams: saturated fat;
- 0 grams: trans fat;
- 6 grams: protein;
- 4 grams: sugars;
- 572 milligrams: sodium;
- 17 grams: fat;
- 5 grams: monounsaturated fat;
- 9 grams: polyunsaturated fat;

348. Warm Potato Salad

Serving: 2 servings | Prep: | Cook: | Ready in: 35mins

Ingredients

- 1 pound tiny new potatoes or other, larger boiling potatoes
- 12 ounces whole red pepper or 11 ounces ready-cut peppers (2 1/2 to 3 cups)
- 3 ounces shallots (6 tablespoons minced)
- 1 small bunch tarragon, enough for 2 tablespoons minced
- 1 tablespoon balsamic vinegar
- 1 tablespoon olive oil
- 1 tablespoon Dijon mustard
- ⅓ cup nonfat plain yogurt
- ¼ teaspoon salt

- Freshly ground black pepper to taste

Direction

- Scrub potatoes. Cook tiny potatoes whole in water to cover. Cube large potatoes, and cook the same way. The whole potatoes will take 10 to 20 minutes, depending on size; the cubed potatoes 7 to 10 minutes.
- Wash, trim, seed and dice the red peppers; mince the shallots.
- Wash, dry and mince the tarragon.
- Whisk vinegar, oil and mustard; stir in yogurt, red pepper, shallots and tarragon.
- When potatoes are cooked, drain; dice whole potatoes, and add to salad. Season with salt and black pepper.

Nutrition Information

- 307: calories;
- 0 grams: trans fat;
- 49 grams: carbohydrates;
- 435 milligrams: sodium;
- 2 grams: polyunsaturated fat;
- 16 grams: sugars;
- 11 grams: protein;
- 9 grams: dietary fiber;
- 1 gram: saturated fat;
- 5 grams: monounsaturated fat;

349. Warm Shrimp And Beans

Serving: 4 servings | Prep: | Cook: | Ready in: 1hours15mins

Ingredients

- ½ pound dried cannellini beans
- Salt and freshly ground black pepper
- 7 tablespoons extra-virgin olive oil
- 20 jumbo shrimp, shelled and deveined
- 2 large garlic cloves, chopped
- 1 tablespoon chopped fresh rosemary leaves
- 1 cup diced ripe tomatoes

Direction

- Cover beans with cold water to a depth of 2 inches above the beans. Soak for 4 hours or overnight.
- Drain the beans and place in a saucepan. Cover with cold water to a depth of 2 inches above the beans, bring to a boil, skim the surface, then lower the heat to medium. Cook the beans until they are tender, about 45 minutes. Drain, reserving 1/3 cup of the cooking liquid. Season the beans with salt and pepper to taste.
- Have four plates ready. Heat 2 tablespoons of the oil in a large skillet, add the shrimp and stir in the oil until golden on both sides, approximately 2 to 3 minutes. Add the garlic, rosemary, tomatoes, beans, reserved 1/3 cup of liquid from the beans and salt and pepper to taste. Cook, stirring gently for 2 minutes. Remove from heat and add remaining oil.
- Divide among the plates, arranging five shrimp on each like spokes of a wheel and mounding the bean mixture in the center. Serve.

Nutrition Information

- 438: calories;
- 17 grams: monounsaturated fat;
- 3 grams: polyunsaturated fat;
- 9 grams: dietary fiber;
- 2 grams: sugars;
- 19 grams: protein;
- 374 milligrams: sodium;
- 0 grams: trans fat;
- 25 grams: fat;
- 4 grams: saturated fat;
- 37 grams: carbohydrates;

350. Watermelon Or Cantaloupe Agua Fresca

Serving: Four servings | Prep: | Cook: | Ready in: 1hours

Ingredients

- 4 cups diced, peeled ripe watermelon or cantaloupe
- 3 cups water
- 2 to 3 teaspoons fresh lime juice
- 1 tablespoon sugar

Direction

- Blend together the watermelon or cantaloupe with 1 1/2 cups of the water, the lime juice and the sugar at high speed until smooth. Strain through a medium strainer into a large pitcher or bowl. Stir in the remaining water. Refrigerate for 1 hour or longer. Fill a glass with ice, pour in the agua fresca, garnish with a mint sprig, and serve.

Nutrition Information

- 59: calories;
- 0 grams: polyunsaturated fat;
- 15 grams: carbohydrates;
- 1 gram: protein;
- 13 grams: sugars;
- 9 milligrams: sodium;

351. White Bean And Shrimp Salad

Serving: Four servings | Prep: | Cook: | Ready in: 3hours40mins

Ingredients

- ½ pound white beans
- 1 teaspoon salt, plus more to taste
- 1 bay leaf
- 1 pound medium-size shrimp, shelled and cleaned
- ½ teaspoon cayenne pepper
- ¼ cup fresh lemon juice
- 2 tablespoons olive oil
- 1 clove garlic, peeled and minced
- 1 white onion, peeled and minced
- ¼ cup minced parsley
- 1 tomato, seeded and cut into 1/2-inch dice
- 1 teaspoon freshly ground pepper, plus more to taste

Direction

- Cover the beans with cold water. Set aside to soak overnight. Drain, rinse under cold water and place in a heavy-bottomed pot. Add 2 cups cold water, 1/2 teaspoon salt and the bay leaf. Simmer until tender, about 1 1/2 hours.
- Place the shrimp in a large nonstick skillet. Add the cayenne and cook over medium-low heat until the shrimp is cooked through, about 5 minutes. Set aside to cool.
- Combine the lemon juice and olive oil in a large glass or ceramic bowl. Add the garlic, onion and parsley. Add the beans, shrimp and tomato. Toss to combine. Season to taste with the remaining 1/2 teaspoon of salt and the pepper. Cover and refrigerate for at least 2 hours, and up to 6, before serving.

Nutrition Information

- 356: calories;
- 0 grams: trans fat;
- 5 grams: monounsaturated fat;
- 4 grams: sugars;
- 30 grams: protein;
- 656 milligrams: sodium;
- 9 grams: fat;
- 1 gram: polyunsaturated fat;
- 42 grams: carbohydrates;
- 10 grams: dietary fiber;

352. White Bean Burgers

Serving: 6 patties | Prep: | Cook: | Ready in: 2hours30mins

Ingredients

- 2 cans white beans, drained and rinsed
- 2 tablespoons extra virgin olive oil
- 1 small onion, finely chopped
- Salt to taste
- 2 to 3 large garlic cloves (to taste), green shoots removed, minced
- ⅔ cup finely grated carrot
- 3 tablespoons freshly squeezed lemon juice
- ¼ cup finely chopped parsley
- 2 teaspoons minced fresh sage or thyme
- ½ cup fresh bread crumbs
- 1 egg, beaten
- Freshly ground pepper to taste
- Whole grain hamburger buns and the condiments of your choice

Direction

- Heat 1 tablespoon of the olive oil in a medium-size skillet and add the onion. Cook, stirring, until tender, about 5 minutes. Add a pinch of salt, the garlic and the grated carrot, and continue to cook for another minute or two, until fragrant and the carrot has softened slightly. Remove from the heat.
- In a food processor fitted with the steel blade, puree the beans with the lemon juice. Transfer to a bowl and stir in the onion mixture, the parsley, sage or thyme, the bread crumbs and the egg. Season to taste. Shape into patties, ½- to ¾-inch thick. Set on a parchment-covered baking sheet and cover with plastic wrap. Refrigerate for 1 to 2 hours.
- Heat the remaining oil in a large, heavy skillet or on a griddle over medium heat and brown the patties for 4 minutes on each side, being very careful when you turn them over. An offset spatula works well for this. Serve on whole grain buns, with the condiments of your choice.

Nutrition Information

- 219: calories;
- 5 grams: fat;
- 1 gram: polyunsaturated fat;
- 0 grams: trans fat;
- 3 grams: monounsaturated fat;
- 7 grams: dietary fiber;
- 2 grams: sugars;
- 386 milligrams: sodium;
- 34 grams: carbohydrates;
- 11 grams: protein;

353. White Bean And Yogurt Green Goddess

Serving: 1 cup, about 6 to 8 servings | Prep: | Cook: | Ready in: 5mins

Ingredients

- 1 small garlic clove, halved, green shoot removed
- ½ cup cooked white beans, drained and rinsed if using canned beans
- ½ cup whole milk or 2 percent Greek yogurt or regular yogurt
- 1 ice cube, if using Greek yogurt
- 1 tablespoon chopped fresh tarragon
- 2 tablespoons chopped fresh parsley
- 1 tablespoon chopped fresh chives
- 1 tablespoon fresh lemon juice
- Salt to taste
- 2 tablespoons extra-virgin olive oil

Direction

- Process garlic in a food processor fitted with a steel blade until minced garlic is adhering to sides. Stop processor and scrape down. Add beans, yogurt, ice cube, tarragon, parsley and chives and process until smooth. With machine running, add lemon juice, salt, and olive oil and process until mixture is smooth. Taste and adjust seasoning.

- Scrape into a bowl. Serve as a dip or use with crisp salads (it's a bit too thick for delicate lettuces like spring mixes).

Nutrition Information

- 81: calories;
- 5 grams: carbohydrates;
- 2 grams: sugars;
- 3 grams: protein;
- 0 grams: polyunsaturated fat;
- 1 gram: dietary fiber;
- 150 milligrams: sodium;

354. White Beans With Clams

Serving: 4 to 6 servings | Prep: | Cook: | Ready in: 1hours55mins

Ingredients

- For the beans:
- 1 pound large white dried beans
- 2 onions, peeled and cut in halves
- 4 cloves garlic, peeled
- 2 carrots, scraped and cut in half crosswise
- 2 sprigs parsley
- 2 bay leaves
- Few strands saffron
- Coarse salt
- For the clams:
- 6 tablespoons olive oil
- 2 tablespoons minced onion
- 4 cloves garlic, minced
- 2 dozen very small clams, at room temperature
- 1 tablespoon paprika
- 2 tablespoons minced parsley
- ½ cup dry white wine
- ½ dried red chili pepper, crumbled
- Coarse salt and freshly ground pepper to taste

Direction

- Soak the beans overnight. The following day, drain them and cover with cold water. Add the onions, garlic, carrots, parsley sprigs and bay leaves. Bring to boil, add one cup cold water to cut the boil, then return to a boil, cover and simmer very slowly one-and-a-half to two hours, or until beans are tender.
- When the beans are almost tender, start preparing the clams. Heat the oil in a skillet and sauté the onion and garlic until the onion is wilted. Add the clams and cook over medium high heat, stirring frequently, until they open. Sprinkle in the paprika and the parsley. Add the wine, chili pepper, salt (if necessary), and pepper. Cook 5 minutes more.
- Stir saffron and salt into the beans, add clams with all liquid in the pan. Shake to mix in clams and liquid. Cover and cook for five minutes.
- Serve the beans in soup bowls with the clams arranged on top.

Nutrition Information

- 457: calories;
- 15 grams: fat;
- 10 grams: monounsaturated fat;
- 14 grams: dietary fiber;
- 24 grams: protein;
- 513 milligrams: sodium;
- 2 grams: polyunsaturated fat;
- 0 grams: trans fat;
- 56 grams: carbohydrates;
- 5 grams: sugars;

355. White Spice Poundcake

Serving: 10 servings | Prep: | Cook: | Ready in: 1hours

Ingredients

- Oil for greasing the pan
- Flour for dusting the pan
- ¼ cup milk

- 4 large egg whites, about 1/2 cup
- 2 teaspoons brandy
- 2 cups sifted cake flour
- 1 cup sugar
- 1 teaspoon baking powder
- ½ teaspoon salt
- ½ teaspoon cinnamon
- ½ teaspoon cloves
- 1 ½ teaspoons unsweetened cocoa
- 16 tablespoons (2 sticks) softened unsalted butter

Direction

- Preheat the oven to 350 degrees. Grease and flour one 6-cup fluted tube pan or loaf pan; if using a loaf pan, grease, line the bottom with parchment or wax paper, and then grease again and flour.
- In a medium-size bowl, lightly combine the milk, egg whites and brandy.
- In a large mixing bowl combine the dry ingredients and mix on low speed for 30 seconds to blend. Add the butter and half of the egg mixture. Mix on low speed until the dry ingredients are moistened. Increase to medium speed (high speed if using a hand mixer) and beat for 1 minute to aerate. Scrape down the sides. Add the remaining egg mixture in two batches, beating for 20 seconds after each addition to incorporate the ingredients. Scrape down the sides.
- Scrape the batter into the prepared pan and smooth the surface with a spatula. The batter will almost fill the pan. Bake 40 to 50 minutes in a fluted tube pan (45 to 55 minutes in a loaf pan) or until a wire cake tester inserted in the center comes out clean and the cake springs back when pressed lightly in the center. (The cake should start to shrink from the sides of the pan only after removal from the oven.)
- For an attractive split down the middle of the crust when using a loaf pan, wait until the natural split is about to develop (about 20 minutes) and then with a lightly greased sharp knife or single-edged razor blade make a shallow mark 6 inches long down the middle of the cake. This must be done quickly so the oven door does not remain open very long or the cake will fall. When the cake splits, it will open along the mark.
- Let the cake cool in the pan on a rack for 10 minutes and invert onto a greased wire rack. If baked in a loaf pan, to keep the bottom from splitting reinvert so the top is up. Cool completely before wrapping airtight.

Nutrition Information

- 368: calories;
- 20 grams: sugars;
- 12 grams: saturated fat;
- 1 gram: dietary fiber;
- 6 grams: monounsaturated fat;
- 43 grams: carbohydrates;
- 4 grams: protein;
- 181 milligrams: sodium;

356. White Or Pink Beans With Beet Greens And Parmesan

Serving: 4 servings | Prep: | Cook: | Ready in: 2hours15mins

Ingredients

- 2 tablespoons extra virgin olive oil
- 1 large red onion, finely chopped
- 2 to 4 garlic cloves (to taste), minced
- ½ pound white or pink beans (1 1/8 cups), soaked in 1 quart water for 4 hours or overnight
- 6 cups water
- A bouquet garni made with a bay leaf, a few sprigs each parsley and thyme, and 2 good-size Parmesan rinds
- Salt to taste
- 1 generous bunch beet greens (about 3/4 pound), stemmed, washed well in 2 changes of water and coarsely chopped

- Freshly ground pepper
- Freshly grated Parmesan for serving

Direction

- Heat the olive oil over medium heat in a large, heavy soup pot or Dutch oven and add the onion. Cook, stirring often, until the onion is tender, about 5 minutes, and add the garlic. Cook, stirring, until it is fragrant, 30 seconds to a minute. Drain the beans and add to the pot, along with 6 cups water (or enough to cover the beans by at least an inch) and the bouquet garni. Bring to a gentle boil, add salt to taste, cover and simmer 1 1/2 to 2 hours, until the beans are soft and fragrant. Taste, adjust salt, and add pepper. Remove the bouquet garni.
- Stir in the beet greens and simmer 5 to 10 minutes. Serve in wide bowls and pass freshly grated Parmesan for sprinkling.

Nutrition Information

- 101: calories;
- 7 grams: fat;
- 1 gram: polyunsaturated fat;
- 9 grams: carbohydrates;
- 2 grams: sugars;
- 3 grams: protein;
- 5 grams: monounsaturated fat;
- 4 grams: dietary fiber;
- 1268 milligrams: sodium;

357. Whole Grain Blueberry Buckle

Serving: 1 8-inch cake, serving 9 to 12 | Prep: | Cook: | Ready in: 1hours30mins

Ingredients

- For the topping
- 20 grams rolled oats (about 3 tablespoons, approximately)
- 60 grams quinoa flour (1/2 cup, approximately; grind quinoa in a spice mill to make the flour)
- 1/2 teaspoon freshly grated nutmeg
- 50 grams unrefined turbinado sugar (1/4 cup, approximately)
- 1/8 teaspoon salt (to taste)
- 60 grams cold unsalted butter, cut into 1/2-inch pieces (4 tablespoons/2 ounces)
- For the cake
- 125 grams whole-wheat flour (1 cup, approximately)
- 65 grams unbleached all-purpose flour (1/2 cup, approximately)
- 5 grams baking powder (1 teaspoon, approximately)
- 1 gram baking soda (1/4 teaspoon, approximately)
- 3 grams fine sea salt (scant 1/2 teaspoon, approximately)
- 90 grams unsalted butter, preferably French-style such as Plugrà, at room temperature (6 tablespoons/3 ounces)
- 120 grams sugar, preferably organic (scant 1/2 cup, approximately)
- 1 teaspoon finely grated lemon zest
- 2 eggs, at room temperature
- 130 grams buttermilk or kefir (1/2 cup)
- 350 grams blueberries (2 1/4 cups, approximately/ 2 boxes), divided

Direction

- Preheat oven to 350 degrees. Butter a 9-inch square baking pan and cover bottom with parchment. Butter parchment.
- Make the crumble topping. Place oats, quinoa flour, turbinado sugar, salt, and nutmeg in a food processor fitted with the steel blade and pulse several times to combine. Add cold butter and pulse until butter is evenly distributed in throughoutthroughout the grain mix. The mixture should have a crumbly consistency. Place in freezer while you make the ix up cake batter.
- Sift together flours, baking powder, baking soda and salt. In a standing mixer fitted with

the paddle attachment, or in a bowl with electric beaters, cream butter, sugar, and lemon zest on medium speed for 3 to 5 minutes, until fluffy. Add eggs, one at a time, scraping down bowl between each addition.

- On low speed, add flour mixture in 3 batchesadditions, adding buttermilk or kefir between each addition. Scrape down bowl between each addition. Remove beaters and gently fold in half the blueberries.
- Scrape batter into prepared pan and spread evenly. Distribute remaining blueberries over the top. Sprinkle crumble topping over the blueberries.
- Bake 50 to 55 minutes, until golden and firm when pressed gently in the middle.

Nutrition Information

- 257: calories;
- 210 milligrams: sodium;
- 3 grams: dietary fiber;
- 0 grams: trans fat;
- 1 gram: polyunsaturated fat;
- 35 grams: carbohydrates;
- 18 grams: sugars;
- 4 grams: protein;
- 12 grams: fat;
- 7 grams: saturated fat;

358. Whole Wheat Focaccia

Serving: 1 large focaccia or 2 smaller focacce, 12 to 15 pieces | Prep: | Cook: | Ready in: 4hours

Ingredients

- 2 teaspoons (8 grams) active dry yeast
- 1 teaspoon (5 grams) sugar
- 1 ½ cups (340 grams) lukewarm water
- 2 tablespoons (25 grams) olive oil, plus 1 to 2 tablespoons (25 grams) for drizzling
- 250 grams (approximately 2 cups) whole-wheat flour
- 200 to 220 grams (approximately 1 2/3 to 1 3/4 cups) unbleached all-purpose flour or bread flour, plus additional as needed for kneading
- 1 ¾ teaspoons (13 grams) salt
- Simple Toppings
- Coarse sea salt
- 2 to 4 tablespoons chopped fresh rosemary, thyme or sage
- Pitted black olives
- Roasted red peppers, diced or sliced

Direction

-
-
-

359. Whole Wheat Seeded Loaves

Serving: | Prep: | Cook: | Ready in: 5hours15mins

Ingredients

- 25 grams sunflower seeds (approximately 2 tablespoons plus 1 teaspoon)
- 25 grams sesame seeds (approximately 2 1/2 tablespoons)
- 25 grams flax seeds (approximately 2 1/2 tablespoons)
- 25 grams rolled oats (approximately 1/4 cup)
- 25 grams pumpkin seeds (approximately 2 tablespoons)
- 180 grams water (approximately 3/4 cup) plus about 60 grams additional water
- 170 grams bread flour or unbleached all-purpose flour (approximately 1 1/3 cups)
- 170 grams lukewarm water (approximately 3/4 cup less 2 teaspoons)
- 4 grams dry yeast (approximately 1 teaspoon)
- 250 grams whole-wheat flour (approximately 2 cups) or 125 grams bread flour and 125 grams whole-wheat flour
- 12 grams sea salt (approximately 1 1/2 teaspoons)

Direction

- Mix seeds and oats together with 180 grams of water in a medium mixing bowl; cover with plastic wrap and and let soak overnight in the refrigerator.
- Combine 170 grams bread flour or all-purpose flour, 170 grams lukewarm water, and yeast in bowl of a standing mixer and mix together until well combined. Cover with plastic and leave to ferment at room temperature for two hours or until it doubles in volume. Meanwhile, remove bowl with nuts and seeds from the refrigerator, drain and bring to room temperature.
- Add drained seeds, 250 grams whole-wheat flour and sea salt to the starter. Start mixing on medium speed. The dough should come together in the first minute. If it does not and you see dry ingredients in the bottom of the bowl, add about 1/4 cup of water. Mix dough for 5 minutes on medium speed, then turn the speed up to medium-high and mix 5 to 7 minutes more, or until dough is elastic.
- Cover bowl with plastic wrap and set in a warm spot to rise for 1 hour.
- Dust work surface lightly with flour and scrape out dough. Weigh dough and divide into 2 equal pieces. Shape each piece into a ball or into oblong pointed loaves. (For oblong loaves, first shape into balls, cover with a towel or lightly with plastic and let rest for 15 minutes. Then press the dough out to a rectangle about 3/4 inch thick. Take the side closest to you and fold lengthwise halfway to the center of the loaf. Lightly press down to seal. Take the top flap and bring it toward you over the first fold to the middle of the loaf and lightly press down to seal. Flip over so seam is on the bottom and roll back and forth with both hands to form an oblong loaf with pointy ends. Place on a sheet pan lined with parchment paper and repeat with the remaining dough. Cover with a towel and place in a warm spot for one hour.)
- Preheat oven to 450 degrees with a pizza stone on the middle rack and a small sheet pan on bottom of the oven for 30 to 45 minutes. Have 1 cup water ready in a small cup or a glass. (If you have a large pizza stone, you can bake both loaves at once. If you have a standard home pizza stone, bake one loaf at a time and place the other loaf in the refrigerator to slow down the fermentation.) Dust a pizza peel or flat baking sheet lightly with flour, semolina or cornmeal and place one loaf on top. Using a razor blade or a moistened bread knife, make a 1/2-inch deep horizontal cut down the middle of loaf from one end to the other, or if the loaves are round make 2 slashes across top. Slide loaf onto pizza stone and close oven door. Wait 30 seconds, then open oven door quickly and pour water onto the sheet pan on the bottom of the oven to create steam. After 5 minutes take the sheet pan out of the oven. Bake for a total of 30 to 35 minutes, until loaf is dark brown and sounds hollow when you tap the bottom. Transfer loaf to a wire rack to cool completely for 45 minutes. Repeat with other loaf.

Nutrition Information

- 266: calories;
- 4 grams: polyunsaturated fat;
- 43 grams: carbohydrates;
- 6 grams: dietary fiber;
- 10 grams: protein;
- 7 grams: fat;
- 1 gram: saturated fat;
- 0 grams: sugars;
- 2 grams: monounsaturated fat;
- 279 milligrams: sodium;

360. Whoopie Pies

Serving: 6 pies | Prep: | Cook: | Ready in: 1hours

Ingredients

- For the cakes

- ¼ pound (1 stick) butter, at room temperature
- 1 cup light brown sugar
- 1 large egg
- 1 teaspoon vanilla extract
- 1 ¼ teaspoons baking soda
- 1 teaspoon sea salt
- 2 cups all-purpose flour
- ½ cup cocoa
- 1 cup buttermilk
- For the buttercream filling
- 3 large egg whites
- ¾ cup sugar
- ½ pound butter (2 sticks), at room temperature
- ¾ teaspoon vanilla
- ¼ teaspoon sea salt

Direction

- For the cakes: Preheat oven to 350 degrees. In a mixing bowl, cream together the butter and brown sugar. Add the egg and vanilla extract and beat until light and creamy. In a separate bowl, whisk together the baking soda, salt, flour and cocoa. Add dry ingredients to butter mixture in three parts, alternating with buttermilk, and combining well after each addition.
- Using an ice cream scoop or a spoon, scoop out 12 1/4-cup mounds of batter and place about 6 inches apart on a parchment-lined baking sheet. Bake until tops are puffed and cakes spring back when touched, 12 to 14 minutes. Remove from oven and cool completely before filling.
- For the buttercream filling: For best results, follow directions carefully, paying attention to required temperatures. Fill bottom half of a double boiler (or a medium saucepan) with an inch or two of water, and bring to a boil over high heat. In top half of double boiler (or a metal bowl), combine egg whites and sugar. Place over simmering water and whisk just until sugar is dissolved and temperature reaches 180 degrees on an instant-read thermometer.
- Using a whisk attachment on a heavy-duty mixer, whisk egg whites and sugar on high until they double in volume and become thick and shiny. Continue to whisk until cool. Reduce speed to medium and begin to add butter about 1/2 tablespoon at a time, until all the butter is incorporated. Add vanilla and salt. If mixture looks curdled, continue to whisk until it is smooth. Increase speed to high and whisk for 1 more minute. Use immediately or place in an airtight container and chill for up to 3 days, whisking buttercream again before using.
- For assembly: Using an ice cream scoop or spoon, place 1/4 cup buttercream on flat side of each of 6 cakes, spreading it to edges. Top filled half with another cake to sandwich the buttercream. Store in an airtight container at room temperature for up to 3 days, or wrap individually and freeze for up to 3 months.

Nutrition Information

- 602: calories;
- 23 grams: saturated fat;
- 9 grams: monounsaturated fat;
- 38 grams: sugars;
- 388 milligrams: sodium;
- 8 grams: protein;
- 36 grams: fat;
- 1 gram: trans fat;
- 2 grams: polyunsaturated fat;
- 65 grams: carbohydrates;
- 3 grams: dietary fiber;

361. Yogurt Or Buttermilk Soup With Spinach And Grains

Serving: 6 to 8 servings | Prep: | Cook: | Ready in: 1hours30mins

Ingredients

- ¾ pound (1 generous bunch) spinach, stemmed and washed in 2 changes of water, or 6 ounces baby spinach, rinsed

- 1 ½ cups finely diced cucumber (2 Persian cucumbers)
- Salt to taste
- 5 cups plain low-fat yogurt (free of gums and stabilizers) or buttermilk, or a mixture of the two
- 1 cup finely diced celery
- 1 to 2 garlic cloves (to taste), finely minced or puréed with a little salt in a mortar and pestle
- 2 tablespoons freshly squeezed lemon juice (more to taste)
- 1 cup cooked barley, spelt, kamut or farro
- ⅔ cup diced radishes
- Freshly ground pepper to taste (optional)
- ½ teaspoon sumac (more to taste)
- 2 tablespoons chopped cilantro
- Optional
- 1 ripe Hass avocado, cut in small dice

Direction

- Place the cucumber in a bowl and sprinkle with salt. Toss and place in a strainer set over the bowl. Allow to drain for 15 minutes. Rinse if desired and drain on paper towels.
- Meanwhile, steam the spinach above 1 inch of boiling water until wilted, 1 to 2 minutes, moving the leaves around with tongs once to ensure that they steam evenly. Rinse with cold water and squeeze out excess moisture. Chop medium-fine.
- Combine all the ingredients in a bowl. Thin out with ice water if desired. Season to taste with salt and pepper. Chill for one hour or longer.

Nutrition Information

- 179: calories;
- 6 grams: fat;
- 3 grams: monounsaturated fat;
- 11 grams: protein;
- 668 milligrams: sodium;
- 2 grams: saturated fat;
- 1 gram: polyunsaturated fat;
- 22 grams: carbohydrates;
- 4 grams: dietary fiber;
- 12 grams: sugars;

362. Zarela Martinez's Ropa Vieja

Serving: 8 to 10 servings | Prep: | Cook: | Ready in: 2hours30mins

Ingredients

- 3 pounds flank steak
- 1 ½ cups water
- 8 cloves garlic (6 whole and peeled, 2 sliced and peeled)
- 6 whole black peppercorns
- Salt to taste
- 8 fresh poblano peppers
- ⅓ cup lard, bacon drippings or vegetable oil
- 1 large onion, halved and sliced 1/8-inch thick
- Flour tortillas

Direction

- Cut the flank steak in half horizontally so it will fit into a large Dutch oven. Place it in the pot and cover it with the water. Add the six whole cloves of garlic, along with the peppercorns and salt as desired. Place over low heat and bring the liquid to a simmer. Cover the Dutch oven and continue cooking over low heat, turning the meat occasionally, until it is tender and well done, about 1 1/2 to 2 hours.
- While the meat is stewing, heat the broiler. Rinse and dry the peppers. Arrange them in a broiler pan about four inches from the flame. Roast them, turning frequently, until they are evenly blistered and charred on all sides. Transfer to a paper bag, seal it and let the peppers sit until cool enough to handle.
- Remove the cooled peppers from the bag and slice off the top of each. Scrape out the seeds and slip off the skins with your fingers (wear rubber gloves if your hands are sensitive).

Slice each pepper lengthwise into strips an eighth of an inch wide. Set aside.

- When the meat is tender, remove the Dutch oven from the heat and let the meat cool in its own broth. When it cools enough to handle, remove it from the broth and place it on a cutting board. Slice the meat across the grain into strips about two inches across. Using your fingers, pull the meat into fine shreds. Return it to the cooking broth.
- Heat the lard or other fat in a large heavy skillet over medium heat until it is rippling. Crush the sliced garlic cloves and add to the hot fat. Saute for one minute, stirring frequently. Add the sliced onion and saute, stirring frequently, until it is somewhat soft, about three minutes. Add the reserved pepper strips to the pan and continue sauteing and stirring for about two minutes.
- Using a slotted spoon, transfer the peppers, onion and garlic to the Dutch oven. Cook the meat mixture, uncovered, over medium heat, stirring frequently, until the flavors are blended, about 10 to 15 minutes. Serve the meat hot, rolled up in heated flour tortillas.

363. Zrazy Zawijane (Stuffed Rolls Of Beef)

Serving: 6 servings | Prep: | Cook: | Ready in: 2hours55mins

Ingredients

- 1 four-inch piece of stale French bread, crust removed
- 1 Polish-style dill pickle
- 3 thick slices of slab bacon
- 6 thin slices rump or round steak, about 4 ounces each
- 2 medium-size onions, peeled, halved and very thinly sliced
- Salt and freshly ground black pepper to taste
- 1 ½ cups chicken or beef broth
- 2 Polish dried mushrooms, or 1/2 ounce Italian dried porcini
- ¼ cup or more all-purpose flour
- 2 tablespoons cooking oil
- 2 tablespoons unsalted butter

Direction

- Preheat oven to 350 degrees.
- Slice the bread lengthwise into six pieces, each one as thick as an index finger. Slice the pickle lengthwise into six fingers. Cut each bacon slice in half crosswise.
- Place a steak slice between two pieces of plastic wrap or wax paper and pound evenly until it is very thin. Distribute a few onion slices over center of meat, add a finger of bread, one of pickle and a half slice of bacon. Sprinkle a very little salt (the bacon will add salt) and some pepper over all. Wrap the steak slice around the stuffing and tie or fasten with toothpicks. Repeat with remaining steak slices.
- Bring the chicken or beef stock to a slow simmer and add the dried mushrooms. (If using Italian mushrooms, soak them first in warm water for 20 minutes, then rinse to rid them of sand.) Remove from heat and let mushrooms steep in hot stock for at least 20 minutes.
- Roll beef rolls in the flour.
- Heat one tablespoon of oil and one of butter in a skillet over medium-high heat until butter foam subsides. Add remaining sliced onion and cook, stirring and tossing slices until onion is thoroughly browned; remove to an ovenproof dish. Add remaining butter and oil to the pan and brown the beef rolls evenly on all sides. When rolls are thoroughly browned and crisp on all sides, add to the dish with the onions. Distribute onions over and around beef rolls.
- Add stock and mushrooms, and bring to a gentle simmer on top of the stove. Place in oven and bake about two hours, or until the beef rolls are fork tender and the braising liquid has reduced to a syrupy gravy.

Nutrition Information

- 379: calories;
- 1 gram: dietary fiber;
- 29 grams: protein;
- 24 grams: fat;
- 11 grams: carbohydrates;
- 3 grams: polyunsaturated fat;
- 2 grams: sugars;
- 590 milligrams: sodium;
- 8 grams: saturated fat;
- 0 grams: trans fat;

364. Zucchini Panzanella With Sun Dried Tomatoes

Serving: Four servings | Prep: | Cook: | Ready in: 35mins

Ingredients

- 3 cups stale Italian or French bread, cut into 1 1/2-inch cubes
- 1 cup water
- ¼ cup sun-dried tomatoes (not packed in oil)
- 2 small zucchini, trimmed and diced fine
- ½ small red onion, peeled and diced fine
- ¼ cup chopped fresh basil leaves
- 1 large clove garlic, peeled and minced
- 1 teaspoon grated lemon zest
- 2 tablespoons fresh lemon juice
- 2 teaspoons olive oil
- 1 teaspoon salt
- Freshly ground pepper to taste
- ¼ cup chopped Italian parsley

Direction

- Place the bread in a medium bowl and pour the water over it. Squeeze the bread into the water until saturated. Let stand for 15 minutes.
- Meanwhile, place the sun-dried tomatoes in a small saucepan and cover with water. Bring to a boil over medium heat. Reduce heat and simmer until the tomatoes are soft, about 5 minutes. Drain and finely chop.
- Squeeze the excess water from the bread and coarsely chop. Place in a bowl and toss with the tomatoes, zucchini, onion, basil and garlic. Add the lemon zest, lemon juice, olive oil, salt and pepper. Toss in the parsley. Serve as a salad or stuffing for chicken or trout.

Nutrition Information

- 151: calories;
- 4 grams: fat;
- 2 grams: dietary fiber;
- 26 grams: carbohydrates;
- 5 grams: sugars;
- 429 milligrams: sodium;
- 1 gram: polyunsaturated fat;
- 0 grams: trans fat;
- 6 grams: protein;

365. Zucchini Phyllo Pizza

Serving: 3 to 4 servings | Prep: | Cook: | Ready in: 40mins

Ingredients

- ½ cup freshly grated Parmesan or asiago cheese
- ¼ cup mixed, chopped fresh herbs like savory, thyme, parsley and basil
- 2 tablespoons unsalted butter, melted
- 2 tablespoons canola oil
- ½ package phyllo dough (12 sheets, defrosted according to package directions)
- 6 teaspoons wheat germ
- 1 medium green zucchini, thinly sliced
- ½ sweet red onion, chopped fine
- 1 medium yellow zucchini or summer squash, thinly sliced

Direction

- Preheat oven to 400 degrees. Place cheese and herbs in a small bowl and set aside.

- Combine melted butter and oil and, with a pastry brush, lightly grease a baking sheet. Place 2 sheets of phyllo, one on top of the other, on the baking sheet. Brush lightly with the oil and butter mixture, sprinkle with 2 tablespoons of the herb-cheese mixture and 1 teaspoon of wheat germ. Repeat 5 more times, until all the sheets have been used, ending with a layer of phyllo. Brush this top sheet with the oil and butter.
- Leaving a 1 1/2-inch border free, sprinkle the onion on the top sheet. Place the green and yellow zucchini, in alternating rows, overlapping as necessary. Sprinkle with remaining cheese, herbs and wheat germ. Drizzle with any remaining oil and butter.
- Bake 15 to 20 minutes, or until phyllo is lightly browned and the cheese has melted. Remove to cooling rack and cut into 3-inch squares.

Nutrition Information

- 362: calories;
- 20 grams: fat;
- 0 grams: trans fat;
- 35 grams: carbohydrates;
- 4 grams: dietary fiber;
- 7 grams: saturated fat;
- 9 grams: monounsaturated fat;
- 3 grams: sugars;
- 11 grams: protein;
- 445 milligrams: sodium;

Index

A

Ale 62,92,111,220,221

Amaranth 5,128

Apple 3,4,6,7,35,47,66,148,168,210,211

Apricot 3,4,11,32,33,60

Arborio rice 165,167

Artichoke 3,4,6,14,69,152,183

Asparagus 3,4,6,15,72,164

Avocado 3,5,15,16,46,50,119

B

Bacon 4,66

Banana 5,7,101,224

Barley 3,18

Basil 3,4,17,19,59

Bay leaf 88

Beans 3,4,5,7,8,30,77,93,121,205,229,232,233

Beef 3,4,8,20,75,239

Biscuits 5,137

Blini 3,20

Blueberry 3,8,28,29,234

Bran 3,12

Bread 4,6,60,181,182

Broccoli 3,6,7,13,142,156,165,204

Broth 5,7,103,188

Buckwheat 3,5,32,103

Burger 6,7,8,147,219,231

Butter 3,4,7,8,10,29,35,36,37,52,77,95,97,98,109,143,168,193,213,214,216,234,237

C

Cabbage 3,4,6,38,70,163,180

Cake 5,6,7,100,183,224,225

Calvados 223

Capers 3,6,48,177

Caramel 6,7,164,185

Cardamom 5,100

Carrot 3,4,5,6,7,24,77,125,142,155,159,169,184,198,227

Cauliflower 3,5,6,7,18,106,170,189

Cava 118

Cayenne pepper 28,112,125,185

Celery 3,6,7,26,156,199

Champ 3,40,183,195

Chard 3,4,7,27,31,40,72,207,213

Cheese 3,4,5,6,10,22,23,82,122,127,130,143,150,166

Cherry 3,5,25,41,109

Chicken 3,4,5,6,42,43,44,45,46,47,48,63,85,87,109,112,119,146,154,167

Chickpea 3,4,5,33,58,84,129

Chinese cabbage 223

Chipotle 5,119

Chips 4,78

Chives 5,116

Chocolate 4,5,7,65,97,224

Cinnamon 3,4,51,71

Clams 5,8,114,232

Clementine 216

Coconut 5,128

Cod 3,7,53,54,196

Cognac 141,219

Cola 3,14

Coleslaw 7,199

Collar 7,189

Coriander 6,175

Couscous 4,57,58,59,74

Crab 5,7,97,193

Cranberry 6,154

Cream 3,4,5,6,25,29,45,59,112,135,164

Crumble 4,22,23,81,82,101,152,173

Cucumber 3,4,24,61,62

Cumin 7,211

Curry 3,4,7,51,64,188,227

Custard 4,71

D

Dal 7,188

Dandelion 4,65

Dijon mustard 20,28,68,77,81,84,122,127,152,176,200,210,222,228

Duck 4,66,67,76

E

Egg 3,4,5,7,15,68,127,184,193,203

F

Farfalle 4,69,70

Fennel 3,4,6,26,73,74,82,90,148

Feta 4,72,91

Fig 3,4,6,16,74,82,172

Fish 3,4,5,16,88,125,185,226

Flank 3,30

Fleur de sel 23

Flour 5,101,232,238

Focaccia 4,8,76,235

French bread 38,60,239,240

Fruit 4,5,60,66,135

G

Game 4,78

Garlic 3,4,5,6,7,10,79,82,109,124,148,171,179,196,199

Gin 3,4,6,7,36,47,81,154,158,168,175,177,185,211

Gorgonzola 4,59,88

Grain 8,234,237

Grapefruit 7,195

Grapes 12

Gratin 3,4,5,6,7,14,79,82,120,149,189,210,217

Guacamole 4,7,93,211

H

Ham 5,135

Harissa 5,104

Heart 6,183

Herbs 3,5,6,7,33,101,168,203,204

Honey 4,5,33,96,97

Horseradish 7,192

J

Jam 3,48

Jus 96,118,119,121

K

Kale 4,5,6,7,70,101,181,227

Kohlrabi 5,102

L

Lamb 4,5,7,56,89,95,104,197

Leek 5,14,107,108

Leftover turkey 215

Lemon 4,5,54,71,87,108,109,110,117,132,189

Lentils 5,113

Lettuce 227

Lime 3,4,5,7,46,49,76,112,118,119,185

Ling 5,113,133

Lobster 3,4,7,17,18,57,192

M

Mascarpone 162

Mayonnaise 3,54

Meat 5,7,119,178,187

Melon 4,5,62,118

Meringue 4,71

Millet 3,5,7,38,120,227

Mince 141,194,195

Mint 4,5,61,123

Mirin 4,92

Monkfish 5,6,116,150

Morel 6,7,164,218

Muffins 3,4,5,36,81,101

Mushroom 4,5,6,7,84,114,126,136,179,181,184,186,204,207,219

Mussels 5,137

Mustard 4,5,89,97

N

Nectarine 7,184

Noodles 5,103,127

Nut 1,9,10,11,12,13,14,15,16,17,18,19,21,22,23,25,26,27,28,29,30,31,32,33,34,35,36,37,38,39,40,41,42,43,44,45,46,47,48,49,50,51,52,53,54,55,56,57,58,59,60,61,62,63,64,65,66,67,68,69,70,71,72,73,74,75,76,77,78,79,80,81,83,84,85,86,87,88,89,91,92,93,94,95,96,97,98,99,100,101,103,104,105,106,107,108,109,110,111,112,113,114,115,116,117,118,119,120,121,122,123,124,125,126,127,128,130,131,132,133,134,135,136,137,138,140,141,142,144,145,146,147,148,149,150,152,153,154,156,157,158,159,160,161,162,163,164,165,166,167,168,169,170,171,172,173,174,175,176,177,178,179,180,181,182,183,184,186,187,188,189,190,191,192,193,194,195,196,197,198,199,200,201,202,203,204,205,206,207,208,210,211,212,213,214,216,217,218,219,220,221,222,223,224,225,227,228,229,230,231,232,233,234,235,236,237,238,240,241

O

Oatmeal 3,6,7,52,182,216

Oats 5,128

Octopus 5,129

Oil 4,5,6,38,76,84,90,105,106,107,120,129,132,146,161,182,189,202,207,210,217,219,232

Okra 4,58

Olive 3,4,5,6,7,21,38,42,48,57,74,76,122,129,154,161,173,189,210

Onion 3,4,6,7,38,65,69,148,155,201

Orange 4,5,7,73,74,130,195,208

Oyster 5,7,133,186

P

Pancakes 7,216

Pancetta 4,6,82,152,168

Papaya 3,5,50,134

Paprika 3,46

Parfait 5,118

Parmesan 4,5,6,8,12,13,14,18,20,21,26,27,31,32,38,39,69,70,71,73,80,82,83,84,90,102,103,105,106,107,109,110,121,133,135,138,139,140,149,157,161,165,166,172,180,182,189,196,202,207,217,233,234,240

Parsley 5,6,127,135,170

Parsnip 6,169

Pasta 3,5,7,10,136,137,218

Peach 4,6,60,153

Pear 3,4,6,9,66,168

Peas 3,4,5,6,28,35,43,50,64,69,72,119,139,140

Pecorino 69,70,189

Peel 9,16,31,52,79,83,100,102,114,115,116,143,146,151,152,153,155,156,171,227

Penne 5,139

Pepper 3,5,7,13,19,34,43,49,94,98,122,135,154,201,204,211

Pheasant 6,141

Pie 3,4,6,7,8,29,57,83,143,154,187,225,236

Pineapple 7,196

Pizza 3,4,6,8,32,90,145,150,240

Plantain 6,146

Plum 5,6,101,153

Polenta 4,6,57,91,172

Pomegranate 3,4,6,27,65,169

Porcini 4,91

Pork 3,6,7,31,39,147,148,200

Port 5,136

Potato 3,4,5,6,7,31,73,82,115,116,140,143,149,150,151,152,155,169,172,183,211,212,228

Prosciutto 5,113

Prune 3,6,7,9,48,153,212

Pumpkin 4,5,6,7,81,108,112,154,155,166,194,213,220,224,225

Q

Quinoa 3,5,6,26,101,159

R

Rabbit 6,160

Radicchio 6,161

Radish 4,82

Raisins 3,4,12,59

Raita 4,61

Raspberry 6,162

Ratatouille 6,163

Rhubarb 6,164

Rice 3,6,7,13,20,26,50,51,140,184,203,204,221

Ricotta 3,20

Rigatoni 4,59

Risotto 3,4,5,6,13,18,26,57,102,161,164,165,166

Rosemary 4,6,55,150

Rum 7,200

S

Sage 3,37

Salad 3,4,5,6,7,15,16,18,22,26,28,38,45,51,62,67,68,72,74,77,82,84,91,97,101,111,117,125,135,152,176,190,193,195,210,222,227,228,230

Salmon 3,6,54,177

Salsa 3,4,6,41,50,87,177

Salt 4,9,15,16,17,18,21,23,24,25,26,27,28,31,32,33,35,36,37,38,40,42,43,44,45,50,53,54,55,56,58,59,61,62,63,68,69,70,72,74,76,77,79,80,82,83,84,85,86,87,89,90,91,92,93,96,97,100,101,102,103,104,105,106,107,108,109,111,113,114,115,116,117,119,120,121,123,125,127,128,129,131,132,136,138,139,140,141,143,147,148,150,151,152,154,155,156,157,158,159,161,163,166,170,172,174,175,176,177,179,180,181,182,183,184,185,186,187,189,190,193,194,195,196,197,198,199,201,202,203,204,205,206,207,210,211,212,213,214,215,217,218,219,220,221,222,227,228,229,231,233,238,239

Sausage 3,5,6,39,48,139,179

Savory 6,181,182

Scallop 5,6,7,129,183,184,185

Seeds 4,5,27,89,128

Seville orange 195

Shallot 6,150,171,179

Sole 5,7,132,194

Sorbet 4,5,7,25,74,118,134,215

Soup 3,4,5,6,7,8,25,27,46,55,61,108,111,119,155,156,157,158,169,171,196,208,220,237

Soy sauce 24,103,142

Spaghetti 7,196

Spices 4,6,7,75,151,211

Spinach 3,4,6,7,8,14,24,67,140,175,181,184,198,201,202,204,206,237

Squash 3,4,5,6,7,36,37,80,105,121,158,180,189,213

Squid 7,208

Steak 3,19

Stew 3,4,5,27,56,116

Stock 7,215

Strawberry 7,208

Stuffing 3,6,7,17,179,186

Sugar 3,35

Swiss chard 31,40,72,112,207,213,214,217

Swordfish 7,214

Syrup 5,6,123,163

T

Tabasco 31,61,178,197,221,222

Taco 3,6,40,177

Tahini 6,170

Tangerine 7,215

Tarragon 3,6,17,167

Tea 228

Thai basil 193,203,204,205

Thyme 5,7,117,205

Tofu 3,6,7,24,142,175,190

Tomatillo 6,146,177

Tomato 3,4,5,6,7,8,16,34,42,55,58,73,87,88,109,126,127,131,135,1 36,137,160,166,193,196,210,213,218,240

Turkey 7,220

Turmeric 6,7,175,221

Turnip 6,7,142,192

V

Veal 7,222,223

Vegan 7,224

Vegetables 3,6,7,10,172,223

Venison 7,225

ıegar 7,227

ıs 17

4,7,62,91,230

ı,66,160,222

Worcestershire sauce 20,79,80,120,178,191,197

Z

Zest 36,71,110

L

lasagna 79,105,106,107

Conclusion

Thank you again for downloading this book!

I hope you enjoyed reading about my book!

If you enjoyed this book, please take the time to share your thoughts and post a review on Amazon. It'd be greatly appreciated!

Write me an honest review about the book – I truly value your opinion and thoughts and I will incorporate them into my next book, which is already underway.

Thank you!

If you have any questions, **feel free to contact at:** *author@thymerecipes.com*

Doris Naquin

thymerecipes.com

Printed in Great Britain
by Amazon

Plantain 6,146

Plum 5,6,101,153

Polenta 4,6,57,91,172

Pomegranate 3,4,6,27,65,169

Porcini 4,91

Pork 3,6,7,31,39,147,148,200

Port 5,136

Potato 3,4,5,6,7,31,73,82,115,116,140,143,149,150,151,152,155,169,172,183,211,212,228

Prosciutto 5,113

Prune 3,6,7,9,48,153,212

Pumpkin 4,5,6,7,81,108,112,154,155,166,194,213,220,224,225

Q

Quinoa 3,5,6,26,101,159

R

Rabbit 6,160

Radicchio 6,161

Radish 4,82

Raisins 3,4,12,59

Raita 4,61

Raspberry 6,162

Ratatouille 6,163

Rhubarb 6,164

Rice 3,6,7,13,20,26,50,51,140,184,203,204,221

Ricotta 3,20

Rigatoni 4,59

Risotto 3,4,5,6,13,18,26,57,102,161,164,165,166

Rosemary 4,6,55,150

Rum 7,200

S

Sage 3,37

Salad 3,4,5,6,7,15,16,18,22,26,28,38,45,51,62,67,68,72,74,77,82,84,91,97,101,111,117,125,135,152,176,190,193,195,210,222,227,228,230

Salmon 3,6,54,177

Salsa 3,4,6,41,50,87,177

Salt 4,9,15,16,17,18,21,23,24,25,26,27,28,31,32,33,35,36,37,38,40,42,43,44,45,50,53,54,55,56,58,59,61,62,63,68,69,70,72,74,76,77,79,80,82,83,84,85,86,87,89,90,91,92,93,96,97,100,101,102,103,104,105,106,107,108,109,111,113,114,115,116,117,119,120,121,123,125,127,128,129,131,132,136,138,139,140,141,143,147,148,150,151,152,154,155,156,157,158,159,161,163,166,170,172,174,175,176,177,179,180,181,182,183,184,185,186,187,189,190,193,194,195,196,197,198,199,201,202,203,204,205,206,207,210,211,212,213,214,215,217,218,219,220,221,222,227,228,229,231,233,238,239

Sausage 3,5,6,39,48,139,179

Savory 6,181,182

Scallop 5,6,7,129,183,184,185

Seeds 4,5,27,89,128

Seville orange 195

Shallot 6,150,171,179

Sole 5,7,132,194

Sorbet 4,5,7,25,74,118,134,215

Soup 3,4,5,6,7,8,25,27,46,55,61,108,111,119,155,156,157,158,169,171,196,208,220,237

Soy sauce 24,103,142

Spaghetti 7,196

Spices 4,6,7,75,151,211

Spinach 3,4,6,7,8,14,24,67,140,175,181,184,198,201,202,204,206,237

Squash 3,4,5,6,7,36,37,80,105,121,158,180,189,213

Squid 7,208

Steak 3,19

Stew 3,4,5,27,56,116

Stock 7,215

Strawberry 7,208

Stuffing 3,6,7,17,179,186

Sugar 3,35

Swiss chard 31,40,72,112,207,213,214,217

Swordfish 7,214

Syrup 5,6,123,163

T

Tabasco 31,61,178,197,221,222

Taco 3,6,40,177

Tahini 6,170

Tangerine 7,215

Tarragon 3,6,17,167

Tea 228

Thai basil 193,203,204,205

Thyme 5,7,117,205

Tofu 3,6,7,24,142,175,190

Tomatillo 6,146,177

Tomato 3,4,5,6,7,8,16,34,42,55,58,73,87,88,109,126,127,131,135,136,137,160,166,193,196,210,213,218,240

Turkey 7,220

Turmeric 6,7,175,221

Turnip 6,7,142,192

V

Veal 7,222,223

Vegan 7,224

Vegetables 3,6,7,10,172,223

Venison 7,225

Vinegar 7,227

W

Watercress 17

Watermelon 4,7,62,91,230

Whisky 5,99

Wine 3,4,6,7,18,39,66,160,222

Worcestershire sauce 20,79,80,120,178,191,197

Z

Zest 36,71,110

L

lasagna 79,105,106,107

Conclusion

Thank you again for downloading this book!

I hope you enjoyed reading about my book!

If you enjoyed this book, please take the time to share your thoughts and post a review on Amazon. It'd be greatly appreciated!

Write me an honest review about the book – I truly value your opinion and thoughts and I will incorporate them into my next book, which is already underway.

Thank you!

If you have any questions, **feel free to contact at:** author@thymerecipes.com

Doris Naquin

thymerecipes.com

Printed in Great Britain
by Amazon